WELCOME.

The Cake Mix Doctor Is In.

• • •

DEEPLY CHOCOLATE ALMOND CAKE
P26

LETHAL PEPPERMINT
CHOCOLATE CAKE P30

Hope you're hungry. On the pages that follow are color photos of more than 150 completed, delicious cakes. All began with a mix. All were assembled and baked in lightning-fast speed. And all have their own twists that give them from-scratch taste. So savor with your eyes and then get baking!

BUTTERMILK DEVIL'S FOOD CAKE
P28

CHOCOLATE PRALINE CAKE
P33

DARN GOOD CHOCOLATE CAKE
P36

MILK CHOCOLATE POUND CAKE
P38

CHOCOLATE PISTACHIO CAKE
P40

STACY'S CHOCOLATE CHIP CAKE
P42

CHOCOLATE MARBLE CAKE WITH
SHINY CHOCOLATE GLAZE P44

MISSISSIPPI MUD CAKE
P46

TURTLE CAKE
P48

CHOCOLATE-COVERED
CHERRY CAKE P50

CHOCOLATE SHEET CAKE WITH
PEANUT BUTTER FROSTING P52

OLD-FASHIONED COLA CAKE
P55

WHITE CHOCOLATE
POUND CAKE P58

SOUR CREAM CHOCOLATE
CUPCAKES P60

STRAWBERRY CAKE
P64

TRIPLE-DECKER STRAWBERRY
CAKE P67

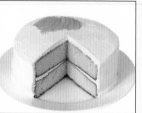

PEACHES AND CREAM CAKE
P70

BANANA CAKE WITH
QUICK CARAMEL FROSTING P72

HUMMINGBIRD CAKE
P74

BUTTER LAYER CAKE WITH
SWEET LIME CURD P76

FRESH ORANGE CAKE
P79

FESTIVE CRAN-ORANGE CAKE
P81

SUSAN'S LEMON CAKE
P83

FAVORITE APRICOT NECTAR CAKE
P85

PLUM AND CARDAMOM CAKE
P87

APPLESAUCE SPICE CAKE
P89

PINEAPPLE INSIDE-OUT CAKE
P92

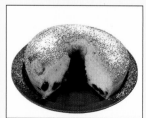

BLUEBERRY MUFFIN CAKE
P94

LEMON CHIP PICNIC CAKE
P96

OLD-FASHIONED
PEAR AND GINGER CAKE P98

UPSIDE-DOWN APPLE
SKILLET CAKE P100

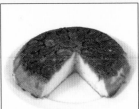

UPSIDE-DOWN BANANAS
FOSTER CAKE P102

MOM'S LAYER CAKE WITH FLUFFY
CHOCOLATE FROSTING P106

CARROT CAKE
P109

CARAMEL CAKE
P112

SWEET POTATO CAKE
P114

TENNESSE JAM CAKE
P116

GRANDMA'S COCONUT
ICEBOX CAKE P118

SNICKERDOODLE CAKE
P121

CHARLESTON POPPY SEED CAKE
P124

LEMON BUTTERMILK POPPY SEED
CAKE P127

ALMOND CREAM CHEESE
POUND CAKE P129

ZUCCHINI SPICE CAKE WITH
PENUCHE FROSTING P131

PECAN PIE CAKE
P133

MACADAMIA FUDGE TORTE
P136

BANANA PUDDING CAKE
P139

TOASTED COCONUT
SOUR CREAM CAKE P142

OLD-FASHIONED PRUNE CAKE WITH
HOT BUTTERMILK GLAZE P144

EASY TIRAMISU
P146

FINGER LICKIN' GOOD CAKE
P150

QUICK RED VELVET CAKE
P152

TOMATO SOUP SPICE CAKE
P156

LEMON-LIME CAKE WITH
PINEAPPLE CURD P158

FIDDLER ON THE ROOF CAKE
P161

INCREDIBLE MELTED
ICE-CREAM CAKE P163

FIVE-FLAVOR CAKE
P165

ORANGE DREAMSICLE CAKE
P167

CHOCOLATE BETTER THAN ? CAKE
P169

BETTER THAN ? CAKE
P171

EARTHQUAKE CAKE
P173

HORNET'S NEST CAKE
P175

HOLY COW CAKE
P177

FRIENDSHIP CAKE
P179

LOVE CAKE
P184

MT. VERNON CAKE
P187

IRISH ALMOND AND
CARAWAY CAKE P190

BRIDE'S CAKE WITH WHITE
CHOCOLATE FROSTING P192

BIRTHDAY CAKE CONES
P195

RED, WHITE, AND BLUE ANGEL
FOOD ICE-CREAM CAKE P197

CANNOLI CAKE
P199

DEVILISHLY GOOD
CHOCOLATE CAKE P202

PUMPKIN ROULADE
P204

PUMPKIN PIE CRUMBLE CAKE
P207

HOLIDAY YULE LOG
P209

AMBROSIA CAKE
P212

SNOWBALLS
P215

GINGERBREAD HOUSE
P218

NEW YORK–STYLE CHEESECAKE
P224

PUMPKIN SPICE CHEESECAKE
P227

FRESH LIME CHEESECAKE
P230

SWEET-TART CHERRY
CHEESECAKE P232

CHOCOLATE MOCHA SWIRL
CHEESECAKE P234

TOFFEE CRUNCH CHEESECAKE
P236

MINDY'S RICOTTA CHEESECAKE
P238

GOOEY BUTTER CAKE
P240

ALMOND GOOEY BUTTER CAKE
P242

CHOCOLATE MARBLE GOOEY
BUTTER CAKE P244

LEMON CHESS GOOEY
BUTTER CAKE P247

COCONUT-PECAN GOOEY
BUTTER CAKE P250

CINNAMON-CHOCOLATE-APRICOT
COFFEE CAKE P254

KATHY'S CINNAMON BREAKFAST CAKE P257

SOCK-IT-TO-ME CAKE P260

MATTIE'S ORANGE CINNAMON POPPY SEED CAKE P262

MOM'S CHOCOLATE SYRUP CAKE P264

HONEY BUN CAKE P266

HAPPY VALLEY CHERRY CAKE P269

BLUEBERRY STREUSEL COFFEE CAKE P272

APPLE SOUR CREAM KUCHEN P274

FRESH PEACH PECAN KUCHEN P276

PUMPKIN SPICE CAKE P278

RIPE BANANA LOAVES P280

HARVEY WALLBANGER CAKE P284

CHOCOLATE KAHLUA CAKE P286

DOUBLE-CHOCOLATE RUM CAKE P289

BACARDI RUM CAKE P292

ORANGE RUM ZUM CAKE P294

PINA COLADA CAKE P296

FUZZY NAVEL CAKE P298

KENTUCKY BUTTERMILK RAISIN CAKE P300

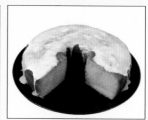
AMARETTO CAKE P303

CHOCOLATE GRAPPA CAKE
P306

JACK APPLE PECAN SPICE CAKE
P308

LEMON CHEESE BARS
P312

APRICOT ALMOND SQUARES
P314

RASPBERRY MERINGUE BARS
P316

CINNAMON BLUEBERRY
CRUMBLE BARS P318

CRANBERRY OAT
CRUMBLE BARS P320

STICKY PECAN PIE BARS
P322

BUTTERSCOTCH CASHEW
SCOTCHIES P324

PEANUT BUTTER CHOCOLATE
BARS P326

CHOCOLATE-ALMOND-COCONUT
BARS P328

CANDY BARS
P330

RUM BALLS
P332

DOUBLE-CHOCOLATE CHEWIES
P324

CHOCOLATE MOCHA CHEWIES
P337

WHITE CHOCOLATE CHEWIES
P340

CHUNKY OATMEAL MACADAMIA
COOKIES P342

APPLESAUCE RAISIN COOKIES
P344

ORANGE SPICE COOKIES
P346

COOKIE POPS
P348

CHOCOLATE MACADAMIA BISCOTTI
P350

LEMON PECAN BISCOTTI
P352

CHOCOLATE CUSTARD ICEBOX
CAKE P356

CHERRY DUMP CAKE
P358

APPLE WALNUT CRISP
P360

SOUR CREAM PEAR BUCKLE
P362

NINA'S STRAWBERRY CRISP
P364

PUNCH BOWL CAKE
P366

CHOCOLATE PUNCH BOWL CAKE
P368

FRUIT PIZZA
P370

BETTER-FOR-YOU-POUND CAKE
P374

STRAWBERRY APPLESAUCE CAKE
P376

ZESTY CRANBERRY CAKE
P378

PEAR AND TOASTED PECAN
BUTTERMILK CAKE P380

CLASSIC ORANGE CHIFFON CAKE
P383

APRICOT LEMON CHIFFON CAKE
P386

DARK CHOCOLATE CHIFFON CAKE
P389

ORANGE ALMOND ANGEL
FOOD CAKE P391

CHOCOLATE-SPECKLED PEPPERMINT
ANGEL FOOD CAKE P393

CINNAMON AND PINEAPPLE
CARROT SHEET CAKE P395

the Cake mix Doctor...

by ANNE BYRN

Photographs by Anthony Loew

WORKMAN PUBLISHING, NEW YORK

For Bebe

Library of Congress Cataloging-in-Publication Data
Byrn, Anne.
The cake mix doctor/by Anne Byrn; photographs by Anthony Loew.
p. cm.
Includes bibliographical references and index.
ISBN 0-7611-1790-3(hc)—ISBN 0-7611-1719-9(pb)
1. Cake. I. Title.
TX771. B97 1999 99-33167
641.8'653—dc21 CIP

Cover and book design by Paul Hanson with Janet Vicario
Front cover and interior photographs by Anthony Loew
Cakes baked by Jennifer Aaronson

Workman books are available at special discounts when purchased in bulk for premiums and
sales promotions as well as for fund-raising or educational use. Special editions or book excerpts can be
created to specification. For details contact the Special Sales Director at the address below.

Workman Publishing Company, Inc.
708 Broadway
New York, NY 10003-9555
www.workmanweb.com
First Printing October 1999
10 9 8 7 6 5 4 3 2 1

Acknowledgments

• • •

Just as various flavors, textures, and techniques go into baking a stellar cake, so have the efforts of many talented people been essential in the making of this cake book. From family and friends in Nashville to cake bakers across the country to an editor, publisher, and production team in New York, everyone who touched The Cake Mix Doctor has contributed to its success. And I offer them my heartfelt thanks.

On the home front, this book would have never been completed without my husband, John, who unselfishly spent his evenings and weekends feeding, bathing, driving, walking, and amusing our three children while I baked and wrote. He was always eager to sample yet another cake, as were my critical but loveable daughters Kathleen and Litton. Baby John offered his thumbs up and down from a high chair and broke a family tradition in that he savored chocolate cake before his first birthday! Thanks, too, must go to my support team—parents Bebe and Bill Byrn, sister Ginger Byrn, sister and brother-in-law Susan and Mark Anderson, as well as Dorothy Dearth and Diane Hooper, who kept the kids and house in order.

My radio co-host and friend Mindy Merrell not only helped test recipes, but she offered encouragement, fresh ideas, and energy. Kathy Sellers, too, spent a good part of the winter rummaging through recipe files for ideas, and she jumped right in when I needed help testing. And Katharine Ray was both enthusiastic and patient when it came to reviewing my recipes.

I must thank the experts—Pam Becker and Kay Emel-Powell—at General Mills, Betty Crocker test kitchen; Sandra Carpenter, a Columbus, Ohio, home economist who works with Duncan Hines and Cindy Young, a Cincinnati home economist who formerly worked there; and Sandy Nieman and Marlene Johnson at the Pillsbury Company. I also thank my friend and food science guru Shirley Corriher of Atlanta for helping me understand how a cake mix works.

I thank those hundreds of Middle Tennessee cooks who generously responded to the first Cake Mix Doctor story in *The Tennessean*, as well as the residential lending department of First American National Bank in Nashville, who sampled and critiqued many, many cakes. Thanks to food historian John Egerton of Nashville for his thoughts on the Red Velvet Cake, to Louise Durman at the *Knoxville News-Sentinel*, Susan Puckett at the *Atlanta Journal-Constitution,* and Cathy Barber at the *Dallas Morning News* for their recipe feedback. A big hug to Southern food writers Martha Pearl Villas of Charlotte, North Carolina, and Damon Fowler of Savannah, Georgia, for sharing their favorite cake mix renditions. A deep chocolate thank you to Rita Richardson of Nashville, my daughter's French teacher, for explaining how the word "ganache" translates, and to Jill Gosden Pollock in Chicago for her invaluable bake sale tips.

The folks at Workman Publishing have made this project a pleasure. My hat goes off to Peter Workman and his fine family. Thanks to my editor Suzanne Rafer, who has been a cheerleader from the get-go. She has been dedicated and thoughtful, toting the manuscript home and baking cakes on the weekend. It has been a joy to work with Suzanne and her able assistant Kylie Foxx, who found the sharpest knife in Manhattan to slice the cakes on this cover, and a few fingers, too! I feel most fortunate to have been in the artistic hands of design director Paul Hanson, who transformed an idea into a stunning package complete with chocolate-colored type! Thanks, too, to Janet Vicario for fine-tuning the design, to Jennifer Aaronson, who baked the cakes on the cover and those in the color insert, and to photographer Anthony Loew, who made the cakes and this mother of three look gorgeous. Thanks to make-up whiz Mark Lindsey for the glamour I lacked.

Many thanks to copy editor Evie Righter—for the tedious task of copy editing me. Someone had to do it, and Evie, you did a beautiful job. Also at Workman I thank Janet Harris, Jennifer Mandel, and the sales staff, as well as Andrea Glickson, Ellen Morgenstern, and the publicity department for their constant enthusiasm.

Finally, I tip my hat to cake queen Rose Levy Beranbaum, who suggested I go to Workman with the book idea. And also to my agent Nancy Crossman, who from the first moment, that first phone call in August 1998, understood the idea and worked with me to hone my proposal so that this book might find its home and these recipes might be shared with you.

Anne Byrn
Nashville, Tennessee

Contents

• • •

Introduction
PAGE 1

DOCTORING CAKE MIXES

Cake Mix 101
PAGE 4

HOW TO USE THIS BOOK

Everything you need to know, from choosing a mix to tips on baking and frosting a cake. Plus some cake-mix history.

Chocolate Cakes
PAGE 24

Think dessert, think chocolate. Rich Buttermilk Devil's Food Cake with White Chocolate Frosting, Milk Chocolate Pound Cake, Chocolate Sheet Cake with Peanut Butter Frosting. Dark, dense, and delicious.

Cakes with Fruit
PAGE 62

Create a tropical springtime buzz with the lively Hummingbird Cake. Sweeten a summer picnic with Peaches and Cream Cake. Toast a golden afternoon tea with a Festive Cran-Orange Cake. These fruit-filled cakes are sure to bring a smile.

Strike It Rich Cakes
PAGE 104

Decidedly rich, decidedly decadent. Dazzle kids and parents alike with Mom's Layer Cake with Fluffy Chocolate Frosting or the fragrant Caramel Cake or Carrot Cake with Fresh Orange Cream Cheese Frosting. These moist, aromatic desserts are sure to spell success regardless of the occasion.

Cake-Mix Classics
PAGE 148

These are the cakes that started it all, the tried-and-true crowd pleasers that brought cake-mix doctoring into the kitchen. Surprise a sweetheart with a deep crimson Quick Red Velvet Cake. Shake things up with the pecan- and coconut-studded Earthquake Cake. Or evoke memories of childhood trips to the candy shop with a Five-Flavor Cake. Whichever you choose, it's sure to be a hit!

Special Occasion Cakes

PAGE 182

For that day that comes only once in a lifetime, bake a beautiful Bride's Cake with Raspberry Filling and White Chocolate Frosting. Create Birthday Cake Cones for a children's party. Celebrate America's independence with a cool Red, White, and Blue Angel Food Ice-Cream Cake. Make the winter season extra festive with a yummy Holiday Yule Log and a Gingerbread House everyone in the family can build together. Any occasion is a cake occasion, but the holidays should definitely be special.

Cheesecakes and Gooey Cakes

PAGE 222

Creamy cheesecakes topped with sweet-tart cherries or flavored with pureed pumpkin. Rich butter cakes marbled with chocolate or blended with coconut and pecans. These are the cakes that sweet tooths crave and leave us calling out for seconds.

Coffee Cakes

PAGE 252

A steaming cup of freshly brewed coffee and a thick slice of homemade cake is the sweetest way to start the day. Wake up to Kathy's Cinnamon Breakfast Cake or fresh Apple Sour Cream Kuchen. Or, for a weekend afternoon treat, dig into a piece of Honey Bun Cake with a scoop of vanilla ice cream to top it off. Whether greeting the morning sun or hiding out from the rain, coffee and cake always satisfies.

Cakes with Spirit

PAGE 282

Nothing is more delectable than a moist, dense cake infused with the heady perfume of a favorite liquor. Some draw their inspiration from time-worn traditions, like the deeply flavored Bacardi Rum Cake. Others are new twists on popular mixed drinks—the Piña Colada and the Fuzzy Navel become intriguing desserts in cake form.

Incredible Bars and Comforting Cookies

PAGE 310

Whether for family gatherings, school bake sales, or just snacking, there is nothing more satisfying than cookies and bars. Packed up in a lunchbox, Peanut Butter Chocolate Bars, Cinnamon Blueberry Crumble Bars, and Chunky Oatmeal Macadamia Cookies are like a hug away from home.

This Can't Contain Cake Mix

PAGE 354

These desserts take cake mix where it's rarely gone before. Crave something crumbly and sweet? Bake up Nina's Strawberry Crisp or a Sour Cream Pear Buckle. Or for the truly unexpected, turn a mix into a trifle-like Punch Bowl Cake or chewy-crusted Fruit Pizza. The possibilities are endless.

Lighter Cakes

PAGE 372

For the warm summer days when something sweet is in order, but something heavy is not, whip up a fruity Apricot Lemon Chiffon Cake. Or when looking to cut back on fat but not on flavor, try a slice of Better-For-You Pound Cake with a cool glass of iced tea. Any way you slice them, these cakes will taste great and won't weigh you down.

Just the Basics

PAGE 397

Recipes for plain layers and Bundt and tube cakes to doctor with your favorite flavorings and frostings.

Frostings, Glazes, and One Compote

PAGE 414

Any cake—doctored or otherwise— deserves the best from-scratch finishes and these are definitely the best. Easy, quick, and luscious buttercreams, cream cheese frostings, glazes, and more.

Conversion Table

PAGE 439

Bibliography

PAGE 440

Index

PAGE 443

Doctoring Cake Mixes

• • •

On the day before Thanksgiving I stood in the checkout line of the local grocery store with no turkey, no onions, no celery, no cranberries, and no sweet potatoes in my basket. Only cake mix. Boxes upon boxes of devil's food, lemon, spice, yellow, and white. "What is this crazed woman feeding her family?" my curious fellow shoppers must have wondered as they queued up, their eyes darting from tabloid headlines to candy bars to the contents of my shopping cart. Had they asked, I would have been pleased to tell them that no, what I was buying didn't represent the entire Thanksgiving meal. However, by the next day these mixes would be the basis of cakes that would be the stars of the dessert table at our traditional family feast. My mother would roast the turkey, my aunt Mary Jo would make cornbread dressing, my sister Ginger would stir together a cranberry relish, and I would

bake cakes. A lot of them, with great ease, and in no time flat. There was a pumpkin roulade and a custardy pumpkin pie cake, as well as a banana-pineapple layer cake, a chocolate Kahlúa cake, and a delightful toasted coconut cake that is served right from the pan.

At the time, I was up to my eyebrows in batter, bowls, and beaters in testing recipes for *The Cake Mix Doctor.* My relatives embraced the situation in true Southern style—bring on the cake! On Thanksgiving, all was gobbled up.

This book began as a newspaper headline in early summer 1998. I wrote a food story in Nashville's morning newspaper, *The Tennessean,* on how to jazz up cake mixes using fresh lemon zest, or chocolate chips, or a spoonful of rum, apricot nectar, almond extract, even cherry pie filling. The story was entitled *The Cake Doctor Is In,* and it included not only my favorite recipes but a brief history of the cake mix at a milestone—50 years of age. I incorporated tips for turning each cake-baking session into a resounding success, and I invited readers to send me their favorite recipes to print in a sequel.

Within a week 500 recipes had arrived via fax, mail, and computer. And then the sequel ran. More recipes poured in. And then, to my fortune, Suzanne Rafer and Peter Workman at Workman Publishing understood this strong connection between the supermarket cake mix and the American kitchen. *The Cake Mix Doctor* had a home.

Left untouched, cake mixes may be ho-hum. But with a dash of creativity (yours), a tub of richness (eggs, butter, cream from the grocer), and a cupful of inspiration (this book), cake mixes turn out truly wonderful creations. When you doctor them up and work your magic on them as I explain in this book, they are not only different creatures, they become your own signature desserts.

Cake mixes play a huge role in a style of cooking firmly planted on American kitchen linoleum—speed scratch. No sifting of flour, no creaming of butter, no adding eggs, one at a time. Beginning cooks master it, average cooks revel in it, and advanced cooks may feel themselves too good for it until they taste one of these one-bowl wonders, and then they clamor for the recipe! Want a yellow layer cake with fluffy choco-

late frosting that tastes like the one Mom made for your eighth birthday? It's here. Want a drop-dead caramel cake that doesn't take three hours to assemble? It's here. Want a white chocolate pound cake to serve your sweetheart on Valentine's Day? It's here. Want a devil's food cake so devilishly good your chocolate-snob sister will turn her head? It's here, crowned with a creamy white chocolate frosting.

Creating these recipes and modifying those sent in by newspaper readers and friends across the country was enormous fun. It was disastrous for my figure, but each morning that I walked into the kitchen and lined up the mixes, eggs, oil, flavorings, cream cheese, and chocolate on the counter, I felt an eagerness to produce yet another dazzling cake. And considering that I was relatively new to the cake-mix game, this was a revelation. Up until then, I thought cake-mix cakes had outrageous titles—Better Than Sex Cake and Pea Pickin' Cake—and contained more than their fair share of whipped topping, crushed pineapple, food colorings, and candy. Many do. But to some cooks, this is the mystique, so I have devoted an entire chapter to these zany, but delicious, kinds of recipes.

And to many cooks, especially today's younger generation, mixes *are* a homemade cake, as compared to a bakery cake not baked at home. Purists may flinch, but when you fire up the oven, rev up the mixer, count fresh eggs, and soften a little butter, you are baking. These mixes might not be pedigree *génoise*, but they're prepared in a fraction of the time.

In addition to shortening preparation time, cake mixes are a reliable friend. Cakes "from scratch" require some practice to pull off, and you fuss over the ingredients—the right flour, room-temperature butter. Yet the doctored-up mixes are easily assembled using the dump method in which all the ingredients are mixed in one bowl. And they bake up looking pretty time after time. Plus, cake mixes adapt to new ingredients, be it a can of cherry pie filling or a handful of fresh strawberries. Tweak them with the right number of eggs and a suitable amount of fat and liquid, and they bake up not only into cakes, but into bars, cookies, cheesecakes, crisps, pies, even a gingerbread house.

Cake mixes adapt to varying oven temperatures and pan sizes, too. They withstand overbeating and, oddly, their steel-belted toughness is melded with an amazingly patient quality that allows them to bake up perfect even with too little beating! Mixes look stunning, svelte, and tall baked in a tube pan in spite of being yanked out of the oven minutes too soon. And most magically of all, cake mixes contain marvelous emulsifiers that seal in moisture and keep your cake lip-smacking good on the kitchen counter for many days.

Baking need not be an ordeal calling for a multitude of pans, an open calendar, and a refrigerator stocked with gourmet ingredients. It can take place on the spur of the moment, with a cake mix and a modest pantry. And when you have home-baked cake on the kitchen counter you raise the comfort level of your household. Especially when the frosting is homemade.

My mother once told me, as mothers often share nuggets of wisdom with their daughters: "You can get away with baking a cake from a mix, but you absolutely must make homemade frosting." I'm sure at the time she said this her kitchen was mayhem. Dinner was bubbling on the stove, a young child was tugging at her hemline, the telephone was ringing, and the dog was barking. A cake-mix cake was in the oven, but at the same time the butter was softening for her famous frosting.

I never thought that statement would relate to my life. But as I worked on recipes for this book project, including my favorite from-scratch chocolate, caramel, peanut butter, and orange cream cheese frostings to bedeck cake-mix cakes, Mother's words rang true, indeed. Just because you're busy doesn't mean you don't have time to bake cakes—for Thanksgiving, holidays, everyday. Enjoy!

Cake Mix 101: How to Use This Book

• • •

How do you start with an empty bowl and wind up with a triple-layer cake in less than half the time it takes to bake that cake from scratch? Use a mix. How can you create a cake so memorable that people will search for a business card, cocktail napkin, or the back of the electric bill just to write down the recipe? Doctor up that mix.

Cake mixes are a fixture in the American kitchen pantry—used by more than 60 percent of households. And they can be your prescription for dazzling family, friends, and business colleagues with your baking prowess. The Cake Mix Doctor is ready to show you her secrets for baking box cakes that taste as if they're not.

Choosing a Cake Mix

You might think that selecting a cake mix is a minor decision, that a cake mix is a cake mix, right? So wrong. Not only are there slightly different sizes of cake mixes—most are for two-layer cakes and some are for one-layer cakes—there are various manufacturers. And flavors vary with the manufacturer. Some of the yellow cakes, for example, have an overtone of coconut. One white mix has a decidedly cherry taste. These are nuances of that particular cake mix, researched and developed within the company and offered to consumer taste panels for sampling. Some mixes even contain animal fats such as lard or beef fat, so you must read the label. Although reading a cake-mix label can be daunting, it educates you. And being a more informed consumer makes you a better cook. The first ingredient listed will be sugar, since there is a high concentration of sugar in cake mixes and it weighs the most. From there you'll have flour, some vegetable shortening (or other fat), leavenings, emulsifiers, and a grocery cart of flavorings, colorings, binders, thickeners, and possibly dough conditioners.

In fact, before you bake, taste your way around—bake cakes from several kinds of mixes. And taste before frosting to find the mix that you like best.

PUDDING-IN-THE-MIX CAKES

Pillsbury executives noticed that many of the Bake-Off contest winning recipes called for a package of instant pudding mix. (Ironically, Duncan Hines for years had been running a pound cake recipe calling for pudding mix on the side of its box.) So in 1977 Pillsbury decided to go one better and offer to the consumer a cake mix with the pudding built in. Now both Pillsbury and General Mills' Betty Crocker cake mixes contain pudding inside. No, they don't prepare a batch of vanilla pudding and condense it in the mix. All the components for pudding are there in the mix and listed on the ingredient panel. But how does a pudding-enhanced mix affect cake recipes?

Well, the test kitchens will tell you it won't affect your end results much at all as long as you ease up on the sour cream and become accustomed to a moist, wet cake. You'll find a few recipes out there that instruct you to reduce the eggs by one and to cut back on the oil a bit if you are using one of the pudding-in-the-mix cakes. But I adhere to a more rigid strategy:

• *First,* don't use a mix with pudding inside if you're following a recipe that calls for instant pudding as an ingredient, and many in this book do.

• *Second,* cake mixes with pudding will be heavier, and very moist, so if you want a light layer cake and are planning on placing a filling between the layers and then adding frosting, they're not your best bet. The bottom layer will be quite wet.

• *And last,* pudding cakes tend to shrink upon cooling. This may not bother you, but if you like well-shaped cakes that don't shrink back, then you might be disappointed with the appearance of a pudding-in-the-mix cake.

WHAT ELSE IS IN A MIX?

Sit tight and put on your chemistry hat. Cake mixes do contain all the same ingredients that a from-scratch cake has— flour, sugar, leavening (baking powder or baking soda), fat, salt, and flavorings. But

Cake Habits

*A*ccording to a recent ACNielsen survey (1998), the most popular flavor of cake mix is yellow, followed by white, then devil's food. Other favorites in descending order include golden, German chocolate, lemon, carrot, French vanilla, and chocolate.

ACNielsen also offers some insight as to what type of cake mix we purchase most often—the layer cake without pudding, followed by the specialty cake (including pudding cakes, angel food, pound, chiffon, Bundt, and snack cakes), then smaller mixes under 10 ounces. Most cake-mix buyers are from "maturing families" containing at least one child between 6 and 12 years of age. They're followed by the "established families" with at least one child over the age of 12. A close third comes from "empty nesters"—adults over 55 with no children at home—and "new families"— at least one child under 6 years of age. Interestingly, most of the specialty cakes—angel food and pudding cakes—are purchased by "empty nesters." The folks least interested in purchasing a cake mix? Singles, regardless of their age.

---

cake mixes contain much more. That is because cake mixes have been road tested like those steel-belted tires on your car. They've been tested over and over in corporate kitchens to make them as friendly as possible, ready for the tiniest slip-up from the consumer.

Cake mixes will still perform—bake up pretty and taste good—even if you add too little liquid or too much (see 10 Steps to Sensational Cakes, page 16). They will work whether you beat them by hand or with a turbo-charged commercial mixer, although somewhere in between is best. They will work if you pour the batter into the wrong-size pan, although you might not get the volume you'd anticipated. In other words, cake mixes are beloved by millions because they're reliable old friends, and you had better believe that 50 years of corporate research and development and test-kitchen alchemy made them that way. So what are their secrets? Emulsifiers and a kitchen sink of leavening agents.

• **Emulsifiers.** These are ingredients that keep fat and liquid in a cake mix from separating. Think of emulsifiers as skilled party hosts. They mingle, introducing two guests—fat and water, for example—who don't know each other, and work the room making sure everyone is chatting and the party is one thick and happy batter. Without them, the guests might separate, moving into their own more familiar circles with their own conversations. In a cake mix, the emulsifiers are mono- and diglycerides, sodium-stearoyl lactylate, polyglycerol esters, propylene glycol monoesters, soy lecithin, polysorbate 60, and many more. In the cake batter these emulsifiers hold the ingredients together, not letting them leave the party! The air bubbles are in the fat and the leavening is with the flour so when the two are brought together you have a better distribution of leavening. This makes possible a sweet cake that bakes up evenly, is light, and rises high in the pan. Plus, the cake stays moist for days on the kitchen counter. In a from-scratch cake, however, the only emulsifier is the egg yolk.

So does it matter what type of fat you use with emulsifiers? Food chemist and author Shirley Corriher says any fat will do, but vegetable oil will give you an especially moist cake. It should come as no surprise that on the back of most cake-mix boxes, you're asked to add vegetable oil, not butter or margarine or solid shortening. However, I think that butter adds a great deal of flavor and texture to a cake mix.

• **Leavening.** In our home pantries we have baking powder or baking soda to aid in the rising of cake or quick breads or muffins. But in the cake-mix laboratory scientists can add all sorts of other leavenings—such as dicalcium phosphate and monocalcium phosphate—to make the cake rise. It is this integrated system of leavening that works wonders, compensating for consumer mistakes and producing a cake rising high in the pan time after time.

• **Colorings.** All the colorings used in cake-mix manufacture are considered GRAS, or Generally Recognized As Safe by the Food and Drug Administration. They are called either dyes or lakes on the box, and the latter dissolve better in fat. In yellow cake you'll find both yellow and red coloring. And some recipes here, such as the Quick Red Velvet Cake, call for the addition of even more food coloring.

• **Flavorings.** If it were a perfect world, we could buy a cake mix with natural flavorings and colorings. The one factor that contributes most to that "cake-mix taste" many people associate with box cakes is artificial flavoring, namely vanillin. But you can camouflage much of its too-powerful flavor effect by adding bold-tasting ingredients like coffee, pure almond extract, pure vanilla extract, lime or orange zest, chocolate, and boozy things like sherry, rum, and bourbon to the batter.

CAKE-MIX TASTE

This "cake-mix taste" is the only downside I have found to baking with mixes. There are a few mixes in gourmet markets that don't contain artificial ingredients like vanillin, but they don't bake as well as a supermarket cake mix. I found these mixes to be a time-consuming process, beginning with creaming cold butter with sugar, then adding eggs, one at a time, pouring in dissolved chocolate, if called for, and finally flour. It's much like baking a cake from scratch, but at least with a scratch cake you open a cookbook, spoon into the sack of flour, measure sugar, and do other tangible tasks that signal that you are baking a cake from scratch and this is a hallowed event! Maybe someday we busy cooks will have it all in one box. However, I think that no matter what, we'll still want the pleasure that a little doctoring brings.

The Cake Mix Pantry

With a cake mix and basic ingredients close at hand, baking great cakes is a snap. Here are some of the items I turn to.

KEY INGREDIENTS AT A GLANCE

• **Cake mixes:** Keep on hand two devil's food mixes, two yellow mixes, two white mixes, one spice mix, one lemon mix, and one orange mix.

• **Butter:** I add lightly salted butter. Whereas unsalted butter is preferable in scratch cakes, I feel the salt in the butter helps balance the high sugar content of the cake mixes and, ironically, gives the cakes more of a homemade taste. Since butter is difficult to blend into dry cake mix, the recipes call for melted butter. Margarine, on the other hand, is not recommended unless it is specifically called for in a recipe, such as the Old-Fashioned Cola Cake. That's because butter has superior flavor and in light cakes facilitates browning. Butter is a must for frostings. If you absolutely have to use margarine for health reasons, make sure it is a stick margarine that has more than 65 percent vegetable oil. Spreads will not yield the same results.

• *Milk:* Many recipes in this book will simply say "milk." Others will list "whole milk." The reasoning is simple. When whole milk is specified, that means the extra fat in the whole milk is crucial to the mouthfeel of the recipe. If not specified, simply use whatever milk you have in the refrigerator. And in my recipes, the milk does not have to be at room temperature; it may be added cold.

• *Eggs:* Keep a dozen large size on hand. You can add them to the batter straight from the refrigerator.

• *Nuts:* Store almonds, pecans, walnuts, and other nuts in the freezer to extend their shelf life. If you plan on adding untoasted nuts to a recipe, add them straight from the freezer. If you plan on adding them toasted for more flavor, see Toasting Nuts, page 134), and thaw 10 minutes before toasting.

• *Coconut:* The best coconut is fresh, but that's not reasonable for busy cooks. So keep the next best thing around— unsweetened grated coconut—in the freezer. It thaws in minutes and can be sprinkled on cakes for garnish or added to cake mixes to turn them into something quite exotic. The sweetened coconut in the can is okay in a pinch, but it doesn't have the flavor that the frozen coconut has.

• *Vegetable oil:* The addition of vegetable oil is critical to these cake recipes. Oil works with the built-in emulsifiers to give you a moist, tender cake. But not all vegetable oils will do. Select the lighter, flavorless oils like canola and soybean oil, instead of heavier, more fragrant oils like olive.

• *Chocolate:* A key ingredient to cake doctoring—you just can't keep enough chocolate on hand. Semisweet or bittersweet is useful chopped, grated, or melted into a chocolate swirl. German chocolate can be grated into a batter with marvelous results. White chocolate, although technically not chocolate because it doesn't contain any chocolate liquor, melds beautifully into cakes and frostings. Chocolate chips are multipurpose and best for toppings and folding into cakes, bars, and cookies. Chocolate syrup, too, is a quick addition to marble cakes or cheesecakes. And unsweetened cocoa powder gives a mighty punch to devil's food cake mixes and impromptu frostings.

• *Extracts:* Be sure to buy pure vanilla and almond extracts as well as pure fruit extracts like orange and lemon. Cake mixes contain a ready supply of artificial flavorings, so you must take care that what you add is of the best quality.

• **Spices:** Keep your favorite spices on hand. I like ground cinnamon, cardamom, ginger, and nutmeg, and whole poppy seeds. Buy them in small amounts, for the longer spices sit on the pantry shelf, the less flavorful they are.

THE EXTENDED PANTRY: REFRIGERATOR

• **Buttermilk:** Most often low-fat. If you can't find it in your supermarket, use buttermilk powder, following the package instructions for reconstituting.

• **Sour cream:** Full-fat for a rich taste and velvety texture.

• **Yogurt:** Plain, lemon, and vanilla full-, low-, or nonfat. Use your imagination when choosing the flavor; yogurt adds richness, moisture, and tenderness to these recipes.

• **Cream cheese:** Full-fat works best, but you may substitute reduced-fat (neufchâtel) or fat-free.

• **Citrus:** Oranges, lemons, and limes. Use both the juice and the grated zest.

FREEZER

• **Fruit:** Keep strawberries, raspberries, sliced peeled peaches, and cranberries.

CUPBOARD

• **Sugar:** Granulated, confectioners', and light and dark brown sugar.

• **Dried fruit:** Raisins, cranberries, cherries, currants, and prunes.

• **Canned fruits:** Varieties such as pineapple, blueberries, peaches, pears, or mandarin oranges, in light syrup (not pie fillings).

• **Instant coffee powder**

Equipment to Have on Hand

FOR BAKING

• **Pans:** Three words—buy good pans. You'll need two or three 9-inch pans, a 13- by 9-inch metal pan, a 12-cup Bundt pan, a 10-inch tube pan, and some other pans like a 9- to 10-inch springform, baking sheets, and cupcake pans for preparing the recipes in this book. Choose shiny aluminum or aluminized steel (with better heat distribution). The best bakeware has a folded construction to prevent warping.

• *Mixer:* Use a hand mixer or an electric stand mixer for these recipes. Save your big heavy-duty restaurant-style mixer for from-scratch cake recipes.

• *Bowls:* Either stainless steel or glass bowls are best. You will need several large bowls, a few medium, and a small bowl for these recipes.

• *Spatulas:* You can't have too many rubber spatulas. They are invaluable for scraping down the sides of the bowl when you are blending cake batter, as well as smoothing the top of cake batter, getting melted chocolate and butter out of a glass dish or saucepan, and spreading fillings onto cake layers. One good flexible metal icing spatula is a must for frosting cakes. A metal spatula with a bend to it, for frosting a sheet cake in the pan, is nice but not essential.

• *Racks:* Choose stainless-steel cooling racks because they don't rust and last a lifetime.

• *Sharp serrated knife:* This makes slicing cake layers in half a breeze. Also good for slicing cake.

• *Mister:* Fill a stainless-steel mister with vegetable oil and you don't need to buy those aerosol vegetable oil cooking sprays that can overbrown the edges.

• *Shakers:* Fill these stainless-steel canisters with flour or confectioners' sugar to make sprinkling surfaces a breeze.

• *Doodads:* A pastry comb will enhance the appearance of frosted layer cakes. Run it around the sides of a frosted cake to make ridges. Stencils, placed on top of an unfrosted cake, create a pretty pattern when dusted with confectioners' sugar or cocoa powder; carefully lift off. Toothpicks or wooden skewers help to determine a cake's doneness. And drinking straws or chopsticks poke large holes into cakes so syrups and glazes can seep into the crumb.

FOR STORING:
LONG-TERM OR
SHORT-TERM

• *Plastic cake saver:* This is an oh-so-handy tool if you do a lot of cake toting to your work, school, or dinner get-togethers. You frost or glaze the cake right on the saver base, fit the top over the cake, and seal it shut. With room in between the frosting and the top of the cake saver, you have no messes.

• **Glass cake dome or bell:** This glass cake stand or cover looks beautiful on your kitchen counter, and it does its job well, protecting the cake from drying out and yet keeping the frosting surface intact. It's perfect for all cakes that can be left unrefrigerated.

• **Waxed paper:** Just the right wrap to lay across the top of a cream cheese frosting that has had 30 minutes to firm up uncovered in the refrigerator. It keeps the moisture in but doesn't stick to the frosting. Unfortunately, waxed paper doesn't stick to the sides of a plate, so you'll need to tape it to the plate should you want a secure fit. And waxed paper doesn't provide an effective moisture barrier, so it's useless for freezing cakes.

• **Aluminum foil:** The best protector in the freezer, especially when you use heavy-duty foil. Good for keeping out moisture in the refrigerator, too, but be careful not to use it with acidic cakes like ones with strawberry or lemon. Aluminum foil is also nice for the 13- by 9-inch cakes that store in their pan, for it can mold onto the side of the pan, creating a seal.

• **Plastic wrap:** A good all-purpose wrap for cakes with no glaze or frosting. Good for wrapping up single slices of cake. Per-

fect for refrigerator storage, but not for use in the freezer.

Ready to Bake

OVEN TEMPERATURE AND RACK POSITION

The recipes in this book were tested in General Electric, Frigidaire, and Five Star electric ranges. The oven temperature of 350°F is the general rule of thumb, but you will find a few variations. Some Bundt or tube cake recipes call for 325°F. Pans with a dark finish and glass pans need the lower heat of 325°F to prevent overbrowning. And when you are baking cake layers larger than 9 inches to stack for wedding cakes, you'll want to reduce the temperature to 325°F so the layers bake evenly and don't dome in the middle.

For most cakes, the rack should be positioned in the middle of the oven. Although most of the cakes in this book are easily baked on a single rack, a few may need a second one. Three-layer cakes, for example. For ovens that aren't large enough to bake three layers on one center rack, place two layers on the center rack and one layer in the center of the top rack, making sure there is plenty of air circulation around the pans. Some Bundt and

Pan Grease

*C*indy Young of Cincinnati, who worked for many years testing recipes for Duncan Hines, passes along a recipe for something called *"pan grease."* No, it's not what your mechanic finds underneath your car, it's what test kitchen cooks use to swab the multitude of pans they use for baking cakes. To make pan grease, combine 2 cups solid vegetable shortening and 1 cup all-purpose flour with a wooden spoon or electric mixer. Cover this with plastic wrap and store at room temperature for up to 6 months. Wipe this onto pans with a pastry brush or paper towel, and it cuts the preparation time in half.

tube cakes that take nearly an hour to bake may need to be placed on the lower rack so they don't overbrown.

THE ART OF GREASING AND FLOURING

I can't say enough about the old-fashioned method of greasing pans with solid vegetable shortening and then flouring them. This imparts no flavor to the cake and forms a nice, firm, easily frosted crust. I have found the easiest way to grease with solid shortening is to dab a paper towel into the container. You'll need about 1 tablespoon shortening for two layer pans or a 13- by 9-inch pan, and slightly more for a Bundt or tube pan. Once it's greased, sprinkle a tablespoon of flour into the pan, tilting it to allow the flour to coat the sides. If greasing layer pans, pour the excess into the remaining pan, gently tapping the first pan to release the extra. Repeat the process. Tap out the excess flour over a sink or trash can.

When preparing a Bundt or tube pan, a mister makes the job infinitely easier. You can use supermarket vegetable oil spray or vegetable oil and flour sprays, but they contain propellants and produce a dark, heavy crust on your cake. A solution is to buy a nonaerosol sprayer. One is called QuickMist and is sold at Williams-Sonoma stores. You fill the container half full of vegetable oil, pump the container about 15 times to build up pressure, and then spray.

Roulade recipes, on the other hand, need a lining of buttered parchment paper on the bottom of baking pan. This allows easy removal of the large cake from the pan, and you can just peel the parchment off the cake after it is inverted and before it is rolled.

High-Altitude Baking

An area with an altitude over 3,500 feet is considered high altitude. This is where there is less air pressure and less humidity, and these two factors create havoc for cake bakers. The reduction in air pressure causes less resistance to the leavening action in the batter. Thus, cake batter may overflow from the pan, the cake may bake right out of the pan, or it may fall flat.

In high-altitude baking, you don't want as tender a cake because it will overrise, so be wary of cakes with a lot of added sugar and oil. Often a little flour is added to a recipe to make it heavier. The oven temperature should be increased so that the batter sets up more quickly and doesn't overflow.

Layer cakes should be baked in 9-inch pans, never 8-inch or they would overflow. And absolutely do not bake cakes that have marshmallows added to the mix. They'll blow up from the high sugar content. Finally, grease the pans well because high-altitude cakes are more likely to stick.

Don't think it's only the residents of Denver who must take all this into consideration. Other high-altitude areas include the mountainous region of eastern North Carolina, the plains of western Kansas, and Albuquerque, N.M., where much of the high-altitude baking research is conducted. Whereas only 20 percent of the U.S. population now lives in high-altitude areas, this is expected to increase as baby boomers retire to these areas.

MIXING

One of the beauties of a cake mix is that you snip open the packet and out it pours into your bowl, no sifting or stirring required. If there are any lumps in the mix, rest assured most will smooth out on beating and they will all bake out in the oven.

Another plus for cake mixes is that you don't have to plan ahead. There's no removing butter and eggs from the refrigerator to come to room temperature. Eggs can be added cold to the batter and all at the same time, for they are not your source of leavening. Therefore it doesn't matter, as it does in a from-scratch cake, that they be a little warm to achieve maximum volume. Cake mixes don't call for creaming the butter either. Since the mix contains emulsifiers, fats are not the only reason the cake will stay moist. When you use fat consider what it will add flavor-wise to the cake. If you want flavor—such as a buttery taste in a white mix—by all means add butter (just melt and pour in). But if it's a deep chocolate flavor you're aiming for, you might as well add a flavorless vegetable oil.

Once everything is in the bowl, mix on the lowest speed of your electric mixer for 30 seconds to 1 minute, or until combined. Then turn off the machine and scrape the bowl with a rubber spatula. Now, here is where test kitchen home economists will differ. Some say it's okay to then increase the speed of your mixer to medium and beat 2 minutes more. Others say that's unnecessary, and that the increased speed may cause tunneling (alleys in the finished cake) and the cake to lose volume in the oven. I take the approach of mixing 2 minutes more on medium because I like the look of the smooth and thickened batter after this mixing. In addition, emotionally I feel I am baking a cake if I hear that mixer running!

But don't beat on medium past 2 to 3 minutes. Follow the times listed on these recipes. And save your commercial mixer for the scratch cakes.

The recipes in this book have been tested with both hand-held electric mixers and small electric stand mixers, but not with more elaborate commercial-type stand mixers. The reasoning is simple—cake-mix batters do not need the long, laborious creaming that scratch batters must have to achieve volume. These recipes call for blending on low speed for 1 minute to incorporate ingredients, and then blending 2 minutes more on medium speed to lighten the batter. Ingredients like chocolate chips, nuts, and coconut are then folded in. The only thing you need to be sure you do when using a hand-held mixer on some of these stiffer batters is to get the beaters down far enough so they mix all those ingredients that might cling to the bottom of the bowl. Stir once or twice on the bottom as you scrape the sides of the bowl and that should take care of it.

TESTS FOR DONENESS

Here are some good tests for cake doneness. Although test kitchens rely on the toothpick method first, I begin with the color method.

• The color of a baked white cake should be light brown, yellow cake should be golden brown, and chocolate cakes should deepen in color.

• Press lightly with your fingertips in the center of the cake. It should just spring back and not indent.

• The cake should just be starting to pull away from the sides of the pan.

10 Steps to Sensational Cakes

1. Preheat your oven for 10 to 15 minutes before you plan to bake.

2. Buy an oven thermometer and check your oven routinely to see if it is baking at the correct temperature. If cakes are browning quickly, it may run hot. If cakes are not done by the maximum baking time, it may run cold.

3. Place the oven rack in the center position.

4. Read the recipe and be sure to use the correct pan size.

5. Measure liquid by placing a liquid-ingredient measuring cup on the kitchen counter, pouring liquid in the cup, and checking the measurement at eye level.

6. Measure dry ingredients (sugar, for example) by spooning them into dry measuring cups and leveling off the top with a dinner knife. When you measure brown sugar, pack it into the cup before leveling it off.

7. Blend the batter for the time specified, and use a hand or standard mixer set on low or medium speed. If beating by hand, beat at the rate of 150 strokes per minute, resting as needed.

8. Check the cake for doneness, looking for browning in light-colored cakes, pressing the top to see if it springs back, seeing if the cake is starting to pull away from the sides of the pan, and inserting a toothpick in the center to see if it comes out clean.

9. Allow 10 to 15 minutes for cake layers to cool before inverting onto a rack. Tube and Bundt cakes need 20 minutes.

10. Unless the cake is to be glazed while hot, let layer, Bundt, tube, and sheet cakes cool completely, then frost.

• Carefully stick a toothpick or wooden skewer in the center of the cake. It should come out clean.

• You can smell when a cake is baked, but it takes a little experience to train your nose.

TURNING THE CAKE OUT OF THE PAN

About 10 to 15 minutes is the right amount of time to let a layer pan rest on a cooling rack before you invert the cake out of the pan. Any longer than that and what you used to grease the pan will set up and the cake may stick. Any time shorter than that and the hot cake may split.

For tube and Bundt pans, and for 13- by 9-inch cakes you want to remove from the pan to frost, you'll need to let these cakes rest 20 minutes.

By running a dinner knife around the edges of a cake layer or sheet pan before inverting it, you make the task of releasing the cake from the pan easier. Do the same thing with a long, sharp knife for tube and Bundt pans, although with Bundt pans all you really need is to tap and rotate the pan, then invert it. Tilt the pan at a 45-degree angle and tap it against the surface of the counter and the cake should come out more easily.

You'll want to invert layer and sheet cakes twice if you're planning on frosting them. That's because if you let the cake rest top side down on the rack, lines will form as the cake cools and as you try to pull the cake from the rack the entire top may come off. Invert tube cakes, too, twice so that the fuller top side is up. Bundt pans, however, need just one flip onto a rack to cool, for their fluted edge is what you want to see on the serving platter.

FROSTING THE CAKE

What's the right term—frosting or icing? For consistency in this book, I have labeled all the frostings and what might be called icings, simply as frostings. And the verb of choice is to "frost" a cake. Those mixes of confectioners' sugar with a little liquid, I call glazes.

There is no right or wrong frosting or glaze for a cake. Use your preference to select something that will complement what you have baked. As a general rule, however, caramel frostings and others that set up firm are best with softer-textured cakes. And it's the dense, oilier cakes that are best with the fluffier icings, like cream cheese or buttercream. You want to also play up corresponding flavors in the cakes and frostings: For example, serve a Cinnamon Buttercream with a spice cake, or a Peppermint Buttercream with a chocolate cake.

You need not pull your hair out when frosting a cake. Here are some steps to keeping the process sane.

1. Brush all the crumbs from the sides of the cake layers with a soft pastry brush. You can freeze the cake for 20 minutes to make it easier to frost.

2. Place a dab of frosting or corn syrup in the center of the platter to secure the bottom cake layer to the platter. Choose the thickest layer and place it right side up on the platter.

3. To keep the edges of the serving platter clean, ease 4 strips of waxed paper, about 3 inches wide and a foot long, under the layer so that they form a square. These will catch the run-off frosting.

4. Apply a first thin coat of frosting, ½ to ¾ cup or about ¼ inch thick, to the first layer. If the top is lopsided, build it up with some of the frosting. Stack the second layer on top of it so that both layers are right side up.

5. Spread a thin layer of frosting on the top of the cake to seal crumbs and repair imperfections; then apply a thin layer around the sides.

6. Apply a second, thicker, more decorative layer of frosting to the top and sides. For smooth sides, hold the spat-ula tight against the cake with one hand and turn the cake with the other. On the top of the cake, make decorative ridges or swirls with the end of a thin metal spatula.

7. Once the cake is frosted, gently ease the paper strips out from underneath the cake. If you didn't use paper strips, clean up the platter with a wet paper towel.

8. If you frosted with whipped cream or cream cheese and don't want the cake to dry out in the refrigerator, cover the whole cake with a cake dome or with a large inverted saucepan.

9. If you are frosting a cake in the summertime in a hot kitchen, you may want to assemble the cake differently so that it doesn't slide. Place the first layer bottom side up, and frost it; then place the second layer bottom side down on top of it, so the flat surfaces are next to each other. Frost the sides and top as you normally would.

10. If the cake is fragile, and you are worried that the frosting is heavy and will tear the cake, place the layer in the freezer for a few minutes to firm up. And remember that if you dust the cake with confectioners' sugar, do so at the last minute or the sugar will be absorbed into the cake.

STORING THE CAKE:
SHORT-TERM AND LONG-TERM

The good news is that cake-mix cakes are good keepers. If wrapped properly they will last up to a week (if you haven't gobbled them up by then) at room temperature or in the refrigerator, and they will stay fresh up to 6 months in a chest freezer.

The bad news is that many people don't wrap cakes in the right material, so they compromise the flavor of the cake. The refrigerator can rob a poorly wrapped cake of moisture. The freezer can rob a poorly wrapped cake of moisture and flavor. There are ways to wrap and store cakes successfully. But before you wrap, remember that it's easier to wrap a cake if the frosting is hard. That's not a problem for caramel frosting, which hardens as it cools, but it is a problem for the butter-cream and cream cheese frostings that are soft to the touch. Chill them uncovered at least 20 minutes before covering so that the packaging material doesn't pull the frosting off the cake. Allow a cake to cool completely before freezing it.

If the frozen cake has a creamy frosting or a filling containing eggs, then it must be thawed in the refrigerator from 8 hours to overnight. Otherwise, you can thaw a cake on the counter overnight. If the cake layers are frozen unfrosted, and you want to thaw them to frost, follow a procedure recommended by Pillsbury's Sandy Nieman: Thaw them three-quarters of the way covered, then uncover and complete the thawing. This allows the layers to dry out so the frosting will adhere to them.

Cake-Mix History

● ● ●

Long before many of us had savored our first bite of birthday cake, American scientists and flour manufacturers were putting together a cake mix. Although the first mixes were not on grocery store shelves until after World War II, the mix had been evolving since the 1920s. A Mr. McCollum of New Brunswick, New Jersey, developed a corn muffin mix in 1920, and a pie-crust mix two years later.

That same decade, the Duff Company of Pittsburgh, a molasses manufacturer, was successful in drying molasses in a huge vacuum oven, and it was the catalyst for their gingerbread mix in 1929. Duff went on to introduce white, spice, and devil's food cakes in the 1930s. In fact, a consumer cake mix was pending when World War II broke out. But wartime shortages put this on hold, and the big flour manufacturers instead developed baking mixes to feed the troops. Unfortunately, these mixes had an eternal shelf life and that's where they belonged. Their inferior flavor was due to poor dry milk, powdered eggs, and yeast. Luckily for consumers, the com-panies spent from 1943 to 1948 in research and development, fine-tuning the flavor and packaging of those early mixes.

With postwar households, it seemed, the revamped cake mix couldn't miss. Reunited families were prospering. Many women stayed in the workforce, and many of the ones who chose domestic life didn't know how to bake. Plus, rationing-weary consumers were a captive audience for new products. But in what form? The hottest controversy in those days was whether to add the eggs (powdered) or allow the cook to add her own fresh eggs.

In the end, General Mills and Pillsbury decided on a complete mix including eggs, but they would reformulate down the road as the companies learned the home cook indeed wanted to add eggs. Duncan Hines, coming into the game three years after its competitors, would in the end have the right formula. Their Three Star Special, so named because you could make a white, yellow, or chocolate cake from the same mix, called for consumers to add their own fresh eggs. It captured 48 percent of the market in just three weeks.

But clever marketing efforts ensured the success of the cake mix, especially as the manufacturers developed a face behind the name. For Pillsbury, it was a fictitious Ann Pillsbury. For General Mills, it was the legendary Betty Crocker. And for Duncan Hines, it was simply Duncan Hines, the only real person behind the name. Hines was a well-known restaurant critic from Kentucky who sold the rights to his name to Nebraska Consolidated Mills and later to Procter & Gamble.

Today, Ann has been replaced by the giggling Doughboy, Betty has gone through numerous reincarnations, and Duncan is to the consumer just another corporate name on the box.

In the half century that cake mixes have lined the supermarket baking aisle, they have experienced explosive growth and subtle transformations—with dry eggs, then without, a few mainstay flavors, then more specialty flavors, then bars, cakes with pudding, microwave cakes, and most recently, low-fat cakes. Mixes have been reformulated to contain shortenings that require less mixing time, need more liquid, and stay moister. And quality ingredients such as premium chocolate have been added to boost consumer appeal.

Along the way, glitches in packaging and distribution have been ironed out. Cake mixes travel well. General Mills' research and development department even designed a machine to simulate the jiggling of train movement. And at Pillsbury a senior home economist took the testing on the road, literally. She loaded Lemon Gold Cake Mix into the trunk of her car and drove the box around in a 3,000-mile circle in the state of Montana. A thermometer registered the highs and lows of the trip, and the effect of high altitude on the mix was noted.

Distribution has changed since those early days, too. Manufacturers used to sell to regional supermarkets, and had the chance to roll out a new mix a bit at a time, gauging consumer feedback along the way. Nowadays marketing must be strategically planned. And research and development of a new cake mix is crucial. Any mistakes in formulation can be costly in what has become a hyper-competitive industry. Just as Pillsbury launched a cake mix with pudding inside, so did General Mills. Just as one signs on Hershey's chocolate, the other enlists Jell-O gelatin. Whatever the companies can do to catch the 45-second attention span of today's busy shopper is what will be rolled out next.

But the mix that most consumers want to buy, according to ACNielsen, isn't tutti-frutti or banana-rum-a-rama. It's yellow, followed by white, then devil's food. And ironically these were the first mixes to come our way, some 50 years ago.

Cake-Mix Time Line

1842   Jay Fowler of Baltimore patents self-rising flour, the beginning
of the mix.

1920   Corn-muffin mix developed by Mr. McCollum of New Brunswick, N.J.,
who tests products at church suppers.

1921   General Mills creates the Betty Crocker persona.

1929   The Duff Company of Pittsburgh, a molasses manufacturer, creates
gingerbread mix, drying molasses in a vacuum oven. Also introduces
white, spice, and devil's food cake mixes between 1930 and 1936.

1943   General Mills begins Betty Crocker cake-mix research.

1943   Baking mixes, plagued by poor packaging, tested for use in the U.S.
armed forces by industry and government team.

1946   Duncan Hines, experimental cake-mix testing begins.

1947   General Mills introduces single-layer Betty Crocker ginger cake mix.

1948   General Mills introduces devil's food and party cake mixes.

1948   Pillsbury introduces a white layer cake mix, and a chocolate
fudge cake mix a month later.

1949   Grand National Recipe and Baking Contest from
Pillsbury; first Bake-Off.

1951   Duncan Hines' first cake mix—the Three Star Special—stuns
competitors as it captures 48 percent of the market in 3 weeks.

1951   Pillsbury introduces a yellow cake mix.

1952   Betty Crocker yellow and white cake mixes come onto the market.

1952   Pillsbury angel food cake mix arrives.

1954   Betty Crocker's Answer Cake offers foil pan, mix, and frosting for busy consumer; discontinued by 1968.

1955   Michigan's Chelsea Milling introduces Jiffy cake mixes in yellow, white, and devil's food.

1956   Procter & Gamble buys Duncan Hines mixes from Nebraska Consolidated Mills in Omaha.

1958   Betty Crocker unveils the chiffon-cake mix.

1964   Betty Crocker reformulates mix, adding new emulsified shortenings.

1966   Tunnel of Fudge Cake puts the Bundt pan on the map.

1967   New Pillsbury mix cuts the mixing time in half.

1971   Pillsbury Bake-Off winner Pecan Pie Surprise Bars uses mix and begins bar-mania.

1974   Pillsbury Bake-Off winner Chocolate Cherry Bars brings cake-mix doctoring to the forefront.

1977   Pillsbury introduces pudding-in-the-mix layer cakes. General Mills follows.

1983   The Friendship Cake, calling for mix and a fruit starter, most requested recipe from Betty Crocker test kitchens.

1988   Pillsbury Bake-Off winner Chocolate Praline Layer Cake epitomizes the indulgent 1980s.

1996   Pillsbury offers $1 million for grand prize at Bake-Off.

1998   Aurora Foods of Columbus, Ohio, buys Duncan Hines cake mixes from P&G.

Aurora Foods (Duncan Hines); Chelsea Milling; General Mills; The Pillsbury Company.

Also thanks to: Gerot, Paul S. *Convenience, Ease and Success from the Oven: The Story of Prepared Cake Mixes*. Article written for executives of the Pillsbury Company.

Trager, James. *The Food Chronology*. New York: Henry Holt, 1995.

Chocolate Cakes

• • •

They won't tell you this in biology class, but there are other things besides hair color and height that are hereditary. Another is a love for chocolate.

You see, I inherited my love for chocolate from my mother, who doesn't consider dessert fit to eat unless it is made of chocolate—preferably dark and semisweet chocolate. And when my mother gets a hankering for chocolate, she makes a chocolate sheet cake with a hot chocolate frosting and toasted pecans, or a deep chocolate cream pie. She prefers intense flavors that yield intense satisfaction.

I understand that predicament, when dessert just doesn't seem like dessert unless it is chocolate. I've gotten a great deal more open-minded about this, and have fallen in love with many a nonchocolate cake in this book. But in a pinch, it'll be the chocolate cupcake or the chocolate sauce that I run to. And my younger daughter, Litton, is the same way. Her sister, Kathleen, will eagerly accept a slice of lemon cake or the whitest, blandest cake imaginable, but Litton? No, she'll wrinkle her nose and do the chocolate whine: "Don't we have anything chocolate?" I pity the poor man who must listen to that as Litton gets older, for I know from experience it's not a craving that passes with time. So for those of you who inherited the chocolate bug or for those newcomers who have just been bitten, here are some extravagantly rich and decidedly chocolate cakes to suit you. And they offer a little for everyone.

For those birthdays when only chocolate cake is in order, do make Buttermilk Devil's Food Cake with White Chocolate Frosting, or Lethal Peppermint Chocolate Cake, or Chocolate Sheet Cake with Peanut Butter Frosting, or Deeply Chocolate Almond Cake with Chocolate Cream Cheese Frosting. And don't forget Sour Cream Chocolate Cupcakes with Sour Cream Chocolate Frosting for the little ones to tote to a school party.

For the suppers with neighbors, carry along a Chocolate Pistachio Cake, Darn Good Chocolate Cake, Stacy's Chocolate Chip Cake, or Chocolate Marble Cake with Shiny Chocolate Glaze. And when a sheet cake is in order, bake Chocolate-Covered Cherry Cake, Mississippi Mud Cake, or Old-Fashioned Cola Cake.

If it's a faint (heaven forbid!) taste of chocolate you prefer, then opt for a Milk Chocolate Pound Cake. If it's the sweetest, gooiest chocolate dessert you're after, try the Turtle Cake or Chocolate Praline Cake.

So for all of us who inherited the chocolate gene and for those folks who just have to put up with us—enjoy!

DEEPLY CHOCOLATE ALMOND CAKE WITH CHOCOLATE CREAM CHEESE FROSTING

The only thing more delicious than one slice of this cake is a second slice of this cake. But fear not! Only the frosting is a calorie-buster. The rich almond-scented cake is made with buttermilk, vegetable oil, and just three eggs. Bake it a day ahead of serving so the flavors have time to meld.

SERVES: 16

PREPARATION TIME: 10 MINUTES

BAKING TIME: 28 TO 30 MINUTES

ASSEMBLY TIME: 20 MINUTES

Solid vegetable shortening for greasing the pans

Flour for dusting the pans

1 ounce unsweetened chocolate, coarsely chopped

⅓ cup water

1 package (18.25 ounces) plain devil's food cake mix

1 cup buttermilk

½ cup vegetable oil, such as canola, corn, safflower, soybean, or sunflower

3 large eggs

1 teaspoon pure almond extract

Chocolate Cream Cheese Frosting (page 421), made with pure almond extract

1. Place a rack in the center of the oven and preheat the oven to 350°F. Generously grease two 9-inch round cake pans with solid vegetable shortening, then dust with flour. Shake out the excess flour. Set the pans aside.

2. Heat the chopped chocolate and water in a small saucepan over low heat until melted, stirring constantly. Set the pan aside to cool for 10 minutes.

3. Place the cake mix, buttermilk, oil, eggs, almond extract, and melted chocolate mixture in a large mixing bowl. Blend with an electric mixer on low speed for 1 minute. Stop the machine and scrape down the sides of the bowl with a rubber spatula. Increase the mixer speed to medium and beat 2 minutes more, scraping the sides down again if needed. The batter should look thick and combined. Divide the batter between the prepared pans, smoothing it out with the rubber spatula. Place the pans in the oven side by side.

4. Bake the cakes until they spring back when lightly pressed with your finger and just start to pull away from the sides of the pan, 28 to 30 minutes. Remove the pans from the oven and place them on wire racks to cool for 5 minutes. Run a dinner knife around the edge of each layer and invert each onto a rack, then invert them again onto another rack so that the cakes are right side up. Cool completely, 30 minutes.

5. Meanwhile, prepare the Chocolate Cream Cheese Frosting.

6. Place one cake layer, right side up, on a serving platter. Spread the top with frosting. Place the second layer, right side up, on top of the first layer and frost the top and sides of the cake with clean, smooth strokes.

❋ *Place this cake, uncovered, in the refrigerator until the frosting sets, 20 minutes. Cover the cake with waxed paper and store in the refrigerator for up to 1 week. Or freeze it, wrapped in aluminum foil, for up to 6 months. Thaw the cake overnight in the refrigerator before serving.*

R

the Cake Doctor says...

It's the unsweetened chocolate added to this cake mix that improves the flavor. For an even more intense chocolate flavor, dust the pans with unsweetened cocoa powder instead of flour.

BUTTERMILK DEVIL'S FOOD CAKE WITH WHITE CHOCOLATE FROSTING

My husband, John, celebrates his birthday a week before Christmas. And while this may have curtailed the number of birthday presents he received as a child, it only enhanced what type of birthday cake would come his way. In December, his cake  has usually been either coconut or deep, dark chocolate. On his most recent birthday, I made him this devil's food cake moistened with buttermilk and intensified with unsweetened cocoa. Then I spread the middle, top, and sides with a creamy white chocolate frosting. It was stunning, festive, and delicious, especially when served with peppermint ice cream.

SERVES: 16

PREPARATION TIME: 10 MINUTES

BAKING TIME: 28 TO 30 MINUTES

ASSEMBLY TIME: 20 MINUTES

Solid vegetable shortening for greasing
the pans
Flour for dusting the pans
1 package (18.25 ounces) plain devil's food
cake mix
3 tablespoons unsweetened cocoa powder
1⅓ cups buttermilk
½ cup vegetable oil, such as canola, corn,
safflower, soybean, or sunflower
3 large eggs
1 teaspoon pure vanilla extract
White Chocolate Frosting (page 424)

R

the Cake Doctor says...

Cocoa is a great way to add some extra chocolate punch to a devil's food cake mix. I prefer devil's food mixes compared to other chocolate cake mixes because they are more intense and the brownish-black color of the cake resembles a from-scratch cake more closely. If you want even more intensity, substitute 1 tablespoon instant coffee powder for one of the tablespoons of cocoa.

1. Place a rack in the center of the oven and preheat the oven to 350°F. Generously grease two 9-inch round cake pans with solid vegetable shortening, then dust with flour. Shake out the excess flour. Set the pans aside.

2. Place the cake mix, cocoa powder, buttermilk, oil, eggs, and vanilla in a large mixing bowl. Blend with an electric mixer on low speed for 1 minute. Stop the machine and scrape down the sides of the bowl with a rubber spatula. Increase the mixer speed to medium and beat 2 minutes more, scraping the sides down again if needed. The batter should look well blended. Divide the batter between the prepared pans, smoothing it out with the rubber spatula. Place the pans in the oven side by side.

3. Bake the cakes until they spring back when lightly pressed with your finger and just start to pull away from the sides of the pan, 28 to 30 minutes. Remove the pans from the oven and place them on wire racks to cool for 10 minutes. Run a dinner knife around the edge of each layer and invert each onto a rack, then invert them again onto another rack so that the cakes are right side up. Cool completely, 30 minutes.

4. Meanwhile, prepare the White Chocolate Frosting.

5. Place one cake layer, right side up, on a serving platter. Spread the top with frosting. Place the second layer, right side up, on top of the first layer and frost the top and sides of the cake with clean, smooth strokes.

❋ *Place this cake, uncovered, in the refrigerator until the frosting sets, 20 minutes. Cover the cake with waxed paper and store, in the refrigerator, for up to 1 week. Or freeze, wrapped in aluminum foil, for up to 6 months. Thaw the cake overnight in the refrigerator before serving.*

LETHAL PEPPERMINT CHOCOLATE CAKE

I was raised on King Leo peppermint sticks. We used to stick them into a juicy orange and suck them like a straw. We used to crush them into homemade peppermint ice cream, churned on the patio outside. This cake is an ode to my childhood.  Based on the buttermilk devil's food recipe on page 28, it has a layer of Peppermint Buttercream Frosting sandwiched in between the cake layers. Then the entire lethal confection is enrobed with a peppermint-infused Chocolate Ganache. It's over the top, and I love it!

SERVES: 16
PREPARATION TIME: 10 MINUTES
BAKING TIME: 28 TO 30 MINUTES
ASSEMBLY TIME: 25 MINUTES

Chocolate Ganache (page 428)
1 tablespoon peppermint schnapps
Solid vegetable shortening for greasing the
     pans
Flour for dusting the pans
1 package (18.25 ounces) plain devil's food
     cake mix
3 tablespoons unsweetened cocoa powder
1⅓ cups buttermilk
½ cup vegetable oil, such as canola, corn,
     safflower, soybean, or sunflower
3 large eggs
1 teaspoon pure vanilla extract
½ recipe Peppermint Buttercream Frosting
     (page 418)

1. Prepare the Chocolate Ganache, adding the peppermint schnapps after all the chocolate has melted. Let the ganache cool.

R

the Cake Doctor says...

You can make the Chocolate Ganache and Peppermint Buttercream Frosting early in the day. If you don't want to add peppermint schnapps to them, use ½ teaspoon peppermint extract instead. Then, just bake and cool the chocolate layers and you're ready to assemble the cake.

2. Place a rack in the center of the oven and preheat the oven to 350°F. Generously grease two 9-inch round cake pans with solid vegetable shortening, then dust with flour. Shake out the excess flour. Set the pans aside.

3. Place the cake mix, cocoa powder, buttermilk, oil, eggs, and vanilla in a large mixing bowl. Blend with an electric mixer on low speed for 1 minute. Stop the machine and scrape down the sides of the bowl with a rubber spatula. Increase the mixer speed to medium and beat 2 minutes more, scraping the sides down again if needed. The batter should look thick and combined. Divide the batter between the prepared pans, smoothing it out with the rubber spatula. Place the pans in the oven side by side.

4. Bake the cakes until they spring back when lightly pressed with your finger and just start to pull away from the sides of the pan, 28 to 30 minutes. Remove the pans from the oven and place them on wire racks to cool for 10 minutes. Run a dinner knife around the edge of each layer and invert each onto a rack, then invert them again onto another rack so that the cakes are right side up. Cool completely, 30 minutes more.

5. Meanwhile, prepare half a recipe of Peppermint Buttercream Frosting.

6. Place one cake layer, right side up, on a serving platter. Spread the top with Peppermint Buttercream Frosting. Place the second layer, right side up, on top of the first layer and frost the top and sides of the cake with Chocolate Ganache that has cooled until it is spreadable. Work with clean, smooth strokes. Chill the cake until ready to serve.

✸ *Place this cake, uncovered, in the refrigerator until the frosting sets, 20 minutes. Cover the cake with waxed paper and store in the refrigerator for up to 1 week. Or freeze it, wrapped in aluminum foil, for up to 6 months. Thaw the cake overnight in the refrigerator before serving.*

Ganache

Making ganache for the first time is an eye-opening experience. You will wonder what took you so long to savor the simplicity of hot whipping cream and chopped semisweet chocolate stirred together in this mysterious and irresistible chocolate sauce. Ask a pastry chef what ganache is and he or she will answer a chocolate cake filling, frosting, or the center of a truffle. But consult a French dictionary and you'll find the word means "old fool." Is this because any old fool is able to assemble this easy ganache? You decide.

Begin with whipping (heavy) cream in a saucepan. Bring it to a boil, then remove it from the heat and pour it over chopped chocolate in a mixing bowl. Stir and add a tablespoon of liqueur, if desired. Then serve warm as a stunning glaze over cake or ice cream. Or cool to use as a spread on cake layers as a luxurious frosting, or whip on high speed with an electric mixer for a whipped ganache frosting. Or simply cover the ganache with plastic wrap and let it get quite cold in the refrigerator. Scoop the ganache up with a melon baller into truffles and roll them in unsweetened cocoa powder.

Ganache purists insist the ratio of cream to chocolate needs to vary with the end result. For example,

- for that glaze, use equal parts cream and chocolate (1 cup cream to 8 ounces chocolate)

- for the frosting, use about 1 cup cream to about 12 ounces chocolate

- for the whipped ganache, use more cream than chocolate—1 cup cream to 4 ounces chocolate

- for the truffles, use 1 cup cream to 16 ounces chocolate

Ganache can be wrapped with plastic wrap and refrigerated up to 5 days or frozen up to 6 months.

CHOCOLATE PRALINE CAKE

Here's a show-stopper of a dessert, a fancy layered thing with a quick praline of butter, brown sugar, cream, and pecans in the bottom of the pans and chocolate batter on top. You sandwich the layers with sweetened whipped cream, and, well, it's a winner! In fact, this cake is adapted from a 1988 Pillsbury Bake-Off contest winner. And whereas this cake works well with a pudding-enhanced mix, if you want to use plain devil's food cake mix, that works, too!

SERVES: 16
PREPARATION TIME: 12 MINUTES
BAKING TIME: 35 TO 37 MINUTES
ASSEMBLY TIME: 15 MINUTES

8 tablespoons (1 stick) butter, cut up
¼ cup heavy (whipping) cream
1 cup packed light brown sugar
¾ cup chopped pecans
1 package (18.25 ounces) devil's food cake
    mix with pudding
1 cup water
½ cup vegetable oil, such as canola,
    corn, safflower, soybean,
    or sunflower
3 large eggs
Sweetened Cream (page 432)
1 square (1 ounce) semisweet chocolate,
    for garnish

1. Place a rack in the center of the oven and preheat the oven to 325°F. Set aside two 9-inch round cake pans.

2. Place the butter, cream, and brown sugar in a small heavy saucepan. Cook

Melting Chocolate

It seems an easy task to just melt some chocolate. But chocolate is a clever and finicky ingredient:

- If you must add liquid, chocolate needs more than 1 tablespoon moisture per ounce of chocolate to melt smoothly. Too little liquid will cause the chocolate to seize up and look curdled.

- Don't put a lid on a pan of melting chocolate or the condensation will drip down into your chocolate and will cause it to seize.

- If chocolate seizes, remove the pan from the heat and try whisking in 1 teaspoon of a light vegetable (canola, corn, safflower, soybean, or sunflower) oil for each ounce of chocolate. This should smooth it out.

- Use low heat, preferably a double boiler with the simmering water level in the bottom pan at least ½ inch below the top pan.

- In actuality, a lot of people now melt chocolate in the microwave. Chop the chocolate first into pieces so it melts evenly and quickly. If you must use high power, do so for only 30 seconds and then stir. Medium power is safer; melt from 30 seconds to 1½ minutes, depending on the amount of chocolate you are melting. Open the door and stir the chocolate a couple of times as it melts. Microwaved chocolate will retain its shape, so stir it to see if it has really melted.

over low heat, stirring, until the butter is melted, 3 minutes. Pour the mixture evenly into the cake pans and sprinkle it evenly with the chopped pecans. Set the pans aside.

3. Place the cake mix, water, oil, and eggs in a large mixing bowl. Blend with an electric mixer on low speed for 1 minute. Stop the machine and scrape down the sides of the bowl with a rubber spatula. Increase

the mixer speed to medium and beat 2 minutes more, scraping the sides down again if needed. The batter should look well combined. Divide the batter between the prepared pans, pouring it over the pecan mixture, then smoothing it out with the rubber spatula. Place the pans in the oven side by side.

4. Bake the cakes until they spring back when lightly pressed with your finger, 35 to 37 minutes. Remove the pans from the oven and place them on wire racks to cool for 10 minutes. Run a dinner knife around the edge of each layer and invert each onto a rack to cool, praline side up.

5. Meanwhile, prepare the Sweetened Cream. Grate the semisweet chocolate for the garnish.

6. Place one cake layer, praline side up, on a serving platter and spread half of the Sweetened Cream on top. Place the second layer, praline side up, on top of the first and frost the top of it with the remaining Sweetened Cream, working with clean, smooth strokes. Scatter the grated chocolate on top of the cake. Slice and serve.

✳ *Store this cake, covered loosely in waxed paper, in the refrigerator for up to 3 days.*

the Cake Doctor says...

For a cake that totes easily to dinners away from home, bake this cake in a 13- by 9-inch baking pan for 55 minutes. Cool the cake for 10 minutes in the pan and then invert the cake onto a serving platter. Let the cake cool completely, frost it with Sweetened Cream, and garnish it with the grated chocolate.

DARN GOOD CHOCOLATE CAKE

My mother says she got this recipe from my aunt Louise Grissim some twenty-five years ago, but we can't track down its exact origin. What sets it apart from other chocolate cakes is the irresistible chocolatey aroma that permeates the kitchen as it bakes. And so with a cold glass of milk, you fork into a warm bite and mutter, "This is darn good chocolate cake" . . . thus confirming its name!

SERVES: 16

PREPARATION TIME: 10 MINUTES

BAKING TIME: 45 TO 50 MINUTES

Vegetable oil spray for misting the pan
Flour for dusting the pan
1 package (18.25 ounces) plain devil's food
    or dark chocolate fudge cake mix
1 package (3.9 ounces) chocolate instant
    pudding mix
4 large eggs
1 cup sour cream
½ cup warm water
½ cup vegetable oil, such as canola, corn,
    safflower, soybean, or sunflower
1½ cups semisweet chocolate chips

1. Place a rack in the center of the oven and preheat the oven to 350°F. Lightly mist a 12-cup Bundt pan with vegetable oil spray, then dust with flour. Shake out the excess flour. Set the pan aside.

2. Place the cake mix, pudding mix, eggs, sour cream, warm water, and oil in a large mixing bowl. Blend with an electric mixer on low speed for 1 minute. Stop the machine and scrape down the sides of the bowl with a rubber spatula. Increase the mixer speed to medium and beat 2 to 3 minutes more, scraping the sides down again if needed. The batter should look thick and well combined. Fold in the chocolate chips, making sure they are well distributed throughout the batter. Pour the batter into the prepared pan, smoothing it out with the rubber spatula. Place the pan in the oven.

3. Bake the cake until it springs back when lightly pressed with your finger and just starts to pull away from the sides of the pan, 45 to 50 minutes. Remove the pan from the oven and place it on a wire rack to cool for 20 minutes. Run a long, sharp knife around the edge of the cake and invert it onto the rack to cool completely, 20 minutes more. Or invert it onto a serving platter to slice and serve while still warm.

✹ *Store this cake, covered in aluminum foil or plastic wrap, at room temperature for up to 1 week. Or freeze it, wrapped in foil, for up to 6 months. Thaw the cake overnight on the counter before serving.*

the Cake Doctor says...

Use a plain devil's food or dark chocolate fudge cake mix for this recipe. Adding the pudding mix separately gives more moisture and chocolate flavor to the final result; the sour cream lends richness. And the Cake Doctor loves adding semisweet chips to a recipe, especially when the batter is nice and thick like this one and the chips stay suspended throughout the cake. Try mini chips for a variation.

MILK CHOCOLATE POUND CAKE

There's something energizing about a milk chocolate candy bar eaten in the afternoon just when you need a little pick-me-up to get you through the day.

In this pound-type cake, you've got the delicate, comforting flavor of milk chocolate that seems to say, "Sit down and enjoy me." But if you're looking for an intense chocolate experience, be forewarned, the chocolate taste here is deliciously understated.

SERVES: 16

PREPARATION TIME: 15 MINUTES

BAKING TIME:

55 TO 60 MINUTES

R the Cake Doctor says...

For a more pronounced chocolate flavor, substitute 6 ounces semisweet chocolate for the milk chocolate. Grate it as directed.

Vegetable oil spray for misting the pan
Flour for dusting the pan
4 bars (1.55 ounces each) milk chocolate
1 package (18.25 ounces) plain yellow
    cake mix
1 package (3.4 ounces) vanilla instant
    pudding mix
1 cup sour cream
½ cup vegetable oil, such as canola,
    corn, safflower, soybean,
    or sunflower
4 large eggs
1 teaspoon pure vanilla extract
2 teaspoons confectioners' sugar

1. Place a rack in the center of the oven and preheat the oven to 350°F. Lightly mist a 12-cup Bundt pan with vegetable oil spray, then dust with flour. Shake out the excess flour. Set the pan aside.

2. Break up the milk chocolate bars into 1-inch pieces and place them in a food processor fitted with the steel blade. Pulse on and off 12 to 15 times until the candy is grated but not a powder. (Some pieces may be large and some may be small.) Set the bowl aside.

3. Place the cake mix, pudding mix, sour cream, oil, eggs, and vanilla in a large mixing bowl. Blend with an electric mixer on low speed for 1 minute. Stop the machine and scrape down the sides of the bowl with a rubber spatula. Increase the mixer speed to medium and beat 2 minutes more, scraping the sides down again if needed.

The batter should look thick and smooth. Fold in the grated chocolate until it is well distributed. Pour the batter into the prepared pan, smoothing it out with the rubber spatula. Place the pan in the oven.

4. Bake the cake until it is golden brown and springs back when lightly pressed with your finger, 55 to 60 minutes. Remove the pan from the oven and place it on a wire rack to cool for 20 minutes. Run a long, sharp knife around the edge of the cake and invert it onto the rack to cool completely, 20 minutes more.

5. Place the cake on a serving platter and sift the confectioners' sugar over the top.

✱ *Store this cake, covered in plastic wrap or aluminum foil, at room temperature for up to 1 week. Or freeze it, wrapped in foil, for up to 6 months. Thaw the cake overnight on the counter before serving.*

A Chocolate Story

The word chocolate, I've read, comes from two Mexican words—"choco," meaning sound or noise, and "atle," meaning water. The Mexicans beat chocolate with water to make a frothy drink, which was the beverage of choice in the royal household. Emperor Montezuma is said to have consumed it as an aphrodisiac before entering his harem. And to no one's surprise, when chocolate was imported into Spain in the beginning of the seventeenth century, chocolate drinks were very much in vogue. Within fifty years, the rest of Europe had its hands on chocolate, and sipped it as a tranquilizer, digestive, and for most any ailment. No wonder!

CHOCOLATE PISTACHIO CAKE

What a wonderful combination of flavors—chocolate and pistachio! And what a simple and dazzling cake to prepare. It's far easier to pull together than it looks on the platter.

First chocolate chips and pecans are scattered in the pan, and then a swirled pistachio and chocolate batter is poured over. Once baked, the chips and pecans form a delectable crust, which is just the right foil for the soft, velvety cake. If you like, pour Shiny Chocolate Glaze over the cake for the crowning touch.

SERVES: 16

PREPARATION TIME: 15 MINUTES

BAKING TIME: 55 TO 60 MINUTES

Vegetable oil spray for misting the pan
Flour for dusting the pan
½ cup chopped pecans
½ cup semisweet chocolate chips
1 package (18.25 ounces) plain white cake mix
1 package (3.4 ounces) pistachio instant pudding mix
½ cup sugar
1 cup water
½ cup vegetable oil, such as canola, corn, safflower, soybean, or sunflower
4 large eggs
½ cup chocolate syrup
Shiny Chocolate Glaze (page 435; optional)

1. Place a rack in the center of the oven and preheat the oven to 350°F. Lightly mist a 12-cup Bundt pan with vegetable oil spray, then dust with flour. Shake out the excess flour. Sprinkle the pecans and chocolate chips evenly in the bottom of the pan. Set the pan aside.

2. Place the cake mix, pudding mix, sugar, water, oil, and eggs in a large mixing bowl. Blend with an electric mixer on low speed for 1 minute. Stop the machine and scrape down the sides of the bowl with a rubber spatula. Increase the mixer speed to medium and beat 2 minutes more. The batter should look thick and smooth. Remove 1 cup of the batter to a small bowl. Pour the chocolate syrup into the small bowl and stir until the mixture is well combined. Set aside.

3. Pour the remaining batter into the prepared pan. Pour the chocolate batter over the top, trying to keep the chocolate batter away from the edges of the pan. Swirl the chocolate batter into the white batter using a dinner knife. Place the pan in the oven.

4. Bake the cake until it is golden brown and springs back when lightly pressed with your finger, 55 to 60 minutes. Remove the pan from the oven and place it on a wire rack to cool for 20 minutes. Run a long, sharp knife around the edge of the cake and invert it onto a rack to cool completely, 20 minutes more.

5. To serve, place the cake onto a serving platter and slice. Or, if desired, glaze the cooled cake with Shiny Chocolate Glaze.

✳ *Store this cake, covered loosely in plastic wrap or aluminum foil, at room temperature for up to 1 week. Or freeze it, wrapped in foil, for up to 6 months. Thaw the cake overnight on the counter before serving.*

R
the Cake Doctor says...

You can also make this cake with a yellow cake mix, but the green color of the pistachio-flavored batter won't be as vivid.

STACY'S CHOCOLATE CHIP CAKE

Stacy Ross is a great Nashville cook and mom who knows a wonderful recipe when she sees it. This is a recipe she has used for years, making big batches when she's planning a party or it's time for gift giving. All I know is that I made it for my mother, who is fussy about cakes, and she kept coming back into the kitchen to cut off another slice. Bake the cake in a tube pan or in loaves. Both freeze well.

SERVES: 16

PREPARATION TIME: 15 MINUTES

BAKING TIME: 58 TO 60 MINUTES FOR A TUBE PAN; 50 TO 52 MINUTES FOR 8-INCH LOAVES

Vegetable oil spray for misting the pan
Flour for dusting the pan
1 bar (4 ounces) German chocolate
1 package (18.25 ounces) plain yellow
    cake mix
1 package (3.4 ounces) vanilla instant
    pudding mix
1 cup whole milk
1 cup vegetable oil, such as canola,
    corn, safflower, soybean,
    or sunflower
4 large eggs
1 package (6 ounces; 1 cup) semisweet
    chocolate chips

1. Place a rack in the center of the oven and preheat the oven to 325°F. Lightly mist a 10-inch tube pan (or three 8-inch loaf pans) with vegetable oil spray, then dust with flour. Shake out the excess flour. Set the pan aside.

2. Break the German chocolate bar into four pieces. Grate the bar using a food processor or a hand grater until the bar is finely grated. (If you are using a food processor, insert the steel blade and drop the chocolate pieces into the processor one at a time.) Set the grated chocolate aside.

3. Place the cake mix, pudding mix, milk, oil, and eggs in a large mixing bowl. Blend with an electric mixer on low speed for 1 minute. Stop the machine, fold in the grated chocolate, and scrape down the sides of the bowl with a rubber spatula. Increase the mixer speed to medium and beat 2 minutes more, scraping the sides down again if needed. Fold in the chocolate chips. The batter should look well blended, and the chocolate chips should be evenly distributed. Pour the batter into the prepared tube pan (or divide it equally among the loaf pans), smoothing it out with the rubber spatula. Place the pan in the oven.

4. Bake the cake until it is golden brown and springs back when lightly pressed with your finger, 58 to 60 minutes for a tube pan (50 to 52 minutes for loaf pans). Remove the pan from the oven and place it on a wire rack to cool for 20 minutes for a tube pan (5 minutes for loaf pans). Run a long, sharp knife around the edge of the cake and invert it onto a rack, then invert it again onto another rack so that it is right side up. Allow the cake to cool completely, 30 minutes more, then serve. (Cool loaves out of the pans, on their sides.)

✳ *Store this cake, covered in aluminum foil or plastic wrap, at room temperature for up to 1 week. Or freeze it, wrapped in foil, for up to 6 months. Thaw the cake overnight on the counter before serving.*

the Cake Doctor says...

One wonderful contribution that a pudding mix makes is to help suspend chocolate chips in a cake batter. Moisture, too, comes from the pudding mix, along with the large proportion of oil and whole milk. Two chocolates add richness and a delightful contrast in flavor.

CHOCOLATE MARBLE CAKE WITH SHINY CHOCOLATE GLAZE

The trick to creating a marbled look in this chocolate cake is to gently drag the chocolate batter through the yellow batter with a knife until the batter is just swirled. I remember the fascination I had with marbled foods when I was just learning to cook; there was something artistic in combining two different batters just as they went into the oven. So swirl away with this easy cake.

And if you're a fan of German chocolate, substitute it for the semisweet.

SERVES: 16
PREPARATION TIME: 12 MINUTES
BAKING TIME: 40 TO 45 MINUTES
ASSEMBLY TIME: 10 MINUTES

Vegetable oil spray for misting the pan
Flour for dusting the pan
1 package (18.25 ounces) plain yellow
    cake mix
1 cup sour cream
½ cup vegetable oil, such as canola,
    corn, safflower, soybean,
    or sunflower
4 tablespoons (½ stick) butter,
    melted
4 large eggs
1 teaspoon pure almond extract
2 squares (1 ounce each) semisweet
    chocolate, coarsely chopped
1 tablespoon milk
1 tablespoon water
Shiny Chocolate Glaze (page 435)

R
the Cake Doctor says...

Save time by using the microwave oven to melt both the butter and the chocolate called for in this batter. Melt them separately, using a glass measuring cup. Melt the 4 tablespoons butter on high power for about 30 seconds; the 2 squares chopped chocolate with the milk and water on high power for 30 seconds to 1 minute. Be careful not to let the chocolate burn. If the chocolate still retains its shape, stir with a wooden spoon until smooth.

1. Place a rack in the center of the oven and preheat the oven to 350°F. Lightly mist a 10-inch tube pan with vegetable oil spray, then dust with flour. Shake out the excess flour. Set the pan aside.

2. Place the cake mix, sour cream, oil, melted butter, eggs, and almond extract in a large mixing bowl. Blend with an electric mixer on low speed for 1 minute. Stop the machine and scrape down the sides of the bowl with a rubber spatula. Increase the mixer speed to medium and beat 2 minutes more, scraping the sides down again if needed. The batter should look well blended.

3. Meanwhile, melt the semisweet chocolate with the milk and water in a small saucepan over medium heat, stirring often, until the chocolate is melted and smooth. Cool slightly.

4. Pour the batter into the prepared pan, smoothing it out with the rubber spatula. Drop the chocolate mixture by spoonfuls over the batter. Marble the batter by swirling the chocolate lightly through it with a knife. Place the pan in the oven.

5. Bake the cake until it is golden brown and springs back when lightly pressed with your finger, 40 to 45 minutes. Remove the pan from the oven and place it on a wire rack to cool for 20 minutes.

6. Meanwhile, prepare the Shiny Chocolate Glaze.

7. Run a long, sharp knife around the edge of the cake and invert it onto a rack, then invert it again onto a serving platter, so that it is right side up. Pour the chocolate glaze over the top of the cake and let it drizzle down the sides. Allow the cake to cool completely, 30 minutes more, then serve.

✳ *Store this cake, covered in aluminum foil or plastic wrap, at room temperature for up to 1 week. Or freeze it, wrapped in foil, for up to 6 months. Thaw the cake overnight on the counter before serving.*

MISSISSIPPI MUD CAKE

If you judged a recipe solely on its title, you wouldn't go much farther here. Nothing seems too appetizing about a cake full of messy mud from the mighty Mississippi River. But step back and think about a precocious Southern cook who has just concocted a deep, dark, and moist chocolate cake. The cake is topped with marshmallows and a heavy, almost candy-like chocolate frosting. She takes one look and says in her best drawl, "Why, mercy me, that looks just like Mississippi mud," and so the name sticks. It's similar to the classic Old-Fashioned Cola Cake (page 55) except

that this cake is darker and marshmallows aren't added to the batter before baking; marshmallow creme is spread over the hot cake right after it comes out of the oven.

....

SERVES: 20

PREPARATION TIME: 5 MINUTES

BAKING TIME: 40 TO 42 MINUTES

ASSEMBLY TIME: 15 MINUTES

....

Vegetable oil spray for misting the pan
1 package (18.25 ounces) plain devil's food
  cake mix
8 tablespoons (1 stick) butter or margarine,
  melted
1½ cups buttermilk
2 large eggs
1 teaspoon pure vanilla extract
1 jar (7 ounces) marshmallow creme
Chocolate Pan Frosting (page 429)
1 cup chopped toasted pecans (see Toasting
  Nuts, page 134)

1. Place a rack in the center of the oven and preheat the oven to 350°F. Lightly mist a 13- by 9-inch baking pan with vegetable oil spray. Set the pan aside.

2. Place the cake mix, melted butter, buttermilk, eggs, and vanilla in a large mixing bowl. Blend with an electric mixer on low speed for 1 minute. Stop the machine and scrape down the sides of the bowl with a rubber spatula. Increase the mixer speed to medium and beat 2 minutes more, scraping the sides down again if needed. The batter should look well blended. Pour the batter into the prepared pan, smoothing it out with the rubber spatula. Place the pan in the oven.

3. Bake the cake until it springs back when lightly pressed with your finger, 40 to 42 minutes. Remove the pan from the oven and place it on a wire rack to cool. Spread the warm cake with the marshmallow creme.

4. Prepare the Chocolate Pan Frosting.

5. Pour the hot frosting on top of the marshmallow creme and spread it out with a spatula so that the frosting reaches the edges of the cake. Scatter the top with the toasted pecans. Cool the cake for 20 minutes before serving.

✱ *Store this cake, covered in aluminum foil, at room temperature for up to 1 week. Or freeze it, wrapped in foil, for up to 6 months. Thaw the cake overnight on the counter before serving.*

the Cake Doctor says...

Instead of disappearing marshmallows in this cake, you've got a layer of marshmallow creme that makes quite a statement! It creates a nice spongy, sweet contrast to the crunchy toasted pecans. If you would like to substitute marshmallows for the creme, use about 1½ cups of the mini variety. The hot frosting will melt the marshmallows.

TURTLE CAKE

Turtle Cake exists in countless variations. So named because containing caramel, pecans, and chocolate, it resembles the famous candy,  this recipe is better than the rest. Why? Because it is frosted with a quick glaze of melted chocolate chips and sprinkled with toasted pecans. No doubt about it, this cake is for serious sweet-lovers; it's so ooey-gooey it makes my teeth ache just to think about it!

SERVES: 20

PREPARATION TIME: 10 MINUTES

BAKING TIME: 50 TO 55 MINUTES

ASSEMBLY TIME: 5 MINUTES

Vegetable oil spray for misting the pan

1 package (14 ounces) vanilla caramels

1 can (5 ounces) evaporated milk

1 package (18.25 ounces) German chocolate cake mix with pudding

1¼ cups water

¾ cup (1½ sticks) butter, melted

2 large eggs

1 bag (12 ounces; 2 cups) semisweet chocolate chips

2 cups chopped pecans

1. Place a rack in the center of the oven and preheat the oven to 350°F. Lightly mist a 13- by 9-inch baking pan with vegetable oil spray. Set the pan aside.

2. Place the caramels and evaporated milk in a small saucepan over low heat. Stir and cook until the caramels melt, 4 to 5 minutes. Cover to keep warm and set the pan aside.

3. Place the cake mix, water, melted butter, and eggs in a large mixing bowl. Blend with an electric mixer on low speed for 1 minute. Stop the machine and scrape

R
the Cake Doctor says...

This cake follows the "more is better" theory, which is okay every now and then! German chocolate cakes ordinarily bake up pale and tasteless but this one is a doozy, amplified by caramel, chocolate, butter, and toasted pecans.

down the sides of the bowl with a rubber spatula. Increase the mixer speed to medium and beat 2 minutes more, scraping the sides down again if needed. The batter should look well blended. Pour half of the batter into the prepared pan, smoothing it out with the rubber spatula. Place the pan in the oven.

4. Bake the cake until it begins to puff around the edges but the center is still soft, 13 to 15 minutes. Remove the pan from the oven, but leave the oven on.

5. Pour the caramel mixture over the cake and spread it out to the edges of the pan with a rubber spatula. Sprinkle the top with 1 cup of the chocolate chips and 1 cup of the pecans. Pour the remaining cake batter evenly over the top and carefully spread it out to the edges of the

pan with the rubber spatula. Place the pan in the oven.

6. Bake the cake until it springs back when lightly pressed with your finger and just starts to pull away from the sides of the pan, 35 to 40 minutes more. Remove the pan from the oven, but leave the oven on. Place the pan on a wire rack to cool while you prepare the toppings.

7. Place the remaining 1 cup pecans in a pie plate and toast them in the oven for 3 to 4 minutes. Remove them from the oven.

8. Melt the remaining 1 cup chocolate chips in a small saucepan over low heat (or in a microwave oven) until melted and smooth. Spread the melted chocolate over the cake with a rubber spatula, then sprinkle the toasted pecans over the chocolate glaze. Allow the cake to cool for 20 minutes more before slicing it.

✳ *Store this cake, covered in waxed paper, at room temperature for up to 5 days or in the refrigerator for up to 1 week. Or freeze it, wrapped in aluminum foil, for up to 6 months. Thaw the cake overnight on the counter before serving.*

CHOCOLATE-COVERED CHERRY CAKE

Here is one of those crazy recipes you look at and think, How will this work? Four ingredients? No oil? No liquid? Trust me. This cake works because of the cherry pie filling. It not only adds body, but also provides liquid (serving as a substitute for any oil) and moistness. This cake stays fresh for days. Plus, the partnership between chocolate and cherries is tried and true—just think of the candy by the same name!

    After testing several versions of this recipe, I found out the original has been around for years and was the grand prize winner of the 1974 Pillsbury Bake-Off contest. I have added a to-die-for homemade chocolate glaze.

SERVES: 20
PREPARATION TIME: 7 MINUTES
BAKING TIME: 30 TO 35 MINUTES
ASSEMBLY TIME: 10 MINUTES

CAKE:

Vegetable oil spray for misting the pan
1 package (18.25 ounces) plain devil's
    food cake mix or devil's food mix with
    pudding
1 can (21 ounces) cherry pie filling
2 large eggs
1 teaspoon pure almond extract

CHOCOLATE GLAZE:

1 cup sugar
⅓ cup butter
⅓ cup whole milk
1 package (6 ounces; 1 cup) semisweet
    chocolate chips

the Cake Doctor says...

Emulsifiers in the cake mix work together with the cherry pie filling to keep the cake moist for days.

1. Place a rack in the center of the oven and preheat the oven to 350°F. Lightly mist a 13- by 9-inch baking pan with vegetable oil spray. Set the pan aside.

2. Place the cake mix, cherry pie filling, eggs, and almond extract in a large mixing bowl. Blend with an electric mixer on low speed for 1 minute. Stop the machine and scrape down the sides of the bowl with a rubber spatula. Increase the mixer speed to medium and beat 2 minutes more, scraping the sides down again if needed. The batter should look thick and well blended. Pour the batter into the prepared pan, smoothing the top with the rubber spatula. Place the pan in the oven.

3. Bake the cake until it springs back when lightly pressed with your finger and just starts to pull away from the sides of the pan, 30 to 35 minutes. Remove the pan from the oven and place it on a wire rack while you prepare the glaze.

4. For the glaze, place the sugar, butter, and milk in a small saucepan over medium-low heat and cook, stirring constantly, until the mixture comes to a boil. Boil, stirring constantly, for 1 minute. Remove the pan from the heat and stir in the chocolate chips. When the chips have melted and the glaze is smooth, pour it over the warm cake so that it covers the entire surface. The glaze will be thin but will firm up. Cool the cake for 20 minutes more before cutting it into squares and serving.

✳ *Store this cake, covered in aluminum foil, at room temperature for up to 5 days or in the refrigerator for up to 1 week. Or freeze the cake, wrapped in foil, for up to 6 months. Thaw the cake overnight on the counter before serving.*

CHOCOLATE SHEET CAKE WITH PEANUT BUTTER FROSTING

"**T**aste me," this sturdy sheet cake seems to be calling out. The compatible flavors of chocolate and peanut butter unite to form one memorable cake, capable of traveling well right in its pan.

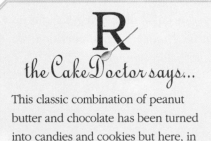

R
the Cake Doctor says...

This classic combination of peanut butter and chocolate has been turned into candies and cookies but here, in cake form, it is sublime. For added interest and a little texture, substitute crunchy peanut butter for the smooth.

SERVES: 20

PREPARATION TIME: 10 MINUTES

BAKING TIME: 40 TO 45 MINUTES

ASSEMBLY TIME: 10 MINUTES

Vegetable oil spray for misting the pan

*1 package (18.25 ounces) plain devil's food
　cake mix*

2 tablespoons unsweetened cocoa powder

1⅓ cups buttermilk

*½ cup vegetable oil, such as canola, corn,
　safflower, soybean, or sunflower*

3 large eggs

1 teaspoon pure vanilla extract

Peanut Butter Frosting (page 427)

1. Place a rack in the center of the oven and preheat the oven to 350°F. Lightly mist a 13- by 9-inch baking pan with vegetable oil spray. Set the pan aside.

2. Place the cake mix, cocoa powder, buttermilk, oil, eggs, and vanilla in a large mixing bowl. Blend with an electric

Devil's Food

If angel food cake is the gentle and soft dessert you bake for ladies' luncheons and children's teas, then its opposite—the devil's food—seems the right dessert for every other occasion. For naughty devil's food is built on deep chocolate flavors and has a big coarse crumb, nothing for the timid. Slather it with a frosting of more deep chocolate or of milder white chocolate. And the only thing more delicious than a devil's food cake is another slice of devil's food cake.

Fortunately for cake doctoring, it's easy to improvise and improve on a devil's food cake mix. Add up to 3 tablespoons unsweetened cocoa powder for a more decided chocolate punch. Or do the trick with a square (1 ounce) of unsweetened chocolate melted with ⅓ cup boiling water. You can also add a tablespoon of instant coffee powder for an extra kick, especially if you're frosting the cake with a sweet, fluffy mocha-infused buttercream frosting. But you absolutely must add buttermilk to this cake. It assures you a moist cake and compensates for your addition of cocoa, which can dry out cake batter. Plus, the acidity in buttermilk naturally complements chocolate.

There you have it: A naughty but delicious chocolate cake. Worthy of one slice, two, even three. So sell your soul to the devil.

mixer on low speed for 1 minute. Stop the machine and scrape down the sides of the bowl with a rubber spatula. Increase the mixer speed to medium and beat 2 minutes more, scraping the sides down again if needed. The batter should look thick and combined. Pour the batter into the prepared pan, smoothing it out with the rubber spatula. Place the pan in the oven.

3. Bake the cake until it springs back when lightly pressed with your finger and just starts to pull away from the sides of the pan, 40 to 45 minutes. Remove the pan from the oven and place it on a wire rack to cool for 30 minutes.

4. Meanwhile, prepare the Peanut Butter Frosting.

5. Frost the top of the cake, spreading the frosting out to the edges with a rubber spatula. Slice and serve.

✱   *Store this cake, covered in aluminum foil or plastic wrap, at room temperature for up to 3 days or in the refrigerator for up* *to 1 week. Or freeze it, wrapped in foil, for up to 6 months. Thaw the cake overnight on the counter before serving.*

Tips on Working with Chocolate

- Supermarket baking chocolate works well in the frostings and cakes in this book.

- Semisweet and bittersweet chocolates are interchangeable for recipes in this book.

- Do not substitute chocolate chips—either semisweet or white—when the recipe calls for simply semisweet or white chocolate. Use bar chocolate. The chips have a tighter consistency because they have been specially formulated to withstand heat and not melt. Frostings and glazes made from them are not as creamy.

- Chocolate in a recipe may cause it to bake more quickly. For these reasons you want to keep your eyes on that chocolate cake in the oven. Don't let it overbake!

- Cocoa powder is an excellent addition to a cake-mix cake, and you can add

up to 3 tablespoons (the equivalent of 1 ounce of unsweetened chocolate) to give the mix more flavor. Use unsweetened cocoa powder, not Dutch-process cocoa, which has been treated with an alkali to make it more soluble and more delicate in flavor.

- Milk chocolate is fine when you want a mild chocolate flavor, but it doesn't have the intensity or the shelf life of either semisweet or unsweetened chocolate.

- White chocolate isn't chocolate at all, for it contains no chocolate liquor (just cocoa butter, milk, and flavorings). But it does have a creamy consistency that works well in frostings, and its milky flavor contrasts nicely with a deep chocolate cake.

- It's easy to amplify the chocolate taste by adding pure vanilla extract, dark rum, or toasted nuts.

OLD-FASHIONED COLA CAKE

Drinking a Coca-Cola is just the beginning. Southern cooks are prone to pour Coke onto hams before they bake them, make gelatin salads out of it, and, yes, pour it into a cake mix and frosting. This cola cake recipe has been around for a long time, but perhaps not made with a mix. Begin with a white cake mix, moisten it with the cola of your choice (Coke, Pepsi, or RC) and buttermilk, and then add the customary miniature marshmallows. And if you think that's not sweet enough, wait until you try the frosting. Yum!

SERVES: 20
PREPARATION TIME: 5 MINUTES
BAKING TIME: 40 TO 42 MINUTES
ASSEMBLY TIME: 15 MINUTES

CAKE:

Vegetable oil spray for misting the pan
1 package (18.25 ounces) plain white
   cake mix
4 tablespoons unsweetened cocoa powder
8 tablespoons (1 stick) butter or margarine,
   melted
1 cup cola
½ cup buttermilk
2 large eggs
1 teaspoon pure vanilla extract
1½ cups miniature marshmallows

COLA FROSTING:

8 tablespoons (1 stick) butter or
   margarine
4 tablespoons unsweetened cocoa powder
⅓ cup cola
4 cups confectioners' sugar, sifted
1 cup chopped pecans

R

the Cake Doctor says...

From-scratch cola cakes are not as dark and chocolatey as devil's food cakes, so for this easy version I start with a plain white cake mix and flavor it with unsweetened cocoa powder. The marshmallows melt into the cake batter as it bakes, making sweet, sticky pockets. And the two-egg cake bakes up rich and dense with the addition of butter and buttermilk. The cola frosting is a dandy, too, much the same as the Chocolate Pan Frosting (page 429). For added flavor, toast your pecans before folding them into the frosting.

1. Place a rack in the oven and preheat the oven to 350°F. Lightly mist a 13- by 9-inch baking pan with vegetable oil spray. Set the pan aside.

2. Place the cake mix, cocoa powder, melted butter, cola, buttermilk, eggs, and vanilla in a large mixing bowl. Blend with an electric mixer on low speed for 1 minute. Stop the machine and scrape down the sides of the bowl with a rubber spatula. Increase the mixer speed to medium and beat 2 minutes more, scraping the sides down again if needed. The

batter should look well blended. Fold in the marshmallows. Pour the batter into the prepared pan, smoothing it out with the rubber spatula. Place the pan in the oven.

3. Bake the cake until it springs back when lightly pressed with your finger and just starts to pull away from the sides of the pan, 40 to 42 minutes. Remove the pan from the oven and place it on a wire rack to cool for 15 minutes.

4. Meanwhile, prepare the frosting. Place the butter in a medium saucepan over low heat. As the butter melts, stir in the cocoa powder and cola. Let the mixture come just to a boil, stirring constantly, and then remove it from the heat. Stir in the confectioners' sugar until the frosting is thickened and smooth. Fold in the pecans.

5. Pour the frosting over the top of the cake, spreading it out with a rubber spatula so that it reaches the edges of the cake. Cool the cake for 20 minutes before serving.

✳ *Store this cake, covered in aluminum foil, at room temperature for up to 1 week. Or freeze it, wrapped in foil, for up to 6 months. Thaw the cake overnight on the counter before serving.*

Marshmallows

Ever wonder how marshmallows got their name?

They were once sweet treats made from the roots of the marsh mallow plant (known as *Althaea officinalis*), and the pharaohs of ancient Egypt were especially fond of them. Today marshmallows are no longer constructed from the plant that gave them a name. Instead, they're made of corn syrup, sugar, and gelatin. And they're associated with some of America's most child-friendly recipes: They are toasted and sandwiched into campfire food like s'mores; they crown whipped sweet potato casserole; they are stirred into the classic cola cake, spread atop Mississippi Mud Cake, dropped into hot cocoa. How can a child or an adult possibly resist marshmallows?

15 Cakes to Tote to a Potluck

1. Carrot Cake with Fresh Orange Cream Cheese Frosting (page 109)

2. Old-Fashioned Cola Cake (page 55)

3. Stacy's Chocolate Chip Cake (page 42)

4. Grandma's Coconut Icebox Cake (page 118)

5. Darn Good Chocolate Cake (page 36)

6. Easy Tiramisù (page 146)

7. Banana Pudding Cake (page 139)

8. Tennessee Jam Cake (page 116)

9. Amaretto Cake (page 303)

10. Pumpkin Pie Crumble Cake (page 207)

11. Gooey Butter Cake (page 240)

12. Lemon Chip Picnic Cake (page 96)

13. Strawberry Cake with Strawberry Cream Cheese Frosting (page 64)

14. Old-Fashioned Pear and Ginger Cake (page 98)

15. Punch Bowl Cake (page 366)

WHITE CHOCOLATE POUND CAKE

These are lovely loaves to wrap up with a pretty ribbon for a special friend. Or serve thick slices plain or with a scoop of your favorite ice cream. Or tuck them in the freezer to pull out when fresh berries come into the markets. It's amazing how the consistency of this cake mimics the tight-grained consistency of a from-scratch pound cake.

SERVES: 18

PREPARATION TIME: 15 MINUTES

BAKING TIME:
40 TO 45 MINUTES

Vegetable oil spray for misting the pans
Flour for dusting the pans
6 ounces white chocolate,
    coarsely chopped
1 package (18.25 ounces) plain white
    cake mix
8 tablespoons (1 stick) butter, melted
1 cup whole milk
3 large eggs
1 teaspoon pure vanilla extract

1. Place a rack in the center of the oven and preheat the oven to 350°F. Lightly mist three 8-inch loaf pans with vegetable oil spray, then dust with flour. Shake out the excess flour. Set the pans aside.

2. Heat the chopped white chocolate in a small saucepan over low heat until melted, stirring constantly. Set aside to cool slightly.

R

the Cake Doctor says...

This batter also bakes up nicely in layers. Bake two 9-inch layers about 28 to 30 minutes, then frost as desired.

3. Place the cake mix, melted butter, milk, eggs, vanilla, and slightly cooled white chocolate in a large mixing bowl. Blend with an electric mixer on low speed for 1 minute. Stop the machine and scrape down the sides of the bowl with a rubber spatula. Increase the mixer speed to medium and beat 2 minutes more, scraping the sides down again if needed. The batter should look well blended. Divide the batter evenly among the prepared pans, smoothing it out with the rubber spatula. Place the pans in the oven side by side.

4. Bake the loaves until they are light brown and spring back when lightly pressed with your finger, 40 to 45 minutes. Remove the pans from the oven and place them on wire racks to cool for 10 minutes. Run a dinner knife around the edge of the loaves and invert them onto racks. Turn on one side and let cool completely, 35 to 40 minutes, before serving.

✳ *Store these loaves, covered in aluminum foil or plastic wrap, at room temperature for up to 4 days or in the refrigerator for up to 1 week. Or freeze the loaves, wrapped in foil, for up to 6 months. Thaw them overnight in the refrigerator before serving.*

SOUR CREAM CHOCOLATE CUPCAKES WITH SOUR CREAM CHOCOLATE FROSTING

Chocolate cake mixes are just not flavored intensely enough for me, so I added unsweetened cocoa powder to give this recipe an extra hit of choco-  late! If you prefer a milder flavor, opt for just a tablespoon of cocoa, or none at all. Cupcakes should satisfy you with just four or five bites, and believe me, these cupcakes are all satisfaction with sour cream in the mix and in the frosting.

MAKES 18 TO 20 CUPCAKES
(2½ INCHES EACH)
PREPARATION TIME: 10 MINUTES
BAKING TIME: 28 TO 30 MINUTES
ASSEMBLY TIME: 20 MINUTES

1 package (18.25 ounces) plain devil's food
　　cake mix
2 tablespoons unsweetened cocoa powder
1 cup sour cream
½ cup vegetable oil, such as canola, corn,
　　safflower, soybean, or sunflower
½ cup water
3 large eggs
1 teaspoon pure vanilla extract
Sour Cream Chocolate Frosting (page 425)

1. Place a rack in the center of the oven and preheat the oven to 350°F. Line cupcake pans with 18 to 20 paper liners. Set the pans aside.

2. Place the cake mix, cocoa powder, sour cream, oil, water, eggs, and vanilla in a large mixing bowl. Blend with an electric mixer on low speed for 1 minute. Stop the machine and scrape down the sides of the bowl with a rubber spatula. Increase the mixer speed to medium and beat 2 minutes more, scraping the sides down again if needed. Pour the batter into the lined cupcake pans, filling each cupcake liner three-quarters of the way full. Place the pans in the oven.

3. Bake the cupcakes until they spring back when lightly pressed with your finger and a toothpick inserted in the center comes out clean, 28 to 30 minutes. Remove the pans from the oven and place them on wire racks to cool for 5 minutes. Run a dinner knife around the edges of the cupcake liners, pick them up carefully with your fingertips, and place the cupcakes on a wire rack to cool completely, 15 minutes.

4. Meanwhile, prepare the Sour Cream Chocolate Frosting.

5. Spread the tops of the cupcakes with the frosting. Place the cupcakes on a tray and place the tray in the refrigerator for 30 minutes so that the frosting will set. Bring the cupcakes to room temperature before serving.

✳ *Place the cupcakes, uncovered, in the refrigerator until the frosting sets, 30 minutes. Cover them with waxed paper and store in the refrigerator for up to 3 days. Or, freeze them, wrapped in aluminum foil, for up to 6 months. Thaw the cupcakes overnight in the refrigerator before serving.*

R
the Cake Doctor says...

Sour cream lends this batter both a nice acidic bite and a moist crumb.

Cakes with Fruit

• • •

It's fitting that fruit—the useful and sweet part of a plant—is not only nutritious but tastes good, too. Crisp pears and apples fuel our bodies. Soft and supple peaches and plums offer pleasure on a summer picnic. And that sleek banana, whether sliced atop morning cereal, stashed in a lunchbox, or spread with peanut butter for a snack, is nutrient-dense and beckoning.

Team these delicious fruits with cakes, and you have a long-standing and successful relationship, even if the nutritional attributes fly out the window as you add butter and cream to the recipes! Cakes of fresh strawberries, cakes of oranges, cakes of lemon, cakes of pineapple, cakes studded with blueberries, cakes enlivened with apricot nectar, and cakes jam-packed with bananas. We can't get enough.

A cake with fruit seems to transcend generations, more so than one made with chocolate. I think of the orange cake my grandmother used to bake around the holidays and the lush fruitcakes jammed with raisins and candied fruit that we used to soak in bourbon-saturated cheesecloth at the close of the year.

Thus, an entire book could be written on cakes filled with fruit. You'll see throughout this book—not just in this chapter—other recipes containing fruits, whether they are fresh, canned, frozen, or dried. In this chapter, however, I offer cakes where the fruit cries forth and makes a statement. You have the beloved Hummingbird Cake with its banana and pineapple; a butter layer cake filled with a tart but sweet lime curd; fast and fabulous upside-down cakes of apples or bananas; and bright pink strawberry cakes that children clamor for on their birthdays.

In each of these cakes there are myriad ways you could substitute another fruit for the one listed. That is the beauty of cooking with fruits: Pears work instead of apples and peaches instead of pears and lemon juice works instead of orange or you might opt for lime. Possibilities, possibilities.

So with an eye on what's in season or just what's in your pantry, set forth with these friendly fruit-and-cake combinations. The fruit will lend flavor, moisture to extend the storage time, and a special sweetness enjoyed by folks of all ages.

STRAWBERRY CAKE WITH STRAWBERRY CREAM CHEESE FROSTING

hirley Lambert of Tullahoma, Tennessee, takes strawberry cake seriously. So seriously that she adds only fresh strawberries to this dazzling pink cake, along with coconut and chopped pecans. Now, this type of cake has been around for some time. It's based on a white cake mix to which you add strawberry gelatin and berries. But of the countless cakes of this genre I have tasted, this is my favorite.

SERVES: 16

PREPARATION TIME: 10 MINUTES

BAKING TIME: 28 TO 30 MINUTES

ASSEMBLY TIME: 20 MINUTES

CAKE:

Solid vegetable shortening for greasing the pans

Flour for dusting the pans

1 package (18.25 ounces) plain white cake mix

1 package (3 ounces) strawberry gelatin

1 cup mashed fresh strawberries with juice (1½ cups whole berries)

1 cup vegetable oil, such as canola, corn, safflower, soybean, or sunflower

½ cup whole milk

4 large eggs

1 cup frozen unsweetened grated coconut, thawed

½ cup chopped pecans

STRAWBERRY CREAM CHEESE FROSTING:

1 package (8 ounces) cream cheese, at room
temperature

8 tablespoons (1 stick) butter, at room
temperature

3½ cups confectioners' sugar, sifted

¾ cup fresh ripe strawberries, rinsed,
capped, and mashed to make ½ cup,
then drained well

½ cup frozen unsweetened grated coconut,
thawed

½ cup chopped pecans

1. Place a rack in the center of the oven and preheat the oven to 350°F. Lightly grease three 9-inch round cake pans with solid vegetable shortening, then dust with flour. Shake out the excess flour. Set the pans aside.

2. Place the cake mix, strawberry gelatin, mashed strawberries and juice, oil, milk, and eggs in a large mixing bowl and blend with an electric mixer on low speed for 1 minute. Stop the machine and scrape down the sides of the bowl with a rubber spatula. Increase the mixer speed to medium and beat for 2 minutes more, scraping the sides down again if needed. The strawberries should be well blended into the batter. Fold in the coconut and pecans. Divide the bat-

R
the Cake Doctor says...

You won't recognize the white cake mix after adding strawberry gelatin and fresh berries. Add the rich cream cheese frosting, and this cake is blue ribbon potential. This is a superior cake, perfect for birthday parties and baby showers.

ter among the prepared pans and place them in the oven; if your oven is not large enough, place two pans on the center rack and place the third pan in the center of the highest rack.

3. Bake the cakes until they are light brown and just start to pull away from the sides of the pan, 28 to 30 minutes. Be careful not to overcook the layer on the highest oven rack. Remove the pans from the oven and place them on wire racks to cool for 10 minutes. Run a dinner knife around the edge of each layer and invert each onto a rack, then invert again onto another rack so that the cakes are right side up. Allow them to cool completely, 30 minutes more.

4. Meanwhile, prepare the frosting. Combine the cream cheese and butter in a medium bowl with an electric mixer on low speed for about 30 seconds. Stop the machine and add the sugar and drained strawberries. Blend the frosting on low until the sugar has been incorporated. Then raise the speed to medium and mix the frosting another minute or until the frosting lightens and is well combined. Fold in the coconut and pecans.

5. To assemble, place one cake layer, right side up, on a serving platter. Spread the top with frosting. Add another cake layer, right side up, and frost the top.

Repeat this process with the third layer and frost the top. Use the remaining frosting to frost the sides, working with clean, smooth strokes. Serve at once or chill the cake for later serving.

❋ *Place this cake, uncovered, in the refrigerator until the frosting sets, 20 minutes. Cover the cake with waxed paper and store, in the refrigerator, for up to 1 week. Or freeze it, wrapped in aluminum foil, for up to 6 months. Thaw the cake overnight in the refrigerator before serving.*

TRIPLE-DECKER STRAWBERRY CAKE

Pretty in pink is an apt way to describe this blushing cake from Dianne Nanney of Adams, Tennessee. Serve it up for birthdays and baby showers. This is a basic way to make strawberry cake, using three layers. Frost only the tops with a simple sugar, butter, and berry mixture, to give the cake the look of a torte.

If you like a heavier strawberry cake, bake Strawberry Cake with Strawberry Cream Cheese Frosting (page 64).

SERVES: 16

PREPARATION TIME: 10 MINUTES

BAKING TIME: 33 TO 35 MINUTES

ASSEMBLY TIME: 15 MINUTES

CAKE:

Solid vegetable shortening for greasing the pans

Flour for dusting the pans

1 package (18.25 ounces) plain white cake mix

1 package (3 ounces) strawberry gelatin

4 tablespoons all-purpose flour

1 cup vegetable oil, such as canola, corn, safflower, soybean, or sunflower

½ cup granulated sugar

½ cup whole milk

4 large eggs

½ cup finely chopped fresh strawberries and juice

FROSTING:

8 tablespoons (1 stick) butter, at room temperature

4 cups confectioners' sugar, sifted, or more if needed

½ cup finely chopped fresh strawberries and juice, or more if needed

1 cup halved fresh strawberries, for garnish

R

the Cake Doctor says...

When fresh strawberries are in season, by all means use them! Otherwise, try the individually frozen berries (thawed), not packed in any syrup. The flour in this recipe serves to help soak up the excess moisture that comes from the strawberries. The modest amount of sugar added makes the cake more tender.

1. Place a rack in the center of the oven and preheat the oven to 350°F. Lightly grease three 9-inch round cake pans with solid vegetable shortening, then dust with flour. Shake out the excess flour. Set the pans aside.

2. Place the cake mix, strawberry gelatin, flour, oil, sugar, milk, eggs, and strawberries and juice in a large mixing bowl and blend with an electric mixer on low speed for 1 minute. Stop the machine and scrape down the sides of the bowl with a rubber spatula. Increase the mixer speed to medium and beat for 2 minutes more, scraping the sides down again if needed. The strawberries should be well blended into the batter. Divide the batter among the prepared pans and place them in the oven;

if your oven is not large enough, place two pans on the center rack and place the third pan in the center of the highest rack.

3. Bake the cakes until they spring back when lightly pressed with your finger and just start to pull away from the sides of the pan, 33 to 35 minutes. Be careful not to overcook the layer on the highest oven rack. Remove the pans from the oven and place them on wire racks to cool for 10 minutes. Run a dinner knife around the edge of each layer and invert each onto a rack, then invert again onto another rack so that the cakes are right side up. Allow to cool completely, 30 minutes more.

4. Meanwhile, prepare the frosting. Place the softened butter in a large mixing bowl and blend it with an electric mixer on low speed until fluffy, 20 seconds. Stop the machine and add 4 cups confectioners' sugar and ½ cup strawberries and juice. Blend on low speed until the frosting is creamy and of a spreadable consistency. If it is too thin, add more sugar. If it is too thick, add more strawberries.

5. To assemble, place one cake layer, right side up, on a serving platter. Spread the top with frosting. Add another layer, right side up, on top of the first and frost the top. Repeat this process with the third layer and frost the top; the cake should now resemble a torte with the sides left unfrosted. Decorate the top attractively with the halved strawberries. Serve at once or chill the cake for later serving.

❋ *Place this cake, uncovered, in the refrigerator until the frosting sets, 20 min-* *utes. Cover the cake with waxed paper and store in the refrigerator for up to 1 week. Or freeze it, wrapped in aluminum foil, for up to 6 months. Thaw the cake overnight in the refrigerator before serving.*

15 Beautiful Birthday Cakes

1. Hummingbird Cake (page 74)

2. Strawberry Cake with Strawberry Cream Cheese Frosting (page 64)

3. Triple-Decker Strawberry Cake (page 67)

4. Mom's Layer Cake with Fluffy Chocolate Frosting (page 106)

5. Buttermilk Devil's Food Cake with White Chocolate Frosting (page 28)

6. Birthday Cake Cones (page 195)

7. Banana Cake with Quick Caramel Frosting (page 72)

8. Grandma's Coconut Icebox Cake (page 118)

9. Tennessee Jam Cake (page 116)

10. Carrot Cake with Fresh Orange Cream Cheese Frosting (page 109)

11. Caramel Cake (page 112)

12. Peaches and Cream Cake (page 70)

13. Lethal Peppermint Chocolate Cake (page 30)

14. Quick Red Velvet Cake (page 152)

15. Butter Layer Cake with Sweet Lime Curd (page 76)

PEACHES AND CREAM CAKE

It's the dead of winter. You dream of summer. You ache for a taste of something that will remind you of warmer weather. So look no farther than your pantry for the answer—canned peaches. Oh sure, fresh peaches would taste fabulous in this cake, especially if you save some fragrant slices, toss them with sugar and a little lemon juice, and spoon them seductively over the cake before you slice it. But in a pinch, canned peaches taste great, and they're far more interesting than out-of-season fresh peaches.

SERVES: 16

PREPARATION TIME: 10 MINUTES

BAKING TIME: 28 TO 32 MINUTES

ASSEMBLY TIME: 15 MINUTES

*Solid vegetable shortening for greasing
    the pans*
Flour for dusting the pans
*1 can (29 ounces) peach halves,
    packed in heavy syrup, drained,
    and syrup reserved*
*1 package (18.25 ounces) plain yellow
    cake mix*
*8 tablespoons (1 stick) butter,
    melted*
4 large eggs
1 teaspoon pure vanilla extract
Sweetened Cream (page 432)

1. Place a rack in the center of the oven and preheat the oven to 350°F. Generously grease two 9-inch round cake pans with solid vegetable shortening, then dust with flour. Shake out the excess flour. Set the pans aside.

2. Place about 8 of the peach halves in a food processor fitted with the steel blade and process until smooth. This should measure about 1½ cups. Reserve ½ cup syrup and the remaining peach halves.

3. Place the cake mix, peach puree, melted butter, eggs, and vanilla in a large mixing bowl. Blend with an electric mixer on low speed for 1 minute. Stop the machine and scrape down the sides of the bowl with a rubber spatula. Increase the mixer speed to medium and beat 2 to 3 minutes more, scraping the sides down again if needed. The batter should look well blended. Divide the batter between the prepared pans, smoothing it with the rubber spatula. Place the pans in the oven side by side.

4. Bake the cakes until they are golden brown and spring back when lightly pressed with your finger, 28 to 32 minutes. Remove the pans from the oven and place them on wire racks to cool for 10 minutes. Run a dinner knife around the edge of each layer and invert each onto a rack, then invert them again onto another rack so that the cakes are right side up. While the layers are still warm, poke holes in the top of them with a toothpick or wooden skewer. Carefully pour the reserved peach syrup over the layers (¼ cup over each) so that the cake soaks up all the juice. Let the layers cool completely.

5. Meanwhile, prepare the Sweetened Cream and reserve in the refrigerator. Cut the remaining peach halves into ½-inch-thick slices.

6. Place one cake layer, right side up, on a serving platter. Spread the top with cream frosting. Place the second layer, right side up, on top of the first and frost the top and sides of the cake with clean, smooth strokes. Arrange the peach slices attractively on top of the cake.

✱ *Store this cake, loosely covered in plastic wrap or waxed paper, for up to 1 week in the refrigerator.*

the Cake Doctor says...

The peach puree and syrup make this an incredibly moist cake. You must begin with a cake mix that does not contain pudding or you will have a soggy mess! If you like a more whimsical look, don't frost the sides of the cake, just the middle and top.

BANANA CAKE WITH QUICK CARAMEL FROSTING

This delightful combination of flavors—the fruity spiciness of the bananas, the sweetness of the caramel frosting, and the salty taste of the toasted pecans—is one of my favorites. Prepare this cake for most any occasion and you will not regret it. Sherry Williams of Hendersonville,  Tennessee, came up with the basic idea. I added a little *crème de banane*, plus my favorite quick caramel frosting and pecan garnish.

SERVES: 16

PREPARATION TIME: 10 MINUTES

BAKING TIME: 30 TO 32 MINUTES

ASSEMBLY TIME: 20 MINUTES

Solid vegetable shortening for greasing the pans

Flour for dusting the pans

1 package (18.25 ounces) plain yellow cake mix

½ cup packed light brown sugar

1 teaspoon ground cinnamon

2 medium-size ripe bananas, peeled and mashed (about 1 cup)

1 cup water

½ cup vegetable oil, such as canola, corn, safflower, soybean, or sunflower

3 large eggs

2 teaspoons crème de banane *liqueur* (optional)

Quick Caramel Frosting (page 430)

1 cup chopped pecans, toasted (see Toasting Nuts, page 134)

1. Place a rack in the center of the oven and preheat the oven to 350°F. Lightly grease two 9-inch round cake pans with solid vegetable shortening, then dust with flour. Shake out the excess flour. Set the pans aside.

R

the Cake Doctor says...

This cake is absolutely so good no one will know you've used a mix. Credit the rich bananas, as well as the added light brown sugar and cinnamon, with improving the cake flavor and texture. And the caramel frosting is a tried-and-true winner. It is like donning that little black dress and adding a string of cultured pearls, just the right accompaniment and so classy.

2. Place the cake mix, brown sugar, and cinnamon in a large mixing bowl. Add the mashed bananas, water, oil, eggs, and *crème de banane* liqueur (if desired). Blend with an electric mixer on low speed for 1 minute. Stop the machine and scrape down the sides of the bowl with a rubber spatula. Increase the mixer speed to medium and beat for 2 minutes more, scraping the sides down again if needed. The batter should look well blended and the bananas should be well pureed. Divide the batter between the prepared pans. Place the pans in the oven side by side.

3. Bake the cakes until they are lightly browned and a toothpick inserted in the center of each layer comes out clean, 30 to 32 minutes. Remove the pans from the oven and place them on wire racks to cool for 10 minutes. Run a dinner knife around the edge of each layer and invert each onto a rack, then invert again onto another rack so that the cakes are right side up. Allow them to cool completely, 30 minutes more.

4. Prepare the Quick Caramel Frosting. This will take only 5 to 10 minutes; therefore, time the frosting preparation so that the cake has cooled enough and is ready to frost.

5. When the cake layers are cool, transfer one layer, right side up, to a serving platter. Frost the top of the layer with the warm frosting, working quickly because it will firm up as it cools. Place the second layer, right side up, on top of the first layer and frost the top and sides of the cake, making sure to work quickly with clean, smooth strokes. While the frosting is still warm, sprinkle the toasted pecans on top of the cake so that they cling to the frosting. Let the cake cool at least 1 hour for easier slicing.

✻ *Store this cake, covered in plastic wrap, at room temperature for up to 1 week. Or freeze, in aluminum foil, for up to 6 months. Thaw the cake overnight on the counter before serving.*

HUMMINGBIRD CAKE

This wonderful banana-pineapple cake has been around for nearly 30 years, and I used to think its name came from the fact that when you tasted it the flavor was so good it caused you to hum. But Southern food writers Martha Pearl Villas and her son Jim Villas say the cake might have been so named because it is so sweet, and hummingbirds are known for their love of sugar water. I briefly thought about renaming this cake the Banana Banshee Cake when my infant, John, wailed impatiently as he watched me slather on the frosting. But once I fed him a nibble, a smile broke through and he was humming.

SERVES: 16
PREPARATION TIME: 10 MINUTES
BAKING TIME:
30 TO 32 MINUTES
ASSEMBLY TIME: 20 MINUTES

Solid vegetable shortening for greasing
    the pans
Flour for dusting the pans
1 package (18.25 ounces) plain yellow
    cake mix
1 can (8 ounces) crushed pineapple packed
    in juice, undrained
2 medium or 3 small ripe bananas, peeled
    and mashed (1 cup)
½ cup water
½ cup vegetable oil, such as canola,
    corn, safflower, soybean, or
    sunflower
3 large eggs
1 teaspoon pure vanilla extract
1 teaspoon ground cinnamon
Cream Cheese Frosting (page 420)
½ cup chopped pecans, toasted
    (see Toasting Nuts, page 134)

R

the Cake Doctor says...

You can make this cake with a pudding-enhanced mix, but it will be a heavier cake than if you use a mix without pudding added to it. Both the pineapple and the bananas add a lot of weight to the cake. Be sure to toast the pecans before sprinkling them on the frosting. Toasting is such a simple step and it brings out the flavor in the nuts.

1. Place a rack in the center of the oven and preheat the oven to 350°F. Lightly grease two 9-inch round cake pans with solid vegetable shortening, then dust with flour. Shake out the excess flour. Set the pans aside.

2. Place the cake mix, pineapple with its juice, mashed bananas, water, oil, eggs, vanilla, and cinnamon in a large bowl. Blend with an electric mixer on low speed for 1 minute. Stop the machine and scrape down the sides of the bowl with a rubber spatula. Increase the mixer speed to medium and beat for 2 minutes more, scraping the sides down again if needed. The batter should look thick and the fruit well blended. Divide the batter between the prepared pans, smoothing it down

with the rubber spatula. Place the pans in the oven side by side.

3. Bake the cakes until they are golden brown and spring back when lightly pressed with your finger, 30 to 32 minutes. Remove the pans from the oven and place them on wire racks to cool for 10 minutes. Run a dinner knife around the edge of each layer and invert each onto a rack, then invert them again onto another rack so the cakes are right side up. Allow them to cool completely, 30 minutes more.

4. Meanwhile, prepare the Cream Cheese Frosting.

5. When the cake layers have cooled completely, place one layer, right side up, on a serving platter and spread the top with frosting. Place the second layer on top of the first and then spread the top and sides of the cake with frosting using clean, smooth strokes. Sprinkle the toasted pecans on top of the cake. Serve at once or chill the cake for serving later.

✱ *Place this cake, uncovered, in the refrigerator until the frosting sets, 20 minutes. Cover the cake with waxed paper and store in the refrigerator for up to 1 week. Or freeze it, wrapped in aluminum foil, for up to 6 months. Thaw the cake overnight in the refrigerator before serving.*

BUTTER LAYER CAKE WITH SWEET LIME CURD

Let me smell fresh lime juice and my mind meanders to the tropics. And so with one foot on a sandy beach and another foot at home in the comfort of my mother's kitchen, this cake was born. The exquisite curd can just as easily be made with lemons or oranges should they be at hand.

SERVES: 16

PREPARATION TIME: 10 MINUTES

BAKING TIME: 27 TO 29 MINUTES

ASSEMBLY TIME: 25 MINUTES

CAKE:

*Solid vegetable shortening for greasing
    the pans*

Flour for dusting the pans

*1 package (18.25 ounces) plain white
    cake mix*

1 cup whole milk

8 tablespoons (1 stick) butter, melted

3 large eggs

2 teaspoons pure vanilla extract

LIME CURD:

¾ cup sugar

¼ cup cornstarch

1 cup water

2 large egg yolks, lightly beaten

2 tablespoons butter

1 tablespoon grated lime zest (from 3 limes)

5 tablespoons fresh lime juice (from 3 limes)

Buttercream Frosting (page 416)

1. Place a rack in the center of the oven and preheat the oven to 350°F. Generously grease two 9-inch round cake pans with solid vegetable shortening, then dust with flour. Shake out the excess flour. Set the pans aside.

2. Place the cake mix, milk, melted butter, eggs, and vanilla in a large mixing bowl. Blend with an electric mixer on low speed for 1 minute. Stop the machine and scrape down the sides of the bowl with a rubber spatula. Increase the mixer speed to medium and beat 2 to 3 minutes more, scraping the sides down again if needed. The batter should look well combined and thick. Divide the batter between the prepared pans, smoothing it out with the rubber spatula. Place the pans in the oven side by side.

3. Bake the cakes until they are golden brown and spring back when lightly pressed with your finger, 27 to 29 minutes. Remove the pans from the oven and place them on wire racks to cool for 10 minutes. Run a dinner knife around the edge of each layer and invert each onto a rack, then invert again onto another rack so that the cakes are right side up. Allow them to cool completely, 30 minutes more.

4. Meanwhile, prepare the lime curd. Combine the sugar and cornstarch in a 2-quart saucepan. Gradually whisk in the water. Place the pan over medium heat and cook, stirring constantly, until the mixture thickens and comes to a boil, 3 to 4 minutes. Boil, stirring, for 1 minute more. Remove the pan from the heat. Spoon about ½ cup of the hot mixture into a small bowl with the egg yolks and stir quickly until combined. Stirring constantly, turn the egg mixture into the saucepan. Return the pan to medium heat and cook, stirring, until the curd is thickened and lemon colored, 1 to 2 min-utes. Remove the pan from the heat and stir in the butter, lime zest, and lime juice. Cool.

5. Meanwhile, prepare the Buttercream Frosting.

6. To assemble, transfer one cake layer, right side up, onto a serving platter, and spread with lime curd to within ¾ inch of the edge. Top with the second cake layer, right side up. Frost the sides and the top of the cake with Buttercream Frosting, using clean, smooth strokes. Slice and serve.

✱ *Place the cake, uncovered, in the refrigerator until the frosting sets, 20 minutes. Cover the cake with waxed paper and store in the refrigerator for up to 3 days. Or freeze it, wrapped in aluminum foil, for up to 6 months. Thaw the cake overnight in the refrigerator before serving.*

the Cake Doctor says...

Save time by preparing this cake with a mix and spend that time you saved whipping up a from-scratch curd filling. It's a little tedious, on and off the heat, but in less than 15 minutes you'll have a filling that truly takes a box cake to another stratosphere!

Add Zest to Your Cakes

The perfumed outermost layer of citrus fruits is called the zest. In the case of lemons it is yellow, limes it is green, and with oranges it is orange. Underneath the zest is a bitter white pith. Together, the zest and pith make up the rind, a general term for the outside of a fruit that isn't always limited to citrus (how about watermelon rind). What makes the zest attractive in recipes is its color and the aromatic oils found in it that can lift an ordinary cake to higher levels. From an average-size lemon, you'll get about 2 teaspoons finely grated zest, whereas larger ones will yield nearly a tablespoon and smaller lemons will give up only a teaspoon. Limes, on the other hand, are more stingy. It's hard to get more than a teaspoon or two of grated zest from a lime. Oranges are generous.

There are two schools of thought to zesting but both agree on the following: You must not include the bitter pith, which is found underneath the zest.

- One method is to peel the lemon or other fruit with a sharp potato peeler, working from the stem end to the blossom end in long pulls. Then pile these strips on top of each other on a cutting board and with a sharp knife mince them. You can also use a zester with this same method. This gizmo removes the zest in narrow shreds. You just need to dice these shreds into pieces for most cake recipes.

- A second method (which I revert to in a pinch) is to use an old-fashioned stand cheese grater. Place a sheet of waxed paper under the grater and with the lemon or orange in your hand, rub the fruit against the small sharp holes. This must be the side that is not as large as you would use for shredding cheese and not the smallest holes either. Measure what's on the waxed paper and add to the recipe as directed.

And don't forget the fruit juice, too: Whenever a cake recipe calls for either zest or juice of a citrus fruit, use them both! This is a great way to add even more punch. Most lemons yield about 2 to 3 tablespoons juice, limes about 1 tablespoon of juice, and an orange, depending on the size and variety, will provide anywhere from 2 tablespoons to ½ cup juice.

FRESH ORANGE CAKE

You don't need fancy ingredients in this simple recipe, which is scrumptious in winter when fresh citrus comes into season. Just add vegetable oil, sugar, eggs, vanilla, and fresh orange juice and zest to a yellow cake mix. Ever so moist, this cake improves as it rests on the kitchen counter. It's good for packing in lunches and toting to potluck suppers. For a dazzling variation, bake the cake in two 9-inch layers and, instead of using the glaze, enrobe them in Fresh Orange Cream Cheese Frosting (page 422).

SERVES: 16
PREPARATION TIME: 10 MINUTES
BAKING TIME: 45 TO 47 MINUTES
ASSEMBLY TIME: 5 MINUTES

CAKE:

Vegetable oil spray for misting the pan
Flour for dusting the pan
1 package (18.25 ounces) yellow cake mix
    with pudding
1 cup fresh orange juice (from about 5
    medium oranges) or from the carton
½ cup vegetable oil, such as canola, corn,
    safflower, soybean, or sunflower
¼ cup granulated sugar
1 teaspoon pure vanilla extract
4 large eggs

GLAZE:

1 cup confectioners' sugar, sifted
3 tablespoons fresh orange juice (from about
    1 medium orange)
1 teaspoon fresh grated orange zest (from
    about 1 medium orange)

R

the Cake Doctor says...

Added sugar makes this cake more tender, and the orange juice and zest pack a flavor punch. This is a good example of how a pudding-enhanced cake mix can work to your advantage and save you time. The Cake Doctor says orange cakes please children and build strong, positive food memories.

1. Place a rack in the center of the oven and preheat the oven to 350°F. Lightly mist a 12-cup Bundt pan with vegetable oil spray, then dust with flour. Shake out the excess flour. Set the pan aside.

2. Place the cake mix, orange juice, oil, sugar, vanilla, and eggs in a large mixing bowl. Blend with an electric mixer on low speed for 1 minute. Stop the machine and scrape down the sides of the bowl with a rubber spatula. Increase the mixer speed to medium and beat for 2 minutes more, scraping the sides down again if needed. The batter should look thick and well blended. Pour the batter into the prepared pan and place it in the oven.

3. Bake the cake until it is golden brown and just starts to pull away from the sides of the pan, 45 to 47 minutes. Remove the pan from the oven and place it on a wire rack to cool for 20 minutes. Run a long, sharp knife around the edge of the cake and invert it onto a rack to cool completely, 30 minutes more.

4. Meanwhile, prepare the glaze. Combine the confectioners' sugar, fresh orange juice, and orange zest in a small bowl and stir with a wooden spoon until smooth.

5. Place the cake on a serving platter and pour the glaze over the top, letting it drizzle down the sides and into the center. Let the glaze set for a few minutes before slicing.

✱ *Store this cake under a glass cake dome or covered in plastic wrap at room temperature for up to 1 week. Or freeze it, wrapped in aluminum foil, for up to 6 months. Thaw the cake overnight on the counter before serving.*

FESTIVE CRAN-ORANGE CAKE

Years ago, a local bakery started combining orange zest and dried, sweetened cranberries in a sweetened bread round and baking it at the onset of the holiday season. Just like that cranberry-orange bread, this cake is sure to be appreciated for its festive ingredients. Although the glaze for this cake is the same as the one for Fresh Orange Cake (page 79), I like to top it off with long, thin strips of orange zest.

SERVES: 16
PREPARATION TIME: 10 MINUTES
BAKING TIME: 45 TO 47 MINUTES
ASSEMBLY TIME: 5 MINUTES

CAKE:

Vegetable oil spray for misting the pan
Flour for dusting the pan
1 package (18.25 ounces) yellow cake mix
        with pudding
1 cup fresh orange juice (from about 5
        medium oranges) or from the carton
½ cup vegetable oil, such as canola, corn,
        safflower, soybean, or sunflower
¼ cup granulated sugar
4 large eggs
1 cup chopped sweetened dried cranberries

GLAZE AND GARNISH:

1 cup confectioners' sugar, sifted
3 tablespoons fresh orange juice (from about
        1 medium orange)
Thin strips of orange zest (from about 1
        medium orange)
10 to 15 long thin strips (3 inches each,
        if possible) fresh orange zest
        (from 1 medium orange), for garnish

1. Place a rack in the center of the oven and preheat the oven to 350°F. Lightly mist

R

the Cake Doctor says...

I love sweetened dried cranberries in any kind of baked good—cookie, pie, or cake. A fast way to chop them before adding them to this cake batter is to mist your knife with a vegetable oil spray and chop away. No sticking to the blade!

a 12-cup Bundt pan with vegetable oil spray, then dust with flour. Shake out the excess flour. Set the pan aside.

2. Place the cake mix, orange juice, oil, sugar, and eggs in a large mixing bowl and blend with an electric mixer on low speed for 1 minute. Stop the machine and scrape down the sides of the bowl with a rubber spatula. Increase the mixer speed to medium and beat for 2 minutes longer, scraping the sides down again if needed. The batter should look thick and well blended. Fold in the dried cranberries. Pour the batter into the prepared pan and place it in the oven.

3. Bake the cake until it is golden brown and just starts to pull away from the sides of the pan, 45 to 47 minutes. Remove the pan from the oven and place it on a wire rack to cool for 20 minutes. Run a long, sharp knife around the edge of the cake and invert it onto a rack to cool for 30 minutes longer.

4. Meanwhile, prepare the Orange Glaze. Combine the confectioners' sugar and the fresh orange juice in a small bowl and stir with a wooden spoon until smooth.

5. Place the cake on a serving platter and pour the glaze over the top, letting it drizzle down the sides and into the center. Decorate the top with the zest strips. Let the glaze set for a few minutes before slicing.

✱ *Store this cake under a glass cake dome or covered in plastic wrap at room temperature for up to 1 week. Or freeze it, wrapped in aluminum foil, for up to 6 months. Thaw the cake overnight on the counter before serving.*

SUSAN'S LEMON CAKE

My sister, Susan Anderson, of Atlanta, prepares this easy lemon cake to tote to picnics and family get-togethers in the mountains. Even in hot weather children would rather have a  slice of it than eat ice cream. Who knows why? Perhaps because it is moist and has that perfect balance of sweet and tart.

....

SERVES: 16

PREPARATION TIME: 5 TO 7 MINUTES

BAKING TIME: 40 MINUTES

ASSEMBLY TIME: 5 MINUTES

....

CAKE:

Vegetable oil spray for misting the pan

Flour for dusting the pan

1 package (18.25 ounces) plain yellow cake mix

1 package (3 ounces) lemon gelatin

⅔ cup vegetable oil, such as canola, corn, safflower, soybean, or sunflower

⅔ cup hot water

4 large eggs

GLAZE:

2 cups confectioners' sugar, sifted

2 tablespoons fresh lemon juice (from 1 lemon)

1 teaspoon finely grated lemon zest (from 1 lemon)

1. Place a rack in the center of the oven and preheat the oven to 350°F. Lightly mist a 12-cup Bundt pan with vegetable oil spray, then dust with flour. Shake out excess flour. Set the pan aside.

2. Place the cake mix, gelatin, oil, water, and eggs in a large mixing bowl and beat with an electric mixer on low speed for 1 minute. Stop the machine and scrape down the sides of the bowl with a rubber spatula. Increase the mixer speed to medium and beat for 2 minutes more, scraping the sides down if needed. The batter should look thick and well blended. Pour the batter into the prepared pan, smoothing the top with the rubber spatula, and place the pan in the oven.

3. Bake the cake until it is light brown and just starts to pull away from the sides of the pan, about 40 minutes. Remove the pan from the oven and place it on a wire rack to cool for 10 minutes.

4. Meanwhile, prepare the glaze. Combine the confectioners' sugar, lemon juice, and lemon zest in a small bowl and stir with a wooden spoon until smooth.

5. Run a long, sharp knife around the edge of the cake and invert it onto a serving platter. Spoon the glaze evenly over the warm cake so that it drizzles down the sides and into the center. Slice and serve warm, or let it cool before slicing.

R

the Cake Doctor says...

Lemon is the key. You can transform a simple cake mix into majesty by adding a little lemon juice and zest to both enliven dull flavors and mask an artificial cake mix taste. Feeling inspired? Try lime, orange, and other citrus flavors.

✳ *Store this cake, covered in plastic wrap or placed under a glass cake dome, at room temperature for up to 1 week. Or freeze it, wrapped in aluminum foil, for up to 6 months. Thaw the cake overnight on the counter before serving.*

FAVORITE APRICOT NECTAR CAKE

This was a favorite recipe long before I baked cakes from scratch. Because you poke holes in the cake and spoon on a warm, tart glaze of apricot nectar, the cake is so moist you'd swear it was some high-falutin sponge cake with a simple syrup swabbed on. And this cake is delicious at any temperature—warm, cold, or right from the freezer.

SERVES: 16

PREPARATION TIME: 10 MINUTES

BAKING TIME: 40 TO 42 MINUTES

ASSEMBLY TIME: 5 MINUTES

CAKE:

Vegetable oil spray for misting the pan

Flour for dusting the pan

1 package (18.25 ounces) plain yellow cake mix

1 package (3 ounces) lemon gelatin

¾ cup canned apricot nectar

¾ cup vegetable oil, such as canola, corn, safflower, soybean, or sunflower

Grated zest of 1 lemon (1 teaspoon)

4 large eggs

GLAZE:

¾ cup confectioners' sugar, sifted

2 tablespoons fresh lemon juice (from 1 lemon)

4 tablespoons canned apricot nectar, or more as needed

1. Place a rack in the center of the oven and preheat the oven to 325°F. Lightly mist a 12-cup Bundt pan with vegetable oil spray, then dust with flour. Shake out the excess flour. Set the pan aside.

2. Place the yellow cake mix, gelatin, apricot nectar, oil, lemon zest, and eggs in

R

the Cake Doctor says...

Apricot nectar masks the "cake-mix taste" in this old standby. Lemon gelatin adds both dazzling color and a richer texture. Lemon zest and juice in the cake and glaze contribute a freshness that also overcomes cake-mix taste. It's a winner!

a large mixing bowl. Blend with an electric mixer on low speed for 1 minute. Stop the machine and scrape down the sides of the bowl with a rubber spatula. Increase the mixer speed to medium and beat for 2 to 3 minutes more, scraping the sides down again if needed. The batter should look thick and smooth. Pour the batter into the prepared pan. Place the pan in the oven.

3. Bake the cake until it is light brown and springs back when lightly pressed with your finger, 40 to 42 minutes. Remove the pan from the oven and place it on a wire rack to cool for 10 minutes.

4. Prepare the glaze. Combine the confectioners' sugar, lemon juice, and apricot nectar in a small saucepan and heat over medium-low heat, stirring, until the sugar has dissolved, 3 to 4 minutes.

5. Run a long, sharp knife around the edge of the cake and invert it onto a serving platter. While the cake is still warm, poke holes in the top with a toothpick or long wooden skewer. Spoon the glaze onto the cake so that it seeps down into the holes. Let the cake cool before slicing.

✸ *Store this cake, covered in plastic wrap or under a glass cake dome, at room temperature for up to 1 week. Or freeze it, wrapped in aluminum foil, for up to 6 months. Thaw the cake overnight on the counter before serving.*

PLUM AND CARDAMOM CAKE

I've often wondered what got into someone to dump a couple of jars of baby food into a cake mix. Had the child outgrown strained fruits, and these two lone jars remained on the pantry shelf? Or was the cook just sleep-deprived, half-crazed, and desperate as most parents are and decided one more trip to the supermarket would do her in? She needed a cake for the dinner party and, by gosh, it would be with strained plums! Anyway, this recipe has been around for years, but not with the addition of ground cardamom, which I think adds a whole new dimension to baby food cookery. And if you can get your hands on some fresh dark red or purple plums, slice and sweeten them with a little sugar and spoon them over the top of the cake.

....

SERVES: 16

PREPARATION TIME: 20 MINUTES

BAKING TIME: 40 TO 45 MINUTES

....

Vegetable oil spray for misting the pan
Flour for dusting the pan
1 package (18.25 ounces) plain yellow
     cake mix
1 cup sour cream
1 cup strained plums (two 4-ounce baby food
     jars) or 1 cup pureed fresh, peeled plums
⅓ cup vegetable oil, such as canola, corn,
     safflower, soybean, or sunflower
¼ cup sugar
4 large eggs
1 teaspoon ground cardamom

R

the Cake Doctor says...

This is nothing more than a basic sour cream cake recipe, with plums added as the liquid. You need the extra sugar because plums are a tart fruit. For a change, try a white cake mix instead of yellow for a more pristine color and more delicate flavor.

1. Place a rack in the center of the oven and preheat the oven to 350°F. Generously mist a 12-cup Bundt pan with vegetable oil spray, then dust with flour. Shake out the excess flour. Set the pan aside.

2. Place the cake mix, sour cream, strained plums, oil, sugar, eggs, and cardamom in a large mixing bowl. Blend with an electric mixer on low speed for 1 minute. Stop the machine and scrape down the sides of the bowl with a rubber spatula. Increase the mixer speed to medium and beat 2 to 3 minutes more, scraping the sides down again if needed. The batter should look well combined and thick. Pour the batter into the prepared pan, smoothing it out with the rubber spatula. Place the pan in the oven.

3. Bake the cake until it is golden brown and just starts to pull away from the sides of the pan, 40 to 45 minutes. Remove the pan from the oven and place it on a wire rack to cool for 20 minutes. Run a long, sharp knife around the edge of the cake and invert it onto a rack to finish cooling. Or invert it onto a serving platter to slice and serve while still warm.

✳ *Allow this cake to cool completely, then store it, covered in plastic wrap or under a glass cake dome at room temperature, for up to 1 week. Or freeze it, wrapped in aluminum foil, for up to 6 months. Thaw the cake overnight on the counter before serving.*

APPLESAUCE SPICE CAKE

I picked up a box of spice cake mix in the grocery store, thinking of the obvious re-dos like carrot cake and prune cake and Tennessee Jam Cake. But it wasn't until I was driving home that I thought, eureka! Applesauce Spice Cake! Applesauce and buttermilk meld so easily into cake mix batters, and the spices are already in the mix. The recipe was out of my head and on paper in less time than it took me to unload the car. And that cake was in and out of the oven in about an hour.

R the Cake Doctor says...

In order to arrive at a dense, moist cake, I reduced the number of eggs, added butter for flavor and browning, and added shortening for some lightness and volume. Applesauce, chopped apple, and pecans provided texture; and for that little something extra, I added lemon zest. This is a moist cake that seems to get even more moist as it stands. If it's a cake you want to keep on the kitchen counter, dust it with confectioners' sugar. If you want to make a big show, spoon the rich caramel glaze over the top.

....

SERVES: 16

PREPARATION TIME: 15 MINUTES

BAKING TIME: 50 TO 55 MINUTES

ASSEMBLY TIME (IF USING THE
BROWN SUGAR GLAZE):
10 MINUTES

....

Apple Picking

*I*f you think all apples were created equal, get your hands on a
Bramley apple. I did while living
in England for a year. A neophyte, I
bought the fragrant, tart apples at the
local market, cut them up for apple
pie, and within minutes in a hot
oven, the apples had disintegrated! I
thought this was a cooking apple.

Cooking apples in the U.S. are
more firmly textured, and for baking
into pies and cakes I tend to favor the
Jonathans with their white flesh and
ability to stay together in nice chunks.
Yorks, Staymans, and Arkansas
Blacks are also good cookers, and
they remain intact, whereas the flavorful Rome Beauty is more of an
applesauce apple or can be added to a
cake when it matters not if you get a
bite of apple. And then there is the
ubiquitous Golden Delicious, which
works well in pies, cakes, sauce, and
even out of hand. I'll admit when a full
range of apples no longer comes into
our market, I search for the bags of
Golden Delicious that have been
grown in North Carolina and, later in
the year, Michigan. They're a better
value than the loose apples, and they
have much more flavor.

Vegetable oil spray for misting the pan
Flour for dusting the pan
1 package (18.25 ounces) plain spice
     cake mix
1 cup sweetened applesauce
½ cup buttermilk
⅓ cup butter, at room temperature
⅓ cup solid vegetable shortening
1 teaspoon pure vanilla extract
1 teaspoon finely grated lemon zest
     (from 1 lemon)
2 large eggs
1 cup chopped peeled apple
½ cup chopped pecans
2 teaspoons sifted confectioners' sugar
     (for dusting) or Brown Sugar Caramel
     Glaze (page 437)

1. Place a rack in the center of the oven
and preheat the oven to 350°F. Lightly
mist a 12-cup Bundt pan with vegetable
oil spray, then dust with flour. Shake out
the excess flour. Set the pan aside.

2. Place the cake mix, applesauce, buttermilk, butter, shortening, vanilla, lemon
zest, and eggs in a large mixing bowl.
Blend with an electric mixer on low speed
for 1 minute. Stop the machine and
scrape down the sides of the bowl with a
rubber spatula. Increase the mixer speed
to medium and beat for 2 minutes more,
scraping the sides down again if needed.

The batter should look well blended. Fold in the apple and pecans. Pour the batter into the prepared pan, smoothing it out with the rubber spatula. Place the pan in the oven.

3. Bake the cake until it is golden brown and springs back when lightly pressed with your finger, 50 to 55 minutes. Remove the pan from the oven and place it on a wire rack to cool for 20 minutes. Run a long, sharp knife around the edge of the cake and invert it onto the rack so that the cake is right side up. Allow it to cool completely, 30 minutes more.

4. Place the cake on a serving platter and serve it dusted with confectioners' sugar. Or spoon the Brown Sugar Caramel Glaze over the top, letting it drizzle down the sides and into the center.

❋ *Store this cake, covered in plastic wrap or under a glass cake dome, at room temperature for up to 1 week. Or freeze it, unglazed, wrapped in aluminum foil, for up to 6 months. Thaw the cake overnight on the counter before glazing and serving.*

PINEAPPLE INSIDE-OUT CAKE

Linda Clemons of Mount Juliet, Tennessee, shared this favorite recipe of hers, a delightful combination of lemon and pineapple. The cake is extremely moist, made with crushed pineapple, and you place more pineapple on top of the cake after it has been glazed. When I taste this cake, I think of potluck suppers at church or in the neighborhood and the multitude of pretty cakes lined up on checkered tablecloths. This cake outshines the rest.

SERVES: 16

PREPARATION TIME: 10 MINUTES

BAKING TIME: 48 TO 50 MINUTES

ASSEMBLY TIME: 5 MINUTES

Solid vegetable shortening for greasing
    the pan
Flour for dusting the pan
1 package (18.25 ounces) plain lemon
    cake mix
1 can (15.25 ounces) crushed pineapple
    packed in juice (divided into two 1-cup
    portions)
¼ cup granulated sugar
½ cup vegetable oil, such as canola, corn,
    safflower, soybean, or sunflower
4 large eggs
1 cup confectioners' sugar, sifted
1 tablespoon fresh lemon juice

1. Place a rack in the center of the oven and preheat the oven to 350°F. Lightly grease a 10-inch tube pan with solid vegetable shortening, then dust with flour. Shake out the excess flour. Set the pan aside.

R

the Cake Doctor says...

Pineapple and lemon have a natural affinity for each other. So what better way to play up the cake's strong lemon flavor than with a glaze made of lemon juice, sugar, and pineapple juice? The crushed pineapple here makes a moist cake, as does other fruit, like mashed bananas and applesauce.

2. Place the cake mix, 1 cup undrained crushed pineapple, sugar, oil, and eggs in a large mixing bowl and blend with an electric mixer on low speed for 1 minute. Stop the machine and scrape down the sides of the bowl with a rubber spatula. Increase the mixer speed to medium and beat for 2 minutes more, scraping the sides down again if needed. The pineapple should be well blended into the batter. Pour the batter into the prepared pan, smoothing the top with the rubber spatula. Place the pan in the oven.

3. Bake the cake until it springs back when lightly pressed with your finger and just starts to pull away from the sides of the pan, 48 to 50 minutes. Remove the pan from the oven and place the pan on a wire rack to cool for 15 minutes. Run a long, sharp knife around the edge of the cake and invert it onto a rack, then invert onto another rack so the cake is right side up. Allow it to cool completely, 30 minutes more.

4. Meanwhile, prepare the glaze. First, drain the remaining 1 cup crushed pineapple and reserve the juice. Combine the confectioners' sugar, 2 tablespoons of the reserved pineapple juice, and the lemon juice in a small bowl and stir with a wooden spoon until smooth.

5. Place the cake on a serving platter. Spoon the glaze onto the cooled cake. Spoon the remaining 1 cup drained pineapple on top of the glaze. Slice and serve.

✳ *Store this cake, covered in plastic wrap or under a glass cake dome, at room temperature for up to 1 week. The remaining 1 cup crushed pineapple will keep, covered, in the refrigerator for up to 1 week.*

BLUEBERRY MUFFIN CAKE

SERVES: 16

PREPARATION TIME: 15 MINUTES

BAKING TIME: 45 TO 50 MINUTES

This cake is for my younger daughter, Litton, who loves muffins, especially when they're packed with blueberries. I remember that affection for anything blueberry—muffins, pancakes, waffles—when I was young. When Litton quizzed me one afternoon as to what was available to snack on, I said I had some special Blueberry Muffin Cake. She laughed at such a silly name, but after a bite she declared, "Mommy, you were correct. This tastes just like a blueberry muffin."

Solid vegetable shortening for greasing
the pan
Flour for dusting the pan
1 package (18.25 ounces) plain yellow or
white cake mix
1 package (3.4 ounces) vanilla instant
pudding mix
1 cup low-fat vanilla yogurt
½ cup vegetable oil, such as canola, corn,
safflower, soybean, or sunflower
¼ cup water
1 teaspoon ground cinnamon
4 large eggs
1 cup fresh blueberries, rinsed and
drained
2 teaspoons confectioners' sugar
(for dusting; optional)

1. Place a rack in the center of the oven and preheat the oven to 350°F. Lightly grease a 10-inch tube pan with solid veg-

R

the Cake Doctor says...

If fresh blueberries are not in season, use thawed frozen berries but omit the water in the cake as these berries are so watery on their own. Also, you could just as well use a can of wild blueberries, as long as it is well drained. For variation, add a teaspoon of grated orange zest and use the juice of 1 large orange to moisten up confectioners' sugar for a fast glaze. *Voilà!* A blueberry-orange muffin cake.

etable shortening, then dust with flour. Shake out the excess flour. Set the pan aside.

2. Measure out 2 tablespoons of the cake mix and reserve it. Place the remaining cake mix, pudding mix, yogurt, oil, water, cinnamon, and eggs in a large mixing bowl. Blend with an electric mixer on low speed for 1 minute. Stop the machine and scrape down the sides of the bowl with a rubber spatula. Increase the mixer speed to medium and beat for 2 minutes more, scraping the sides down again if needed. The batter should look thick and well blended.

3. Toss the blueberries with the reserved cake mix.

4. Pour two-thirds of the batter into the prepared pan. Scatter the blueberries over the batter. Spread the remaining batter over the blueberries so that it covers the fruit. Place the pan in the oven.

5. Bake the cake until it is golden brown on top and just starts to pull away from the sides of the pan, 45 to 50 minutes. Remove the pan from the oven and place the pan on a wire rack to cool for 20 minutes. Run a long, sharp knife around the edge of the cake and invert it onto a rack, then onto another rack so that the cake is right side up, Allow it to cool completely, 30 minutes more.

6. Place the cake on a serving platter, dust with confectioners' sugar (if desired), and serve.

✽ *Allow this cake to cool completely, then store it, covered in plastic wrap, at room temperature for up to 1 week. Or freeze, wrapped in aluminum foil, for up to 6 months. Thaw the cake overnight on the counter before serving.*

LEMON CHIP PICNIC CAKE

SERVES: 20

PREPARATION TIME: 10 MINUTES

BAKING TIME:

45 TO 47 MINUTES

ASSEMBLY TIME: 5 MINUTES

Pastry chefs have long known the power of the sugar syrup, swabbed onto cake layers to keep them moist and flavorful. Well, here you have a delightful, down-home take on a light lemon genoise, except this cake contains miniature semisweet chocolate chips and is baked in a 13- by 9-inch pan. Once you take the cake from the oven, prick holes in it with a wooden skewer and pour a warm syrup of lemon juice, sugar, water, and melted butter over the top.

    Tote this on a spring picnic with a bowlful of fresh sweet strawberries and cream.

CAKE:

Vegetable oil spray for misting the pan

1 package (18.25 ounces) plain yellow cake mix

1 package (3.4 ounces) lemon instant pudding mix

¾ cup vegetable oil, such as canola, corn, safflower, soybean, or sunflower

¾ cup water

4 large eggs

1 cup miniature semisweet chocolate chips

LEMON GLAZE:

¼ cup water

¼ cup fresh lemon juice (from 2 lemons)

2 tablespoons butter

2 cups confectioners' sugar, sifted

1. Place a rack in the center of the oven and preheat the oven to 350°F. Lightly mist a 13- by 9-inch baking pan with vegetable oil spray. Set the pan aside.

2. Place the cake mix, pudding mix, oil, water, and eggs in a large mixing bowl. Blend with an electric mixer on low speed for 1 minute. Stop the machine and scrape down the sides of the bowl with a rubber spatula. Increase the mixer speed to medium and beat for 2 minutes more, scraping the sides down again if needed. The batter should look thick and well blended, and the pudding mix should be dissolved. Fold in the chocolate chips. Pour the batter evenly into the prepared pan and smooth the top with the rubber spatula. Place the pan in the oven.

3. Bake the cake until it is golden brown and springs back when lightly pressed with your finger, 45 to 47 minutes. Remove the pan from the oven and place it on a wire rack to cool while you prepare the glaze.

4. Prepare the lemon glaze. Place the water, lemon juice, and butter in a saucepan and heat over low heat until the butter melts, 2 to 3 minutes. Remove the saucepan from the heat, and stir in the confectioners' sugar until well blended. Return the pan to the heat, bring the glaze to a boil, and cook until it looks smooth, 1 to 2 minutes. Remove the glaze from the heat.

the Cake Doctor says...

This is a fabulous, moist cake, even better the next day or the day after. Credit emulsifiers in the mix that soak up the water and oil. The lemon-chocolate combination works well together. For more intensity, add a teaspoon of grated lemon zest to the glaze.

5. Prick holes all over the top of the cake with a toothpick or wooden skewer and pour the hot glaze over the top, spreading it with the back of a spoon to reach all sides. Allow the cake to cool about 20 minutes before cutting it into squares and serving.

✳ *Store this cake, covered in aluminum foil, at room temperature for up to 1 week. Or freeze it, wrapped in foil, for up to 6 months. Thaw the cake overnight on the counter before serving.*

OLD-FASHIONED PEAR AND GINGER CAKE

This cake sat on my kitchen counter still warm from the oven when my friend Mindy Merrell stopped by the house. Without asking, I served Mindy up a slice, even though it was barely 9:00 A.M. "Wow!" was her response. "That is a great cake, so homey, so com-forting." What recipe needs more introduc-tion? The goodies—pears, brown sugar, and butter—are on the bottom. So be sure to flip the slice onto the plate so they rest on top. And an added bonus—you don't have to grease the pan!

SERVES: 20
PREPARATION TIME: 18 MINUTES
BAKING TIME: 43 TO 46 MINUTES

¾ cup packed dark brown sugar

6 tablespoons (¾ stick) butter, melted

1 can (29 ounces) pear halves, packed in heavy syrup, drained, and syrup reserved

1 package (18.25 ounces) plain spice cake mix

1 cup buttermilk

⅓ cup reserved pear syrup

⅓ cup vegetable oil, such as canola, corn, safflower, soybean, or sunflower

3 large eggs

1 teaspoon ground ginger

½ teaspoon ground cinnamon

Vanilla ice cream, for serving

1. Place a rack in the center of the oven and preheat the oven to 350°F.

2. Place the brown sugar and melted butter in the bottom of a 13- by 9-inch baking pan. Blend with a rubber spatula. Use the spatula to spread the mixture across the bottom of the pan to form a thin layer. Cut each pear half into 4 slices and arrange the slices, rounded side up, in rows on top of the brown sugar and butter mixture.

3. Place the cake mix, buttermilk, pear syrup, oil, eggs, ginger, and cinnamon in a large mixing bowl. Blend with an electric mixer on low speed for 1 minute. Stop the machine and scrape down the sides of the bowl with a rubber spatula. Increase the mixer speed to medium and beat 2 to 3 minutes more, scraping the sides down again if needed. The batter should look well combined. Pour the batter over the pears, smoothing it out with the rubber spatula. Place the pan in the oven.

4. Bake the cake until it springs back when lightly pressed with your finger and just starts to pull away from the sides of the pan, 43 to 46 minutes. Remove the pan from the oven and place it on a wire rack to cool for 10 minutes.

5. Cut the cake into squares and invert them onto serving plates so that the pears are on the top. Serve warm with ice cream. Or, cool and serve at room temperature later in the day.

✳ *Store this cake, covered in aluminum foil, for up to several days at room temperature.*

R
the Cake Doctor says...

Ground ginger is an amazing flavor enhancer here, transforming an ordinary spice cake mix into grandmother's gingerbread. Even if you think you don't like ginger, you will here, especially when it is mingled with the sweet pears and the gutsy dark brown sugar.

UPSIDE-DOWN
APPLE SKILLET CAKE

This dessert is reminiscent of the Appalachian Mountains, where family cooks have for a long time baked cakes using little more than fresh apples, a simple spice cake batter, and a well-seasoned cast-iron skillet. I don't know what's more delicious—this cake warm with ice cream or cold the next morning for breakfast. If you don't have a cast-iron skillet, use a 10-inch skillet that is at least 2 inches deep and has an ovenproof handle.

SERVES: 16
PREPARATION TIME: 15 MINUTES
BAKING TIME: 43 TO 47 MINUTES

TOPPING:

⅓ cup butter

1 cup packed light brown sugar

1 teaspoon ground cinnamon

4 medium apples such as Jonathans or Golden Delicious, peeled, cored, and sliced ¼-inch thick (3 cups sliced)

CAKE:

1 package (18.25 ounces) plain spice cake mix

8 tablespoons (1 stick) butter, melted

1 cup buttermilk

⅓ cup dark corn syrup

2 large eggs

1 teaspoon ground cinnamon

1. Place a rack in the center of the oven and preheat the oven to 350°F.

2. Prepare the topping. Place butter in a 10-inch cast-iron skillet and heat the skillet over low heat to melt the butter. Remove the skillet from the heat, and with a fork stir in the brown sugar and cinnamon. Using the fork, spread the mixture out evenly in the bottom of the skillet.

R

the Cake Doctor says...

To bake skillet cakes, or cornbread, or biscuits in a cast-iron skillet, the pan needs to be cared for properly so the food doesn't stick and, in the case of skillet cakes, so they release from the pan without a struggle. You want the pores of the skillet so oil-saturated they create their own natural nonstick finish.

I know some folks who are deeply religious about their cast iron. They fry bacon in them each day and never, ever, wash them with anything but hot water and a stiff brush. I think it's fine to use a little mild dishwashing soap, as long as you scrub gently. Then, rinse the skillet, dry it with a towel, and let it rest on top of the stove for several hours before storing in the cabinet. Cast-iron pans are happiest when they're left out on the stove or are hanging overhead for ready use. There's an old saying: Smile at your cast-iron skillet and it should smile back!

Arrange the apple slices over the bottom of the skillet.

3. Place the cake mix, melted butter, buttermilk, corn syrup, eggs, and cinnamon in a large mixing bowl. Blend with an electric mixer on low speed for 1 minute. Stop the machine and scrape down the sides of the bowl with a rubber spatula. Increase the mixer speed to medium and beat for 2 minutes more, scraping the sides down again if needed. The batter should look creamy and smooth. Pour the batter on top of the apples in the skillet, smoothing it out with the rubber spatula. Place the skillet in the oven.

4. Bake the cake until it rises high in the skillet and springs back when lightly pressed with your finger, 43 to 47 minutes. Remove the skillet from the oven and run a long, sharp knife around the edges. Carefully invert the skillet onto a heatproof serving plate. The cake should release itself from the skillet. If it does not, simply run the knife around the side of the pan one more time and let the skillet rest on the plate until the cake releases. Lift off the skillet. This cake is best served warm, with vanilla ice cream or whipped cream, so slice and serve at once.

✸ *If serving this cake later in the day, let it cool on a platter and cover it with plastic wrap. For longer storage, wrap it in plastic wrap or aluminum foil and refrigerate for up to 1 week. Slice and serve it at room temperature or reheat it, uncovered, in a microwave oven on high power for about 30 seconds.*

UPSIDE-DOWN BANANAS FOSTER CAKE

The classic dessert by this name originated at Brennan's Restaurant in New Orleans. It's fun to transport those same flavors—bananas, rum, brown sugar, cinnamon, and butter— into a quick skillet cake.  Mountain cooks have long used cast-iron skillets to bake bread and cakes. The skillets conduct heat evenly, and their shiny black sides create a most delicious crust. Feel free to substitute whatever fruit you have on hand, such as canned pineapple, fresh pears, sweet cherries, or summer's ripe peaches. But do be sure to serve this cake warm with a spoonful of vanilla ice cream or whipped cream.

....

SERVES: 16
PREPARATION TIME: 15 MINUTES
BAKING TIME: 43 TO 47 MINUTES

....

TOPPING:

⅓ cup butter

1 cup packed light brown sugar

½ teaspoon ground cinnamon

2 tablespoons light rum

3 cups sliced bananas, cut on the diagonal
        about ⅓ inch thick (from 3 large bananas)

CAKE:

1 package (18.5 ounces) butter recipe golden
        cake mix

8 tablespoons (1 stick) butter, melted

1½ cups whole milk

2 large eggs

4 teaspoons fresh lemon juice

1. Place a rack in the center of the oven and preheat the oven to 350°F.

2. Prepare the topping. Place the butter in a 10-inch cast-iron skillet and heat the skillet over low heat to melt the butter. Remove the skillet from the heat and, with a fork, stir in the brown sugar, cinnamon, and rum. Using the fork, spread the mixture out evenly in the bottom of the skillet. Arrange the banana slices over the bottom of the skillet so they cover it well.

3. Place the cake mix, melted butter, milk, eggs, and lemon juice in a large mixing bowl. Blend with an electric mixer on low speed for 1 minute. Stop the machine and scrape down the sides of the bowl with a rubber spatula. Increase the mixer speed to medium and beat for 2 minutes more, scraping the sides down again if needed. The batter should look creamy and smooth. Pour the batter on top of the bananas in the skillet, smoothing it out with the rubber spatula. Place the skillet in the oven.

4. Bake the cake until it rises high in the skillet and springs back when lightly pressed with your finger, 43 to 47 minutes. Remove the skillet from the oven and run a long sharp knife around the edge. Carefully invert the skillet onto a heatproof serving plate. The cake should release itself from the skillet. If it does not, simply run the knife around the side of the pan one more time and let the skillet rest on the plate until the cake releases.

Lift off the skillet. This cake is best served warm, with vanilla ice cream or whipped cream, so slice and serve at once.

✱ *If serving this cake later in the day, let it cool on a platter and cover it with plastic wrap. For longer storage, wrap in plastic wrap or aluminum foil and refrigerate for up to 1 week. Slice and serve it at room temperature or reheat it, uncovered, in a microwave oven on high power for about 30 seconds.*

the Cake Doctor says...

Use either a butter recipe golden cake mix or a plain yellow cake mix in this recipe. The butter recipe golden cake mix seems to have a finer, more delicate grain, which complements the crusty crunch of the cake exterior once it is baked in cast iron. Lemon juice marries well with fresh bananas and adds acidity to the cake mix, improving flavor.

Strike It Rich Cakes

• • •

These are the cakes I turn to when I'm not counting calories or fat grams or the number of times I walk over to the cake platter and cut another slice. This chapter and its decadent recipes are all about enjoyment and the pleasure they give me. And that is what good and rich cakes should provide—pleasure.

When I think of the cakes I remember the most, they weren't the angel food cake with fresh berries my mother made for company or some fat-free apple cake recipe I had to test for a newspaper food story. They were pound cakes that oozed with butter at the seam or layer cakes sandwiched with creamy buttercream frosting or carrot cake so rich you wish you'd skipped lunch just to be able to finish the entire piece!

Fat serves various purposes in cake baking, namely providing flavor in the case of butter, giving a moist and tender crumb in the case of the oil in that carrot cake, and fat also makes us feel satisfied. Who feels hungry after a slice of Zucchini Spice Cake with Penuche Frosting? And who could possibly be peckish after a wedge of Sweet Potato Cake with Coconut Pecan Cream Cheese Frosting?

Clearly the task is to make it through the entire slice of Grandma's Coconut Icebox Cake because it tastes so good. Good cooks will savor each and every forkful of Tennessee Jam Cake just to determine what is in that caramel frosting. As the saying goes, it's a tough job but someone's got to do it.

And luckily for the style of cooking found in this book, the rich flavors of cream cheese, coconut, pudding, caramel, butter, and sour cream work well with cake mixes. Cake mixes are only improved with the addition of these ingredients, but they must be added in proper proportion. Just enough is the right philosophy. Just enough sour cream to make the mix wet and rich. Just enough cream cheese to add some punch but not overwhelm. Fat works, but fat must work in concert with other ingredients.

Thank goodness the trends have reversed and people truly want to have their cake and eat it too. We may be making sacrifices at the front end of the meal, having smaller portions of meat, more salad, and less butter on our bread, but we're wallowing in dessert. And loving it. It didn't take long for us to realize that fat substitutes just don't work. They can never replace those flavors we truly enjoy and that make us feel so good.

MOM'S LAYER CAKE WITH FLUFFY CHOCOLATE FROSTING

This is the closest you'll get to scratch-butter-cake taste when using a mix. It's the one I'm holding on the cover of this book. The flavors in the cake will bring back memories of birthday parties of yesteryear—light yellow layers, fluffy chocolate frosting, and that essential glass of cold milk. You couldn't keep your hands out of the mixing bowl as a child and you won't be able to as an adult! Instead of Fluffy Chocolate Frosting you could also use Chocolate Pan Frosting (page 429) or Fresh Orange Cream Cheese Frosting (page 422). If you want to give the cake a particularly festive look, add chocolate curls (see box, facing page).

....

SERVES: 16
PREPARATION TIME:
5 TO 7 MINUTES
BAKING TIME: 27 TO 29 MINUTES
ASSEMBLY TIME:
15 TO 20 MINUTES

....

*Solid vegetable shortening for greasing
    the pans*
Flour for dusting the pans
*1 package (18.25 ounces) plain white
    cake mix*
1 cup whole milk
8 tablespoons (1 stick) butter, melted
3 large eggs
2 teaspoons pure vanilla extract
Fluffy Chocolate Frosting (page 426)

Chocolate Curls

When you want to lend your cakes a more upscale look, add curls. They look professional, but you needn't seek professional help. Just begin with an 8-ounce block of either semisweet or white chocolate purchased from a specialty shop or your local bakery. Most supermarkets don't stock these large blocks, and you need this size to create the ribbonlike curls.

Place the chocolate block on a plate in a warm spot—by a sunny window, on top of the stove toward the back (not on a burner), on top of the refrigerator—for about an hour, just to lightly soften it. Drag a sharp vegetable peeler down one side of the chocolate in one motion from top to bottom so you create curls. They will vary in size, and some may just look like splinters, but that doesn't matter. Use several handfuls of these curls on top of your frosted cake, then make some more curls to freeze in a zipper-lock bag; they'll keep for up to 1 month.

If you are making curls to use later in the day, transfer them to a sheet of aluminum foil, and refrigerate so they don't soften and lose their shape. The remaining chocolate can be wrapped tightly and returned to the pantry to be used in future desserts.

1. Place a rack in the center of the oven and preheat the oven to 350°F. Generously grease two 9-inch round cake pans with solid vegetable shortening, then dust with flour. Shake out the excess flour. Set the pans aside.

2. Place the cake mix, milk, melted butter, eggs, and vanilla in a large mixing bowl. Blend with an electric mixer on low speed for 1 minute. Stop the machine and scrape down the sides of the bowl with a rubber spatula. Increase the mixer speed to medium and beat 2 minutes more, scraping the sides down again if needed. The batter should look well blended. Divide the batter between the prepared pans, smoothing it out with the rubber spatula. Place the pans in the oven side by side.

3. Bake the cakes until they are golden brown and spring back when lightly pressed with your finger, 27 to 29 minutes. Remove the pans from the oven and place them on wire racks to cool for 10 minutes. Run a dinner knife around the edge of each layer and invert each onto a rack, then invert them again onto another rack so that the cakes are right side up. Allow them to cool completely, 30 minutes more.

4. Meanwhile, prepare the Fluffy Chocolate Frosting.

5. Place one cake layer, right side up, on a serving platter. Spread the top with frosting. Place the second layer, right side up, on top of the first layer and frost the top and sides of the cake with clean, smooth strokes.

✳ *Place this cake, uncovered, in the refrigerator until the frosting sets, 20 minutes. Cover the cake with waxed paper or place under a glass cake dome and store at room temperature for up to 4 days. Or freeze it, wrapped in aluminum foil, for up to 6 months. Thaw the cake overnight in the refrigerator before serving.*

the Cake Doctor says...

When you want clear flavors to shine through, you must begin with the most simple of mixes—the white cake mix. Choose one that does not include pudding, and use whole eggs, not just whites as directed on the back of the box. Add melted butter for fat, flavor, and color. The cake will bake up fragrant and have the most delicate golden brown color. To save time, melt the butter, cut into tablespoons, in a glass measuring cup in the microwave oven set on high for 1 minute. And use whole milk and pure vanilla extract, just as you would in a from-scratch cake.

CARROT CAKE WITH FRESH ORANGE CREAM CHEESE FROSTING

This is one pretty cake. That's what you'll say to yourself as you smooth the delectable frosting on so effortlessly. This is one scrumptious cake. That's what you'll say to yourself as you take a bite, then another. Fresh orange juice and zest in the creamy frosting are the perfect partners for a spicy carrot cake. There's even a little orange juice in the cake batter. But if you'd rather, opt for the Cinnamon Buttercream Frosting (page 416) to frost the cake.

SERVES: 16
PREPARATION TIME: 10 MINUTES
BAKING TIME: 30 TO 35 MINUTES
ASSEMBLY TIME: 15 MINUTES

*Solid vegetable shortening for greasing
    the pans*
Flour for dusting the pans
*1 package (18.25 ounces) plain yellow
    cake mix*
*1 package (3.4 ounces) vanilla instant
    pudding mix*
⅔ cup fresh orange juice
*½ cup vegetable oil, such as canola, corn,
    safflower, soybean, or sunflower*
4 large eggs
2 teaspoons ground cinnamon
3 cups grated carrots (5 medium carrots)
½ cup raisins
½ cup chopped walnuts or pecans
*Fresh Orange Cream Cheese Frosting
    (page 422)*

R

the Cake Doctor says...

You have so many flavors and textures going on in this carrot cake, from sweet to spicy and from crunchy to soft and moist, that it's pretty hard to tell you've even used a mix. And then you enrobe the entire cake in the seductive orange frosting. It's a thumbs-up recipe, all the way!

1. Place a rack in the center of the oven and preheat the oven to 350°F. Generously grease two 9-inch round cake pans with solid vegetable shortening. Dust with flour, then shake out the excess flour. Set the pans aside.

2. Place the cake mix, pudding mix, orange juice, oil, eggs, and cinnamon in a large bowl. Blend with an electric mixer on low speed for 1 minute. Stop the machine and scrape down the sides of the bowl with a rubber spatula. Increase the mixer speed to medium and beat 2 minutes more, scraping the sides down again if needed. The batter should look thick and well blended. Gently fold in the carrots, raisins, and nuts with a rubber spatula. Divide the batter between the prepared pans, smoothing it out with the

rubber spatula. Place the pans in the oven side by side.

3. Bake the cakes until they are golden brown and spring back when lightly pressed with your finger, 30 to 35 minutes. Remove the pans from the oven and place them on wire racks to cool for 10 minutes. Run a dinner knife around the edges of each layer and invert each onto a rack, then invert each again onto another rack so that the cakes are right side up. Allow them to cool completely, 30 minutes more.

4. Meanwhile, prepare the Fresh Orange Cream Cheese Frosting.

5. Place one cake layer, right side up, on a serving platter. Spread the top with frosting. Place the second layer, right side up, on top of the first layer and frost the top and sides of the cake with clean, smooth strokes.

❋ *Place this cake, uncovered, in the refrigerator until the frosting sets, 20 minutes. Cover the cake with waxed paper and store in the refrigerator for up to 1 week. Or freeze it, wrapped in aluminum foil, for up to 6 months. Thaw the cake in the refrigerator before serving.*

Carrot Cakes

*R*emember when every dessert you saw—in the deli, on the airplane, in the white tablecloth restaurant—was carrot cake? And if I had to guess why carrot cakes came on so strong and appealed to so many I would say the vegetarian movement or the same deli influence that also gave us cheesecake. And yet, according to Jean Anderson in *The American Century Cookbook,* the first carrot cake was developed much earlier than the 1970s when carrot cakes were hot. A recipe for carrot cake was published in 1929 in *The 20th Century Bride's Cookbook,* by members of a Wichita, Kansas, women's club. Anderson says it wasn't until Pillsbury staged a nationwide contest to find an original carrot cake recipe that this early formula surfaced. And she adds that the carrot cake is thought to be a descendant of the carrot puddings of England and Europe. Thus, immigrants combined their love of sweet carrot desserts with American flours to produce the carrot cake we know today. With the addition of cinnamon and the generous proportion of oil, the carrot cake is a beloved spicy and moist cake. And it is customarily frosted with a cream cheese frosting.

And there are infinite ways to jazz up carrot cake. Here are four:

* **Pineapple filling:** Cook 2 cups diced fresh pineapple and ½ cup sugar over low heat until tender. Add ¼ cup pineapple juice and 2 tablespoons cornstarch, stir, and bring to a boil. Remove from the stove immediately and cool.

* **Macadamia nuts:** Instead of the usual walnuts or pecans, press chopped macadamia nuts onto the sides and top of the frosted cake.

* **Orange marmalade glaze:** Heat some marmalade and brush it over the top and sides of the cake layers. Then proceed with frosting the cake.

* **Ginger:** Add a pinch to the batter and 2 tablespoons chopped crystallized ginger to the frosting.

CARAMEL CAKE

This is birthday cake material, pure and simple. Candles look great on it, and people of all ages beg for a slice. Most any ice cream goes with Caramel Cake, but our favorites are peach and a super-rich vanilla. The frosting is a streamlined version of an old-fashioned method in which the caramel is first made by cooking granulated sugar in a cast-iron skillet. The old method creates delicious results, but the frosting is heavy and a lot of trouble. This cake and frosting are lighter on your palate and can be prepared in a fraction of the time. And the results are fragrant and scrumptious.

SERVES: 16

PREPARATION TIME: 5 TO 7 MINUTES

BAKING TIME: 27 TO 29 MINUTES

ASSEMBLY TIME: 20 MINUTES

Solid vegetable shortening for greasing the pans
Flour for dusting the pans
1 package (18.25 ounces) plain white cake mix
1 cup whole milk
8 tablespoons (1 stick) butter, melted
3 large eggs
2 teaspoons pure vanilla extract
Quick Caramel Frosting (page 430)

1. Place a rack in the center of the oven and preheat the oven to 350°F. Generously grease two 9-inch round cake pans with solid vegetable shortening, then dust with flour. Shake out the excess flour. Set the pans aside.

2. Place the cake mix, milk, melted butter, eggs, and vanilla extract in a large mixing bowl. Blend with an electric mixer on low speed for 1 minute. Stop the machine and scrape down the sides of the bowl with a rubber spatula. Increase the mixer speed to medium and beat 2 minutes more, scraping the sides down again if needed. The batter should look well blended. Divide the batter between the prepared pans, smoothing it out with the rubber spatula. Place the pans in the oven side by side.

3. Bake the cakes until they are golden brown and spring back when lightly pressed with your finger, 27 to 29 minutes. Remove the pans from the oven and place them on wire racks to cool for 10 minutes. Run a dinner knife around the edge of each layer and invert each onto a rack, then invert them again onto another rack so that the cakes are right side up. Allow them to cool completely, 30 minutes more.

4. Meanwhile, prepare the Quick Caramel Frosting.

5. Place one cake layer, right side up, on a serving platter. Spread the top with the warm frosting. Place the second layer, right side up, on top of the first layer and frost the top and sides of the cake with clean, smooth strokes. Work quickly, as the frosting will set. (If the frosting gets too hard to work with, place the pan back over low heat for 1 minute, stirring constantly, to soften it up.) Once the frosting has set, slice and serve.

✱ *Store this cake, covered in plastic wrap or aluminum foil, at room temperature for up to 1 week or freeze, wrapped in foil, for up to 6 months. Thaw the cake overnight on the counter before serving.*

the Cake Doctor says...

Work quickly when frosting this cake. The cake layers should be cool to the touch, but the frosting should be warm to hot. For the smoothest spreading, use a long, thin palette knife or rubber spatula. If the frosting begins to set up, return it to low heat and stir until it thins out.

SWEET POTATO CAKE WITH COCONUT PECAN CREAM CHEESE FROSTING

Sweet potatoes are the darlings of the produce bin, packed with vitamins and nutrients. But in this rich cake, you had better count on them just for flavor. The cake is based on a spice cake mix, and is easy to prepare because it contains little more than the mix.

SERVES: 16

PREPARATION TIME: 5 MINUTES

BAKING TIME: 28 TO 31 MINUTES

ASSEMBLY TIME: 20 MINUTES

Solid vegetable shortening for greasing
    the pans
Flour for dusting the pans
1 can (16 ounces) sweet potatoes in heavy
    syrup
1 package (18.25 ounces) plain spice
    cake mix
3 large eggs
⅓ cup vegetable oil, such as canola, corn,
    safflower, soybean, or sunflower
1 teaspoon ground cinnamon
Coconut Pecan Cream Cheese Frosting
    (page 423)

1. Place a rack in the center of the oven and preheat the oven to 350°F. Generously grease two 9-inch round cake pans with solid vegetable shortening, then dust with flour. Shake out the excess flour. Set the pans aside.

2. Mash the sweet potatoes with their heavy syrup in a large mixing bowl using a fork or potato masher. Add the cake

R

the Cake Doctor says...

If you want to use fresh sweet potatoes rather than canned, prepare 1 cup cooked mashed sweet potatoes (1 to 2 sweet potatoes) and add ⅔ cup buttermilk. This is less sweet than the canned version, but just as delicious.

mix, eggs, oil, and cinnamon. Blend with an electric mixer on low speed for 1 minute. Stop the machine and scrape down the sides of the bowl with a rubber spatula. Increase the mixer speed to medium and beat 2 to 3 minutes more, scraping the sides down again if needed. The batter should look well combined and thickened. Divide the batter between the prepared pans, smoothing it out with the rubber spatula. Place the pans in the oven side by side.

3. Bake the cakes until they spring back when lightly pressed with your fingers and just start to pull away from the sides of the pan, 28 to 31 minutes. Remove the pans from the oven and place them on wire racks to cool for 10 minutes. Run a dinner knife around the edge of each layer and invert each onto a rack, then invert them again

onto another rack so that the cakes are right side up. Cool to room temperature.

4. Meanwhile, prepare the Coconut Pecan Cream Cheese Frosting.

5. Place one cake layer, right side up, on a serving platter. Spread the top with frosting. Place the second layer, right side up, on top of the first layer and frost the top and sides of the cake with clean, smooth strokes.

✴ *Place this cake, uncovered, in the refrigerator until the frosting sets, 20 minutes. Cover the cake with waxed paper and store in the refrigerator for up to 1 week. Or freeze it, wrapped in aluminum foil, for up to 6 months. Thaw the cake overnight in the refrigerator before serving.*

TENNESSEE JAM CAKE

In the heat of summer, fat and fragrant blackberries come into season in fields and along road-sides in Tennessee and other parts of the South. Pick a few, sweeten with sugar, and pour a little fresh cream over them and you have a true delicacy. Pick many and turn them into blackberry jam. That's precisely how this classic dessert came about—a good cook had some jam in the larder, so she sandwiched it in between layers of a simple spice cake. And the crowning glory was a from-scratch caramel frosting. Sheer heaven. Here's my fast version, using a mix and a good-quality store-bought blackberry jam.

SERVES: 16
PREPARATION TIME: 5 TO 7 MINUTES
BAKING TIME: 26 TO 28 MINUTES
ASSEMBLY TIME: 20 MINUTES

*Solid vegetable shortening for greasing
   the pans*
Flour for dusting the pans
*1 package (18.25 ounces) plain spice
   cake mix*
1 cup buttermilk
⅓ cup sweetened applesauce
*⅓ cup vegetable oil, such as canola, corn,
   safflower, soybean, or sunflower*
3 large eggs
¼ teaspoon ground cinnamon
⅔ cup good-quality blackberry jam
Quick Caramel Frosting (page 430)

1. Place a rack in the center of the oven and preheat the oven to 350°F. Generously grease two 9-inch round cake pans with solid vegetable shortening, then dust with flour. Shake out the excess flour. Set the pans aside.

R

the Cake Doctor says...

Buttermilk and applesauce are proof
you don't need a lot of extra fat to
make a cake-mix cake moist. This is
a rich-tasting and flavorful cake,
and it benefits from a little added
cinnamon—but then, I just love
cinnamon.

2. Place the cake mix, buttermilk, applesauce, oil, eggs, and cinnamon in a large
mixing bowl. Blend with an electric mixer
on low speed for 1 minute. Stop the
machine and scrape down the sides of
the bowl with a rubber spatula. Increase
the mixer speed to medium and beat 2
minutes more, scraping the sides down
again if needed. The batter should look
well blended. Divide the batter between
the prepared pans, smoothing it out with
the rubber spatula. Place the pans in the
oven side by side.

3. Bake the cakes until they are light
brown and spring back when lightly
pressed with your finger, 26 to 28 minutes. Remove the pans from the oven and
place them on wire racks to cool for 10
minutes. Run a dinner knife around the
edge of each layer and invert each onto a

rack, then invert them again onto another
rack so that the cakes are right side up.
Allow them to cool completely, 30 minutes
more.

4. Meanwhile, prepare the Quick Caramel
Frosting.

5. Place one cake layer, right side up, on
a serving platter. Spread the top with the
blackberry jam and spread a smooth layer
of warm caramel frosting on top of the
jam, using a rubber spatula. Place the second layer, right side up, on top of the first
layer. Frost the top and sides of the cake
with caramel frosting, using clean,
smooth strokes and working quickly, as
the frosting will set up. (If the frosting gets
too hard to work with, place the pan back
over low heat for 1 minute, stirring constantly, to soften it up.) Once the frosting
has set, slice and serve.

✸   *Store the cake, covered in aluminum
foil, at room temperature for up to 1 week
or freeze it, wrapped in foil, for up to 6
months. Thaw the cake overnight on the
counter before serving.*

GRANDMA'S COCONUT ICEBOX CAKE

O r should this be titled Holiday Garage Coconut Cake? Let me explain. One Christmas we traveled to Lookout Mountain, Georgia, to spend the holidays with my in-laws. As will invariably happen when you are away from home with three small children, an ice storm hit the mountain and we lost power. We had plans for some great cooking—a chocolate yule log cake, a pork roast, and gingerbread cookies for the children to decorate—but instead, we listened to the crashing of heavy ice-laden tree limbs outside and ate sandwiches, cereal, and, thank goodness, this coconut cake. It stayed nice and chilled in the frigid garage!

The recipe came to me from Savannah cook and food writer Damon Lee Fowler, who says his grandmother MaMa made this cake, and it was her specialty. It tastes best if allowed to rest at least three days in the icebox (old wonderful word for refrigerator), and it's superlative after five days, but this requires willpower! I recommend you bake it in the winter and tote it along for insurance if you're planning to travel during an ice storm!

SERVES: 20

PREPARATION TIME:

5 TO 7 MINUTES

BAKING TIME: 27 TO 29 MINUTES

ASSEMBLY TIME: 15 MINUTES

CAKE:

Solid vegetable shortening for greasing
the pans

Flour for dusting the pans

1 package (18.25 ounces) plain white
cake mix

1⅓ cups water

2 tablespoons vegetable oil, such as
canola, corn, safflower, soybean,
or sunflower

3 large eggs

COCONUT FROSTING:

2 cups sugar

2 cups (16 ounces) sour cream

1 package (12 ounces, 3½ cups) frozen
unsweetened grated coconut, thawed

1. Place a rack in the center of the oven and preheat the oven to 350°F. Generously grease two 9-inch round cake pans with solid vegetable shortening, then dust with flour. Shake out the excess flour. Set the pans aside.

the Cake Doctor says...

What makes this cake improve with age are the whole eggs in the batter. And the sour cream–based frosting, which is rich, protects the cake and soaks down into the cake as it chills. The coconut has time to lend its flavors, too, so the coconut flavor of the cake increases daily.

2. Place the cake mix, water, oil, and eggs in a large mixing bowl. Blend with an electric mixer on low speed for 1 minute. Stop the machine and scrape down the sides of the bowl with a rubber spatula. Increase the mixer speed to medium and beat 2 minutes more, scraping the sides down again if needed. The batter should look well blended. Divide the batter between the prepared pans, smoothing it out with the rubber spatula. Place the pans in the oven side by side.

3. Bake the cakes until they are golden brown and spring back when lightly pressed with your finger, 27 to 29 minutes.

4. Meanwhile, prepare the frosting. Combine the sugar, sour cream, and thawed coconut in a medium bowl. Let the mixture rest in the refrigerator until the sugar dissolves, 1 hour, stirring occasionally.

5. Remove the pans from the oven and place them on wire racks to cool for 10 minutes. Run a dinner knife around the edge of each layer and invert each onto a rack, then invert them again onto another rack so that the cakes are right side up. Allow them to cool completely, 30 minutes more.

6. When the sugar has dissolved in the frosting, begin to assemble the cake. Carefully slice the cake layers in half horizontally, using a large, sharp serrated bread knife or a long piece of unflavored dental floss. You will have four layers. Place the bottom half of a cake layer on a serving platter, cut side up. Spread with some of the coconut frosting. Top the bottom half with the matching top of the layer, cut side down. Spread with frosting. Next, add the bottom half of the second layer, cut side up, and spread with frosting. Top the bottom half with the matching top of the layer, cut side down. Spread the top and sides of the entire cake with all of the remaining coconut frosting, using clean, smooth strokes. The frosting should be nice and thick and not run off the sides.

7. Chill the cake, uncovered, until the frosting is firm, 1 hour.

✳ *Store this cake covered with waxed paper taped down along the underside of the platter to keep it snug. It will keep in the refrigerator for up to 1 week.*

SNICKERDOODLE CAKE

Who knows what kids like best about the "snickerdoodle"—the silly name or the lively cinnamon taste? This cake is a take-off on the classic snickerdoodle cookie, which, according to John Mariani in *The Dictionary of American Food & Drink,* is a nineteenth-century New England creation seasoned with cinnamon but also containing nuts and dried fruit. The name comes from a nonsense word meaning "quickly made," implying the cookies are whipped up with ingredients at hand. This cake is a snap to pull together, too—it relies on a cinnamon-scented, basic butter cake recipe and a buttercream frosting that you enliven with more aromatic cinnamon.

R

the Cake Doctor says...

Cinnamon is one of the great tools to use when doctoring up cake mixes. Not only is it well loved by all ages, but it steals the show, capturing your attention with its exotic flavor and marrying well with the butter in the cake and the frosting.

....

SERVES: 16

PREPARATION TIME:

5 TO 7 MINUTES

BAKING TIME:

27 TO 29 MINUTES

ASSEMBLY TIME: 20 MINUTES

....

Enriching White Cake Mix

The package of white cake mix suggests adding egg whites instead of the whole egg. Don't do it. Your cake will only benefit from those yolks, for the yolks add a rich flavor, a nice soft yellow color, and a tender crumb texture. Whole eggs give a white mix more of a homemade taste and look. And do add melted butter to a white cake mix, for some or all of the vegetable oil listed on the box. Melted butter provides flavor, color, and texture as well.

Solid vegetable shortening for greasing
    the pans

Flour for dusting the pans

1 package (18.25 ounces) plain white
    cake mix

1 cup whole milk

8 tablespoons (1 stick) butter, melted

3 large eggs

1 teaspoon pure vanilla extract

2 teaspoons ground cinnamon

Cinnamon Buttercream Frosting
    (page 417)

1. Place a rack in the center of the oven and preheat the oven to 350°F. Generously grease two 9-inch round cake pans with solid vegetable shortening, then dust with flour. Shake out the excess flour. Set the pans aside.

2. Place the cake mix, milk, melted butter, eggs, vanilla, and cinnamon in a large mixing bowl. Blend with an electric mixer on low speed for 1 minute. Stop the machine and scrape down the sides of the bowl with a rubber spatula. Increase the mixer speed to medium and beat 2 minutes more, scraping the sides down again if needed. The batter should look well combined. Divide the batter between the prepared pans, smoothing it out with the rubber spatula. Place the pans in the oven side by side.

3. Bake the cakes until they are golden brown and spring back when lightly pressed with your finger, 27 to 29 minutes. Remove the pans from the oven and place them on wire racks to cool for 10 minutes. Run a dinner knife around the edge of each layer and invert each onto a rack, then invert them again onto another rack so that the cakes are right side up. Allow them to cool completely, 30 minutes more.

4. Meanwhile, prepare the Cinnamon Buttercream Frosting.

5. Place one cake layer, right side up, on a serving platter. Spread the top with frosting. Place the second layer, right side up, on top of the first layer and frost the top and sides of the cake with clean, smooth strokes.

✳ *Place this cake, uncovered, in the refrigerator until the frosting sets, 20 minutes. Cover the cake with waxed paper and store in the refrigerator for up to 1 week. Or freeze it, wrapped in aluminum foil, for up to 6 months. Thaw the cake overnight in the refrigerator before serving.*

CHARLESTON POPPY SEED CAKE

This recipe is adapted from a recipe I received from Teresa Pregnall, also known as the Charleston Cake Lady, who says her poppy seed cake is a mainstay of party menus in her port city. It keeps well, for a week under a cake dome, but you'll probably enjoy it at once. Serve with a nice cup of hot tea and imagine you're down South Carolina way.

SERVES: 16

PREPARATION TIME: 15 MINUTES

BAKING TIME: 45 TO 50 MINUTES

Vegetable oil spray for misting the pan

Flour for dusting the pan

1 package (18.25 ounces) plain white cake mix

1 package (3.4 ounces) vanilla instant pudding mix

⅓ cup poppy seeds

1 cup low-fat vanilla yogurt

½ cup vegetable oil, such as canola, corn, safflower, soybean, or sunflower

½ cup dry sherry

4 large eggs

1 teaspoon grated lemon zest (from 1 lemon)

1. Place a rack in the center of the oven and preheat the oven to 350°F. Lightly mist a 10-inch tube pan with vegetable oil spray, then dust with flour. Shake out the excess flour. Set the pan aside.

Sherry

The first time I saw someone sip sherry it wasn't in Andalusia, where Spanish bartenders serve up glasses of this dry, nutty beverage to swill down with *tapas*. It was in a pub in the southern countryside of England when I was traveling after college. An elderly lady at the table next to mine was sipping sherry from a small wine glass. Her gentleman friend was drinking the same. Their cheeks were flushed and their feet were dancing delightfully under the table. I knew right then that there must be something magical about sherry.

Now, as a cook I know the full story, for sherry is both magical and invaluable in baking. My friends in Savannah and Charleston swear by it, adding sherry to Bundt cakes and cream cakes and soaking dried fruit for sherry fruit cakes.

Sherry is a fortified wine, ranging from a pale gold to a deep walnut color. Its scent is a melange of hazelnuts, toasted pecans, orange peel, and vanilla, so just think about what good things it can do to your cheesecake or coffee cake! And there is another reason why I like sherry— the philosophy behind it. Sherries are blends, not vintages with the wine coming from a specific year. Sherry makers believe that an old, fine wine has the power to educate and improve a younger one.

For baking, choose a medium-sweet sherry, a nutty Amontillado or Oloroso sherry from Spain or a golden sherry from other sherry-producing countries. Save the bone-dry sherries for aperitifs and the sugary cream sherries to sip after dinner. But whatever you do, don't substitute cooking sherry! It contains salt and will ruin the taste of your cake.

2. Place the cake mix, pudding mix, poppy seeds, yogurt, oil, sherry, eggs, and lemon zest in a large mixing bowl. Blend with an electric mixer on low speed for 1 minute. Stop the machine and scrape down the sides of the bowl with a rubber spatula. Increase the mixer speed to medium and beat 2 minutes more, scraping the sides down again if needed. The batter should look well combined and thickened and the poppy seeds should be well distributed. Pour the batter into the prepared pan, smoothing it out with the rubber spatula. Place the pan in the oven.

3. Bake the cake until it is golden brown and springs back when lightly pressed with your finger, 45 to 50 minutes. Remove the pan from the oven and place it on a wire rack to cool for 20 minutes. Run a long, sharp knife around the edge of the cake and invert it onto a rack, then invert it onto another rack so that the cake is right side up. Allow the cake to cool completely, 30 minutes more.

4. Place the cake onto a serving platter and serve.

✳ *Store this cake, covered in aluminum foil or plastic wrap, at room temperature for up to 1 week. Or freeze it, wrapped in foil, for up to 6 months. Thaw the cake overnight on the counter before serving.*

R
the Cake Doctor says...

This recipe reflects many clever tricks for doctoring up a cake mix. For example, a good dose of dry sherry takes away any cake-mix flavor, keeps the cake moist, and makes it a most festive dessert. The yogurt is low in fat and keeps the cake moist. The poppy seeds add texture, and I added a little lemon zest to cut through the sweetness.

LEMON BUTTERMILK POPPY SEED CAKE

When springtime flowers come into bloom and you're planning a meal out of doors, don't forget this delicate, moist poppy seed cake. I created this recipe in much the same mold as the Charleston Poppy Seed Cake, except this one isn't boozy. Buttermilk lends a down-home air to this pretty cake that is as suitable for breakfast as it is for dessert.

SERVES: 16

PREPARATION TIME: 15 MINUTES

BAKING TIME: 45 TO 50 MINUTES

Vegetable oil spray for misting the pan

Flour for dusting the pan

1 package (18.25 ounces) plain white cake mix

1 package (3.4 ounces) vanilla instant pudding mix

⅓ cup poppy seeds

1 cup low-fat vanilla or lemon yogurt

½ cup vegetable oil, such as canola, corn, safflower, soybean, or sunflower

½ cup buttermilk

4 large eggs

2 tablespoons fresh lemon juice (from 1 lemon)

1 teaspoon finely grated lemon zest (from 1 lemon)

1. Place a rack in the center of the oven and preheat the oven to 350°F. Lightly mist a 10-inch tube pan with vegetable oil spray, then dust with flour. Shake out the excess flour. Set the pan aside.

2. Place the cake mix, pudding mix, poppy seeds, yogurt, oil, buttermilk, eggs, lemon juice, and lemon zest in a large mixing bowl. Blend with an electric mixer on low speed for 1 minute. Stop the machine and scrape down the sides of the bowl with a rubber spatula. Increase the mixer speed to medium and beat 2 minutes more, scraping the sides down again if needed. The batter should look thick and well blended and the poppy seeds should be evenly distributed. Pour the batter into the prepared pan, smoothing it out with the rubber spatula. Place the pan in the oven.

3. Bake the cake until it is golden brown and springs back when lightly pressed with your finger, 45 to 50 minutes. Remove the pan from the oven and place it on a wire rack to cool for 20 minutes. Run a long, sharp knife around the edge of the cake and invert it onto a rack, then invert it again onto another rack so that the cake is right side up. Allow the cake to cool completely, 30 minutes more.

4. Place the cake on a serving platter and serve.

✳ *Store this cake, covered in aluminum foil or plastic wrap, at room temperature for up to 1 week. Or freeze it, wrapped in foil, for up to 6 months. Thaw the cake overnight on the counter before serving.*

the Cake Doctor says...

Both fresh lemon juice and lemon zest work wonders in transforming an ordinary white cake mix into this exceptional, lemony cake. Buttermilk adds flavor as well, plus a moist texture.

ALMOND CREAM CHEESE POUND CAKE

oss Beck of Texarkana, Arkansas, devised this rich and moist cake. It's not the traditional pound cake from scratch that so many of us were raised on (or at least wish we were) but in a hurried world, it's a delicious alternative. My husband took this cake into the office one morning, and his co-workers begged for the recipe. Beck says the cake is always good plain but better if served with fresh berries when they are in season. So true.

SERVES: 16

PREPARATION TIME: 10 MINUTES

BAKING TIME: 35 TO 40 MINUTES

Vegetable oil spray for misting the pan
Flour for dusting the pan
1 package (18.5 ounces) butter recipe
  golden cake mix
1 package (8 ounces) cream cheese,
  at room temperature
4 large eggs
½ cup water
½ cup sugar
½ cup vegetable oil, such as canola, corn,
  safflower, soybean, or sunflower
1 teaspoon pure vanilla extract
1 teaspoon pure almond extract

1. Place a rack in the center of the oven and preheat the oven to 350°F. Lightly mist a 10-inch tube pan with vegetable oil spray, then dust with flour. Shake out the excess flour. Set the pan aside.

2. Place the cake mix, cream cheese, eggs, water, sugar, oil, vanilla, and almond extract in a large mixing bowl. Blend with an electric mixer on low speed for 1 minute. Stop the machine and scrape down the sides of the bowl with a rubber spatula. Increase the mixer speed to medium and beat 2 minutes more, scraping the sides down again if needed. The batter should look well blended. Pour the batter into the prepared pan, smoothing it out with the rubber spatula. Place the pan in the oven.

3. Bake the cake until it is golden brown and springs back when lightly pressed with your finger, 35 to 40 minutes. Remove the pan from the oven and place it on a wire rack to cool for 20 minutes. Run a long, sharp knife around the edge of the cake, invert it onto a rack, then invert it onto a serving platter so that it is right side up.

4. Slice the cake while it is still a little warm.

✳ *Store this cake, covered in plastic wrap or under a glass dome, at room temperature for up to 1 week. Or freeze it, wrapped in aluminum foil, for up to 6 months. Thaw the cake overnight on the counter before serving.*

R
the Cake Doctor says...

The recipe for the Almond Cream Cheese Pound Cake calls for ½ cup sugar. By adding some extra sugar (from ¼ to ½ cup) to a cake mix, you'll arrive at a more tender cake. Adding cream cheese will give it richness and texture. And be sure to use the pure extracts that this cake calls for—both vanilla and almond—for clear, distinct, and true flavors.

ZUCCHINI SPICE CAKE WITH PENUCHE FROSTING

When the zucchini grow as large as sub-marines, nearly suffo-cating other vegetables in your garden, it's time to bake with them. Anyone who has put in a patch of zucchini during a warm, wet summer knows how quickly these squash swell overnight. This is a dandy of a cake; and if you don't have grated zucchini, you could just as easily use carrots. The frosting is the icing on the cake, so to speak, for the sweet caramel flavor balances nicely with the spices in the cake.

SERVES: 16

PREPARATION TIME: 10 MINUTES

BAKING TIME: 60 TO 65 MINUTES

ASSEMBLY TIME: 15 MINUTES

Vegetable oil spray for misting the pan

Flour for dusting the pan

1 package (18.25 ounces) plain yellow cake mix

1 package (3.4 ounces) vanilla instant pudding mix

1 cup sour cream

½ cup water

¼ cup vegetable oil, such as canola, corn, safflower, soybean, or sunflower

4 large eggs

1 teaspoon ground cinnamon

½ teaspoon ground nutmeg

¼ teaspoon ground cloves

¼ teaspoon salt

2 cups grated zucchini (from 1 medium zucchini)

Penuche Frosting (page 431)

the Cake Doctor says...

Nutmeg is a silent champion in this spice cake recipe, for the flavor comes through and marries well with the Penuche Frosting. If you don't want to spend the time making a frosting, however, just sift a little confectioners' sugar over the top of the cake before you slice.

1. Place a rack in the center of the oven and preheat the oven to 350°F. Generously mist a 10-inch tube pan with vegetable oil spray, then dust with flour. Shake out the excess flour. Set the pan aside.

2. Place the cake mix, pudding mix, sour cream, water, oil, eggs, cinnamon, nutmeg, cloves, and salt in a large mixing bowl. Blend with an electric mixer on low speed for 1 minute. Stop the machine and scrape down the sides of the bowl with a rubber spatula. Increase the mixer speed to medium and beat 2 to 3 minutes more, scraping the sides down again if needed. The batter should look thick and smooth. Fold in the grated zucchini. Pour the batter into the prepared pan, smoothing it out with the rubber spatula. Place the pan in the oven.

3. Bake the cake until it is light brown and springs back when lightly pressed with your finger, 60 to 65 minutes. Remove the pan from the oven and place it on a wire rack to cool for 20 minutes. Run a long, sharp knife around the edge of the cake and invert it onto a rack, then invert it again onto another rack so that the cake is right side up. Allow to cool completely, 30 minutes more.

4. Meanwhile, prepare the Penuche Frosting.

5. Place the cake on a serving platter. Spread the warm frosting on the top and sides of the cooled cake with clean, smooth strokes. Allow the cake and frosting to cool before slicing.

❉ *Store this cake, covered in aluminum foil or placed under a glass cake dome, at room temperature for up to 1 week. Or freeze the cake, wrapped in foil, for up to 6 months. Thaw the cake overnight on the counter before serving.*

PECAN PIE CAKE

O ne of the best Southern desserts is the pecan pie, made with pecans, butter, corn syrup, brown sugar, egg, and vanilla. This recipe blends pie and cake into one, relying on the cake mix for structure and the basic pecan pie ingredients for flavor. Cut it into gooey squares and serve it on Sundays after lunch, like they do in Georgia pecan country. For a dressy variation, drizzle melted semisweet chocolate over the top before slicing.

SERVES: 20
PREPARATION TIME:
10 TO 12 MINUTES
BAKING TIME:
55 TO 57 MINUTES

1 package (18.25 ounces) plain yellow
    cake mix
8 tablespoons (1 stick) butter, melted
4 large eggs
1½ cups light corn syrup
½ cup packed dark brown sugar
1 teaspoon pure vanilla extract
2 cups chopped pecans, toasted (see
    Toasting Nuts, page 134)
Vanilla ice cream, for serving
    (optional)

1. Place a rack in the center of the oven and preheat the oven to 325°F.

2. Place the cake mix, melted butter, and 1 egg in a large mixing bowl. Blend with an electric mixer on low speed for 1 to 2 minutes, or until well combined and thick. Measure out ⅔ cup of the batter

Toasting Nuts

It's amazing how just a little toasting brings out the full, total flavor of nuts. Here is how long various nuts need to toast in a preheated 350° F oven. Spread them out in one layer on a baking pan. Stir once or twice with a metal spatula or a long wooden spoon while toasting. Remember that chopped nuts will take less time than whole nuts and halves. And be mindful of the nuts. Chef Elizabeth Terry of Elizabeth's on 37th in Savannah, Georgia, has a rule that her cooks cannot leave the kitchen while nuts are toasting. Nuts are too easy to burn, and they will continue to cook and darken once they've been removed from the oven. Terry toasts pecans long enough for them to perfume the air.

Almonds: Whole almonds about 10 minutes, stirring once or twice, until light brown. Slivered almonds 2 to 3 minutes.

Pecans: 4 to 5 minutes, or until you smell them.

Pine nuts: 7 to 8 minutes, or until lightly golden. Or, toast in a heavy cast-iron skillet over low heat for 3 to 5 minutes, shaking the pan frequently, until they turn light brown.

Macadamia nuts: 8 minutes, or until golden brown.

Walnuts: 10 minutes, or until golden.

Hazelnuts (filberts): 20 minutes; rub off skins while nuts are warm.

and reserve. Pat the remaining batter into the bottom of an ungreased 13- by 9-inch baking pan and place it in the oven.

3. Bake until the crust is light brown and puffs up, 15 minutes. Remove the pan from the oven and place it on a rack to cool for 10 minutes. Leave the oven on.

4. Place the reserved crust mixture, corn syrup, dark brown sugar, remaining 3 eggs, and vanilla in the same large mixing bowl. Blend with an electric mixer on low speed for 1 minute. Stop the machine and scrape down the sides of the bowl with a rubber spatula. Increase the mixer speed to medium and beat until the batter is

R

the Cake Doctor says...

Looking for a more dramatic taste?
In the filling, substitute 2 tablespoons
bourbon whiskey for the vanilla extract
and add 1 cup miniature semisweet
chocolate chips when you fold in the
pecans.

well combined and the crust mixture has
blended, 1 minute more, scraping the
sides down again if needed. Fold in the
pecans until they are well distributed.

Pour the pecan mixture on top of the
crust mixture, smoothing it out with the
rubber spatula. Return the pan to the
oven.

5. Bake the cake until the edges are
browned but the center is still a little soft,
40 to 45 minutes. Remove the pan from
the oven and let it cool on a rack for 30
minutes. Slice and serve with vanilla ice
cream, if desired.

✻ *Store this cake, covered in aluminum
foil, at room temperature for up to 3 days.
Or freeze it, wrapped in foil, for up to 6
months. Thaw the cake overnight on the
counter before serving.*

MACADAMIA FUDGE TORTE

This recipe from Kurt Wait, of Redwood City, California, was the grand prize winner in the 1996 Pillsbury Bake-Off contest. He was the first million-dollar winner and isn't it ironic that he used a cake mix.

SERVES: 12

PREPARATION TIME: 30 MINUTES

BAKING TIME: 45 TO 50 MINUTES

Vegetable oil spray for misting the pan

FILLING:

⅓ cup low-fat sweetened condensed milk

½ cup semisweet chocolate chips

CAKE:

1 package (18.25 ounces) Pillsbury Moist Supreme Devil's Food Cake Mix (with pudding)

⅓ cup vegetable oil, such as canola, corn, safflower, soybean, or sunflower

1½ teaspoons ground cinnamon

1 can (16 ounces) sliced pears in light syrup, drained

2 large eggs

⅓ cup chopped macadamia nuts or pecans

2 teaspoons water

SAUCE:

1 jar (17 ounces) butterscotch caramel fudge ice-cream topping

⅓ cup milk

Vanilla ice cream, for serving

1. Place a rack in the center of the oven and preheat the oven to 350°F. Lightly mist a 9- or 10-inch springform pan with vegetable oil spray. Set the pan aside.

2. For the filling, place the condensed milk and chocolate chips in a small

R

the Cake Doctor says...

This recipe calls for a cake mix with pudding. If you wish to substitute a cake mix without pudding, add an extra egg and ½ cup vegetable oil.

saucepan over medium-low heat. Heat, stirring, until the chocolate is melted, 2 to 3 minutes. Set the pan aside.

3. Place the cake mix, oil, and cinnamon in a large mixing bowl. Blend with an electric mixer on low speed for 20 to 30 seconds. The mixture will be crumbly. Set the bowl aside. Place the pears in a blender or food processor fitted with the metal blade and blend until smooth.

4. Place 2½ cups of the cake-mix mixture, the pureed pears, and the eggs in a large mixing bowl. Set the remaining cake-mix mixture aside. Blend with an electric mixture on low speed until moistened, 1 minute. Stop the machine and scrape down the sides of the bowl with a rubber spatula. Increase the mixer speed to medium and beat 2 minutes more, scraping the sides down as needed. The batter should look thick and smooth. Pour the batter into the prepared pan,

smoothing it out with the rubber spatula. Drop the filling by spoonfuls over the batter. Stir the nuts and water into the remaining cake-mix mixture and sprinkle this over the filling. Place the pan in the oven.

5. Bake the cake until it springs back when lightly pressed with your finger, 45 to 50 minutes. Remove the pan from the oven and place it on a wire rack to cool for 10 minutes. Remove the sides of the pan. Allow the cake to cool completely, 1½ hours more.

6. For the sauce, place the ice-cream topping and milk in a small saucepan over medium-low heat. Stir and cook until well blended, 3 to 4 minutes.

7. Spoon 2 tablespoons of warm sauce onto each plate and top with a slice of cake and a scoop of vanilla ice cream.

✳ *Store this cake, unsauced, covered in plastic wrap, in the refrigerator for up to 1 week. Or freeze it, wrapped in aluminum foil, for up to 6 months. Thaw the cake overnight in the refrigerator before serving. Prepare the sauce right before serving.*

The Legendary Pillsbury Bake-Off

In 1949, when American families were prospering after World War II, The Pillsbury Co. launched its first cooking contest—the 1949 Grand National Recipe and Baking Contest to commemorate its eightieth birthday. The emphasis was on recipe swapping with your neighbor, but the scene was a glitzy one—the event was staged at the elegant Waldorf-Astoria Hotel in New York City. The winner was a Theodora Smafield of Michigan, who created No-Knead Water-Rising Twists, a peculiar recipe made by wrapping the dough in a kitchen towel and plunging it in warm water to rise.

Macadamia Fudge Torte

But what began as a publicity stunt was such a huge success that Pillsbury executives repeated the contest the next year, and the next. And the Pillsbury Bake-Off, as it is called a half century later, now offers a hefty monetary prize to the lucky winner and acts as a prognosticator as to what Americans are really cooking.

For example, in the 1950s recipes called for pantry staples because one-car families often created desserts with what they had on hand. In the 1960s, with more women entering the work force and an emphasis on saving time, Pillsbury welcomed cake mix entries. In the 1970s, the Bake-Off switched to an every-other-year appearance, and winning recipes were invariably bar cookies or squares what with a new interest in health and exercise. More sophisticated, indulgent flavors made headlines at the Bake-Off in the 1980s, epitomized by the decadent Chocolate Praline Layer Cake in 1988.

But it wasn't until 1996 that a cake mix really drew a reaction from the judges: cook Kurt Wait from Redwood City, California, prepared an elegant chocolate cake—Macadamia Fudge Torte—using a mix. He would take home enough money for his son's college education, and then some—$1 million. The grand prizes are still set at a cool million. (See page 136 for Wait's recipe.)

BANANA PUDDING CAKE

I first envisioned a Bundt cake containing bananas and pudding mix that would taste just like a banana pudding, but what I got was a cake that tasted like mediocre banana bread. So, I thought, what if I created a layered dessert in which the cake is on the bottom, the bananas and pudding are on the top, and whipped cream and crumbled vanilla wafers are on top of that? Bingo. Now that was a Banana Pudding Cake!

....

SERVES: 20
PREPARATION TIME: 10 MINUTES
BAKING TIME: 30 TO 33 MINUTES
ASSEMBLY TIME: 5 MINUTES

....

CAKE:

Vegetable oil spray for misting the pan

1 package (18.25 ounces) plain yellow
      cake mix

8 tablespoons (1 stick) butter, melted

1 cup whole milk

3 large eggs

1 teaspoon pure vanilla extract

PUDDING:

1 package (5.1 ounces) vanilla instant
      pudding mix

3 cups whole milk

4 tablespoons (½ stick) butter, cut up

2 teaspoons pure vanilla extract

4 cups sliced bananas (3 large bananas)

TOPPING:

Sweetened Cream (page 432) or 1 container
      (12 ounces) frozen whipped topping,
      thawed

½ cup crushed vanilla wafer cookies (10 to
      12 cookies)

R

the Cake Doctor says...

This dessert is comfort food at its finest, but should you want to upscale the cake, add 1 tablespoon *crème de banane* liqueur to the pudding mixture. Use real whipped, sweetened cream; scatter lightly toasted macadamia nuts (page 134) on top; and crown with white chocolate shavings.

1. Place a rack in the center of the oven and preheat the oven to 350°F. Lightly mist a 13- by 9-inch baking pan with vegetable oil spray. Set the pan aside.

2. Place the cake mix, butter, milk, eggs, and vanilla in a large mixing bowl. Blend with an electric mixer on low speed for 1 minute. Stop the machine and scrape down the sides of the bowl with a rubber spatula. Increase the mixer speed to medium and beat 2 minutes more, scraping the sides down again if needed. The batter should look thick and well blended. Pour the batter into the prepared pan, smoothing it out with the rubber spatula. Place the pan in the oven.

3. Bake the cake until it is golden brown and springs back when lightly pressed with your finger, 30 to 33 minutes.

Remove the pan from the oven and place it on a wire rack to cool.

4. Meanwhile, prepare the pudding. Place the pudding mix and milk in a medium saucepan. Fold in the butter and vanilla. Cook over low heat, stirring, until the butter melts, 3 to 4 minutes. Remove the pan from the heat and let it cool for about 5 minutes. Fold in the banana slices.

5. Prepare the Sweetened Cream, if desired.

6. To assemble the cake, spoon the pudding and banana mixture on top of the cooled cake, spreading the mixture out to all edges of the cake with the rubber spatula. Cover the pudding with the Sweetened Cream or whipped topping, spreading it out to the edges of the cake with the rubber spatula. Scatter the crushed vanilla wafer cookies over the top. Serve at room temperature.

✴ *Store this cake, covered loosely in waxed paper, in the refrigerator for up to 3 days.*

Whipped Cream

When I was young, my mother would keep a glass bowl full of sweetened whipped cream in the refrigerator. In the summer we would drop a big spoonful on top of fragrant Alabama peaches. In the fall we'd plop the cream atop pumpkin pie. In the doldrums of winter we'd spoon it over our mother's famous chocolate cream pie. And in late spring we'd smear it over strawberries and hot buttered shortcake. And then, there were the in-between times: My mother would dip a spoon into the bowl for no good reason, and I recall the smile on her face. It was a decadent, wonderful childhood. And it was light years before the word "cholesterol" was mentioned.

To this day I'd rather have a spoonful of the real thing—fresh cream, whipped up with sugar—than a whole container of the frozen whipped topping. Yes, the frozen works in a pinch, but it will never, ever, taste as good as fresh. So that is why I urge you to whip your own cream, even if you take shortcuts and bake your cakes using a mix. It takes less than 3 minutes to whip a bowlful of cream to stiff peaks, and it takes far longer than that to thaw a frozen container. Here are my steps to effortless, and memorable, whipped cream:

1. Begin with heavy (whipping) cream. One cup of cream will yield 2 cups whipped.

2. Beat the cream in a stainless steel or glass bowl, never plastic, and chill beaters and bowl in the freezer beforehand for about 2 minutes.

3. Whip just the cream at the electric mixer's highest speed until soft peaks form on the end of the beaters. This is when you can add a little granulated sugar, confectioners' sugar, a smidgen of vanilla, or a bit of booze. Whip again at high speed until the cream forms stiff peaks, but not a second longer as you can easily turn that cream into butter.

4. Fillings need stiffly beaten whipped cream, whereas to dollop whipped cream over a deep chocolate cake or onto an applesauce cake, for instance, you want cream beaten to softer peaks.

5. Be sure to chill the dessert if you top or frost it with whipped cream.

TOASTED COCONUT SOUR CREAM CAKE

T his recipe comes from Billie Pettross of Carthage, Tennessee, who offers something a little different for coconut cake lovers. Instead of the traditional layer cake, this one is baked in a rectangular pan. The cake is moist from sour cream and cream of coconut, then Pettross frosts the cake with a cream cheese frosting. This is the type of cake you'll want to take to community suppers and school picnics.

SERVES: 20

PREPARATION TIME: 5 TO 7 MINUTES

BAKING TIME: 40 TO 42 MINUTES

ASSEMBLY TIME: 15 MINUTES

CAKE:

Vegetable oil spray for misting the pan

1 package (18.25 ounces) plain white
    cake mix

1 cup (8 ounces) sour cream

1 can (8.5 ounces) cream of coconut

¼ cup vegetable oil, such as canola, corn,
    safflower, soybean, or sunflower

3 large eggs

TOASTED COCONUT:

2 cups frozen unsweetened grated coconut,
    thawed

FROSTING:

1 package (8 ounces) cream cheese, at room
    temperature

3¾ cups confectioners' sugar, sifted

2 tablespoons milk

1 teaspoon pure vanilla extract

1. Place a rack in the center of the oven and preheat the oven to 350°F. Lightly mist a 13- by 9-inch baking pan with vegetable oil spray. Set the pan aside.

2. Place the cake mix, sour cream, cream of coconut, oil, and eggs in a large mixing bowl. Blend with an electric mixer on low speed for 1 minute. Stop the machine and scrape down the sides of the bowl with a rubber spatula. Increase the mixer speed to medium and beat 2 minutes more, scraping the sides down again if needed. The batter should look blended; however, flecks of cream of coconut may remain in the batter. Pour the batter into the prepared pan, smoothing it out with the rubber spatula. Place the pan in the oven.

3. Bake the cake until it is light brown and springs back when lightly pressed with your finger, 40 to 42 minutes. Remove the pan from the oven and place it on a wire rack to cool for 20 minutes. Leave the oven on.

4. Place the coconut in a pie plate and let toast in the oven until lightly browned, 4 to 5 minutes.

5. Meanwhile, prepare the frosting. Place the cream cheese in a large mixing bowl and beat with an electric mixer set on low speed until softened, 30 seconds. Stop the machine and add the confectioners' sugar, milk, and vanilla. Beat on low

speed until the ingredients are moistened, 30 seconds more. Scrape the sides down with a rubber spatula, increase the mixer speed to medium, and beat until well combined and fluffy, 2 minutes more.

6. Spread the frosting over the cake, using the rubber spatula to spread the frosting out to the edges of the cake. Sprinkle the top with toasted coconut.

✳ *Store this cake, covered in aluminum foil, in the refrigerator for up to 1 week. Or freeze it, wrapped in foil, for up to 6 months. Thaw the cake overnight on the counter before serving.*

R

the Cake Doctor says...

The trick to making a white cake-mix cake more interesting is to add whole eggs and intense flavorings such as cream of coconut. The cream cheese frosting adds richness, which is a nice balance to the white cake, and I toasted the coconut to gain more flavor. Pettross uses untoasted coconut, however, so suit yourself.

OLD-FASHIONED PRUNE CAKE WITH HOT BUTTERMILK GLAZE

Some of the world's most delicious desserts contain prunes, and I don't mean the infamous prune whip! I mean those rustic prune tarts and ice creams of southwestern France, seasoned with the local Armagnac. A sturdy prune cake American style is also good; solid dessert fare, serve it up warm right from the pan. When I was a child, this was the sort of dessert my mother would make for a casual dinner party. The hot buttermilk glaze is memorable. I recall the magic of watching it bubble up on the stove and then be poured searing hot right onto the cake.

SERVES: 20
PREPARATION TIME: 20 MINUTES
BAKING TIME: 32 TO 35 MINUTES
ASSEMBLY TIME: 10 MINUTES

Vegetable oil spray for misting the pan
1 package (18.25 ounces) yellow cake
*   mix with pudding*
¾ cup buttermilk
¾ cup vegetable oil, such as canola, corn,
*   safflower, soybean, or sunflower*
3 large eggs
1 teaspoon ground cinnamon
½ teaspoon ground allspice
1 cup pitted prunes, chopped
Hot Buttermilk Glaze (page 436)

1. Place a rack in the center of the oven and preheat the oven to 350°F. Lightly

R
the Cake Doctor says...

If you're not crazy about prunes,
substitute chopped dried apricots
or raisins.

mist a 13- by 9-inch baking pan with vegetable oil spray. Set the pan aside.

2. Place the cake mix, buttermilk, oil, eggs, cinnamon, and allspice in a large mixing bowl. Blend with an electric mixer on low speed for 1 minute. Stop the machine and scrape down the sides of the bowl with a rubber spatula. Increase the mixer speed to medium and beat 2 minutes more, scraping the sides down again if needed. The batter should look thick and well blended. Fold in the chopped prunes. Pour the batter into the prepared pan, smoothing it out with the rubber spatula. Place the pan in the oven.

3. Bake the cake until it is golden brown and springs back when lightly pressed with your finger, 32 to 35 minutes. Remove the pan from the oven and place it on a wire rack to cool.

4. Meanwhile, prepare the Hot Buttermilk Glaze.

5. Poke holes all over the top of the cake with a toothpick or wooden skewer and pour the hot glaze over the top, a little at a time, spreading the glaze out with a spoon to reach all edges of the cake. Allow the cake to cool for 20 minutes more before cutting it into squares and serving.

✳ *Store this cake, covered in aluminum foil, at room temperature for up to 1 week or freeze it, wrapped in foil, for up to 6 months. Thaw the cake overnight on the counter before serving.*

EASY TIRAMISU

Nothing is more satisfying after an Italian meal of pasta and salad than a spoonful of *tiramisù*, which means "pick me up" in Italian. This layered, trifle-like dessert could not be better named, for it rejuvenates your taste buds. But I've seen so many complicated versions of the recipe that I decided to devise one using a mix and requiring only one pan. And, in case you live in an area where you cannot get creamy mascarpone cheese, which traditionally makes up the topping, I've found a handy substitute using two items found in the supermarket. *Ciao!*

SERVES: 20

PREPARATION TIME: 10 TO 12 MINUTES

BAKING TIME: 32 TO 35 MINUTES

ASSEMBLY TIME: 5 MINUTES

CAKE:

Vegetable oil spray for misting the pan

1 package (18.25 ounces) plain white cake mix

1⅓ cups water

2 tablespoons vegetable oil, such as canola, corn, safflower, soybean, or sunflower

3 large eggs

1 teaspoon pure vanilla extract

SYRUP:

¾ cup hot water

2 tablespoons instant coffee powder

3 tablespoons granulated sugar

¼ cup Kahlúa or other coffee-flavored liqueur

TOPPING:

2 cups low-fat or nonfat vanilla yogurt

1 package (16 ounces) cream cheese, at room temperature

¼ cup confectioners' sugar

1 teaspoon unsweetened cocoa powder

1. Place a rack in the center of the oven and preheat the oven to 350°F. Lightly mist a 13- by 9-inch baking pan with vegetable oil spray. Set the pan aside.

2. Place the cake mix, water, oil, eggs, and vanilla in a large mixing bowl. Blend with an electric mixer on low speed for 1 minute. Stop the machine and scrape down the sides of the bowl with a rubber spatula. Increase the mixer speed to medium and beat 2 minutes more, scraping the sides down again if needed. The batter should look thick and well blended. Pour the batter into the prepared pan, smoothing it out with the rubber spatula. Place the pan in the oven.

3. Bake the cake until it is golden brown and springs back when lightly pressed with your finger, 32 to 35 minutes. Remove the pan from the oven and place it on a wire rack to cool.

4. Meanwhile, prepare the syrup. Place the hot water, coffee powder, and sugar in a small bowl and stir to combine until the coffee and sugar dissolve. Stir in the coffee liqueur. Poke holes in the cake with a chopstick or drinking straw and spoon the syrup over the cake so that the syrup can seep down into the holes. Set the cake aside.

5. Prepare the topping. Place the yogurt, cream cheese, and confectioners' sugar in a large mixing bowl and blend with an electric mixer on low speed for 1 to 2 minutes. The mixture should look well combined and thick. Spread the topping over the syrup-soaked cake, using the rubber spatula to spread the topping out to the edges of the cake. No more than an hour before serving, sift the cocoa powder over the topping so that it covers the top of the cake. Slice the cake into squares and serve.

✱ *Store this cake, covered in aluminum foil, in the refrigerator for up to 3 days.*

the Cake Doctor says...

When you've got some serious syrup like this for soaking into cake layers, don't be dainty and poke the cake with a toothpick or thin wooden skewer. Poke holes with a chopstick or a drinking straw so that the sweet coffee liquid has a cavern in which to settle.

Cake-Mix Classics

• • •

Every family has them—crazy, loony cousins whom you don't see until that party during the holidays or the baby's christening or a golden wedding anniversary. Well, if this book were a family—and it is—then this chapter would be those cousins.

I couldn't ignore them, excluding them from this book. Doing so would be to put cake-mix cookery up on some pedestal, as if everything has to be frosted with ganache or filled with lemon curd. Much of cake-mix cooking is just plain fun. Much contains a carton of whipped topping. Much includes instant pudding mix, or candy bars, or soda pop, or melted ice cream, or zany flavorings. One cake even calls for condensed canned tomato soup!

These fun-frolicking recipes are some of the most requested. They are classics. Devised by who knows who and passed from friend to friend to friend for years. Food snobs may gasp at the Better Than ? Cake, which has been called Better Than Sex, Better Than Robert Redford, Better Than Just About Anything. It calls for crushed pineapple, vanilla pudding mix, whipped topping, pecans, and coconut. And you know what? It's scrumptious. Another recipe begins with chocolate cake over which you layer caramel ice-cream topping, sweetened condensed milk, crushed candy bars, and whipped topping. It's called Holy Cow Cake, and I think it was named that because the nice preachers' wives didn't want to bake up a cake called Better

Than Sex and cause a rift in the congregation at Wednesday night supper.

Stories, stories, all these cakes have stories. The Earthquake Cake trembles as its bakes. The Finger Lickin' Good Cake contains a can of mandarin oranges and is frosted with pistachio pudding mix and whipped topping, creating a brilliantly colored cake of yellow and a frosting of green that would look stunning and festive for Easter brunch. Friendship Cake is flavored with a wacky fruit starter that bubbles and brews on your counter for five days before you add it to a yellow cake mix. And if you didn't know ahead of time that Orange Dreamsicle Cake contained salad dressing, you'd never guess.

And this chapter is also home to the zany Tomato Soup Spice Cake with Cinnamon Buttercream Frosting, a campy creation using something from your pantry. It is also where you'll find a quick rendition of that perennial favorite—Red Velvet Cake.

In a nutshell, the Quick Red Velvet Cake symbolizes what this chapter of cake-mix cookery is all about. No, it's not prudent to add a bottle or two of red food coloring to cake batter. Scientists assure us that artificial coloring is okay, but our better judgment might overrule. And yet, this is one fun cake. And you're not going to eat it every day. So go ahead, indulge and meet these crazy cake cousins!

FINGER LICKIN' GOOD CAKE

This cake has been given all sorts of crazy names—pea pickin', pig lickin', and finger lickin'—to describe how yummy it is and your reaction once you've tasted it! And whereas the pistachio pudding mix in the frosting sounds a bit bizarre, it's there for taste and color. The vivid green frosting complements the bright yellow color of the cake in a most 1970s retro way!

SERVES: 16

PREPARATION TIME: 10 MINUTES

BAKING TIME: 24 TO 27 MINUTES

ASSEMBLY TIME: 10 MINUTES

CAKE:

*Solid vegetable shortening for greasing
    the pans*

Flour for dusting the pans

*1 package (18.25 ounces) plain yellow
    cake mix*

*1 can (11 ounces) mandarin oranges,
    undrained*

8 tablespoons (1 stick) butter, melted

*¼ cup vegetable oil, such as canola, corn,
    safflower, soybean, or sunflower*

4 large eggs

*Juice drained from 1 can (8 ounces)
    crushed pineapple packed in juice
    (see below)*

FROSTING:

*1 container (12 ounces) frozen whipped top-
    ping, thawed*

*1 package (3.4 ounces) pistachio instant
    pudding mix*

*1 cup frozen unsweetened grated coconut,
    thawed*

*1 can (8 ounces) crushed pineapple packed
    in juice, drained*

1. Place a rack in the center of the oven and preheat the oven to 350°F. Generously grease two 9-inch round cake pans with solid vegetable shortening, then dust with flour. Shake out the excess flour. Set the pans aside.

2. Place the cake mix, mandarin oranges and juice, melted butter, oil, and eggs in a large mixing bowl. Blend with an electric mixer on low speed for 1 minute. Stop the machine and scrape down the sides of the bowl with the rubber spatula. Increase the mixer speed to medium and beat 2 to 3 minutes more, scraping the sides down again if needed. The batter should look well blended and the oranges should be broken up in the batter. Divide the batter between the prepared pans, smoothing it out with the rubber spatula. Place the pans in the oven side by side.

3. Bake the cakes until they are golden brown and spring back when lightly pressed with your finger, 24 to 27 minutes. Remove the pans from the oven and place them on wire racks to cool for 10 minutes. Run a dinner knife around the edge of each layer and invert each onto a rack, then invert them again onto another rack so that the cakes are right side up. While the cakes are still warm, poke holes in the top of each layer with a toothpick or wooden skewer. Pour the pineapple juice over the layers so that the cake soaks up all the juice. Let the layers cool for 30 minutes.

4. Meanwhile, prepare the frosting. Place the thawed whipped topping, pudding mix, coconut, and the drained crushed pineapple in a large mixing bowl. Stir with a wooden spoon until well combined and the pudding mix has dissolved.

5. Place one cake layer, right side up, on a serving platter. Spread the top with frosting. Place the second layer, right side up, on top of the first layer and frost the top and sides of the cake with clean, smooth strokes.

✳ *Store this cake, lightly covered in waxed paper, in the refrigerator for up to 1 week.*

R the Cake Doctor says...

Pouring fruit juice or a fruit syrup over cake layers is a dandy way to keep them moist. In this cake, you use just the juice from the crushed pineapple, and it complements the mandarin orange flavor. Not a pistachio fan? Substitute vanilla instant pudding mix.

QUICK RED VELVET CAKE

When it's Valentine's Day and you're searching for the passionate red cake to bake your loved ones, look no farther than this fun cake. Its base is a box of German chocolate cake mix that's dyed red by an entire bottle of red food coloring. Some recipes for this cake actually call for two bottles! Bedeck it with Cream Cheese Frosting and  sprinkle chopped pecans on top, if desired. So popular is this faintly chocolate cake that some enthusiasts have even created Green Velvet Cakes and Orange Velvet Cakes.

SERVES: 16
PREPARATION TIME: 8 MINUTES
BAKING TIME: 28 TO 30 MINUTES
ASSEMBLY TIME: 15 MINUTES

Solid vegetable shortening for greasing the pans
Flour for dusting the pans
1 package (18.25 ounces) German chocolate cake mix with pudding
1 cup sour cream
½ cup water
¼ cup vegetable oil, such as canola, corn, safflower, soybean, or sunflower
1 bottle (1 ounce) red food coloring
3 large eggs
1 teaspoon pure vanilla extract
Cream Cheese Frosting (page 420)

1. Place a rack in the center of the oven and preheat the oven to 350°F. Generously grease two 9-inch round cake pans with solid vegetable shortening, then dust with flour. Shake out the excess flour. Set the pans aside.

R

the Cake Doctor says...

Red Velvet Cake is all about show. If a vivid red cake is your modus operandi, begin with a white cake mix (all other ingredients remain the same). However, I prefer the chocolatey flavor of the German chocolate mix. You could add more chocolate to suit your taste (2 tablespoons cocoa powder with the cake mix in step 2), but it would muddy up the color.

2. Place the cake mix, sour cream, water, oil, food coloring, eggs, and vanilla in a large mixing bowl. Blend with an electric mixer on low speed for 1 minute. Stop the machine and scrape down the sides of the bowl with the rubber spatula. Increase the mixer speed to medium and beat 2 to 3 minutes more, scraping the sides down again if needed. The batter should look well blended. Divide the batter between the prepared pans, smoothing it out with the rubber spatula. Place the pans in the oven side by side.

3. Bake the cakes until they spring back when lightly pressed with your finger and just start to pull away from the sides of the pans, 28 to 30 minutes. Remove the pans from the oven and place them on wire racks to cool for 10 minutes. Run a dinner knife around the edge of each layer and invert each layer onto a rack, then invert them again onto another rack so that the cakes are right side up. Allow them to cool completely, 30 minutes more.

4. Meanwhile, prepare the Cream Cheese Frosting.

5. Place one cake layer, right side up, on a serving platter. Spread the top with frosting. Place the second layer, right side up, on top of the first layer and frost the top and sides of the cake with clean, smooth strokes.

✻ *Place this cake, uncovered, in the refrigerator until the frosting sets, 20 minutes. Store in a plastic cake saver or covered in waxed paper in the refrigerator, for up to 1 week. Or freeze it, wrapped in aluminum foil, for up to 6 weeks. Thaw the cake overnight in the refrigerator before serving.*

About the Red Velvet Cake

You wonder what would compel someone to dump an entire bottle of red food coloring into cake batter. I had for years shared the Red Velvet Cake recipe as food editor of the *Atlanta Journal-Constitution.* But if you had blindfolded me I could probably not taste the difference between this cake and others, for food coloring offers no flavor.

When it came time to devise a cake-mix version of the Red Velvet Cake, that was no problem. You can easily begin with a German chocolate cake mix, adding sour cream and coloring, but tracking down the history of this odd-ball recipe was a bit more difficult. I telephoned my friend John Egerton, author and food historian, and he admitted to being stumped. Was it Southern or was the South just consumed with it? Was it of the Junior League ilk? Was it a restaurant invention? And then Egerton had an epiphany: "To me there seems no culinary reason why someone would dump

that much food coloring into a cake. And if it wasn't for taste, perhaps it was for exorcism . . . What if a religious person, a little old lady perhaps, with a sense of humor, dyed her cake red to symbolize the devil and brought it to the church supper?" We howled with laughter and imagined the response of the church crowd and visualized how that cake might take hold of a congregation, or an entire town.

But I was still curious. I searched Southern cookbooks for any mention of Red Velvet Cake. Many were Junior League publications, but I found nothing until I looked in *Tennessee Tables,* published by the Junior League of Knoxville in 1982. On page 204 was Regas' Red Velvet Cake, named after a restaurant in town, adding that the cake was a specialty of the restaurant, served to Liberace when he visited in 1970. I called Louise Durman, food editor of the *Knoxville News-Sentinel,* who put aside any thoughts that Knoxville

and the Regas might be the home of the Red Velvet. She said her readers were crazy about the cake and had even baked Green Velvet Cakes for Christmas and a Big Orange Velvet Cake (mostly yellow food coloring mixed with a smidgen of red) prior to the University of Tennessee football team winning the national championship. Durman said the cake possibly originated at the Waldorf-Astoria Hotel in New York City in the 1930s.

So on to the Waldorf I went, where spokespeople there admitted to the connection but not to the birth of the cake. Executive chef John Doherty is all too familiar with the cake, and gets streams of phone calls from anxious cooks in quest of the original recipe. But when Doherty came to the Waldorf twenty-one years ago he had never heard of the Red Velvet Cake. He finally asked one of the callers to send him a recipe so he could give it out to everyone else who calls. And when he opened Oscar's Restaurant in the hotel he thought it would be fun to offer the cake, but in a slightly different preparation. Instead of the artificial red food coloring, which Doherty eschews, he added beet juice to the cake to dye it red naturally, then frosted it with the traditional cream cheese, butter, and sugar mixture and dusted it with cranberry powder. "We're still refining that recipe," he added. The chef plans to bake the cakes, and box and ship them on demand.

By the way, recipes that the Waldorf will claim are the namesake Waldorf Salad, Lobster Newburg, Thousand Island Dressing, and Veal Oscar, named after Oscar Tschirky, maître d'hôtel until the mid-1950s. But no use in telling that to a Red Velvet Cake fan. In home kitchens across the country you can bet that far more Red Velvet Cakes are being prepared than lobster. And at church suppers a little old lady dressed in a devil's outfit is likely to bring a bright red cake, no matter where it originated.

TOMATO SOUP SPICE CAKE WITH CINNAMON BUTTERCREAM FROSTING

Eating a cake containing canned soup might seem weird, but the only give-away to the unusual ingredient in this spice cake is the stunning ruddy color. Bake this cake, studded with raisins and pecans, and topped with the most delectable cinnamon-flavored buttercream frosting imaginable, for your office party and then let everyone guess what the secret ingredient is. They won't have a clue!

SERVES: 16
PREPARATION TIME: 10 MINUTES
BAKING TIME: 28 TO 31 MINUTES
ASSEMBLY TIME: 15 MINUTES

Solid vegetable shortening for greasing the pans
Flour for dusting the pans
1 package (18.25 ounces) plain spice cake mix
1 can (10.75 ounces) condensed tomato soup, undiluted
3 large eggs
⅓ cup vegetable oil, such as canola, corn, safflower, soybean, or sunflower
¼ cup water
½ cup raisins
½ cup chopped pecans
Cinnamon Buttercream Frosting (page 417)

1. Place a rack in the center of the oven and preheat the oven to 350°F. Gener-

R
the CakeDoctor says...

Spice cakes are so versatile and benefit from the addition of liquids like butter-milk, or in this case, concentrated tomato soup! Both give the cake a nice acidic tang.

ously grease two 9-inch round cake pans with solid vegetable shortening, then dust with flour. Shake out the excess flour. Set the pans aside.

2. Place the cake mix, undiluted tomato soup, eggs, oil, and water in a large mixing bowl. Blend with an electric mixer on low speed for 1 minute. Stop the machine and scrape down the sides of the bowl with a rubber spatula. Increase the mixer speed to medium and beat 2 to 3 minutes more, scraping the sides down again if needed. The batter should look well combined and thickened. Fold in the raisins and pecans, making sure they are evenly distributed throughout the batter. Pour the batter evenly into the prepared pans, smoothing it out with the rubber spatula. Place the pans in the oven side by side.

3. Bake the cakes until they spring back when lightly pressed with your finger and

just start to pull away from the sides of the pan, 28 to 31 minutes. Remove the pans from the oven and place them on wire racks to cool for 10 minutes. Run a dinner knife around the edge of each layer and invert each onto a rack, then invert them again onto another rack so that the cakes are right side up. Allow them to cool completely, 30 minutes more.

4. Meanwhile, prepare the Cinnamon Buttercream Frosting. Time the frosting preparation so that the cake has cooled and is ready to frost.

5. Place one cake layer, right side up, on a serving platter. Spread the top with frosting. Place the second layer, right side up, on top of the first layer and frost the top and sides of the cake with clean, smooth strokes.

✳ *Place this cake, uncovered, in the refrigerator until the frosting sets, 20 minutes. Store this cake in a plastic cake saver or covered in waxed paper and store in the refrigerator, for up to 1 week. Or freeze it, wrapped in aluminum foil, for up to 6 months. Thaw the cake overnight on the counter before serving.*

LEMON-LIME CAKE WITH PINEAPPLE CURD

Good Southern cook and author Martha Pearl Villas of Charlotte, North Carolina, was a little hesitant to offer a recipe using a cake mix because, as a purist, she bakes mostly from scratch. But she did have this recipe, "and it's pretty good, real good," she confided. No doubt about it, this cake is more than good; it was a favorite with my young girls even when they didn't know it contained 7-UP! It's a pretty cake, perfect for potluck suppers and barbecues when you want to put something on the table other than chocolate that will dazzle your guests. Prepare the pineapple curd first so that it can cool and thicken while the cake bakes and cools.

SERVES: 16

PREPARATION TIME: 20 MINUTES

BAKING TIME: 20 TO 25 MINUTES

ASSEMBLY TIME: 5 TO 7 MINUTES

PINEAPPLE CURD:

1 can (15.25 ounces) crushed pineapple packed in juice, undrained

8 tablespoons (1 stick) butter, cut into small pieces

3 large eggs

1 tablespoon all-purpose flour

½ cup sugar

1 tablespoon fresh lemon juice

CAKE:

Solid vegetable shortening for greasing
the pans

Flour for dusting the pans

1 package (18.25 ounces) plain lemon
cake mix

1 package (3.4 ounces) vanilla instant
pudding mix

4 large eggs

¾ cup vegetable oil, such as canola,
corn, safflower, soybean,
or sunflower

1 can (12 ounces) 7-UP or lemon-
lime soda

1. Combine the pineapple with its juice, the butter, eggs, flour, sugar, and lemon juice in a medium stainless-steel or enamel-coated saucepan. Cook the mixture, without boiling it, over medium heat, stirring constantly and carefully scraping the bottom and corners of the pan to prevent curdling, until thickened, 6 to 8 minutes.

2. Pour the curd into a bowl and cover with plastic wrap or waxed paper so that it touches the surface. (Doing so prevents the curd surface from hardening.) Refrigerate the curd so that it will cool completely and thicken, about 1 hour. Stir the curd before using it. Store the curd in the refrigerator for up to 4 days.

R

the Cake Doctor says...

Soda adds flavor as well as an element of fun to this cake. I wish I could say the cake rises better because of the carbonation, but that's not the case. The pineapple curd is a yummy filling and a fine way to dress up an ordinary lemon cake mix.

3. Prepare the cake. Place a rack in the center of the oven and preheat the oven to 350°F. Generously grease three 9-inch round cake pans with solid vegetable shortening, then dust with flour. Shake out the excess flour. Set the pans aside.

4. Place the cake mix, pudding mix, eggs, oil, and 7-UP in a large mixing bowl. Blend with an electric mixer on low speed for 1 minute. Stop the machine and scrape down the sides of the bowl with the rubber spatula. Increase the mixer speed to medium and beat 2 to 3 minutes more, scraping the sides down again if needed. The batter should look well combined and thickened. Divide the batter among the prepared pans, smoothing it out with the rubber spatula. Place the pans in the oven; if your oven is not large enough, place two pans on the center rack and place the third pan in the center of the highest rack.

5. Bake the cakes until they spring back when lightly pressed with your finger and just start to pull away from the sides of the pans, 20 to 25 minutes. Be careful not to overbake the layer on the highest oven rack. Remove the pans from the oven and place them on wire racks to cool for 10 minutes. Run a dinner knife around the edge of each layer and invert each onto a rack, then invert them again onto another rack so that the cakes are right side up. Allow them to cool completely, 30 minutes more.

6. Place one cake layer, right side up, on a serving platter. Spread the top of the cake layer with one-third of the pineapple curd. Place the second cake layer, right side up, on top of the first layer covered with the curd and spread the second layer with one-third of the pineapple curd. Top with the remaining cake layer, right side up, and spread it with the remaining pineapple curd.

✱   *Store this cake in a plastic cake saver or covered with waxed paper, in the refrigerator, for up to 1 week.*

FIDDLER ON THE ROOF CAKE

argie Flynt of Madison, Tennessee, sent me this recipe, which she warns is a little more involved than most recipes calling for a cake mix. She's right. But you'll find the sour cream–enriched cake worth the extra fuss. As the song goes in the musical *Fiddler on the Roof,* you'll feel like a rich man, or a rich woman, when you fork into this cake. And the candylike marshmallow frosting is delicious on other cakes as well.

SERVES: 16
PREPARATION TIME: 8 MINUTES
BAKING TIME: 60 TO 65 MINUTES
ASSEMBLY TIME: 10 MINUTES

Vegetable oil spray for misting the pan
Flour for dusting the pan
1 package (18.25 ounces) plain yellow
  cake mix
1 cup (8 ounces) sour cream
¾ cup vegetable oil, such as canola, corn,
  safflower, soybean, or sunflower
½ cup sugar
½ teaspoon pure almond extract
½ teaspoon salt
4 large eggs
¼ cup unsweetened cocoa powder
Chocolate Marshmallow Frosting
  (page 434)

1. Place a rack in the center of the oven and preheat the oven to 350°F. Lightly mist a 12-cup Bundt pan with vegetable oil spray, then dust with flour. Shake out the excess flour. Set the pan aside.

R

the Cake Doctor says...

Pure almond extract is such an effortless way to doctor up a cake mix. And when you're cooking with chocolate, it is a natural partner. For a more dazzling look, scatter toasted slivered almonds (see Toasting Nuts, page 134) onto the frosted cake while it is still warm so that the nuts stay in place.

2. Place the cake mix, sour cream, oil, sugar, almond extract, salt, and eggs in a large mixing bowl. Blend with an electric mixer on low speed for 1 minute. Stop the machine and scrape down the sides of the bowl with a rubber spatula. Increase the mixer speed to medium and beat 2 minutes more, scraping the sides down again if needed. The batter should look well blended. Pour half of the batter into the prepared pan, smoothing it out with the rubber spatula.

3. Add the cocoa powder to the remaining batter and blend with the electric mixer on low speed for 1 minute. Pour this evenly over the batter already in the pan. Run a dinner knife through the batters to swirl them together for a marbleized look. Place the pan in the oven.

4. Bake the cake until it is light brown and springs back when lightly pressed with your finger, 60 to 65 minutes. Remove the pan from the oven and place it on a wire rack to cool for 20 minutes.

5. Meanwhile, prepare the Chocolate Marshmallow Frosting.

6. Run a long, sharp knife around the edge of the cake and invert it onto a serving platter to frost and serve warm. Or invert it onto a rack to cool completely, 30 minutes more. Regardless of whether you want a warm or cooled cake, frost it while the frosting is still warm, spreading the frosting over the top and partially down the sides of the cake with the rubber spatula.

✳ *Store this cake, covered in aluminum foil or plastic wrap, at room temperature for up to 1 week. Or freeze it, wrapped in foil, for up to 6 months. Thaw the cake overnight on the counter before serving.*

INCREDIBLE MELTED ICE-CREAM CAKE

Pillsbury test kitchen home economists have heard it all. When they told me some people were adding melted ice cream to a cake mix, I couldn't believe it. Did someone leave the ice cream on the counter during the commercial break of a compelling movie and forget to put it back in the freezer, and *voilà*—a melted mess? Then mom walks into the kitchen, surveys the mess, and decides to whip up a cake recipe using the melted ice cream as the liquid? Well, that's precisely what I did with this fun recipe. Choose your flavor and let the ice cream melt. The only trick is that you must have 2 cups of melted ice cream. For super-premium ice creams with little overrun, that's 1 pint frozen. But for less expensive brands with a lot of air piped in, you'll need to begin with more than a pint.

SERVES: 16
PREPARATION TIME: 5 TO 7 MINUTES
BAKING TIME: 38 TO 42 MINUTES
ASSEMBLY TIME: 10 MINUTES

Vegetable oil spray for misting the pan
Flour for dusting the pan
1 package (18.25 ounces) plain white
    cake mix
2 cups melted ice cream, your choice of
    flavor
3 large eggs
Chocolate Marshmallow Frosting
    (page 434)

R

the Cake Doctor *says...*

I made this cake with several flavors of ice cream and our favorite was a super-premium from Ben & Jerry's— Cherry Garcia. With cherry and chocolate pieces and the cream and the eggs in the ice cream, you need little else. Your liquid, your fat, and your flavorings are all in the melted ice cream. This recipe works well, too, in a 13- by 9-inch pan.

1. Place a rack in the center of the oven and preheat the oven to 350°F. Lightly mist a 12-cup Bundt pan with vegetable oil spray, then dust with flour. Shake out the excess flour. Set the pan aside.

2. Place the cake mix, melted ice cream, and eggs in a large mixing bowl. Blend with an electric mixer on low speed for 1 minute. Stop the machine and scrape down the sides of the bowl with the rubber spatula. Increase the mixer speed to medium and beat 2 minutes more, scraping the sides down again if needed. The batter should look thick and well blended. Pour the batter into the prepared pan, smoothing the top with the rubber spatula. Place the pan in the oven.

3. Bake the cake until it springs back when lightly pressed with your finger and just starts to pull away from the sides of the pan, 38 to 42 minutes. Remove the pan from the oven and place it on a wire rack to cool for 20 minutes. Run a long, sharp knife around the edge of the cake and invert it onto a small rack, then invert it again onto a second rack so that the cake is right side up to complete cooling, 30 minutes more.

4. Meanwhile, prepare the Chocolate Marshmallow Frosting, or another frosting that would go well with the flavor of the ice cream in the cake. Place the cake on a serving platter and frost the top of the cake with clean, smooth strokes.

✳   *Store this cake in a plastic cake saver or under a glass cake dome at room temperature for up to 1 week. Or freeze it, wrapped in foil, for up to 6 months. Thaw the cake overnight on the counter before serving.*

FIVE-FLAVOR CAKE

If you love the flavor of the Life-savers fruit candies, then you'll fall over backwards for another slice of this cake. I had seen this cake at bake sales and church suppers for years, but I was never crazy about it because the cake itself was dry and lifeless. No more. This buttery version is a winner, so good you'll want to slice into it before you pour over the glaze. If the five-extract butter glaze is too far out for you, opt for a more conservative Brown Sugar Caramel Glaze (page 437).

SERVES: 16
PREPARATION TIME: 8 MINUTES
BAKING TIME: 55 TO 60 MINUTES
ASSEMBLY TIME: 10 MINUTES

CAKE:

Vegetable oil spray for misting
    the pan
Flour for dusting the pan
1 package (18.25 ounces) plain yellow
    cake mix
1 package (3.4 ounces) vanilla instant
    pudding mix
8 tablespoons (1 stick) butter, melted
4 large eggs
1 cup milk
1 teaspoon pure vanilla extract

BUTTER GLAZE:

1 cup sugar
½ cup hot water
8 tablespoons (1 stick) butter, cut up
1 teaspoon pure almond extract
1 teaspoon rum extract
1 teaspoon pure vanilla extract
1 teaspoon coconut extract
1 teaspoon butter-flavored extract

1. Place a rack in the center of the oven and preheat the oven to 350°F. Lightly spray a 10-inch tube pan or 12-cup Bundt pan with vegetable oil spray, then dust with flour. Shake out the excess flour. Set the pan aside.

2. Place the cake mix, pudding mix, melted butter, eggs, milk, and vanilla in a large mixing bowl. Blend with an electric mixer on low speed for 1 minute. Stop the machine and scrape down the sides of the bowl with a rubber spatula. Increase the mixer speed to medium and beat 2 to 3 minutes more, scraping the sides down again if needed. The batter should look well combined and thickened. Pour the batter into the prepared pan, smoothing it out with the rubber spatula. Place the pan in the oven.

3. Bake the cake until it is golden brown and springs back when lightly pressed with your finger, 55 to 60 minutes.

4. Meanwhile, prepare the butter glaze. Place the sugar, hot water, and butter in a small saucepan. Cook over medium heat just until the butter melts and the sugar dissolves, stirring constantly, 2 to 3 minutes. Remove the pan from the heat and stir in the almond, rum, vanilla, coconut, and butter extracts.

5. Remove the pan from the oven and place it on a wire rack to cool for 15 min-

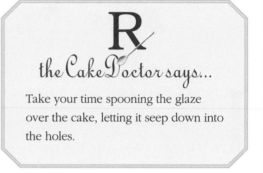

R

the Cake Doctor says...

Take your time spooning the glaze over the cake, letting it seep down into the holes.

utes. Run a long, sharp knife around the edge of the cake and carefully invert it onto a serving platter. If you baked the cake in a tube pan, invert the cake onto a rack, then invert it onto the platter so that it is right side up.

6. Poke holes in the cake with a long skewer. Slowly pour the warm butter glaze over the warm cake, allowing the glaze to soak in. Allow the cake to cool to room temperature before serving.

✳ *Store the cake, covered in waxed paper or under a glass cake dome, at room temperature for up to 1 week. Or freeze the cake, unglazed (do not poke holes in it), wrapped in aluminum foil. Thaw overnight on the counter. Poke holes in the cake and glaze as described in step 6. Allow the cake to mellow at room temperature for 2 hours before serving.*

ORANGE DREAMSICLE CAKE

What a gorgeous cake! It truly bakes like a dream and looks stunning on the serving platter glazed with a simple sugar and orange juice mixture. This is a classic recipe, made with salad dressing (the mayonnaise type) and whipped topping mix, which is found next to the gelatins in the supermarket. Take a bite, savor the tang of the orange zest, and you'll imagine you're eating one of those creamy ice-coated ice-cream pops!

SERVES: 16
PREPARATION TIME: 8 MINUTES
BAKING TIME: 40 TO 45 MINUTES
ASSEMBLY TIME: 2 TO 3 MINUTES

CAKE:

Vegetable oil spray for misting the pan
Flour for dusting the pan
1 package (18.25 ounces) plain yellow cake mix
¾ cup Miracle Whip salad dressing
1 package (1.3 ounces) whipped topping mix
¾ cup fresh orange juice (from 2 medium oranges)
3 large eggs
2 tablespoons freshly grated orange zest

GLAZE:

1½ cups confectioners' sugar, sifted
2 tablespoons fresh orange juice

1. Place a rack in the center of the oven and preheat the oven to 350°F. Lightly spray a 10-inch tube pan with vegetable

R

the Cake Doctor says...

You'll get about 2 tablespoons grated orange zest from 2 medium oranges. First remove the zest, then cut the oranges in half and squeeze the juice into a measuring cup. The mayonnaise-style dressing adds a nice richness to the cake without interfering with the flavor.

oil spray, then dust with flour. Shake out the excess flour. Set the pan aside.

2. Place the cake mix, salad dressing, whipped topping mix, orange juice, eggs, and orange zest in a large mixing bowl. Blend with an electric mixer on low speed for 1 minute. Stop the machine and scrape down the sides of the bowl with the rubber spatula. Increase the mixer speed to medium and beat 2 minutes more, scraping the sides down again if needed. The batter should look well blended and thick. Pour the batter into the prepared pan, smoothing it out with the rubber spatula. Place the pan in the oven.

3. Bake the cake until it springs back when lightly pressed with your finger and just starts to pull away from the sides of

the pan, 40 to 45 minutes. Remove the pan from the oven and place it on a wire rack to cool for 15 minutes. Run a long, sharp knife around the edge of the cake, invert it onto a rack, and invert again onto another rack so that it is right side up. Allow the cake to cool completely, 30 minutes more.

4. Meanwhile, prepare the glaze. Place the confectioners' sugar and orange juice in a small bowl and mix with a spoon until smooth.

5. Place the cake on a serving platter. Spoon the glaze over the top of the cooled cake and let it drizzle into the center and down the sides. Let rest for 20 minutes for the glaze to set, then slice and serve.

❋ *Store this cake, covered in plastic wrap or waxed paper, at room temperature for up to 1 week. Or freeze it, wrapped in aluminum foil, for up to 6 months. Thaw the cake overnight on the counter before serving.*

CHOCOLATE BETTER THAN ? CAKE

Reading the ingredient list of this recipe, you've got to be saying to yourself, "This had better be better than . . ." And it truly is. This cake is crammed with all kinds of good-ies—chocolate chips, nuts, and sour cream. It's a thick, dense cake  and one traditionally covered in a Penuche Frosting. If you prefer a chocolate frosting instead, try the Chocolate Pan Frosting (page 429). For the traditional Better Than ? Cake, see page 171.

SERVES: 16

PREPARATION TIME: 10 MINUTES

BAKING TIME: 50 TO 55 MINUTES

ASSEMBLY TIME: 15 MINUTES

Vegetable oil spray for misting the pan
Flour for dusting the pan
1 package (18.25 ounces) plain devil's food
*   cake mix*
1 package (6 ounces; 1 cup) semisweet
*   chocolate chips*
¾ cup chopped pecans
1 package (3.9 ounces) chocolate instant
*   pudding mix*
1 cup sour cream
½ cup vegetable oil, such as canola, corn,
*   safflower, soybean, or sunflower*
¼ cup water
4 large eggs
1 teaspoon pure vanilla extract
Penuche Frosting (page 431)

1. Place a rack in the center of the oven and preheat the oven to 350°F. Lightly mist a 10-inch tube pan with vegetable oil

R

the Cake Doctor says...

The chocolate chips and pecans are well suspended in this cake. A stiff batter and the extra step of tossing the chips and nuts with a little cake mix (as you would flour them in a from-scratch cake recipe) prevents them from sinking to the bottom of the pan.

spray, then dust with flour. Shake out the excess flour. Set the pan aside.

2. Place 2 tablespoons of the cake mix, the chocolate chips, and the pecans in a small bowl. Stir and set aside.

3. Place the remaining cake mix, along with the chocolate pudding mix, sour cream, oil, water, eggs, and vanilla in a large mixing bowl. Blend with an electric mixer on low speed for 1 minute. Stop the machine and scrape down the sides of the bowl with a rubber spatula. Increase the mixer speed to medium and beat 2 to 3 minutes more, scraping the sides down again if needed. The batter should be thick and well blended. Fold in the chocolate chip and pecan mixture until it is well distributed. Pour the batter into the prepared pan, smoothing the top with the rubber spatula. Place the pan in the oven.

4. Bake the cake until it springs back when lightly pressed with your finger and just starts to pull away from the sides of the pan, 50 to 55 minutes. Remove the pan from the oven and let it cool on a wire rack for 15 minutes. Run a long, sharp knife around the edge of the cake and invert the cake onto a cooling rack, then invert it again onto a serving platter to finish cooling, 20 minutes more.

5. Prepare the Penuche Frosting. Spread the top and sides of the cooled cake with the warm frosting, using clean, smooth strokes. Let the cake stand 30 minutes before slicing and serving.

✳ *Store this cake, covered in aluminum foil, at room temperature for up to 1 week or freeze it, wrapped in foil, for up to 6 months. Thaw overnight in the refrigerator before serving.*

BETTER THAN ? CAKE

People in the past have determined that this cake is better than sex, better than Robert Redford. So what might it be better than now? In myriad versions, this has been a most requested recipe for years from newspaper food section readers. But the cake simply won't work miracles. It's just fun, and no book on cake-mix baking would be complete without it and its chocolate cousin, Chocolate Better Than ? Cake (page 169).

....

SERVES: 20

PREPARATION TIME: 10 MINUTES

BAKING TIME: 28 TO 32 MINUTES

ASSEMBLY TIME: 10 MINUTES

....

CAKE:

Vegetable oil spray for misting the pan

*1 package (18.25 ounces) plain yellow
cake mix*

8 tablespoons (1 stick) butter, melted

1 cup whole milk

3 large eggs

TOPPING:

*1 can (20 ounces) crushed pineapple
packed in juice, undrained*

1 cup sugar

*1 package (5.1 ounces) vanilla instant
pudding mix*

3 cups whole milk

*1 container (8 ounces) frozen whipped
topping, thawed*

*1 cup chopped pecans, toasted
(see Toasting Nuts, page 134)*

*1 package (6 ounces) frozen unsweetened
grated coconut, thawed*

1. Place a rack in the center of the oven and preheat the oven to 350°F. Lightly mist a 13- by 9-inch baking pan with vegetable oil spray. Set the pan aside.

2. Place the cake mix, melted butter, milk, and eggs in a large mixing bowl. Blend with an electric mixer on low speed for 1 minute. Stop the machine and scrape down the sides of the bowl with the rubber spatula. Increase the mixer speed to medium and beat 2 minutes more, scraping the sides down again if needed. The batter should look thick and well blended. Pour the batter into the prepared pan, smoothing the top with the rubber spatula. Place the pan in the oven.

3. Bake the cake until it springs back when lightly pressed with your finger and just starts to pull away from the sides of the pan, 28 to 32 minutes.

4. Meanwhile, prepare the topping. Place the pineapple with its juice and the sugar

the Cake Doctor says...

For maximum flavor from those pecans, go ahead and toast them before you fold them into the whipped topping. And if you enjoy the taste of real whipped cream, by all means, substitute it for the frozen whipped topping (see Sweetened Cream, page 432).

in a medium saucepan over medium heat, and cook, stirring, until the sugar dissolves and the mixture comes just to a boil, 2 minutes. Set the pan aside.

5. Remove the cake from the oven and immediately poke holes in the top of it with a drinking straw or chopstick. Spoon the pineapple and sugar mixture evenly over the top of the cake.

6. Place the pudding mix and cold milk in a large mixing bowl and blend according to the package directions. Spread the pudding over the pineapple layer with a rubber spatula. Place the pan in the refrigerator to chill for 30 minutes.

7. Place the whipped topping, pecans, and coconut in a large mixing bowl and stir gently until the pecans and coconut are well distributed. Spread this whipped topping layer over the pudding layer and return the cake to the refrigerator. Chill the cake until the topping has a chance to set, 30 minutes more. Slice into squares and serve.

✳ *Store this cake, covered in waxed paper, in the refrigerator for up to 1 week. It tastes best if made a day ahead of serving.*

EARTHQUAKE CAKE

Kids will love assembling this easy cake. And parents will like the fact that there are few pans to wash! The cake—studded with coconut and pecans—bakes up shaky and gets its name from its appearance. But never fear, the cake only seems wobbly; it sets up and is delicious. Try the recipe baked into cupcakes. Place a tiny spoonful of the gooey filling on top of each unbaked cupcake.

SERVES: 20
PREPARATION TIME: 10 MINUTES
BAKING TIME: 40 TO 45 MINUTES

R *the Cake Doctor says...*

In a hurry? Then cut a stick of cold butter into 8 pieces and place in a microwave-safe bowl. Microwave on high for 45 seconds, or until almost melted. Add the cream cheese, cut into 6 slices. Zap on high 15 seconds more, then add the confectioners' sugar for the cake's irresistible, gooey filling.

Vegetable oil spray for misting the pan
1 cup frozen unsweetened grated coconut, thawed
1 cup finely chopped pecans or walnuts
1 package (18.25 ounces) German chocolate cake mix (with or without pudding)
1⅓ cups water
½ cup vegetable oil, such as canola, corn, safflower, soybean, or sunflower
3 large eggs
8 tablespoons (1 stick) butter, melted
1 package (8 ounces) cream cheese, at room temperature
4 cups confectioners' sugar, sifted

1. Place a rack in the center of the oven and preheat the oven to 350°F. Lightly mist a 13- by 9-inch baking pan with vegetable oil spray. Set the pan aside.

2. Scatter the coconut and pecans in the bottom of the prepared pan.

3. Combine the cake mix, water, oil, and eggs in a large mixing bowl. Blend with an electric mixer on low speed for 1 minute. Stop the machine and scrape down the sides of the bowl with the rubber spatula. Increase the mixer speed to medium and beat 2 to 3 minutes more, scraping the sides down again if needed. The batter should look well combined. Pour the batter over the coconut and nuts in the pan, smoothing it out with the rubber spatula.

4. Combine the melted butter, cream cheese, and confectioners' sugar in a large bowl. Blend with an electric mixer on low speed for 1 minute. The mixture should look smooth. With a large spoon, place 12 large globs of the topping on top of the cake batter, distributing them well. Place the pan in the oven.

5. Bake the cake until the center jiggles a little when you shake the pan, 40 to 45 minutes. Don't overbake the cake because it will set up as it cools. Remove the pan from the oven and cool the cake in the pan on a wire rack for 30 minutes. Cut into squares and flip them onto a plate so the pecans and coconut are on top.

✲ *Store the cake, covered in aluminum foil, in the refrigerator for up to 1 week. Or freeze it, wrapped in foil, for up to 6 months. Thaw the cake overnight in the refrigerator before serving.*

Cupcakes

Cupcakes are kid friendly. Baked up in those thin pastel-colored paper liners, they're as pretty on a cooling rack as a basket of freshly dyed Easter eggs. And, you eat them with your hands! When you sink your teeth into a frosted cupcake, you're in heaven.

Cupcakes are a cinch to make. You just need to line standard muffin pans for easy removal, preheat the oven to 350°F, and fill the liners about three-quarters full so you have a nice tall cupcake. The cake-mix box will say you'll get two dozen cupcakes, but in reality, it's closer to 18. We love Earthquake cupcakes, with a surprise inside, or simple devil's food cupcakes, with a sour cream and chocolate frosting.

HORNET'S NEST CAKE

Diane Paul of Smyrna, Tennessee, shares this fun cake that really does look like a hornet's nest after it's baked. I know the method seems a bit quirky—you combine dry cake mix and instant pudding, then top with butterscotch chips and chopped pecans. But strangely enough, the cake bakes up to perfection and the surface is pitted with holes like a hornet's nest. It's a hit at school class parties, especially when the class is studying insects!

R the Cake Doctor says...

To create the holey appearance, remember to scatter the chips on before you add the pecans. The chips will sink down into the batter and create holes. Then, sprinkle the pecans on top of the chips.

SERVES: 20

PREPARATION TIME: 5 TO 7 MINUTES

BAKING TIME:

35 TO 40 MINUTES

Vegetable oil spray for misting the pan

1 package (3.4 ounces) vanilla instant
    pudding mix

2 cups whole milk

1 package (18.25 ounces) plain yellow
    cake mix

1 package (11 ounces) butterscotch chips

1 cup chopped pecans

Great Add-Ins

Here are five ingredients to keep on hand for expressway baking.

1. **Lemon curd:** Buy this velvety lemon-flavored filling in the gourmet section of the supermarket. Mix up a lemon-flavored cake mix, add a couple of tablespoons of lemon curd to the batter, bake, cool, then frost with whipped topping to which you have folded in the rest of the jar of lemon curd.

2. **Crème de menthe:** Bake a devil's food cake, brush it with *crème de menthe* when the cake is still warm, then cool and frost with whipped topping to

which you have added a little *crème de menthe*. Garnish with fresh mint leaves.

3. **Seedless raspberry jam:** Swirl this into white cake batter before baking, spread between baked cake layers before frosting, or swirl into white frosting on top of the cake.

4. **Crushed chocolate mint cookies or chocolate sandwich cookies:** Crush and fold into white cake batter or onto the top of a frosted cake.

5. **Eggnog:** Substitute for milk in holiday batters and frostings, using the same amount called for in the recipe.

---

1. Place a rack in the center of the oven and preheat the oven to 350°F. Lightly mist a 13- by 9-inch baking pan with vegetable oil spray. Set the pan aside.

2. Place the pudding mix and milk in a large mixing bowl and blend according to the package directions. Fold in the dry cake mix and stir with a wooden spoon until the batter is combined, although still a little lumpy. Pour the batter into the prepared pan and smooth the top with the rubber spatula. Scatter the butterscotch chips on top of the batter, then sprinkle

the pecans on top of the chips. Place the pan in the oven.

3. Bake the cake until it springs back when lightly pressed with your finger, 35 to 40 minutes. Remove the pan from the oven and let the cake cool in the pan on a wire rack for 30 minutes before serving.

✳ *Store this cake, covered in aluminum foil, at room temperature for up to 1 week. Or freeze it, wrapped in foil, for up to 6 months. Thaw the cake overnight on the counter before serving.*

HOLY COW CAKE

That's what your mouth will say when you take a bite of chocolate cake, caramel, cream cheese, whipped topping, and crunchy Butterfinger candy bar pieces. This is the cake you take to the Halloween party or the potluck when you know there will be lots of children or adults in attendance who adore sweet things. In fact, if you take this cake to a Halloween party (and you should because its color is orange, white, and black), why not rename it the Goblin Good Cake?

....

SERVES: 20
PREPARATION TIME: 5 TO 7 MINUTES
BAKING TIME: 35 TO 38 MINUTES
ASSEMBLY TIME: 10 MINUTES

....

CAKE:

Vegetable oil spray for misting the pan

1 package (18.25 ounces) plain devil's food cake mix

1⅓ cups water

½ cup vegetable oil, such as canola, corn, safflower, soybean, or sunflower

3 large eggs

TOPPING:

1 jar (8 ounces) caramel topping

1 can (14 ounces) sweetened condensed milk

4 Butterfinger candy bars (2.1 ounces each), crushed

1 container (12 ounces) frozen whipped topping, thawed

1 package (8 ounces) cream cheese, at room temperature

1. Place a rack in the center of the oven and preheat the oven to 350°F. Lightly mist a 13- by 9-inch baking pan with vegetable oil spray. Set the pan aside.

2. Place the cake mix, water, oil, and eggs in a large mixing bowl. Blend with an electric mixer on low speed for 1 minute. Stop the machine and scrape down the sides

R

the Cake Doctor says...

If you prefer a less intense chocolate flavor, use a German chocolate cake mix instead. This is a good basic recipe that you can alter to your own taste. For example, instead of Butterfinger pieces, you could crush Heath Bars.

of the bowl with a rubber spatula. Increase the mixer speed to medium and beat 2 minutes more, scraping the sides down again if needed. The batter should look thick and well blended. Pour the batter into the prepared pan, smoothing out the top with the rubber spatula. Place the pan in the oven.

3. Bake the cake until it springs back when lightly pressed with your finger and just starts to pull away from the sides of the pan, 35 to 38 minutes. Remove the pan from the oven and place it on a wire rack. Immediately poke holes in the top of the cake with a drinking straw or chopstick.

4. Prepare the topping. Place the caramel topping and sweetened condensed milk in a small bowl and stir to combine. Spoon this mixture over the warm cake so that it can seep down into the holes. Measure out half of the crushed candy bars and sprinkle the pieces over the cake.

5. Place the whipped topping and cream cheese in a large mixing bowl and blend with an electric mixer on low speed until smooth and combined, 1 minute. Spread the mixture over the top of the candy. Sprinkle the remaining candy pieces on top.

6. Place the pan, uncovered, in the refrigerator to chill the cake for about 20 minutes before cutting it into squares and serving.

✻ *Store this cake, covered in waxed paper, in the refrigerator for up to 1 week.*

On the Cutting Edge

Tired of coating cake pans with shortening and flour? Here are two special ways to coat cake pans:

• For white cakes, brush melted butter over the bottom and sides of the pans. Coat with a tablespoon of granulated sugar and shake out the excess. It gives the cake a crunchy sugar coating and a pretty look if you're not frosting the sides of the cake.

• For chocolate cakes, grease the pan with shortening, but dust it with unsweetened cocoa powder instead of flour.

FRIENDSHIP CAKE

This recipe has been around since the early 1980s, and it's one of those recipes that people just keep asking for in newspaper food pages. But much like a chain letter, it's a recipe you either love or hate. The whole idea  behind this cake is that you prepare a fruit starter at least five days before baking. And, since you need only a quarter of the starter to make one cake, you must give the rest to friends—thus its name! For many years, it was shunned by county extension agents who warned of its safety. Yet, a major cake mix manufacturer actually sent the recipe to a microbiology laboratory, and the

the Cake Doctor says...

This is just the sort of cake you want to undertake if you get snowed in and all your ingredients are ready. The maraschino cherries blend into the cake batter, making the cake a pretty color. The fermenting fruits in the starter add a rich, yeasty flavor. You could just as easily substitute a plain white cake mix with pudding for the yellow.

starter was deemed harmless. So bake a cake for yourself and share the starter with friends!

SERVES: 20

PREPARATION:

5 DAYS OF SIMPLE PREPARATION;

20 MINUTES ON DAY 6 (BAKING DAY)

BAKING TIME:

40 TO 45 MINUTES

FRIENDSHIP STARTER:

3 cups apple juice

½ cup granulated sugar

2 teaspoons fresh lemon juice

1 package (.25 ounce) active dry yeast

1 jar (10 ounces) maraschino cherries,
    undrained

2 cups raisins

1 package (7 ounces; 1¼ cups) dried
    apricots, chopped

1 can (15.25 ounces) crushed pineapple
    packed in juice, undrained

CAKE:

Vegetable oil spray for misting the pan

½ cup packed light brown sugar

½ cup chopped pecans or walnuts

2 tablespoons butter or margarine, at room
    temperature

1 package (18.25 ounces) yellow cake mix
    with pudding

1 jar fruit and juice from the starter
    (about 2 cups)

⅓ cup vegetable oil, such as canola,
    corn, safflower, soybean,
    or sunflower

3 large eggs

1. Day 1: At least 5 days before making the cake, prepare the starter. Place the apple juice in a medium saucepan over

low heat and warm the juice to about 110°F. Pour the warm juice into a 2-quart glass jar with a lid or into a glass bowl and add the sugar, lemon juice, yeast, and cherries. Stir the mixture until the sugar has dissolved. Cover the mixture with the jar lid or with plastic wrap and let it stand at room temperature, stirring twice more that day.

2. Day 2: Stir the mixture twice during the day.

3. Day 3: Stir in the raisins.

4. Day 4: Stir in the apricots.

5. Day 5: Stir in the pineapple with its juice and drain the mixture, reserving the juice. Divide both the fruit and the juice into 4 equal parts (about 1¼ cups fruit and ¾ cup juice in each part). Place one part fruit and one part juice into each of four clean 2-cup jars with lids. Refrigerate until ready to use. The starter will keep for up to 2 weeks.

6. Place a rack in the center of the oven and preheat the oven to 350°F. Lightly mist a 13- by 9-inch baking pan with vegetable oil spray. Set the pan aside.

7. Prepare the cake. Place the brown sugar, nuts, and butter in a small bowl.

Get 20 Servings From a 13" x 9" Pan

Depending on how you slice it, a 13- by 9-inch cake pan can yield anywhere from 16 to 30 pieces of cake. I settle for somewhere in the middle—about 20. Here's how. First cut the cake in half crosswise. Then, cut these 2 halves in half again so that you have 4 crosswise quarters of cake. Now make 5 lengthwise cuts through these quarters of cake, making sure that these are spaced equally apart. There you have it—4 times 5 equals 20.

Mix well with a fork until well blended. Set aside.

8. Place the cake mix, fruit and juice from the starter, oil, and eggs in a large mixing bowl. Blend with an electric mixer on low speed for 1 minute. Stop the machine and scrape down the sides of the bowl with a rubber spatula. Increase the mixer speed to medium and beat 2 to 3 minutes more, scraping the sides down again if needed. The batter should look well combined and thickened. Pour the batter into the prepared pan, smoothing it out with the rubber spatula. Sprinkle the cake batter with the brown sugar and nut mixture. Place the pan in the oven.

9. Bake the cake until it springs back when lightly pressed with your finger and just starts to pull away from the sides of the pan, 40 to 45 minutes. Remove the pan from the oven and place the pan on a wire rack to cool completely, 40 minutes. Cut into squares and serve.

✻ *Store this cake, covered in aluminum foil, at room temperature for up to 1 week. Or freeze it, wrapped in foil, for up to 6 months. Thaw the cake overnight on the counter before serving.*

Special Occasion Cakes

• • •

You don't have to be a statistician to figure out when most people bake a cake. It is for that hallowed occasion of the birthday that the electric mixer starts buzzing, the heirloom cake platter comes out of the cabinet, and candles are arranged just so. My mother always made a big deal out of birthdays. When I was growing up, my sisters and I would not only put in a request for gifts, but we'd decide the menu and the type of birthday cake that suited us. And although as adults we eventually came to some conclusion about our favorite type of cake, as children we craved variety. This year, make it chocolate. Next year, I'll want strawberry, or my name spelled out in birthday cake, or the years spelled out in the candles. And so on. Birthdays are still really special events in my family, which my husband came to learn and love quickly.

Birthdays are not the only occasion when a cake is paramount. Just look at your calendar and you will find all sorts of holidays and festive days when a party cake is in order, from the depths of winter where Valentine's Day seems a bright spot—perfect for a pale pink Love Cake—to George Washington's birthday and other presidential birthday celebrations in February. Into March, St. Patrick's Day deserves an Irish cake (baked with Irish whisky) and May and June celebrations call for something special for Mother's Day and Father's Day.

Bake Birthday Cake Cones for summer birthdays, as well as a make-ahead red, white, and blue ice-cream cake for the Fourth of July.

Into fall, Columbus Day calls for a Cannoli Cake and a Halloween party calls for Devilishly Good Chocolate Cake. And Thanksgiving feasts are complete with either a Pumpkin Roulade, filled with a Sweetened Cream, or a fabulous Pumpkin Pie Crumble Cake, a split personality of a dessert, half of it resembling pie, half cake! Winter holiday cakes turn even more festive with Snowballs, sour cream white cakes enrobed in fluffy marshmallow frosting and grated coconut. Ambrosia Cake is inspired from the Southern fruit dessert called Ambrosia, and it's pretty and regal sitting on the sideboard. As is the Holiday Yule Log, a chocolate cake filled with a brandy cream and frosted to look like an actual log. And lastly, the Gingerbread House puts aside any notion that a cake mix is confined to layers, sheets, tubes, and Bundts. You really can produce a Gingerbread House from a mix, and your children will love you even more for it!

Transforming a cake mix into a special occasion dessert isn't something you'll want to do every day because it's a bit more time-consuming. But then, special occasions don't come around every day. When they do, you are now armed with recipes that will serve you well, that will turn hallowed family days into memories for a lifetime.

LOVE CAKE

Y ou will love this heart-shaped white chocolate cake, covered with a creamy fresh strawberry or raspberry frosting, and garnished with fresh berries and curls of white chocolate. It is perfect for sweethearts of all ages and travels easily to a party at your child's school as well as to the dinner table at the end of an intimate meal with your honey. You bake a heart-shaped cake in two pans, one square and one round. Assembling is easy and explained in step 6.

SERVES 16

PREPARATION TIME: 15 MINUTES

BAKING TIME: 27 TO 30 MINUTES

ASSEMBLY TIME: 15 MINUTES

CAKE:

Solid vegetable shortening for greasing the pans

Flour for dusting the pans

8 tablespoons (1 stick) butter, cut in pieces

1 package (6 ounces) white chocolate, finely chopped

1 package (18.25 ounces) plain white cake mix

1 cup whole milk

3 large eggs

2 teaspoons pure vanilla extract

BERRY BUTTERCREAM FROSTING:

¾ cup fresh strawberries or raspberries, rinsed and drained

8 tablespoons (1 stick) butter, at room temperature

3¾ cups confectioners' sugar, sifted, or more if needed

Milk, if needed

GARNISH:

1 cup fresh small whole strawberries or
raspberries, rinsed and drained
White chocolate curls (see box, page 107)

1. Place a rack in the center of the oven and preheat the oven to 350°F. Generously grease one 9-inch round cake pan and one 9-inch square cake pan with solid vegetable shortening, then dust with flour. Shake out the excess flour. Set the pans aside.

2. Place the butter and white chocolate in a small saucepan over low heat. Cook, stirring, until both have melted, 3 to 4 minutes.

3. Place the cake mix, milk, eggs, vanilla, and melted butter and white chocolate mixture in a large mixing bowl. Blend with an electric mixer on low speed for 1 minute. Stop the machine and scrape down the sides of the bowl with a rubber spatula. Increase the mixer speed to medium and beat 2 minutes more, scraping the sides down again if needed. The batter should look well blended. Divide the batter between the prepared pans, smoothing it out with the rubber spatula. Place the pans in the oven side by side.

4. Bake the cakes until they are light brown and spring back when lightly pressed with your finger, 27 to 30 minutes. Remove the pans from the oven and place them on wire racks to cool for 10 minutes. Run a dinner knife around the edge of each cake and invert each onto a rack, then invert them again onto another rack so that the cakes are right side up. Allow them to cool completely, 30 minutes more.

5. Meanwhile, prepare the Berry Buttercream Frosting. Cut the green caps off the strawberries and puree the strawberries or raspberries in a food processor fitted with the steel blade. You should have about ½ cup puree. If using raspberry puree, rub it through a fine-mesh strainer with the rubber spatula to remove the seeds. Place the butter in a large mixing bowl. Blend with an electric mixer on low speed until fluffy, 30 seconds. Stop the machine, add the sifted confectioners' sugar and berry puree, and blend with the mixer on low speed until the sugar is combined, 1 minute. Increase the mixer speed to medium speed and beat until light and fluffy, 1 minute more. Blend in up to 1 tablespoon milk if the frosting seems too stiff. Add confectioners' sugar, 1 tablespoon at a time, if it seems too thin.

6. Place the square cake layer on a serving platter so that one point faces you. Cut the round cake layer in half and place the halves on adjoining sides of the square, so to form a heart shape. Spread

R

the Cake Doctor says...

White chocolate adds a world of richness to this simple cake. It takes on
the consistency of a pound cake. You
can also make a smaller heart-shaped
cake by using 8-inch pans. The baking time will increase a bit, 30 to 35
minutes.

the frosting on the top and sides of the
cake with clean, smooth strokes.

7. Scatter the chocolate curls on top of
the cake and the fresh berries around it.
Slice and serve.

✳ *Place this cake, uncovered, in the
refrigerator until the frosting sets, 20 minutes. Cover the cake in waxed paper and
store in the refrigerator for up to 4 days. Or
freeze it, wrapped in aluminum foil, for up
to 6 months. Thaw the cake overnight in
the refrigerator before serving.*

MOUNT VERNON CAKE

The Presidents Day holiday commemorates those American presidents who were born in the month of February. Both George Washington and Abraham Lincoln head the list, but William Henry Harrison, president from 1840 to 1844, also celebrated his birthday in February. When we think of Washington, we think of his family home, Mount Vernon, in Virginia. And we think of the story of his cutting down the cherry tree as a lad and admirably admitting to this boyhood prank. This layer cake with a cherry filling is a delicious way to honor our first U.S. president—and those that followed.

SERVES: 16

PREPARATION TIME: 25 MINUTES

BAKING TIME: 20 TO 22 MINUTES

ASSEMBLY TIME: 15 MINUTES

CAKE:

Solid vegetable shortening for greasing the pans

Flour for dusting the pans

1 package (18.25 ounces) plain white cake mix

1 cup sour cream

½ cup vegetable oil, such as canola, corn, safflower, soybean, or sunflower

3 large eggs

CHERRY FILLING:

1 can (16 ounces) pitted tart red cherries

½ cup light corn syrup

¼ cup sugar

2½ tablespoons cornstarch

4 drops red food coloring (optional)

1 teaspoon pure almond extract

TOPPING:

Marshmallow Frosting (page 433)

1. Place a rack in the center of the oven and preheat the oven to 350°F. Generously grease three 9-inch round cake pans with solid vegetable shortening, then dust with flour. Shake out the excess flour. Set the pans aside.

2. Place the cake mix, sour cream, oil, and eggs in a large mixing bowl. Blend with an electric mixer on low speed for 1 minute. Stop the machine and scrape down the sides of the bowl with a rubber spatula. Increase the mixer speed to medium and beat 2 minutes more, scraping the sides down again if needed. The batter should look well blended. Divide the batter among the prepared pans, smoothing it out with the rubber spatula. Place the pans in the oven; if your oven is not large enough, place two pans on the center rack and place the third pan in the center of the highest rack.

3. Bake the cakes until they are light brown and spring back when lightly pressed with your finger, 20 to 22 minutes. Be careful not to overbake the layer on the highest oven rack. Remove the pans from the oven and place them on wire racks to cool for 10 minutes. Run a dinner knife around the edge of the cakes and invert each onto a rack, then invert them again onto another rack so that the cakes are right side up. Allow to cool completely, 30 minutes more.

R

the Cake Doctor says...

Since some white cake mixes have a slight taste of cherry to them already, this filling makes a natural complement. If you don't wish to make the Marshmallow Frosting, substitute Buttercream Frosting (page 416).

4. Meanwhile, prepare the Cherry Filling. Drain the cherries, reserving the liquid. Pour the liquid into a measuring cup. Set the cherries and liquid aside. Combine the corn syrup, sugar, and cornstarch in a small saucepan and stir. Add enough water to the reserved cherry liquid to make 1 cup. Add the cherry liquid and food coloring, if desired, to the saucepan. Cook the mixture over medium heat, stirring constantly, until it is smooth and thickened, 2 to 3 minutes. Remove the pan from the heat and stir in the drained cherries and almond extract. Pour the filling into a medium-size bowl and place, covered, in the refrigerator to chill while you make the frosting.

5. Prepare the Marshmallow Frosting.

6. Place one cake layer, right side up, on a serving platter. Spread the top with half of the Cherry Filling, spreading it with a spatula up to 1 inch from the cake edge. Place the second layer, right side up, on top of the filling. Spread the second layer with the remaining filling, spreading it up to 1 inch from the cake edge. Top the two layers with the remaining cake layer, right side up, and spread frosting on the top and sides of the cake with clean, smooth strokes.

✳ *Store this cake in a cake saver in the refrigerator for up to 1 week.*

IRISH ALMOND AND CARAWAY CAKE

When Americans think of St. Patrick's Day, we envision great slabs of corned beef brisket, a huge pile of cabbage, and rivers of green beer. But in Ireland the holiday is marked by children off from school, a town parade, mass, then heading to the local pub for songs and drink. Cakes in Ireland are wonderful earthy confections made of sturdy flours spiced with nutmeg or ginger and studded with currants and almonds and candied fruit. With true Irish tradition in mind, and an American thirst for something fast and flashy, here is a cake to serve at your St. Patrick's Day party. In Ireland it would be referred to as a seed cake, as caraway seeds are often used along with almonds in buttery cakes. The whisky adds a little kick.

....

SERVES: 16

PREPARATION TIME: 15 MINUTES

BAKING TIME: 48 TO 52 MINUTES

ASSEMBLY TIME: 5 MINUTES

....

R
the Cake Doctor says...

Caraway gives cakes an exotic, faintly licorice taste. The whisky provides an authentic taste of Ireland and marries well with the caraway and lemon. One lemon will yield the teaspoon of grated zest and the 2 tablespoons of juice. If you don't care for caraway seeds, add ½ cup dried currants.

CAKE:

Vegetable oil spray for misting the pan

Flour for dusting the pan

1 package (18.25 ounces) plain yellow
cake mix

1 package (3.4 ounces) vanilla instant
pudding mix

½ cup vegetable oil, such as canola, corn,
safflower, soybean, or sunflower

½ cup water

⅓ cup Irish whisky

4 large eggs

1 cup finely chopped slivered almonds

1 tablespoon caraway seeds

1 teaspoon grated lemon zest

GLAZE:

1 cup confectioners' sugar

2 tablespoons fresh lemon juice

1 tablespoon Irish whisky

1. Place a rack in the center of the oven and preheat the oven to 325°F. Lightly mist a 12-cup Bundt pan with vegetable oil spray, then dust with flour. Shake out the excess flour. Set the pan aside.

2. Place the cake mix, pudding mix, oil, water, whisky, and eggs in a large mixing bowl. Blend with an electric mixer on low speed for 1 minute. Stop the machine and scrape down the sides of the bowl with the rubber spatula. Increase the mixer speed to medium and beat for 2 minutes more, scraping the sides down again if needed. The batter should look thick and well blended. Fold in the almonds, caraway seeds, and lemon zest. Pour the batter into the prepared pan, smoothing it out with the rubber spatula. Place the pan in the oven.

3. Bake the cake until it is golden brown and just starts to pull away from the sides of the pan, 48 to 52 minutes. Remove the pan from the oven and place it on a wire rack to cool for 20 minutes. Run a long, sharp knife around the edge of the cake and invert it onto a rack to cool for 30 minutes more.

4. Meanwhile, prepare the glaze. Combine the confectioners' sugar, lemon juice, and whisky in a small bowl and stir with a wooden spoon until smooth.

5. Slide the cake onto a serving platter and pour the glaze over the cake, letting it drizzle down the sides and into the center. Let the glaze set before slicing the cake.

✳ *Store this cake, covered in plastic wrap, at room temperature for up to 1 week. Or freeze it, wrapped in aluminum foil, for up to 6 months. Thaw the cake overnight on the counter before serving.*

BRIDE'S CAKE WITH RASPBERRY FILLING AND WHITE CHOCOLATE FROSTING

I know caterers who pair raspberries and white chocolate in grand wedding cakes, but grand cakes are not always possible to pull off in your home kitchen. Yet, you can easily handle this recipe for smaller weddings, engagement parties, or bridal showers. The cake bakes up pale, pale yellow but has a lovely flavor, and the filling is just the right complement to the white chocolate frosting.

SERVES: 16

PREPARATION TIME: 15 MINUTES

BAKING TIME:
27 TO 29 MINUTES

ASSEMBLY TIME:
25 MINUTES

Solid vegetable shortening for greasing
   the pans
Flour for dusting the pans
1 package (18.25 ounces) plain white
   cake mix
1 cup whole milk
8 tablespoons (1 stick) butter, melted
3 large eggs
2 teaspoons pure vanilla extract
White Chocolate Frosting
   (page 424)
¼ cup seedless raspberry jam
1 cup fresh raspberries, rinsed
   and drained

R

the Cake Doctor says...

Vary the flavor of this cake by changing the type of jam you sandwich in between the layers. Peach or apricot jam would be delicious.

1. Place a rack in the center of the oven and preheat the oven to 350°F. Generously grease two 9-inch round cake pans with solid vegetable shortening, then dust with flour. Shake out the excess flour. Set the pans aside.

2. Place the cake mix, milk, melted butter, eggs, and vanilla in a large mixing bowl. Blend with an electric mixer on low speed for 1 minute. Stop the machine and scrape down the sides of the bowl with a rubber spatula. Increase the mixer speed to medium and beat 2 minutes more, scraping the sides down again if needed. The batter should look well blended. Divide the batter evenly into the prepared pans, smoothing it out with the rubber spatula. Place the pans in the oven side by side.

3. Bake the cakes until they are light brown and spring back when lightly pressed with your finger, 27 to 29 min-

utes. Remove the pans from the oven and place them on wire racks to cool for 10 minutes. Run a dinner knife around the edge of the cakes and invert each onto a rack, then invert them again onto another rack so that the cakes are right side up. Allow to cool completely, 30 minutes more.

4. Meanwhile, prepare the White Chocolate Frosting.

5. Place one cake layer, right side up, on a serving platter. Spread the top with a thin layer of the White Chocolate Frosting, then spread with the raspberry jam, spreading the jam with a spatula up to 1 inch from the cake edge. Place the second layer, right side up, on top of the jam. Spread frosting on the top and sides of the cake with clean, smooth strokes.

6. Garnish the cake with the fresh raspberries. Slice and serve.

❋ *Place this cake, uncovered, in the refrigerator until the frosting sets, 20 minutes. Cover the cake in waxed paper and store in the refrigerator for up to 1 week. Or freeze it, wrapped in aluminum foil, for up to 6 months. Thaw the cake overnight in the refrigerator before serving.*

Groom's Cake

The most dangerous food in the world is wedding cake.

—American proverb

*P*ity the groom at the wedding, what with all the attention given to the bride. But don't pity the poor groom at the reception afterwards, for his cake is far more interesting than the triple-tiered white wedding cake. The tradition of baking a separate cake for the groom can be traced to the English tradition of baking a whisky-soaked, fruit-laden cake for the wedding. When snowy white, soft wedding cakes came into vogue, what to do with their heavier, and more flavorful, counterparts? Bake them up, too, but say they're for the groom! Nowadays a groom's cake may be like those original wedding cakes, or simply a butter cake soaked in brandy, or a deep, dark chocolate cake. And whereas the bride's cake is for admiring, the groom's cake is for devouring. Better stand in line, though, for there's generally less groom's cake.

15 SHOW-STEALING GROOM'S CAKES

1. Buttermilk Devil's Food Cake with White Chocolate Frosting (page 28)

2. Deeply Chocolate Almond Cake with Chocolate Cream Cheese Frosting (page 26)

3. Chocolate Praline Cake (page 33)

4. Cannoli Cake (page 199)

5. Lethal Peppermint Chocolate Cake (page 30)

6. Ambrosia Cake (page 212)

7. Lemon-Lime Cake with Pineapple Curd (page 158)

8. Hummingbird Cake (page 74)

9. Tennessee Jam Cake (page 116)

10. Caramel Cake (page 112)

11. Carrot Cake with Fresh Orange Cream Cheese Frosting (page 109)

12. Harvey Wallbanger Cake (page 284)

13. Chocolate Grappa Cake (page 306)

14. Double-Chocolate Rum Cake (page 289)

15. Quick Red Velvet Cake (page 152)

BIRTHDAY CAKE CONES

Boy, will you delight the little ones when you present these cones filled with—surprise—cake! This is a fun dessert for birthday parties or other festive occasions—the end of school, the beginning of school, a soccer party, you name it. Simply choose your favorite cake-mix flavor, and prepare it pretty close to the package directions. I've chosen chocolate here and add cinnamon to boost the taste. If you go with white or yellow cake, add a teaspoon of vanilla extract instead. You'll need three muffin pans to bake the 28 cones.

SERVES: 28
PREPARATION TIME: 15 MINUTES
BAKING TIME: 20 TO 25 MINUTES
ASSEMBLY TIME: 15 MINUTES

28 good-quality flat-bottomed ice cream
    cones
1 package (18.25 ounces) plain devil's food
    cake mix
1⅓ cups water
½ cup vegetable oil, such as canola, corn,
    safflower, soybean, or sunflower
3 large eggs
½ teaspoon ground cinnamon
Fluffy Chocolate Frosting (page 426)
1 cup colored sugar sprinkles, for garnish

1. Place a rack in the center of the oven and preheat the oven to 350°F. Wrap a small square of aluminum foil around the base of each of the ice cream cones, and stand the cones in ungreased muffin baking pans. Set the pans aside.

2. Place the cake mix, water, oil, eggs, and cinnamon in a large mixing bowl.

R

the Cake Doctor says...

Don't overfill these cones. If you do, the batter will run down the sides. If you want to make ice cream part of this treat, fill the cones with less batter, bake, and fill in the top of each cone with a scoop of ice cream just before serving. The kids will bite in and find the cake surprise underneath! By the way, the oven baking will crisp up the cones but not burn or discolor them.

Blend with an electric mixer on low speed for 1 minute. Stop the machine and scrape down the sides of the bowl with a rubber spatula. Increase the mixer speed to medium and beat 2 minutes more, scraping the sides down again if needed. The batter should look well blended.

Spoon about ¼ cup of the batter into each ice cream cone, filling it no more than halfway. Place the pans in the oven; if your oven is not large enough, place two pans on the center rack and place the third pan in the center of the highest rack.

3. Bake the cones until the cake springs back when lightly pressed with your finger, 20 to 25 minutes. Be careful not to over-bake the pan on the highest oven rack. Remove the pans from the oven and place them on wire racks to cool for 30 minutes.

4. Meanwhile, prepare the Fluffy Chocolate Frosting.

5. Remove the foil from the base of each cone and frost the tops with frosting. Decorate with sugar sprinkles. Carefully place on a platter and serve.

✴ *Store these cupcakes in a plastic cake saver or under a glass cake dome at room temperature for up to 4 days.*

RED, WHITE, AND BLUE ANGEL FOOD ICE-CREAM CAKE

I've positioned this recipe in the Fourth of July spot in the chapter, but use your imagination as you sandwich ice cream between layers of angel food cake. If you're serving this on the Fourth, opt for strawberry and blueberry for a red, white, and blue effect as I suggest below. If it's Christmas, opt for peppermint and deep, dark chocolate and garnish with peppermint candies and chocolate shavings. And so on. You can, in a pinch, use frozen whipped topping instead of real whipped cream but it won't taste nearly as good. As a timesaver, make the cake up to two days in advance and keep it in the freezer.

....

SERVES: 16

PREPARATION TIME: 5 MINUTES

BAKING TIME: 40 TO 44 MINUTES

ASSEMBLY TIME: 25 MINUTES

FREEZING TIME: 2½ HOURS

....

1 box (16 ounces) angel food cake mix

1¼ cups water

4 cups (2 pints) strawberry ice cream, softened

2 cups (1 pint) blueberry ice cream, softened

Sweetened Cream (page 432)

¼ cup slivered almonds, toasted (Toasting Nuts, page 134)

1 cup fresh small, whole strawberries, rinsed and drained, for garnish

R
the CakeDoctor says...

Here a basic angel food cake is merely the canvas, and you as the artist use interesting, colorful, and flavorful ice creams or sorbets to achieve a beautiful and festive dessert that changes with the season. In this frozen dessert, why would it ever matter if the cake wasn't made from scratch?

1. Remove the top oven rack and move the other rack to the lowest position. Preheat the oven to 350°F. Set aside an ungreased 10-inch tube pan.

2. Prepare the cake mix according to the package instructions, using 1¼ cups water. The batter should look well combined. Pour the batter into the pan, smoothing it out with a rubber spatula. Place the pan in the oven.

3. Bake the cake until it is golden brown and springs back when lightly pressed with your finger, 40 to 44 minutes. Remove the pan from the oven and invert the pan onto the neck of a heatproof glass bottle. Allow it to cool completely, 1 to 1½ hours. Remove the pan from the bottle. Run a long, sharp knife around the edge of the cake and invert it onto a platter that can withstand the freezer.

4. Carefully split the cake horizontally into 4 layers. Place the bottom layer on the platter, and spread with half of the strawberry ice cream. Place the platter in the freezer and freeze until the ice cream is solid, about 15 minutes. Remove the platter from the freezer. Place the second layer on top of the strawberry ice cream and spread the blueberry ice cream on top. Place the platter in the freezer and freeze for 15 minutes, or until the ice cream is solid. Remove the platter from the freezer and add the third layer of cake and spread with the remaining strawberry ice cream. Place the remaining cake layer on top. Cover the cake with plastic wrap and place in the freezer until the cake is quite firm, 2 hours.

5. When the cake is frozen, prepare the Sweetened Cream.

6. Remove the platter from the freezer and spread the top and sides of the cake quickly with the Sweetened Cream, using clean, smooth strokes. Sprinkle the toasted almonds over the top. Garnish with the whole strawberries. Slice and serve at once, or wrap the cake lightly with waxed paper and return the platter to the freezer.

❋ *Store the cake, covered in waxed paper or in a plastic cake saver, in the freezer for up to 2 weeks.*

CANNOLI CAKE

In Italian, the word *cannoli* means "pipes." But in the world of Italian food, cannoli are pipe- or tube-shaped pastries that are deep-fried before being filled with a lovely sweet ricotta cheese mixture. The

cheese filling also often includes cinnamon, chocolate, candied fruit, orange zest, or pistachios; these festive flavors are naturals for a cake recipe. So I've created a cannoli-type filling for a buttery four-layer cake, which is a little more difficult than the other layer cakes in this book but worth the extra time. You choose the frosting, either a rich and classic buttercream or a velvety and wicked ganache. Why not bake

R the Cake Doctor says...

Powerful flavors are at work here, and a simple white cake mix is once again transformed! This blockbuster of a filling has intense orange, Marsala wine, and vanilla flavors, plus the addition of semisweet chocolate. What makes this cake a joy is that it has such good structure that the layers can be halved and filled with this sturdy filling and then be frosted, to stand pretty and tall on the serving platter.

it as a tribute to Christopher Columbus?

....

SERVES: 16

PREPARATION TIME: 20 MINUTES

BAKING TIME:

27 TO 29 MINUTES

ASSEMBLY TIME: 15 MINUTES

....

CANNOLI FILLING:

¾ cup sugar

3 tablespoons cornstarch

¾ cup whole milk

1 container (15 ounces; 1¾ cups) ricotta
    cheese

1 tablespoon grated orange zest (from 1
    orange)

1 tablespoon sweet Marsala wine (optional)

1½ teaspoons pure vanilla extract

½ cup miniature semisweet chocolate chips

CAKE:

Solid vegetable shortening for greasing the
    pans

Flour for dusting the pans

1 package (18.25 ounces) plain white cake
    mix

1 cup whole milk

8 tablespoons (1 stick) butter, melted

3 large eggs

2 teaspoons pure vanilla extract

FROSTING:

Buttercream Frosting (page 416) or Chocolate
    Ganache (page 428)

1. For the filling, place the sugar and cornstarch in a small saucepan and stir in the milk. Cook over low heat, whisking constantly, until the mixture thickens and is bubbly, 5 minutes. Remove the pan from the heat and let the mixture cool slightly. Place the ricotta cheese in a large mixing bowl and blend with an electric mixer on low speed until creamy, 1 minute. Fold in the cooled milk and sugar mixture, orange zest, Marsala wine, if desired, and vanilla. Blend with the mixer on low speed until well combined, 1 minute. Fold in the chocolate chips. Set the bowl aside, covered, in the refrigerator while you bake the cake.

2. Place a rack in the center of the oven and preheat the oven to 350°F. Generously grease two 9-inch round cake pans with solid vegetable shortening, then dust with flour. Shake out the excess flour. Set the pans aside.

3. Place the cake mix, milk, melted butter, eggs, and vanilla in a large mixing bowl. Blend with the mixer on low speed for 1 minute. Stop the machine and scrape down the sides of the bowl with a rubber spatula. Increase the mixer speed to medium and beat 2 minutes more, scraping the sides down again if needed. The batter should look well combined. Divide the batter between the prepared pans, smoothing it out with the rubber spatula. Place the pans in the oven side by side.

4. Bake the cakes until they look golden brown and spring back when lightly pressed with your finger, 27 to 29 minutes. Remove the pans from the oven and place them on wire racks to cool for 10 minutes. Run a dinner knife around the edge of each layer and invert each onto a rack, then invert them again onto another rack so that the cakes are right side up. Allow them to cool completely, 30 minutes more.

5. Meanwhile, prepare either the Buttercream Frosting or the Chocolate Ganache.

6. When the cake layers are cool, slice each in half horizontally using a serrated bread knife. Place the bottom of one layer, cut side up, on a serving platter and frost with a third of the Cannoli Filling. Top with the top of the first layer, cut side down, and frost with another third of the Cannoli Filling. Top with the bottom of the second layer, cut side up, and frost with the remaining third of the Cannoli Filling. Place the top of the second layer, cut side down, on top of the filling. Spread the frosting of your choice on the top and sides of the filled cake with clean, smooth strokes. Chill at least 30 minutes before slicing and serving.

✳ *Store this cake, covered in plastic wrap or waxed paper, in the refrigerator for up to 1 week. Or freeze it, wrapped in aluminum foil, for up to 6 months. Thaw the cake overnight in the refrigerator before serving.*

DEVILISHLY GOOD CHOCOLATE CAKE

If you're having a Halloween party, this is the perfect cake to serve. It's a devil of a chocolate cake topped with Chocolate Pan Frosting, and it looks downright scary surrounded by cobwebs or plastic spiders found at any party store. If you want a more upbeat cake, then frost it with the Butter-cream Frosting (page 416), tinted with orange food coloring.

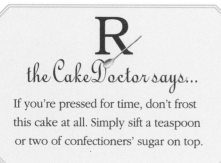

R
the Cake Doctor says...

If you're pressed for time, don't frost this cake at all. Simply sift a teaspoon or two of confectioners' sugar on top.

SERVES: 16
PREPARATION TIME: 15 MINUTES
BAKING TIME: 45 TO 50 MINUTES
ASSEMBLY TIME: 10 MINUTES

Vegetable oil spray for misting the pan
Flour for dusting the pan
1 square (1 ounce) unsweetened chocolate, finely chopped
½ cup water
1 package (18.25 ounces) plain devil's food cake mix
1 package (3.9 ounces) chocolate instant pudding mix
4 large eggs
¾ cup buttermilk
½ cup vegetable oil, such as canola, corn, safflower, soybean, or sunflower
2 teaspoons pure vanilla extract
Chocolate Pan Frosting (page 429)

1. Place a rack in the center of the oven and preheat the oven to 350°F. Lightly mist a 12-cup Bundt pan with vegetable oil spray, then dust with flour. Shake out the excess flour. Set the pan aside.

2. Place the chocolate and water in a small saucepan over low heat. Cook, stirring, until the chocolate is melted, 3 to 4 minutes. Set aside.

3. Place the cake mix, pudding mix, eggs, buttermilk, oil, and vanilla in a large mixing bowl. Fold in the melted chocolate. Blend with an electric mixer on low speed for 1 minute. Stop the machine and scrape down the sides of the bowl with a rubber spatula. Increase the mixer speed to medium and beat 2 to 3 minutes more, scraping the sides down again if needed. The batter should look thick and well combined. Pour the batter into the prepared pan, smoothing it out with the rubber spatula. Place the pan in the oven.

4. Bake the cake until it springs back when lightly pressed with your finger and just starts to pull away from the sides of the pan, 45 to 50 minutes. Remove the pan from the oven and place it on a wire rack to cool for 20 minutes. Run a long, sharp knife around the edge of the cake and invert it onto a rack to complete cooling, 20 minutes more.

5. Meanwhile, prepare the Chocolate Pan Frosting. Transfer the cake to a serving platter and spread the warm frosting over the cooled cake with clean, smooth strokes. Let the frosting set for 20 minutes, then slice and serve.

Hold the Batter!

Kay Emel-Powell of Betty Crocker says the nice thing about cake-mix batter is that it doesn't have to be baked right away. You can mix your ingredients early in the day, cover the bowl with plastic wrap, tuck the batter in the refrigerator, and pour it into pans when you're back home and have time to assemble a cake.

Well, I put those words to the test with the Devilishly Good Chocolate Cake recipe, preparing it one Saturday morning and not baking the batter until 8 P.M. that night. I poured the chilled batter right into the pan and placed it in a preheated oven. It baked for about the same time as that recipe did when made from batter that had not been chilled, and it rose high in the pan and tasted terrific. The frosting is easy to prepare while the cake is cooling.

✳ *Store this cake, covered in aluminum foil or plastic wrap, at room temperature for up to 4 days. Or freeze it, wrapped in foil, for up to 6 months. Thaw the cake overnight on the counter before serving.*

PUMPKIN ROULADE

On Thanksgiving it just seems un-American to serve anything other than pumpkin pie for dessert. But if you can't get enough of that good pumpkin taste, this dessert is for you. Based on the same flavors as pumpkin pie, this roulade captures the attention of cake lovers because it has a spicy spongy cake rolled around a sweet fluffy cream filling. Plus, it's a great do-ahead dessert, chilled and waiting, while the turkey roasts to perfection. Be sure to garnish the cake platter with

R
the Cake Doctor says...

You save time using frozen whipped topping in this easy filling, but should you prefer to make the whipped cream from scratch, begin with 1 cup of heavy cream. If you're bringing this dessert to someone's house, the combination of commercial whipped topping and cream cheese makes a surprisingly delicious and stable filling.

clean evergreen sprigs, pansies, or mum blossoms.

....

SERVES: 16

PREPARATION TIME: 20 MINUTES

BAKING TIME:

15 TO 17 MINUTES

ASSEMBLY TIME: 15 MINUTES

....

CREAMY FILLING:

*1 package (8 ounces) cream cheese, at
    room temperature*

1 cup confectioners' sugar, sifted

½ teaspoon pure vanilla extract

*1 container (8 ounces) frozen whipped
    topping, thawed*

*½ cup chopped almonds or pecans,
    toasted (see Toasting Nuts,
    page 134)*

PUMPKIN ROULADE:

Softened butter for greasing the pan

Parchment paper for the pan

*1 package (18.25 ounces) plain spice
    cake mix*

⅔ cup canned pumpkin

½ cup buttermilk

*⅓ cup vegetable oil, such as canola,
    corn, safflower, soybean, or sunflower*

4 large eggs

½ teaspoon ground cinnamon

½ teaspoon ground nutmeg

Confectioners' sugar for dusting

GARNISH:

2 teaspoons confectioners' sugar

1. For the filling, place the cream cheese, sugar, and vanilla in a large mixing bowl. Beat with the electric mixer on low speed until the ingredients are incorporated, 45 seconds. Stop the machine and add the thawed whipped topping. Beat on low until the filling is well combined and fluffy, 1 minute more. Fold in the almonds or pecans until they are well distributed. Cover the bowl with plastic wrap and place in the refrigerator to chill.

2. Place a rack in the center of the oven and preheat the oven to 350°F. Lightly butter the bottom of a 16½- by 11½- by 1-inch jelly-roll pan and line with enough parchment paper to cover the bottom and still have a couple of inches lapping over at each end. Lightly butter the parchment paper, but do not butter the sides of the pan. Set the pan aside.

3. Place the cake mix, pumpkin, buttermilk, oil, eggs, cinnamon, and nutmeg in a large mixing bowl. Blend with an electric mixer on low speed for 1 minute. Stop the machine and scrape down the sides of the bowl with a rubber spatula. Increase the mixer speed to medium and beat 2 minutes more, scraping the sides down again if needed. The batter should look thick and combined. Pour the batter into the prepared pan, smoothing it out with the rubber spatula. Place the pan in the oven.

4. Bake the cake until it springs back when lightly pressed with your finger and a toothpick inserted in the center comes out clean, 15 to 17 minutes. Remove the pan from the oven and place it on a wire rack while you dust a clean kitchen towel or long sheet of parchment paper with confectioners' sugar. Immediately invert the pan onto the towel and carefully peel off the used parchment that clings to the bottom of the cake. While the cake is still hot, use the towel to help carefully roll the cake into a jelly roll, or roulade. Begin with the long side next to you and roll away from you. Place the roulade, seam side down, wrapped in the kitchen towel or parchment paper, on the counter to cool for 30 minutes. Don't worry if the roulade splits while you are rolling it because you will cover up these blemishes with the filling.

5. When the cake is cool, you are ready to assemble the roulade. Carefully unroll the cake just enough so that you can spread the inside surface generously with the chilled filling. Gently roll the cake back into its roulade shape, carefully pulling the kitchen towel out from under it. Place the roulade seam side down on a serving platter. Cover it with plastic wrap and place the platter in the refrigerator to chill, at least 30 minutes.

6. Before serving, sift confectioners' sugar over the top of the roulade. Slice into serving pieces.

✳ *Store the roulade, covered in waxed paper, in the refrigerator for up to 4 days.*

PUMPKIN PIE CRUMBLE CAKE

This recipe comes from Margaret Neblett of Nashville, who got it from a friend, who got it from a friend in Chicago, and so on. Word spreads when there's a great recipe! This dessert is much like a pie in that it has a cinnamon-enhanced pumpkin filling, but much like a cake with a soft crust. And the crunchy topping is the best of both worlds. Don't be concerned that 1 cup of the cake mix is reserved for the topping. The filling bakes up firm and creamy without it.

SERVES: 18 TO 20
PREPARATION TIME: 15 MINUTES
BAKING TIME: 70 TO 75 MINUTES
ASSEMBLY TIME: 5 MINUTES

Solid vegetable shortening for greasing the pan
Flour for dusting the pan
1 package (18.25 ounces) plain yellow cake mix
8 tablespoons (1 stick) butter or margarine, at room temperature
4 large eggs
2 cans (15 ounces each) pumpkin
1 can (5 ounces) evaporated milk
1¼ cups sugar
2 teaspoons ground cinnamon
4 tablespoons (½ stick) butter or margarine, chilled
1 cup chopped pecans
2 recipes Sweetened Cream (page 432)

1. Place a rack in the center of the oven and preheat the oven to 350°F. Lightly grease a 13- by 9-inch baking pan with solid vegetable shortening, then dust with flour. Shake out the excess flour. Set the pan aside.

2. Measure out 1 cup of the cake mix and reserve for the topping. Place the remaining cake mix, the butter, and 1 egg in a large mixing bowl. Blend with an electric mixer on low speed until well combined, 1 minute. Using your fingertips, press the batter over the bottom of the prepared pan so that it reaches the sides of the pan. Set the pan aside.

3. For the filling, place the pumpkin, evaporated milk, 1 cup sugar, remaining 3 eggs, and cinnamon in the same large mixing bowl used to prepare the batter and with the same beaters (no need to clean either), blend on low speed until combined, 30 seconds. Increase the mixer speed to medium and beat until the mixture lightens in color and texture, 1 to 2 minutes more. Pour the filling over the crust in the pan, spreading to the sides of the pan with a rubber spatula. Set the pan aside.

4. For the topping, place the remaining ¼ cup sugar, the chilled butter, and the reserved cake mix in a clean medium-size mixing bowl. Rinse and dry the beaters. Beat with an electric mixer on low speed until just combined and crumbly, 30 seconds to 1 minute. Stop the machine and stir in the pecans. Use your fingers to thoroughly knead the pecans into the topping

R

the Cake Doctor says...

Originally, this recipe called for margarine, but I think it benefits from the taste of butter.

mixture. Distribute the topping evenly over the filling mixture. Place the pan in the oven.

5. Bake the cake until the center no longer jiggles when you shake the pan and the pecans on top have browned, 70 to 75 minutes. Remove the pan from the oven and let cool slightly on a wire rack, 20 minutes.

6. Prepare two recipes of the Sweetened Cream. Slice the cake into squares and pass the Sweetened Cream to spoon on top.

✳ *Store this cake without the Sweetened Cream on it, covered in aluminum foil or plastic wrap, in the refrigerator for up to 1 week.*

HOLIDAY YULE LOG

When you want that one great cake, that one spectacular ending to a holiday meal, then this yule log is just what the Cake Mix Doctor ordered. It is a French Christmas tradition to bake a *bûche de Noël*, or chocolate sponge cake in the shape of a log. Variations abound, but I prefer a devil's food cake batter, intensified with a tablespoon of instant coffee powder. The filling is simply brandied whipped cream, and the frosting is Chocolate Pan Frosting. Make ahead of the big event, and keep refrigerated. Decorate with plenty of evergreens or holly sprigs.

SERVES: 16
PREPARATION TIME: 30 MINUTES
BAKING TIME: 18 TO 20 MINUTES
ASSEMBLY TIME: 20 MINUTES

BRANDIED WHIPPED CREAM:

2 cups heavy (whipping) cream
⅓ to ½ cup confectioners' sugar, sifted
4 tablespoons brandy, or to taste

CHOCOLATE ROULADE:

Softened butter for greasing the pan
Parchment paper for the pan
1 package (18.25 ounces) plain devil's food cake mix
1 cup buttermilk
½ cup vegetable oil, such as canola, corn, safflower, soybean, or sunflower
4 large eggs
3 tablespoons unsweetened cocoa powder
1 tablespoon instant coffee powder
Confectioners' sugar for dusting

TOPPING:

Chocolate Pan Frosting (page 429)

R

the Cake Doctor says...

Don't think for a moment you've got to be some famous pastry chef to pull off this dessert. It's just a devil's food cake batter poured into a jelly-roll pan and baked as a roulade. But there are two tricks: To get the batter to rise, don't grease the sides of the pan, but do line the pan with parchment paper so the cake turns out easily onto a clean kitchen towel (or more parchment) dusted with confectioners' sugar.

1. Place a clean large mixing bowl and electric mixer beaters in the freezer for a few minutes while you assemble the ingredients for the whipped cream. Pour the heavy cream into the chilled bowl and beat with the electric mixer on high speed until the cream has thickened, 2 minutes. Stop the machine and add the sugar and half of the brandy. Beat the mixture on high for 30 seconds more, then add the remaining brandy to taste, if desired. Beat until stiff peaks form, 1 to 2 minutes more. Cover the bowl with plastic wrap and place in the refrigerator to chill.

2. Place a rack in the center of the oven and preheat the oven to 350°F. Lightly butter the bottom of a 16½- by 11½- by 1-inch jelly-roll pan and cover with enough parchment paper to cover the bottom and still have a couple of inches lapping over at each end. Lightly butter the parchment, but do not butter the sides of the pan. Set the pan aside.

3. Place the cake mix, buttermilk, oil, eggs, cocoa, and coffee powder in a large mixing bowl. Blend with an electric mixer on low speed for 1 minute. Stop the machine and scrape down the sides of the bowl with a rubber spatula. Increase the mixer speed to medium and beat 2 minutes more, scraping the sides down again if needed. The batter should look thick and combined. Pour the batter into the prepared pan, smoothing it out with the rubber spatula. Place the pan in the oven.

4. Bake the cake until it springs back when lightly pressed with your finger and a toothpick inserted in the center comes out clean, 18 to 20 minutes. Remove the pan from the oven and place on a wire rack while you dust a clean kitchen towel or long sheet of parchment paper with confectioners' sugar. Immediately invert the pan onto the towel and carefully peel off the used parchment that clings to the bottom of the cake. While the cake is still hot, use the towel to help carefully roll the cake into a jelly roll, or roulade. Begin with the long side next to you and roll away from you. Place the roulade, seam side down, wrapped in the kitchen towel or parchment paper, on the counter to cool for 30 minutes. Don't worry if the roulade splits while you are rolling it because you will cover up these blemishes with the filling and frosting .

5. Meanwhile, prepare the Chocolate Pan Frosting.

6. When the frosting is made, the filling has chilled, and the cake is cool, you are ready to assemble the log. Reserve 1 cup filling, covered, in the refrigerator. Carefully unroll the cake just enough so that you can spread the inside surface generously with the chilled filling. Gently roll the cake back into its log shape, carefully pulling the kitchen towel out from under it. Place the log seam side down in front of you. Carefully cut off an inch-thick slice from one end. Cut this slice into two halves.

7. Carefully place the log, seam side down, on a serving platter. Sandwich the two cut halves together and place them, cut side down, about a third of the way down the log so that they resemble a knot

on a branch. Attach them to the log with a dab of frosting. Working quickly, spread the frosting over the entire surface of the log with clean strokes, covering the ends. Make the strokes irregular so that the frosting resembles the bark of a tree. Or drag a fork down through the frosting so that the tines of the fork make lines in the batter, also resembling bark. Place the platter in the refrigerator to chill until the frosting has set, 1 hour. Then, lightly cover the log with waxed paper and chill until serving time.

8. Slice into serving pieces and serve, passing the reserved filling to spoon on top.

✳ *Store this roulade, covered in waxed paper, in the refrigerator for up to 4 days.*

AMBROSIA CAKE

When I was a little girl, a crystal punch bowl full of orange sections and coconut sat on the dining room sideboard on Christmas Eve. It waited until everyone had had their fill of turkey and dressing. This heavenly fruit compote was called Ambrosia, and yes, it was food for the gods! For the oranges and coconut played a melody in your mouth. I grew up learning that Ambrosia is never more than coconut and oranges, but then I tasted Ambrosia containing crushed pineapple, and it was this sacrilegious rendition that inspired the delightful holiday layer cake I share here. In this moist coconut-filled cake, the flavors mimic Ambrosia. Prepare the pineapple and orange filling first so that it can cool and thicken while the cake bakes and cools.

R

the Cake Doctor says...

Make the filling up to 1 day ahead of time. The layers will stack better if the filling has been well chilled.

....

SERVES: 16

PREPARATION TIME:
40 MINUTES

BAKING TIME: 18 TO 20 MINUTES

ASSEMBLY TIME:
20 MINUTES

....

PINEAPPLE AND ORANGE FILLING:

1 can (8 ounces) crushed pineapple in juice, drained
1 cup orange juice
1 cup sugar

CAKE:

Solid vegetable shortening for greasing the pans
Flour for dusting the pans
1 package (18.25 ounces) white cake mix with pudding
1¼ cups water
⅓ cup vegetable oil, such as canola, corn, safflower, soybean, or sunflower
3 eggs
1 package (6 ounces; 1¾ cups) frozen unsweetened grated coconut, thawed
Marshmallow Frosting (page 433)

GARNISH:

1 package (6 ounces; 1¾ cups) frozen unsweetened grated coconut, thawed

1. Combine the pineapple, orange juice, and sugar in a medium-size saucepan. Cook over medium heat, stirring constantly, until the mixture is thickened, 20 to 25 minutes.

2. Pour the filling into a bowl and cover with plastic wrap. Refrigerate the filling so that it will cool completely, about 1 hour. Stir the filling before using it.

3. Place a rack in the center of the oven and preheat the oven to 350°F. Generously grease three 9-inch round cake pans with solid vegetable shortening, then dust with flour. Shake out the excess flour. Set the pans aside.

4. Place the cake mix, water, oil, and eggs in a large mixing bowl. Blend with an electric mixer on low speed for 1 minute. Stop the machine and scrape down the sides of the bowl with a rubber spatula. Increase the mixer speed to medium and beat 2 minutes more, scraping down the sides of the bowl if needed. The batter should look well combined and thickened. Fold in the coconut until it is well distributed. Divide the batter among the prepared pans, smoothing it out with the rubber spatula, and place them in the oven; if your oven is not large enough, place two pans on the center rack and place the third pan in the center of the highest rack.

5. Bake the cakes until they spring back when lightly pressed with your finger and just start to pull away from the sides of the pans, 18 to 20 minutes. Be careful not to overbake the layer on the highest oven rack. Remove the pans from the oven and place them on wire racks to cool for 10

minutes. Run a dinner knife around the edge of the cakes and invert each onto a rack, then invert them again onto another rack so that the cakes are right side up. Allow them to cool completely, 30 minutes.

6. Meanwhile, prepare the Marshmallow Frosting.

7. Place one cake layer, right side up, on a serving platter. Spread the top of the cake layer with half of the filling, spreading the filling with a rubber spatula up to 1 inch from the cake edge. Place the second cake layer, right side up, on top of the filling. Spread the second layer with the remaining half of the filling, spreading it up to 1 inch from the cake edge. Top the two layers with the remaining cake layer, right side up, and spread frosting on the top and sides of the cake with clean, smooth strokes. Garnish the cake generously with the coconut, pressing it around the sides and top of the cake. Slice and serve.

✳ *Store this cake, covered in waxed paper or in a cake saver, in the refrigerator for up to 1 week.*

SNOWBALLS

Y ou don't have to be looking out your kitchen window at snow on the ground to enjoy these fun individual cakes that look as if they are balls of snow. They're just a sour cream white sheet cake that has been cut into squares, spread with a creamy frosting, and then  dredged in coconut. The final results are round and very snowballish. But why divulge secrets? Your guests and your children will think that you've created something magical, indeed.

MAKES 48 SNOWBALLS
(2 INCHES EACH)
PREPARATION TIME: 10 MINUTES
BAKING TIME: 35 TO 40 MINUTES
ASSEMBLY TIME: 40 MINUTES

Solid vegetable shortening for greasing
    the pan
Flour for dusting the pan
1 package (18.25 ounces) plain white
    cake mix
1 cup sour cream
½ cup vegetable oil, such as canola, corn,
    safflower, soybean, or sunflower
3 large eggs
1 teaspoon pure vanilla extract
2 recipes Marshmallow Frosting (page 433)
1 package (12 ounces; 3 cups) frozen
    unsweetened grated coconut, thawed

1. Place a rack in the center of the oven and preheat the oven to 350°F. Generously grease a 13- by 9-inch baking pan with solid vegetable shortening, then dust with flour. Shake out the excess flour. Set the pan aside.

R

the Cake Doctor says...

This sour cream white cake recipe is a wonderful and dense formula, perfect for turning into snowballs, or for simply frosting and using as a sheet cake. The snowball process is a little messy at first, but as you continue you'll catch on as to how to keep one hand clean for spreading and the other a bit messy for rolling the snowballs in coconut.

2. Place the cake mix, sour cream, oil, eggs, and vanilla in a large mixing bowl. Blend with an electric mixer on low speed for 1 minute. Stop the machine and scrape down the sides of the bowl with a rubber spatula. Increase the mixer speed to medium and beat 2 minutes more, scraping down the sides of the bowl if needed. The batter should look well combined and thickened. Pour the batter into the prepared pan, smoothing it out with the rubber spatula. Place the pan in the oven.

3. Bake the cake until it is lightly browned and springs back when lightly pressed with your finger, 35 to 40 minutes. Remove the pan from the oven and place it on a wire rack to cool for 20 min-

utes. Run a dinner knife around the edge of the cake and invert it onto a rack, then invert it again onto another rack so that the cake is right side up. Allow it to cool completely, 30 minutes more.

4. Meanwhile, prepare two recipes of the Marshmallow Frosting, using a large saucepan.

5. Place the coconut in a shallow pan. Cut the cake into 48 squares, about 1½ inches each, making 8 slices down the long side of the pan and 6 slices across. Remove the squares and spread each on all sides with some of the Marshmallow Frosting. Roll each frosted square in coconut. Place the snowballs, as you finish them, in a single layer on large serving platters or in a single layer in plastic storage boxes. Continue the process until all the snowballs have been assembled. Cover the platters with waxed paper or place the lids on the storage boxes. Place the snowballs in the refrigerator to chill until firm, about 30 minutes. Serve at once or keep refrigerated until serving time.

✳ *Store the snowballs, lightly covered in waxed paper, in a plastic storage box with a lid in the refrigerator for up to 1 week.*

Wrap It Up

Cakes aren't just for keeping, they're for giving. Whether you are welcoming a new neighbor or celebrating a family event, whole cakes are a blessing. They can feed a crowd, and often they can go right in the freezer for thawing and serving later. Here are some suggestions for ways you can wrap up a whole cake and present it or mail it to a friend.

- *Layer cakes, tubes, and Bundt cakes:* Buy white cake boxes from a local bakery, or order white and colored boxes (even monogrammed) from the Williams-Sonoma catalog. Or, present the cake in a plastic cake saver, which you can purchase at discount and housewares stores.

  Cakes can be frozen right in the cake saver, so they are quite practical. And unlike cake boxes, these cake savers can tote cakes for years so they are cost efficient.

  Another attractive and practical way to wrap a whole, unfrosted cake is to place it on a cardboard cake round, which you can purchase wherever cake-decorating supplies are sold. Wrap the whole cake generously with plastic or clear cellophane, and tie a ribbon at the top.

- *Cake loaves:* Pour the batter into lightweight aluminum pans from the grocery store. Bake, cool in the pan, then wrap in aluminum foil or snap on a plastic lid that now comes with these pans.

- *Bars and brownies:* Cool, cut, and transfer to a pretty paper plate and overwrap in clear cellophane. Tie with a taffeta bow. Or, place bars in aluminum pans with snap-on plastic lids, in decorated boxes from gift shops, in mesh baskets lined with parchment paper, or in straw baskets lined with a new kitchen towel.

- *You've got cake mail:* The sturdier the cake, the better it will survive the rigors of shipping. Bundts, tubes, and loaves are the best mailers. The cake will ship better if it is unfrosted or has just a simple glaze.

  Place the cake on a cardboard cake round, wrap well in plastic wrap, then aluminum foil, and put the cake in a heavy cardboard box surrounded by foam peanuts.

GINGERBREAD HOUSE

As Christmas drew nearer, I wondered if it would be possible to create a gingerbread house from a spice cake mix. The trick would be to make a batter that could be rolled easily but not rise in the oven. And in spite of all the emulsifiers added to keep the mix moist, this house would have to be sturdy, crisp, and dry. Well, I did it! After some tinkering I found that by adding oil, either sorghum or molasses, and ground ginger you have a tight but workable dough that can be rolled and cut into sections of the house. And the ginger in the dough smells wonderful and gets everyone in the holiday mood! Our house ended up looking more like a festive country church than a house. The children decorated it with gobs of hard candies and gumdrops on the sides, and slivered almonds for the roof, and all was well affixed with royal icing. The uncooked royal icing makes this house one meant for visual enjoyment, not for eating.

MAKES 1 GINGERBREAD HOUSE
PREPARATION TIME: 45 MINUTES
BAKING TIME: 15 TO 17 MINUTES
COOLING TIME: OVERNIGHT
ASSEMBLY TIME: 60 MINUTES

CAKE

2 packages (18.25 ounces each) plain spice
*   cake mix*

1 tablespoon ground ginger

1 cup vegetable oil, such as canola, corn,
*   safflower, soybean, or sunflower*

1 cup sorghum syrup or molasses

1 to 2 tablespoons water, if needed

¼ cup all-purpose flour

ROYAL ICING:

5 cups confectioners' sugar, sifted

5 large egg whites

CANDY DECORATIONS:

Assorted peppermint sticks, hard candy mix,
*   licorice, gumdrops, and slivered almonds*

1. Place a rack in the center of the oven and preheat the oven to 375°F. Set aside 3 ungreased baking sheets.

2. Place the cake mix, ginger, oil, and sorghum or molasses in a large mixing bowl. Blend with an electric mixer on low speed until the mixture comes together

into a ball, 1 minute. Stop the machine and add water as needed to make the dough come together and be firm but still workable. Blend again at low speed to incorporate the water.

3. Sprinkle flour over a clean work surface and roll the dough out to a ¼ inch thickness. Using a ruler and a sharp knife, cut six rectangles from the dough, each 7 by 4½ inches. With floured fingers or with a metal spatula, place four of the rectangles on two of the baking sheets. Place the baking sheets in the refrigerator.

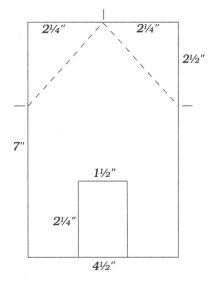

4. Make the peaked roof. Using a ruler and knife, mark the midpoint of one of the short ends of the two remaining rectangles (about 2¼ inches in). From that end, measure and mark 2½ inches along both of the long sides. Place the ruler on the

R

the Cake Doctor says...

It's important that the gingerbread bake long enough to dry it out, and that it have time to cool so that it is dry before assembling.

dough going from the midpoint mark to the mark along one long side to form a corner triangle. Cut away the triangle. Repeat this from the midpoint mark to the mark on the other long side. Mark and cut the remaining rectangle of dough the same way. Carefully place the peaked pieces and the four triangles on the third baking sheet. On the flat end of one of the peaked pieces, cut out a piece 2¼ inches high and 1½ inches wide. This will be the door. Place this door back on the baking sheet. Remove the baking sheets from the refrigerator and place all three in the oven. If your oven is not large enough, place two pans on the center rack and place the third pan in the center of the highest rack.

5. Bake until the dough is lightly brown and firm, 15 to 17 minutes. Be careful not to overbake the sheet on the highest rack. Remove the pans to wire racks to cool for

5 minutes. The dough may puff up but you just need to press it back down with the back of a metal spatula. Carefully slide a spatula underneath the pieces of the house and place them on racks to cool overnight.

6. The next day, prepare the Royal Icing. Place the confectioners' sugar and egg whites in a large mixing bowl. Blend with an electric mixer on low speed for 1 minute. Stop the machine and scrape down the sides of the bowl with a rubber spatula. Increase the mixer speed to medium and beat 2 minutes more, scraping the sides of the bowl down again if needed. The icing should look smooth and thick.

7. When you are ready to assemble the gingerbread house, fill a pastry tube with the Royal Icing, if you have one, or just use a dinner knife. Cover a tray with waxed paper or plastic wrap to protect it. Join one peaked piece and the short side of one side piece with royal icing at the inside corner seam. Support the pieces with small water glasses pushed right up next to them. Do the same for the other peaked piece and side piece, then join the four pieces at the two remaining inside corner seams. Let this frame dry for 1 hour. Place the roof rectangle at an angle over the house and affix along the edges with icing. Place the second roof rectangle at an angle over the house. It will overlap the first. Affix it to the edges and along the top of the roof with icing. If you wish, use the triangles and the royal icing to create a chimney sticking out of the roof. Place the triangles so that the short flat sides form the top of the chimney. Affix the chimney to the roof with royal icing. Seal the tops together with icing. Let this dry for 1 hour. During this time you can pipe or spread royal icing around the house and create candy landscaping, with gumdrops for shrubs and candy canes for a walkway, if desired. If the sides seem secure you can go ahead and decorate the sides and ends with candy, spreading them with a little icing before gently pushing them against the gingerbread.

8. When the roof has dried, spread the roof with icing and sprinkle over lots of slivered almonds to look like roofing tiles. Attach the front door using royal icing, if desired, and decorate the door with candies. Let the house dry out well, a day or so, before transporting it.

✳ *This gingerbread house keeps at room temperature in a dry room for 2 to 3 weeks.*

Cheesecakes and Gooey Cakes

• • •

Y ou would have thought that after tasting hundreds of cakes made from a mix—pinching off a corner of cake on the way out the door in the morning, searching like a hungry child for a bite of something sweet after dinner—my husband would grow jaded. And I'll admit that during the height of testing, at our house it was common to see a dozen aluminum foil–wrapped plates on the counter and a half-dozen plastic-draped cakes in the refrigerator. We shared with friends, family, and John's colleagues at work, but frankly, we were up to our eyebrows in cake. However, when those cheesecakes appeared, well, it seemed as if John had been awakened from a dull, sweet, cake-free slumber. He forked into our New York–style Cheesecake and smiled, then into Mindy's Ricotta Cheesecake and looked amused, then into the Chocolate Mocha Swirl Cheesecake and was intrigued, then into the Pumpkin Spice Cheesecake and was placated. "How did you do this?" he wondered out loud. "This is amazing."

Amazing, yes, to turn a cake mix into a dense and creamy cheesecake, but certainly not difficult. Nor is it tough to begin with a mix and end up with one of the five wonderful Gooey Butter Cakes also in this chapter. Gooey cakes are a cross between a sheet cake and a bar. They're so soft you'll need a fork to savor each bite, but they have the firm crust of a bar cookie. In both, the cake mix, some butter, and an egg form the crust or the foundation for what will be poured on top. It is a perfect slab with which to begin, for the fillings of these two styles of cake are by no means lightweight!

Yes, this chapter should be called "Blow Your Diet" or "Nothing Is Too Rich, Too Sinful . . ." But, alas, I believe almost everyone can enjoy a slice of these cakes in good conscience, even if it is a sliver. And that may be all you want, which is why they are so suitable for feeding a crowd. You can cut the pieces small. You can also bake them ahead of time (they refrigerate well).

I found that these cakes work best baked in a shiny metal 13- by 9-inch baking pan. I also noticed that they bake up with a ridge around the outside, which is what test kitchens refer to as "curbing." It sounds like a traffic violation, doesn't it? Well, I like this curbing because the crusty edges contrast with the smooth and creamy center.

NEW YORK–STYLE CHEESECAKE

When you're tired of the bells and whistles, and you want down-to-earth, honest-to-goodness cheesecake, then this recipe is the one. Without spices and chocolate and flavorings, the true blast of cheesecake flavor comes through. There is a little lemon juice in the filling, and you could easily add some lemon or orange zest, but I tried to keep this one simple!

SERVES: 20

PREPARATION TIME: 15 MINUTES

BAKING TIME:
42 TO 50 MINUTES

CRUST AND FILLING:

Softened butter or solid vegetable shortening
    for greasing the pan

1 package (18.25 ounces) plain white
    cake mix

4 tablespoons (½ stick) butter, melted

4 large eggs

2 packages (8 ounces each) cream cheese,
    at room temperature

1 can (14 ounces) sweetened
    condensed milk

½ cup sour cream

2 tablespoons fresh lemon juice

2 teaspoons pure vanilla extract

TOPPING:

1 cup sour cream

¼ cup sugar

Cheesecake : Not an American Invention

When we think of cheesecake and smile, we most often think of the smooth and creamy cheesecake called either Jewish-style, New York–style, or Lindy's, named after the famous New York City restaurant. The other variation is the Italian cheesecake containing ricotta cheese. And whereas delis and restaurants in America's metropolitan areas have been serving up cheesecake for a century, European cheesecakes have been baked centuries earlier. In fact, the first cheesecake is said to have been baked in the Aegean Islands as early as A.D. 250. Cooks forced cheese through a sieve and combined it with flour and honey before baking. Nowa-

days, cheesecakes can be baked with a cookie crust like the Lindy's style, with a crushed graham cracker crust, with a cake mix as this book suggests, or with no crust at all like those earliest cheesecakes.

But not all cheesecake is made of cream cheese, flavored with vanilla and sugar, and baked. In 1912, a comely actress posed for photographers at a ship's rail in New York harbor, and the gusting wind caused her dress to rise well above accepted levels. According to James Trager in *The Food Chronology*, the ready reporters who caught sight of her exposed flesh referred to it as "cheesecake."

1. Place a rack in the center of the oven and preheat the oven to 325°F. Lightly grease a 13- by 9-inch baking pan with softened butter or vegetable shortening. Set the pan aside.

2. Measure out ½ cup of the cake mix and set aside for the filling.

3. Place the remaining cake mix, the melted butter, and 1 egg in a large mixing bowl. Blend with an electric mixer on low speed for 2 minutes. Stop the machine

and scrape down the sides of the bowl with a rubber spatula. The batter should come together in a ball. With your fingertips, pat the batter evenly over the bottom and 1 inch up the sides of the prepared pan, smoothing it out with your fingers until the top is smooth. Set the pan aside.

4. For the filling, place the cream cheese and the sweetened condensed milk in the same mixing bowl that was used to make the crust, and with the same beaters (no

R

the Cake Doctor says...

Although this cake allows true cheesecake flavor to ring through, it cries out
for a topping of sweetened sliced
peaches or nectarines when they are in
season.

need to clean either) blend with an electric
mixer on low speed until just combined,
30 seconds. Stop the machine and add the
reserved cake mix, the remaining 3 eggs,
the sour cream, lemon juice, and vanilla
and beat on medium speed for 1 minute.
Stop the machine and scrape the sides of
the bowl with a rubber spatula. Pour the
filling onto the crust and spread with the
rubber spatula so that the filling covers
the entire surface and reaches the sides of
the pan. Place the pan in the oven.

5. Bake the cheesecake until it looks
shiny and the center no longer jiggles when
you shake the pan. 35 to 40 minutes.
Remove the pan from the oven while you
prepare the topping. Leave the oven on.

6. For the topping, place the sour cream
and sugar in a small mixing bowl and stir
with a spoon until well combined. Pour
the topping over the cheesecake, and
return the pan to the oven.

7. Bake until the topping sets, 7 to 10
minutes. Remove the pan from the oven
and place it on a wire rack to cool, 30 minutes. Lightly cover the pan with plastic
wrap and place the pan in the refrigerator
to chill for at least 1 hour, but preferably
24 hours for the flavors to meld. Cut into
squares and serve.

✳ *Store this cake, covered in plastic
wrap or aluminum foil, in the refrigerator
for up to 1 week. Or freeze it, wrapped in
foil, for up to 2 months. Thaw the cake
overnight in the refrigerator before serving.*

PUMPKIN SPICE CHEESECAKE

If you're asked to bring dessert to the Thanksgiving feast, this dessert will please both the pumpkin pie fans and those who love cheesecake. You begin with a spice cake mix, and you end up with a dessert that's delicious, keeps well, and feeds plenty. Vary the spices to suit your taste, but don't forget the topping of sour cream and brown sugar.

SERVES: 20
PREPARATION TIME: 15 MINUTES
BAKING TIME: 47 TO 55 MINUTES

CRUST AND FILLING:

Softened butter or solid vegetable shortening
     for greasing the pan
1 package (18.25 ounces) plain spice
     cake mix
4 tablespoons (½ stick) butter, melted
4 large eggs
2 packages (8 ounces each) cream cheese,
     at room temperature
1 can (14 ounces) sweetened
     condensed milk
1 cup canned pumpkin
½ cup packed light brown sugar
½ teaspoon ground cinnamon
¼ teaspoon ground nutmeg
¼ teaspoon ground ginger

TOPPING:

1 cup sour cream
¼ cup packed light brown sugar

R

the Cake Doctor says...

You can substitute pureed unsweetened butternut squash for the pumpkin in this cheesecake. Cut the squash in half lengthwise and remove the seeds and membranes. Peel the halves, then cut the squash into chunks. Place in a large saucepan, add water to cover, and bring to a boil over high heat. Reduce the heat and cook the squash until soft, about 15 minutes. Drain and cool the squash, then puree it in a food processor. You'll need 1 cup for this recipe; enjoy any extra with a little butter and salt as a dinner side dish.

1. Place a rack in the center of the oven and preheat the oven to 325°F. Lightly grease a 13- by 9-inch baking pan with the softened butter or vegetable shortening. Set the pan aside.

2. Measure out ½ cup of the cake mix and set aside for the filling.

3. Place the remaining cake mix, the melted butter, and 1 egg in a large mixing bowl. Blend with an electric mixer on low speed for 2 minutes. Stop the machine and scrape down the sides of the bowl with a rubber spatula. The batter should come together in a ball. With your fingertips, pat the batter evenly over the bottom and 1 inch up the sides of the prepared pan, smoothing it out with your fingers until the top is smooth. Set the pan aside.

4. For the filling, place the cream cheese and the sweetened condensed milk in the same mixing bowl that was used to make the crust, and with the same beaters (no need to clean either) blend with an electric mixer on low speed until just combined, 30 seconds. Stop the machine and add the reserved cake mix, the remaining 3 eggs, the pumpkin, brown sugar, cinnamon, nutmeg, and ginger and beat on medium speed for 1 minute. Stop the machine and scrape down the sides of the bowl with the rubber spatula. Pour the filling onto the crust and spread with the rubber spatula so that the filling covers the entire surface and reaches the sides of the pan. Place the pan in the oven.

5. Bake the cheesecake until it looks shiny and the center no longer jiggles when you shake the pan, 40 to 45 minutes. Remove the pan from the oven while you prepare the topping. Leave the oven on.

6. For the topping, place the sour cream and brown sugar in a small mixing bowl

Don't Overbake Your Cheesecake

Cheesecakes that have been cooked too long are more tough than creamy. Be sure to check for doneness several times during the baking process. The best gauge is to see if the center of the cheesecake looks shiny, and not flat. Then it is done.

- Remember that cheesecakes will continue to cook after they are removed from the oven. If they have cracked, they are overbaked.

- Let cheesecakes cool, then place them in the refrigerator lightly covered with plastic wrap to firm and mature. They will improve in flavor, and they will be easier to slice.

- However, cheesecake tastes best at room temperature. To slice cheesecake, first dip your knife into warm water each time you slice. Wipe it dry before slicing.

and stir with a spoon until well combined. Pour the topping over the cheesecake, and return the pan to the oven.

7. Bake until the topping sets, 7 to 10 minutes. Remove the pan from the oven and place it on a wire rack to cool, 30 minutes. Lightly cover the pan with plastic wrap and place the pan in the refrigerator to chill for at least 1 hour, but preferably 24 hours for the flavors to meld. Cut into squares and serve.

❋ *Store this cake, covered in plastic wrap or aluminum foil, in the refrigerator for up to 1 week. Or freeze it, wrapped in foil, for up to 2 months. Thaw the cake overnight in the refrigerator before serving.*

FRESH LIME CHEESECAKE

When the weather warms and you're looking for a dessert to cap off a dinner from the grill, then think no further than this terrific cheesecake. Key limes are pretty rare, but if you can find these small, round, yellow-flesh limes at a specialty market, their tart juice will really make this dessert. Rest assured, lime is not only a flavor mate for cream cheese, but it's also a refreshing note on which to end a meal.

SERVES: 20

PREPARATION TIME: 15 MINUTES

BAKING TIME: 45 TO 50 MINUTES

Softened butter or solid vegetable shortening for greasing the pan

1 package (18.25 ounces) plain yellow cake mix

4 tablespoons (½ stick) butter, melted

4 large eggs

2 packages (8 ounces each) cream cheese, at room temperature

1 can (14 ounces) sweetened condensed milk

1 tablespoon grated lime zest

½ cup fresh lime juice (from 3 to 5 regular limes or 6 to 10 Key limes)

1 cup Sweetened Cream (page 432) or frozen whipped topping, thawed, for serving

1. Place a rack in the center of the oven and preheat the oven to 325°F. Lightly grease a 13- by 9-inch baking pan with the softened butter or vegetable shortening. Set the pan aside.

2. Measure out ½ cup of the cake mix and set aside for the filling.

3. Place the remaining cake mix, the melted butter, and 1 egg in a large mixing bowl. Blend with an electric mixer on low speed for 2 minutes. Stop the machine and scrape down the sides of the bowl with a rubber spatula. The batter should come together in a ball. With your fingertips, pat the batter evenly over the bottom and 1 inch up the sides of the prepared pan, smoothing it out with your fingers until the top is smooth. Set the pan aside.

4. For the filling, place the cream cheese and the sweetened condensed milk in the same mixing bowl that was used to make the crust, and with the same beaters (no need to clean either) blend with an electric mixer on low speed until just combined, 30 seconds. Stop the machine and add the reserved cake mix, the remaining 3 eggs, the lime zest, and lime juice and beat on medium speed for 1 minute. Stop the machine and scrape down the sides of the bowl with a rubber spatula. Pour the filling onto the crust and spread with the rubber spatula so that the filling covers the entire surface and reaches the sides of the pan. Place the pan in the oven.

5. Bake the cheesecake until it looks shiny and the center no longer jiggles when you shake the pan, 45 to 50 minutes. Remove the pan from the oven and place it on a wire rack to cool, 30 minutes. Lightly cover the pan with plastic wrap and place the pan in the refrigerator to chill for at least 1 hour, but preferably 24 hours for the flavors to meld. Cut into squares and serve with a dollop of Sweetened Cream.

✳ *Store this cake, covered in plastic wrap or aluminum foil, in the refrigerator for up to 1 week. Or freeze it, wrapped in foil, for up to 2 months. Thaw the cake overnight in the refrigerator before serving.*

R

the Cake Doctor says...

If you can purchase bottled Key lime juice, by all means substitute it for the regular fresh lime juice. And if using bottled Key lime juice, you don't really need to buy fresh limes just to add the zest. It can be omitted..

SWEET-TART CHERRY CHEESECAKE

Whereas one of the traditional toppings to cheesecake is cherry pie filling, I think a far more interesting way to meld cherries and cheesecake is to add dried cherries. These tart cherries soak up all  the cheesecake flavor and moisture and after downing just one thin slice, you'd swear you were on your aunt's cherry farm in southern Michigan. Just wait until you taste a spoonful of this dreamy cheesecake!

SERVES: 20

PREPARATION TIME: 15 MINUTES

BAKING TIME: 45 TO 50 MINUTES

Softened butter or solid vegetable
shortening for greasing the pan
1 package (18.25 ounces) plain white
cake mix
4 tablespoons (½ stick) butter, melted
4 large eggs
2 packages (8 ounces each) cream cheese,
at room temperature
1 can (14 ounces) sweetened condensed milk
½ cup sour cream
1 teaspoon pure vanilla extract
½ teaspoon pure almond extract
1 cup finely chopped dried tart cherries

1. Place a rack in the center of the oven and preheat the oven to 325°F. Lightly grease a 13- by 9-inch baking pan with softened butter or vegetable shortening. Set the pan aside.

2. Measure out ½ cup of the cake mix and set aside for the filling.

R

the Cake Doctor says...

White cake mixes take well to the addition of cherries. Although they are not directly in the cake layer here, they seem to spark a better flavor from it.

3. Place the remaining cake mix, the melted butter, and 1 egg in a large mixing bowl. Blend with an electric mixer on low speed for 2 minutes. Stop the machine and scrape down the sides of the bowl with a rubber spatula. The batter should come together in a ball. With your fingertips, pat the batter evenly over the bottom and 1 inch up the sides of the prepared pan, smoothing it out with your fingers until the top is smooth. Set the pan aside.

4. For the filling, place the cream cheese and the sweetened condensed milk in the same mixing bowl that was used to make the crust, and with the same beaters (no need to clean either) blend with an electric mixer on low speed until just combined, 30 seconds. Stop the machine and add the reserved cake mix, the remaining 3 eggs, the sour cream, vanilla and almond extracts, and the cherries and beat on medium speed for 1 minute. Stop the

machine and scrape down the sides of the bowl with a rubber spatula. Pour the filling onto the crust and spread with the rubber spatula so that the filling covers the entire surface and reaches the sides of the pan. Place the pan in the oven.

5. Bake the cheesecake until it looks shiny and the center no longer jiggles when you shake the pan, 45 to 50 minutes. Remove the pan from the oven and place it on a wire rack to cool, 30 minutes. Lightly cover the pan with plastic wrap and place the pan in the refrigerator to chill for at least 1 hour, but preferably 24 hours for the flavors to meld. Cut into squares and serve.

✳ *Store this cake, covered in plastic wrap or aluminum foil, in the refrigerator for up to 1 week. Or freeze it, wrapped in foil, for up to 2 months. Thaw the cake overnight in the refrigerator before serving.*

CHOCOLATE MOCHA SWIRL CHEESECAKE

Pour yourself a cup of coffee, for this cheesecake is about the best partner that steaming cup of java will ever have. Does that make it a coffee cake and a cheesecake? Perhaps. Just depends on what time of day you want to fork into this coffee-scented cheesecake with the chocolate swirl and chocolate crust—in the wee hours of the

morning, during the afternoon, or before bed. It's a winner all day!

SERVES: 20

PREPARATION TIME: 15 MINUTES

BAKING TIME: 35 TO 40 MINUTES

Softened butter or solid vegetable
   shortening for greasing the pan
1 package (18.25 ounces) plain devil's food
   cake mix
4 tablespoons (½ stick) butter, melted
4 large eggs
2 packages (8 ounces each) cream cheese,
   at room temperature
1 can (14 ounces) sweetened condensed milk
½ cup sour cream
2 teaspoons pure vanilla extract
1 tablespoon instant coffee powder
2 ounces semisweet or bittersweet chocolate,
   melted

1. Place a rack in the center of the oven and preheat the oven to 325°F. Lightly grease a 13- by 9-inch baking pan with softened butter or vegetable shortening. Set the pan aside.

2. Measure out ½ cup of the cake mix and set aside for the filling.

3. Place the remaining cake mix, the melted butter, and 1 egg in a large mixing bowl. Blend with an electric mixer on low speed for 2 minutes. Stop the machine and scrape down the sides of the bowl with a rubber spatula. The batter should come together in a ball. With your fingertips, pat the batter evenly over the bottom and 1 inch up the sides of the prepared pan, smoothing it out with your fingers until the top is smooth. Set the pan aside.

4. For the filling, place the cream cheese and the sweetened condensed milk in the same mixing bowl that was used to make the crust, and with the same beaters (no need to clean either) blend with an electric mixer on low speed until just combined, 30 seconds. Stop the machine and add the reserved cake mix, the remaining 3 eggs, the sour cream, vanilla, and coffee powder and beat on medium speed for 1 minute. Stop the machine and scrape down the sides of the bowl with a rubber spatula. Remove 1 cup of the batter, place it in a small bowl, and whisk in the melted chocolate until the mixture is well combined. Set the chocolate mixture aside.

5. Pour the coffee-flavored filling onto the crust and spread with the rubber spatula so that the filling covers the entire surface and reaches the sides of the pan. With a tablespoon, drop chocolate mixture on top

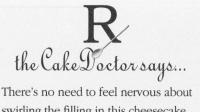

the Cake Doctor says...

There's no need to feel nervous about swirling the filling in this cheesecake. Use a dinner knife to make figure eights, zigzags, or wavy lines to create a marbled look. And don't worry about poking the crust by mistake. It's really pretty sturdy.

of the filling. With a dinner knife, swirl the chocolate mixture around in the batter to create a marbled effect. Place the pan in the oven.

6. Bake the cheesecake until it looks shiny and the center no longer jiggles when you shake the pan, 35 to 40 minutes. Remove the pan from the oven and place it on a wire rack to cool, 30 minutes. Lightly cover the pan with plastic wrap and place the pan in the refrigerator to chill for at least 1 hour, but preferably 24 hours for the flavors to meld. Cut into squares and serve.

✻ *Store this cake, covered in plastic wrap or aluminum foil, in the refrigerator for up to 1 week. Or freeze it, wrapped in foil, for up to 2 months. Thaw the cake overnight in the refrigerator before serving.*

TOFFEE CRUNCH CHEESECAKE

Add chocolate-flavored sweetened condensed milk to the filling, pour a bag of toffee candy chips over the top, and you've got a cheesecake the children will love. In fact, it's a cheesecake the children can bake with you. With a little supervision—heating the oven, running the electric mixer, removing the hot pan from the oven—even young school-children can assemble and bake this cake.

SERVES: 20

PREPARATION TIME: 15 MINUTES

BAKING TIME: 40 TO 45 MINUTES

Softened butter or solid vegetable shortening for greasing the pan

1 package (18.25 ounces) plain yellow cake mix

4 tablespoons (½ stick) butter, melted

4 large eggs

2 packages (8 ounces each) cream cheese, at room temperature

1 can (14 ounces) chocolate sweetened condensed milk

½ cup sour cream

1 teaspoon pure vanilla extract

1 package (6 ounces; 1 cup) toffee chips, such as Heath Bar

1. Place a rack in the center of the oven and preheat the oven to 325°F. Lightly grease a 13- by 9-inch baking pan with softened butter or vegetable shortening. Set the pan aside.

R

the Cake Doctor says...

Want more crunch? Add a handful of chopped unsalted roasted peanuts along with the toffee chips. Want more chocolate? Add a handful of miniature chocolate chips.

2. Measure out ½ cup of the cake mix and set aside for the filling.

3. Place the remaining cake mix, the melted butter, and 1 egg in a large mixing bowl. Blend with an electric mixer on low speed for 2 minutes. Stop the machine and scrape down the sides of the bowl with a rubber spatula. The batter should come together in a ball. With your fingertips, pat the batter evenly over the bottom and 1 inch up the sides of the prepared pan, smoothing it out with your fingers until the top is smooth. Set the pan aside.

4. For the filling, place the cream cheese and the chocolate sweetened condensed milk in the same mixing bowl that was used to make the crust, and with the same beaters (no need to clean either) blend with an electric mixer on low speed until just combined, 30 seconds. Stop the

machine and add the reserved cake mix, the remaining 3 eggs, the sour cream, vanilla, and all but ¼ cup of the toffee chips and beat on medium speed for 1 minute. Stop the machine and scrape down the sides of the bowl with a rubber spatula. Pour the filling onto the crust and spread with the rubber spatula so that the filling covers the entire surface and reaches the sides of the pan. Sprinkle evenly with the remaining toffee chips. Place the pan in the oven.

5. Bake the cheesecake until it looks shiny and the center no longer jiggles when you shake the pan, 40 to 45 minutes. Remove the pan from the oven and place it on a wire rack to cool, 30 minutes. Lightly cover the pan with plastic wrap and place the pan in the refrigerator to chill for at least 1 hour, but preferably 24 hours for the flavors to meld. Cut into squares and serve.

✴ *Store this cake, covered in plastic wrap or aluminum foil, in the refrigerator for up to 1 week. Or freeze it, wrapped in foil, for up to 2 months. Thaw the cake overnight in the refrigerator before serving.*

MINDY'S RICOTTA CHEESECAKE

My friend and tester Mindy Merrell has baked a lot of cheesecakes in her life, and she did her magic on this recipe. It is of the Italian cheesecake school, containing ricotta cheese instead of cream cheese and incorporating flavors like Marsala wine, golden raisins, and almonds. This cake not only bakes up golden and picture-perfect, it is scrumptious as well.

SERVES: 20

PREPARATION TIME: 15 MINUTES

BAKING TIME: 50 TO 55 MINUTES

Softened butter or solid vegetable shortening
    for greasing the pan
1 package (18.25 ounces) plain white cake
    mix
4 tablespoons (½ stick) butter, melted
4 large eggs
2 cups ricotta cheese
1 can (14 ounces) sweetened
    condensed milk
2 tablespoons Marsala wine or medium-
    sweet sherry
1 teaspoon pure vanilla extract
¼ teaspoon pure almond extract
½ cup golden raisins
½ cup sliced almonds

1. Place a rack in the center of the oven and preheat the oven to 325°F. Lightly grease a 13- by 9-inch baking pan with softened butter or vegetable shortening. Set the pan aside.

R

the Cake Doctor says...

If you don't have Marsala wine or sherry, it's okay to omit it completely or substitute fresh-squeezed or from-the-carton orange juice.

2. Measure out ½ cup of the cake mix and set aside for the filling.

3. Place the remaining cake mix, the melted butter, and 1 egg in a large mixing bowl. Blend with an electric mixer on low speed for 2 minutes. Stop the machine and scrape down the sides of the bowl with a rubber spatula. The batter should come together in a ball. With your fingertips, pat the batter evenly over the bottom and 1 inch up the sides of the prepared pan, smoothing it out with your fingers until the top is smooth. Set the pan aside.

4. For the filling, place the ricotta cheese and the sweetened condensed milk in the same mixing bowl that was used to make the crust, and with the same beaters (no need to clean either) blend with an electric mixer on low speed until just combined, 30 seconds to 1 minute. Stop the machine and add the reserved cake mix, the remaining 3 eggs, the Marsala wine, and

the vanilla and almond extracts and beat on medium speed for 1 minute. Stop the machine and scrape down the sides of the bowl with a rubber spatula. Fold in the golden raisins. Pour the filling onto the crust and spread with the rubber spatula so that the filling covers the entire surface and reaches the sides of the pan. Sprinkle the top with the almonds. Place the pan in the oven.

5. Bake the cheesecake until the center no longer jiggles when you shake the pan and the almonds looked toasted, 50 to 55 minutes. Remove the pan from the oven and place it on a wire rack to cool, 30 minutes. Lightly cover the pan with plastic wrap and place the pan in the refrigerator to chill for at least 1 hour, but preferably 24 hours for the flavors to meld. Cut into squares and serve.

✳ *Store this cake, covered in plastic wrap or aluminum foil, in the refrigerator for up to 1 week. Or freeze it, wrapped in foil, for up to 2 months. Thaw the cake overnight in the refrigerator before serving.*

Gooey Butter Cake

Also known as Ooey-Gooey Cake, this little gem has been handed down by word of mouth for years. It's built on a layer of cake mix, butter, and egg that you then cover with a rich filling of cream cheese, eggs, vanilla, confectioners' sugar, and more butter. It's not shy of calories, mind you! Tote it to a picnic or potluck supper, and do experiment with one of the variations on Gooey Butter Cake that follow, or make up your own!

SERVES: 20

PREPARATION TIME:
10 TO 12 MINUTES

BAKING TIME: 45 TO 47 MINUTES

CRUST:

1 package (18.25 ounces) plain yellow
    cake mix
8 tablespoons (1 stick) butter, melted
1 large egg

FILLING:

1 package (8 ounces) cream cheese,
    at room temperature
2 large eggs
1 teaspoon pure vanilla extract
8 tablespoons (1 stick) butter, melted
3¾ cups confectioners' sugar,
    sifted

1. Place a rack in the center of the oven and preheat the oven to 350°F. Set aside an ungreased 13- by 9-inch baking pan.

2. For the crust, place the cake mix, melted butter, and egg in a large mixing bowl. Blend with an electric mixer on low speed for 2 minutes. Stop the machine and scrape down the sides of the bowl with a rubber spatula. The batter should come together in a ball. With your fingertips, pat the batter evenly over the bottom of the pan, smoothing it out with your fingers until the top is smooth. Set the pan aside.

3. For the filling, place the cream cheese in the same mixing bowl that was used to make the crust, and with the same beaters (no need to clean either) blend with an electric mixer on low speed until fluffy, 30 seconds. Stop the machine and add the eggs, vanilla, and melted butter and beat on medium speed for 1 minute. Stop the machine and add the confectioners' sugar. Beat on medium speed until the sugar is well incorporated, 1 minute more. Stop the machine and scrape down the sides of the bowl with a rubber spatula. Pour the filling onto the crust and spread with the rubber spatula so that the filling covers the entire surface and reaches the sides of the pan. Place the pan in the oven.

4. Bake the cake until it is well browned but the center still jiggles when you shake the pan, 45 to 47 minutes. Remove the pan from the oven and place it on a wire rack to cool, 30 minutes. Cut into squares and serve.

✳ *Store this cake, covered in aluminum foil, at room temperature for up to 4 days or in the refrigerator for up to 1 week. Or freeze it, wrapped in foil, for up to 6 months. Thaw the cake overnight in the refrigerator before serving.*

the Cake Doctor says...

Cake mix provides just the right support system for a wonderfully gooey layer on top. What results is a crusty, chewy pastry with an almost pie-like consistency to the filling.

ALMOND GOOEY BUTTER CAKE

By simply adding a little pure almond extract and a handful of slivered almonds, you can turn the basic Gooey Butter Cake into an almond rendition. It's for tried-and-true almond lovers, but then, my children loved it not knowing all the goodies inside!

....

SERVES: 20

PREPARATION TIME: 15 MINUTES

BAKING TIME: 45 TO 47 MINUTES

....

CRUST:

1 package (18.25 ounces) plain yellow
   cake mix

8 tablespoons (1 stick) butter, melted

1 large egg

½ cup slivered almonds

FILLING:

1 package (8 ounces) cream cheese,
   at room temperature

2 large eggs

1 teaspoon pure almond extract

8 tablespoons (1 stick) butter, melted

3¾ cups confectioners' sugar, sifted

1. Place a rack in the center of the oven and preheat the oven to 350°F. Set aside an ungreased 13- by 9-inch baking pan.

2. For the crust, place the cake mix, melted butter, egg, and almonds in a large mixing bowl. Blend with an electric mixer on low speed for 2 minutes. Stop the machine and scrape down the sides of the bowl with a rubber spatula. The batter should come together in a ball. With your fingertips, pat the batter evenly over the bottom of the pan, smoothing it out with your fingers until the top is smooth. Set the pan aside.

3. For the filling, place the cream cheese in the same mixing bowl that was used to make the crust, and with the same beaters (no need to clean either) blend with an

R

the Cake Doctor says...

If you have some almond paste on hand, crumble ¼ cup of it and add it to the crust mix in step 2. Don't go overboard—any more than ¼ cup will cause the crust to burn.

electric mixer on low speed until fluffy, 30 seconds. Stop the machine and add the eggs, almond extract, and melted butter and beat on medium speed for 1 minute. Stop the machine and add the confectioners' sugar. Beat on medium speed until the sugar is well incorporated, 1 minute more.

Stop the machine and scrape down the sides of the bowl with the rubber spatula. Pour the filling onto the crust and spread with the rubber spatula so that the filling covers the entire surface and reaches the sides of the pan. Place the pan in the oven.

4. Bake the cake until it is well browned but the center still jiggles when you shake the pan, 45 to 47 minutes. Remove the pan from the oven and place it on a wire rack to cool, 30 minutes. Cut into squares and serve.

✻ *Store this cake, covered in aluminum foil, at room temperature for up to 4 days or in the refrigerator up to 1 week. Or freeze it, wrapped in foil, for up to 6 months. Thaw the cake overnight in the refrigerator before serving.*

Confectioner's Sugar

Confectioners', or powdered, sugar is a key ingredient in the Gooey Butter Cakes (pages 240 to 251), and in the frostings and glazes later on in this book. It is essentially powdered granulated sugar to which some cornstarch has been added to prevent caking. But inevitably, some lumps remain, in both the XXX sugar and the XXXX slightly finer sugar. That is why, when making frosting, you must first sift or strain it through a fine-mesh sieve. Nothing is more aggravating than lumps in your frosting that you just cannot remove with beating or by mashing with the back of a spoon. It's not as important to sift before adding confectioners' sugar to batters and fillings.

I favor buying confectioners' sugar in the plastic bag instead of the box because the sugar has fewer lumps to begin with. To seal the bag after opening, fold the top back down and attach a piece of tape.

CHOCOLATE MARBLE GOOEY BUTTER CAKE

Marbling was first seen in the 1870s, when molasses or ground spices were used to tint part of a batter that was then swirled with a spoon or knife into the remaining batter and baked.

Later marbled cakes contained chocolate. My favorite marble cakes call for chocolate; and in this easy recipe it is chocolate chips that are melted, mixed with a little batter, and swirled into the gooey butter mixture. It's a keeper.

SERVES: 20

PREPARATION TIME: 15 MINUTES

BAKING TIME:
45 TO 47 MINUTES

CRUST:

1 package (18.25 ounces) plain yellow
    cake mix
8 tablespoons (1 stick) butter, melted
1 large egg

FILLING:

1 package (8 ounces) cream cheese,
    at room temperature
2 large eggs
1 teaspoon pure vanilla extract
8 tablespoons (1 stick) butter, melted
3¾ cups confectioners' sugar, sifted
1 package (6 ounces; 1 cup) semisweet
    chocolate chips

1. Place a rack in the center of the oven and preheat the oven to 350°F. Set aside an ungreased 13- by 9-inch baking pan.

2. For the crust, place the cake mix, melted butter, and egg in a large mixing

15 Cakes to Feed a Crowd

1. Apple Walnut Crisp (page 360)

2. Gooey Butter Cake (page 240)

3. Nina's Strawberry Crisp (page 364)

4. Lemon Chip Picnic Cake (page 96)

5. Old-Fashioned Pear and Ginger Cake (page 98)

6. Chocolate Marble Gooey Butter Cake (opposite page)

7. Punch Bowl Cake (page 366)

8. Banana Pudding Cake (page 139)

9. Easy Tiramisù (page 146)

10. Toasted Coconut Sour Cream Cake (page 142)

11. Fresh Lime Cheesecake (page 230)

12. Cherry Dump Cake (page 358)

13. Chocolate Sheet Cake with Peanut Butter Frosting (page 52)

14. Pumpkin Spice Cheesecake (page 227)

15. Fruit Pizza (page 370)

bowl. Blend with an electric mixer on low speed for 2 minutes. Stop the machine and scrape down the sides of the bowl with a rubber spatula. The batter should come together in a ball. With your fingertips, pat the batter evenly over the bottom of the pan, smoothing it out with your fingers until the top is smooth. Set the pan aside.

3. For the filling, place the cream cheese in the same mixing bowl that was used to make the crust, and with the same beaters (no need to clean either) blend with an electric mixer on low speed until fluffy, 30 seconds. Stop the machine and add the eggs, vanilla, and melted butter and beat on medium speed for 1 minute. Stop the machine and add the confectioners' sugar. Beat on medium speed until the sugar is well incorporated, 1 minute more. Stop the machine and scrape down the sides of the bowl with a rubber spatula.

4. Place the chocolate chips in a small saucepan over low heat. Cook, stirring,

the Cake Doctor says...

For additional flavor, add ½ teaspoon ground cinnamon to the chocolate mixture.

until the chips are melted, 1 to 2 minutes. Measure out 1 cup of the cream cheese filling and fold it into the chocolate mixture, stirring so the batter becomes well combined and all one color. Set aside.

5. Pour the remaining filling onto the crust and spread with the rubber spatula so that the filling covers the entire surface and reaches the sides of the pan. Drop spoonfuls of the chocolate batter over the top of the filling, then swirl them with a dinner knife so the top of the batter has a marbled effect. Be careful not to cut through the crust. Place the pan in the oven.

6. Bake the cake until it is well browned but the center still jiggles when you shake the pan, 45 to 47 minutes. Remove the pan from the oven and place it on a wire rack to cool, 30 minutes. Cut into squares and serve.

✱ *Store this cake, covered in aluminum foil, at room temperature for up to 4 days or in the refrigerator up to 1 week. Or freeze it, wrapped in foil, for up to 6 months. Thaw the cake overnight in the refrigerator before serving.*

LEMON CHESS GOOEY BUTTER CAKE

There is a pie near and dear to Southerners' hearts, and it is called chess pie. When I first tasted Gooey Butter Cake, I was dumbfounded at how much it resembled chess pie. But what it was missing was the acid—either vinegar or lemon juice—and a little cornmeal to give the filling substance and a little grit. So here you have that recipe, using the juice and zest of two large lemons and a small amount of cornmeal.

SERVES: 20
PREPARATION TIME: 15 MINUTES
BAKING TIME: 45 TO 47 MINUTES

CRUST:

1 package (18.25 ounces) plain yellow cake mix
8 tablespoons (1 stick) butter, melted
1 large egg

FILLING:

2 large lemons
1 package (8 ounces) cream cheese, at room temperature
2 large eggs
8 tablespoons (1 stick) butter, melted
2 tablespoons white or yellow cornmeal
3¾ cups confectioners' sugar, sifted

1. Place a rack in the center of the oven and preheat the oven to 350°F. Set aside an ungreased 13- by 9-inch pan.

2. For the crust, place the cake mix, melted butter, and egg in a large mixing bowl. Blend with an electric mixer on low

R the Cake Doctor says...

Some lemons are just so tough and hard (on account of being picked too green) that they don't give up their juice easily. Roll these hard lemons between your palm and the kitchen counter a bit and they should let go of that juice.

speed for 2 minutes. Stop the machine and scrape down the sides of the bowl with a rubber spatula. The batter should come together in a ball. With your fingertips, pat the batter evenly over the bottom of the pan, smoothing it out with your fingers until the top is smooth. Set the pan aside.

3. For the filling, rinse and dry the lemons well. Grate the zest from the lemons and set aside; you should have about 2 teaspoons. Cut the lemons in half, and squeeze the juice into a small bowl; you should have about 6 tablespoons. Set the juice aside.

4. Place the cream cheese in the same mixing bowl that was used to make the crust, and with the same beaters (no need to clean either) blend with an electric mixer on low speed until fluffy, 30 seconds. Stop the machine and add the lemon juice, lemon zest, eggs, melted butter, and cornmeal and beat on medium speed for 1 minute. Stop the machine and add the confectioners' sugar. Beat on medium speed until the sugar is well incorporated, 1 minute more. Stop the machine and scrape down the sides of the bowl with a rubber spatula. Pour the filling onto the crust and spread with the rubber spatula so that the filling covers the entire surface and reaches the sides of the pan. Place the pan in the oven.

5. Bake the cake until it is well browned but the center still jiggles when you shake the pan, 45 to 47 minutes. Remove the pan from the oven and place it on a wire rack to cool, 30 minutes. Cut into squares and serve.

✱ *Store this cake, covered in aluminum foil, at room temperature for up to 4 days or in the refrigerator for up to 1 week. Or freeze it, wrapped in foil, for up to 6 months. Thaw the cake overnight in the refrigerator before serving.*

Baking Cakes in Quantity

What would community suppers do without a sheet cake, also called a sheath cake in our older cookbooks, to feed the long line of hungry folks? Baked in a pan ranging from 13 by 9 inches to as large as a jelly-roll pan, sheet cakes can really dessert the masses. Of course, cooking times will shorten as the depth of the cake decreases and its square footage increases! But the process is much the same—mix, pour, bake, and quickly frost.

Double the Fun: Most of the recipes calling for a 13- by 9-inch baking pan in this book can be produced in quantity. If you want to double the recipe, you'll need an extra large mixing bowl, and you'll need to use a handheld electric mixer. Be sure the ingredients are incorporated first on low. When you stop the machine and scrape down the sides of the bowl with a rubber spatula, scrape the bottom of the bowl, too, to make sure all dry ingredients are blended. Then mix again on medium until the batter is well incorporated. This will take from 3 to 4 minutes with the extra batter. Most ovens will be able to handle two 13- by 9-inch pans on the center rack as long as the pans are placed in the oven with the short side to the back. If your oven cannot accommodate this arrangement, place one pan on the center rack and one above, watching so that the top pan doesn't overbake. To save time frosting cakes in quantity, make your frosting ahead of time and keep it refrigerated.

Fast Toppers: To dress up sheet cakes, frost them with a shimmer of frosting. Then, top with chopped nuts, toffee candy pieces, M&M miniature candies, chopped fresh strawberries, a dusting of confectioners' sugar, or shaved chocolate you make by running a chocolate bar against the big hole side of a hand grater.

COCONUT-PECAN GOOEY BUTTER CAKE

The hint of coconut and pecans in the crust is reminiscent both of pecan pie and of coconut cream pie. This cake sneaks up on you, surprising you with each bite. It's perfect for toting on picnics.

R

the Cake Doctor says...

Sprinkle ½ cup miniature semisweet chocolate chips over this batter before the pan goes into the oven. It makes an already delicious combination even more delicious.

SERVES: 20

PREPARATION TIME: 15 MINUTES

BAKING TIME: 45 TO 47 MINUTES

CRUST:

1 package (18.25 ounces) plain yellow
    cake mix
8 tablespoons (1 stick) butter, melted
1 large egg
1 cup finely chopped pecans
1 cup frozen unsweetened grated coconut,
    thawed

FILLING:

1 package (8 ounces) cream cheese,
    at room temperature
2 large eggs
1 teaspoon pure vanilla extract
8 tablespoons (1 stick) butter, melted
3¾ cups confectioners' sugar,
    sifted

1. Place a rack in the center of the oven and preheat the oven to 350°F. Set aside an ungreased 13- by 9-inch pan.

2. For the crust, place the cake mix, melted butter, egg, pecans, and coconut in a large mixing bowl. Blend with an electric mixer on low speed for 2 minutes. Stop the machine and scrape down the sides of the bowl with a rubber spatula. The batter should come together in a ball. With your fingertips, pat the batter evenly over the bottom of the pan, smoothing it out with your fingers until the top is smooth. Set the pan aside.

3. For the filling, place the cream cheese in the same mixing bowl that was used to make the crust, and with the same beaters (no need to clean either) blend with an electric mixer on low speed until fluffy, 30 seconds. Stop the machine and add the eggs, vanilla, and melted butter and beat on medium speed for 1 minute. Stop the machine and add the confectioners' sugar. Beat on medium speed until the sugar is well incorporated, 1 minute more. Stop the machine and scrape down the sides of the bowl with a rubber spatula. Pour the filling onto the crust and spread with the rubber spatula so that the filling covers the entire surface and reaches the sides of the pan. Place the pan in the oven.

4. Bake the cake until it is well browned but the center still jiggles when you shake the pan, 45 to 47 minutes. Remove the pan from the oven and place it on a wire rack to cool, 30 minutes. Cut into squares and serve.

✽ *Store this cake, covered in aluminum foil, at room temperature for up to 4 days or in the refrigerator for up to 1 week. Or freeze it, wrapped in foil, for up to 6 months. Thaw the cake overnight in the refrigerator before serving.*

Coffee Cakes

• • •

I hadn't yet unpacked all my bags upon moving to England in 1993 when word got out that an American food writer was living in the village. No, they didn't send the food police around to search my kitchen, although I had carefully smuggled some baking chocolate and chili powder through customs! They simply asked me to contribute to the church parish newsletter in the form of a cookery column, from an American point of view, of course.

Here I would be able to write about brownies, and how the Brits loved American brownies! And here I would write about something called the American coffee cake.

Well, the women in the parish were most intrigued with our passion for baking sweet cakes to be eaten in the morning hours with a cup of coffee or tea, because English teatime and the biscuits (cookies), cakes, and sandwiches it includes is a similar ritual. But when the story broke and the sour cream coffee cake recipe I shared was perused by the villagers, there was quite a stir. The phone started ringing. Had an ingredient been left out, they wondered. For how can you make an American coffee cake without any coffee? Very interesting, I thought. It had never occurred to me that readers might think that coffee had been left out of the recipe. And so I explained that these cakes are called "coffee"

15 Bake Sale Winners

1. Cinnamon-Chocolate-Apricot Coffee Cake (page 254)

2. Kathy's Cinnamon Breakfast Cake (page 257)

3. Orange Rum Zum Cake (page 294)

4. Chocolate Kahlúa Cake (page 286)

5. Birthday Cake Cones (page 195)

6. Ripe Banana Loaves (page 280)

7. Susan's Lemon Cake (page 83)

8. Blueberry Streusel Coffee Cake (page 272)

9. Charleston Poppy Seed Cake (page 124)

10. Almond Cream Cheese Pound Cake (page 129)

11. Gooey Butter Cake (page 240)

12. Sock-It-To-Me Cake (page 260)

13. Butterscotch Cashew Scotchies (page 324)

14. Double-Chocolate Chewies (page 334)

15. Cookie Pops (page 348)

cakes only because they are eaten with coffee. You could hear the blush on the other end of the phone; word got around, and the phone stopped ringing.

Coffee cakes are an immensely enjoyable kind of cake because as my experience has proven they do stir conversation! Because they're not all gussied up, like their layer-cake counterparts, oozing with fillings and frostings and goo, their flavors go well with hot beverages and taste appealing in the morning hours. They're simple and yet proper and, ironically, very British! The Honey Bun Cake, the Blueberry Streusel Coffee Cake, the Fresh Peach Pecan Kuchen, the Happy Valley Cherry Cake, Ripe Banana Loaves (with chocolate chips), and even Mom's Chocolate Syrup Cake are perfect with morning coffee, but should a slice be left over, they are scrumptious well into nighttime, too.

CINNAMON-CHOCOLATE-APRICOT COFFEE CAKE

There's something absolutely naughty about eating chocolate and cinnamon and dried apricots in a cake, especially in the morning! But pretend you are on the banks of the Seine in Paris, and you're nibbling on a flaky croissant and inside is chocolate, perhaps a little apricot jam. In your kitchen, it can be Paris every morning with this recipe! Not a big fan of dried apricots? For an equally enticing cake—and one that's even a bit more sophisticated—substitute those marvelous dried cherries from Michigan for the dried apricots. And with this combination, you'd best save a slice for dessert.

....

SERVES: 16
PREPARATION TIME: 15 MINUTES
BAKING TIME: 40 TO 45 MINUTES
ASSEMBLY TIME: 1 MINUTE

....

Vegetable oil spray for misting the pan
Flour for dusting the pan
1 package (18.25 ounces) plain white
    cake mix
¾ cup finely chopped dried apricots
    or dried cherries
½ cup miniature semisweet
    chocolate chips
1 teaspoon ground cinnamon
1 package (3.4 ounces) vanilla instant
    pudding mix
1 cup sour cream
½ cup vegetable oil, such as canola, corn,
    safflower, soybean, or sunflower
¼ cup sugar
4 large eggs
2 teaspoons confectioners' sugar

Cinnamon

It's no wonder that the scent of cinnamon in a coffee cake or layer cake is hard to resist. This aromatic spice was once used in love potions. It's actually the inner bark of a tropical evergreen tree. When harvested during the rainy season, this bark curls up after drying and is cut into lengths of stick cinnamon or ground into cinnamon powder. True cinnamon is referred to as Ceylon cinnamon, but this type of tan-colored ground spice is difficult to find in the U.S., even in gourmet emporiums. We are more familiar with a reddish-brown ground spice we call cinnamon, also known as cassia. Cassia is stronger in flavor than Ceylon cinnamon and less expensive. Cinnamon, either ground or in the sticks, will keep for a long time in a cool, dry, dark place. The world over, cinnamon is used to season both sweet and savory foods, from the meat dishes of Greece to the Moroccan chicken pie called *bastila* to the famous coffee cakes of the United States.

1. Place a rack in the center of the oven and preheat the oven to 350°F. Lightly mist a 12-cup Bundt pan with vegetable oil spray, then dust with flour. Shake out the excess flour. Set the pan aside.

2. For the streusel filling, place 2 tablespoons cake mix, the apricots, chocolate chips, and cinnamon in a small mixing bowl and stir until well combined. Set the bowl aside.

3. Place the remaining cake mix, the pudding mix, sour cream, oil, sugar, and eggs in a large mixing bowl. Blend with an electric mixer on low speed for 1 minute. Stop the machine and scrape down the sides of the bowl with a rubber spatula. Increase the mixer speed to medium and beat 2 minutes more, scraping the sides down again if needed. The batter should look thick and smooth. Pour two-thirds of the batter into the prepared pan and smooth the top with the rubber spatula. Spoon the filling over the batter in the pan. Pour the remaining third of the batter over the filling and smooth it out with the rubber spatula. Place the pan in the oven.

4. Bake the cake until it is light brown and springs back when lightly pressed with your finger, 40 to 45 minutes. Remove the pan from the oven and place it on a wire rack to cool for 20 minutes. Run a long, sharp knife around the edge of the cake and invert it onto a rack to complete cooling. Or transfer the cake to a serving platter to slice and eat while still warm. Sift the confectioners' sugar over the top for garnish.

✳ *Store this cake, covered in aluminum foil or under a glass cake dome, at room temperature for up to 1 week. Or freeze it, wrapped in foil, for up to 6 months. Thaw the cake overnight on the counter before serving.*

R
the Cake Doctor says...

Lightly grease your knife with vegetable oil and dried fruits won't stick to the blade. You will be able to chop about 1 cup fruit without having to re-grease.

KATHY'S CINNAMON BREAKFAST CAKE

This rendition of the famous Sock-It-To-Me Cake, also in this chapter (page 260), uses pudding mix. It is perfect for making ahead of time, when you've got guests coming to town for the weekend or when you're headed to the beach or mountains. The recipe was shared with me by a fine Nashville cook and caterer, Kathy Sellers.

....

SERVES: 16

PREPARATION TIME: 15 MINUTES

BAKING TIME: 58 TO 60 MINUTES

ASSEMBLY TIME: 3 MINUTES

....

Vegetable oil spray for misting the pan

Flour for dusting the pan

FILLING AND CAKE:

⅓ cup packed light brown sugar

2 teaspoons ground cinnamon

½ cup chopped pecans or walnuts

1 package (18.25 ounces) plain yellow cake mix

1 package (3.4 ounces) vanilla instant pudding mix

¾ cup vegetable oil, such as canola, corn, safflower, soybean, or sunflower

¾ cup water

4 large eggs

1 teaspoon pure vanilla extract

GLAZE:

1 cup confectioners' sugar, sifted

2 tablespoons milk

½ teaspoon pure vanilla extract

1. Place a rack in the center of the oven and preheat the oven to 350°F. Lightly mist a 12-cup Bundt pan with vegetable oil spray, then dust with flour. Shake out the excess flour.

R

the Cake Doctor says...

This cake contains a little more vegetable oil than most recipes in this book call for, but the extra oil adds a lot of moisture and contributes to its rich, dense crumb. And by adding the pecans first, they have a chance to toast against the hot edges of the pan and become more flavorful as the cake bakes.

2. For the filling, place the brown sugar and cinnamon in a small bowl and stir until well combined. Set the bowl aside.

3. Sprinkle the pecans in the bottom of the prepared pan. Set the pan aside. Place the cake mix, pudding mix, oil, water, eggs, and vanilla in a large mixing bowl. Blend with an electric mixer on low speed for 1 minute. Stop the machine and scrape down the sides of the bowl with a rubber spatula. Increase the mixer speed to medium and beat 2 minutes more, scraping the sides down again if needed. The batter should look thick and smooth. Pour one third of the batter into the prepared pan. Scatter half of the filling evenly over the batter. Pour another third of the batter evenly over the filling. Scat-

ter the remaining filling over the batter. Pour the remaining batter evenly over the top, smoothing it out with the rubber spatula. Place the pan in the oven.

4. Bake the cake until it is golden brown and springs back when lightly pressed with your finger, 58 to 60 minutes. Remove the pan from the oven and place it on a wire rack to cool for 20 minutes. Run a long, sharp knife around the edge of the cake and invert it onto a rack. Allow it to cool completely, 30 minutes more.

5. Meanwhile, prepare the glaze. Place the confectioners' sugar, milk, and vanilla in a small bowl and stir until smooth. Place the cooled cake on a serving platter and spoon the glaze over the top so that it drizzles down the sides and into the center of the cake. Slice and serve.

✳ *Store this cake, covered in aluminum foil or under a glass cake dome, at room temperature for up to 1 week. Or freeze it, wrapped in foil, for up to 6 months. Thaw the cake overnight on the counter before serving.*

Bake Sale Tips

*J*ill Gosden Pollock, homemaker and mother of two children, has chaired the lucrative bake sale at the St. Chrysostom's Day School in downtown Chicago, and she offers these tips:

• Price the perishable cakes—ones with whipped cream—reasonably so they sell quickly.

• Loaves sell. Assign bakers to bake 4, 5, even 10 loaves instead of the usual 1 or 2. The reasoning? Once you crank up the oven and have the ingredients out, it's easy to double or triple a recipe.

• Stock up on pretty packaging materials, especially clear cellophane paper and cellophane bags with seasonal decorations. Don't think twice about rewrapping baked goods that are donated.

• Labeling is important. To make sure you have a label large enough to include the name of the food, its ingredients, and any cooking instructions, begin with blank self-adhesive nametags.

• What cakes sell best? Coffee cakes "fly out the door." Nothing fancy, just comforting, homey things with crumbs and pecans. Plus, any cakes that appeal to kids—the white cake with chocolate frosting and cookie crumbs—sell well. Also plan on several whole fancy cakes like rum cakes that Mom can cart home and serve to company or give to a needy friend. Don't cut cakes into slices or squares because they sell better whole.

• To tote those whole cakes home, make sure you've got cake boxes from the local bakery or mail-order catalog.

• Consider stocking gift baskets for people who want to bake a cake at another time. Include all the ingredients for the cake, even the pan, and a recipe. Or, do the same for a cookie recipe, including the cutters.

• For those folks who want a little something but not a whole cake, offer a selection of smaller items— cupcakes, muffins, cookies—on a pretty platter.

• Sell coffee, tea, milk, and juice to sip along with those baked goods.

SOCK-IT-TO-ME CAKE

This recipe is my version of one of the classic doctored-up cakes. It imitates the rich, decadent sour cream coffee cake made from scratch. Use a yellow or butter recipe cake mix. Add a smidgen of nutmeg to the filling if you like. And as the name implies, the flavor will sock it to you!

SERVES: 16

PREPARATION TIME: 10 MINUTES

BAKING TIME: 50 TO 55 MINUTES

ASSEMBLY TIME: 3 MINUTES

Vegetable oil spray for misting the pan

Flour for dusting the pan

FILLING AND CAKE:

1 package (18.25 ounces) plain yellow cake mix

2 tablespoons light brown sugar

2 teaspoons ground cinnamon

1 cup finely chopped pecans

1 cup sour cream

⅓ cup vegetable oil, such as canola, corn, safflower, soybean, or sunflower

¼ cup water

¼ cup granulated sugar

4 large eggs

1 teaspoon pure vanilla extract

GLAZE:

1 cup confectioners' sugar, sifted

2 tablespoons milk

1. Place a rack in the center of the oven and preheat the oven to 350°F. Lightly mist a 10-inch tube pan with vegetable oil spray, then dust with flour. Shake out the excess flour. Set the pan aside.

R

the Cake Doctor says...

A little of the cake mix added to the sugar, cinnamon, and pecans helps to hold the filling together.

2. For the filling, place 2 tablespoons cake mix, the brown sugar, cinnamon, and pecans in a small mixing bowl and stir until well combined. Set the bowl aside.

3. Place the remaining cake mix, the sour cream, oil, water, sugar, eggs, and vanilla in a large mixing bowl. Blend with an electric mixer on low speed for 1 minute. Stop the machine and scrape down the sides of the bowl with a rubber spatula. Increase the mixer speed to medium and beat 2 minutes more, scraping the sides down again if needed. The batter should look thick and smooth. Pour half of the batter evenly into the prepared pan, smoothing it out with the rubber spatula. Sprinkle the filling evenly over the batter in the pan. Spoon the remaining batter evenly over the filling, smoothing it out with the rubber spatula. Place the pan in the oven.

4. Bake the cake until it is golden brown and springs back when lightly pressed with your finger, 50 to 55 minutes. Remove the pan from the oven and place it on a wire rack to cool for 20 minutes. Run a long, sharp knife around the edge of the cake and invert it onto a rack, then invert it again onto another rack so that the cake stands right side up. Allow it to cool completely, 30 minutes more.

5. For the glaze, place the confectioners' sugar and milk in a small mixing bowl and stir until smooth. Place the cooled cake on a serving platter and spoon the glaze over the top of the cake. Slice and serve.

✴ *Store this cake, covered in aluminum foil or under a glass cake dome, at room temperature for up to 1 week. Or freeze it, wrapped in foil, for up to 6 months. Thaw the cake overnight on the counter before serving.*

MATTIE'S ORANGE CINNAMON POPPY SEED CAKE

SERVES: 16

PREPARATION TIME: 15 MINUTES

BAKING TIME: 35 TO 38 MINUTES

Here's a speedy recipe from Mattie Gregory of Lebanon, Tennessee, who says this is one of her favorites. It's a wonderful combination—orange juice, cinnamon, and poppy seed—and the trio has an exotic quality when you savor 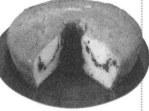 them together in one slice. The cake is a good keeper; just store it in the freezer for up to six months, and it's perfect for welcoming new neighbors.

Vegetable oil spray for misting the pan
Flour for dusting the pan

FILLING:

¼ cup granulated sugar
1 tablespoon packed light brown sugar
4 teaspoons ground cinnamon
1 tablespoon poppy seeds

CAKE:

1 package (18.25 ounces) plain yellow cake
    mix
1 package (3.4 ounces) vanilla instant
    pudding mix
1 cup orange juice
½ cup vegetable oil, such as canola, corn,
    safflower, soybean, or sunflower
4 large eggs

1. Place a rack in the center of the oven and preheat the oven to 350°F. Lightly mist a 10-inch tube pan with vegetable oil spray, then dust with flour. Shake out the excess flour. Set the pan aside.

2. For the filling, place the granulated sugar, light brown sugar, cinnamon, and poppy seeds in a small mixing bowl and stir until well combined. Set the bowl aside.

3. Place the yellow cake mix, pudding mix, orange juice, oil, and eggs in a large mixing bowl. Blend with an electric mixer on low speed for 1 minute. Stop the machine and scrape down the sides of the bowl with a rubber spatula. Increase the mixer speed to medium and beat 2 minutes more, scraping the sides down again if needed. The batter should look thick and smooth. Pour half of the batter into the prepared pan. Scatter half of the filling over the batter and swirl with a dinner knife. Pour the remaining batter evenly over the top, scatter the remaining half of the filling over the batter, and swirl again with the knife. Place the pan in the oven.

4. Bake the cake until it is golden brown and springs back when lightly pressed with your finger, 35 to 38 minutes. Remove the pan from the oven and place it on a wire rack to cool for 20 minutes. Run a long, sharp knife around the edge of the cake and invert it onto a rack, then invert it again onto another rack so that the cake is right side up. Allow it to cool completely, 30 minutes more. To serve, place the cooled cake on a serving platter and slice.

✳ *Store this cake, covered in plastic wrap or aluminum foil, at room temperature for up to 1 week. Or freeze it, wrapped in foil, for up to 6 months. Thaw the cake overnight on the counter before serving.*

R
the Cake Doctor says...

If you're feeding a crowd, bake this cake in a 13- by 9-inch baking pan and slice it into smaller squares.

Mom's Chocolate Syrup Cake

I t's not every day that you want a chocolate cake served before noon, but this cake is different. Sure, it contains chocolate syrup, but it has the simple homespun flavor of a coffee cake, and I think it's perfect to serve with coffee, tea, or a glass of milk. The recipe comes from Nashville writer Susan Chappell, who got it from her mom.

SERVES: 16

PREPARATION TIME: 15 MINUTES

BAKING TIME: 58 TO 60 MINUTES

Vegetable oil spray for misting the pan
Flour for dusting the pan
1 package (18.25 ounces) plain yellow
*　　cake mix*
1 package (3.4 ounces) vanilla instant
*　　pudding mix*
1 cup sour cream
½ cup vegetable oil, such as canola, corn,
*　　safflower, soybean, or sunflower*
4 large eggs
½ cup chocolate syrup
½ cup chopped pecans or walnuts

1. Place a rack in the center of the oven and preheat the oven to 350°F. Lightly mist a 10-inch tube pan with vegetable oil spray, then dust with flour. Shake out the excess flour. Set the pan aside.

2. Place the cake mix, pudding mix, sour cream, oil, and eggs in a large mixing

3. Bake the cake until it is golden brown and springs back when lightly pressed with your finger, 58 to 60 minutes. Remove the pan from the oven and place it on a wire rack to cool for 20 minutes. Run a long, sharp knife around the edge of the cake and invert it onto a rack, then invert it again onto another rack so that the cake is right side up. Allow it to cool completely, 30 minutes more. Slice and serve.

✳ *Store this cake, covered in aluminum foil or plastic wrap, at room temperature for up to 1 week. Or freeze it, wrapped in foil, for up to 6 months. Thaw the cake overnight on the counter before serving.*

R
the Cake Doctor says...

Make sure the chocolate syrup stays in the interior of this cake (by not letting the syrup touch the sides of the pan) so that you have a pretty marbled pattern when you slice it.

bowl. Blend with an electric mixer on low speed for 1 minute. Stop the machine and scrape down the sides of the bowl with a rubber spatula. Increase the mixer speed to medium and beat 2 minutes more, scraping the sides down again if needed. The batter should look thick and smooth. Pour half of the batter into the pan, smoothing it out with the rubber spatula. Pour the chocolate syrup evenly over the batter, making sure not to let the syrup touch the sides of the pan. Pour the remaining batter over the syrup and swirl gently with a knife, making sure to keep the chocolate syrup away from the sides of the pan. Scatter the pecans over the top of the batter. Place the pan in the oven.

HONEY BUN CAKE

My family loves this super-rich coffee cake, which looks and tastes like one big sweet roll. In fact, it was named after the sticky cinnamon roll that's covered in a thin sugar glaze and is known as a "honey bun."

We've eaten this coffee cake for breakfast, for a snack, and we've even topped it with vanilla ice cream for dessert.

SERVES: 20
PREPARATION TIME: 10 MINUTES
BAKING TIME: 38 TO 40 MINUTES
ASSEMBLY TIME: 3 MINUTES

CAKE:

Vegetable oil spray for misting the pan
1 package (18.25 ounces) plain yellow
    cake mix
1 cup sour cream
¾ cup vegetable oil, such as canola, corn,
    safflower, soybean, or sunflower
4 large eggs

FILLING:

⅓ cup honey
⅓ cup packed light brown sugar
1 tablespoon ground cinnamon
½ cup finely chopped pecans (optional)

SUGAR GLAZE:

2 cups confectioners' sugar, sifted
⅓ cup milk
1 teaspoon pure vanilla extract

R

the Cake Doctor says...

This cake is powerfully rich from the addition of sour cream and vegetable oil. Add as much cinnamon to the filling as your palate dictates—bake it the first time with the called for 1 tablespoon, but know you could go as high as 2 tablespoons for a cake that really perfumes the kitchen.

1. Place a rack in the center of the oven and preheat the oven to 350°F. Lightly mist a 13- by 9-inch baking pan with vegetable oil spray. Set the pan aside.

2. Place the cake mix, sour cream, oil, and eggs in a large mixing bowl. Blend with an electric mixer on low speed for 1 minute. Stop the machine and scrape down the sides of the bowl with a rubber spatula. Increase the mixer speed to medium and beat 2 minutes more, scraping the sides down again if needed. The batter should look thick and well blended. Pour the batter into the prepared pan, smoothing it out with the rubber spatula.

3. Add the filling. Drizzle the honey on top of the batter, then sprinkle on the brown sugar, cinnamon, and pecans, if desired. With a dinner knife, swirl through these ingredients to blend them slightly. Place the pan in the oven.

4. Bake the cake until it is golden brown and springs back when lightly pressed with your finger, 38 to 40 minutes. Remove the pan from the oven and place it on a wire rack to cool while you prepare the glaze.

5. For the glaze, place the confectioners' sugar, milk, and vanilla in a small mixing bowl and stir until the mixture is well combined. Pour the glaze over the top of the hot cake in the pan, spreading it to the sides with a spoon. Allow the cake to cool for 20 minutes more before cutting it into squares and serving warm.

✳ *Store this cake, covered in plastic wrap, at room temperature for up to 1 week. Or freeze it, wrapped in aluminum foil, for up to 6 months. Thaw the cake overnight on the counter before serving.*

The Cake Mix Doctor Is In

Q *What happens if I pick the wrong pan size?*

A If the pan is too big, the cake will take less time to bake and it may shrink back while baking. If the pan is too small, the cake will take more time to bake and it may rise over the sides of the pan.

Q *Are you always supposed to grease a pan before baking a cake?*

A Not always. Roulades and angel food cakes call for ungreased sides so the batter can reach up and cling onto the side of the pan, not slide back down.

Q *What are the holes and tunnels in my baked cake?*

A They are round- or sausage-shaped air bubbles trapped in the cake batter. To get rid of them, either sharply tap the filled cake pan several times on the kitchen counter before you place it in the oven or run a knife through the batter in zigzag motions to pop the bubbles. You can avoid tunneling by not overbeating the cake-mix batter or beating it at too high a mixer speed.

Q *How can I cut neat slices from a frosted cake?*

A Moisten the knife blade completely with hot water before each cut, then dry it well. Once you've made a cut, wipe the knife clean with a paper towel and remoisten in hot water. Repeat the process.

Loaf pan

Tube pan

Bundt pan

9-inch round pan

HAPPY VALLEY CHERRY CAKE

Sinclair Baldassari married into a wonderful Italian family, but she has German roots, and this cake was prepared first by her German-born, California-based grandmother. The tart cherries in the sweet batter, and the warm cherry sauce poured over it, give the cake a decidedly German flavor. Baldassari hasn't a clue as to what or where Happy Valley is. And whereas it began as a from-scratch cake, Baldassari has updated this old family recipe to use a cake mix. The cake is sliced in the pan, and pieces are inverted onto serving plates, then topped with a warm cherry sauce. Taste a bite and, just like Baldassari's grandmother, you will want to establish your own family tradition of sharing this delectable cake with each generation.

R
the Cake Doctor says...
The cherries will sink to the bottom of this easy-to-make coffee cake, but don't panic—the cake is inverted and served upside down so the cherries are in full view.

....

SERVES: 20
PREPARATION TIME: 10 MINUTES
BAKING TIME: 43 TO 45 MINUTES
ASSEMBLY TIME: 10 MINUTES

....

CAKE:

Vegetable oil spray for misting the pan

1 package (18.25 ounces) plain lemon cake mix

8 tablespoons (1 stick) butter, melted

1 cup whole milk

3 large eggs

1 can (14½ ounces) pitted tart red cherries, packed in water

CHERRY SAUCE:

⅜ cup cherry water (reserved after draining cherries above)

½ cup water

2 teaspoons fresh lemon juice

¼ cup sugar

1 tablespoon cornstarch

1 teaspoon pure almond extract

1. Place a rack in the center of the oven and preheat the oven to 350°F. Lightly mist a 13- by 9-inch baking pan with vegetable oil spray. Set the pan aside.

2. Place the cake mix, melted butter, milk, and eggs in a large mixing bowl. Blend with an electric mixer on low speed for 1 minute. Stop the machine and scrape down the sides of the bowl with a rubber spatula. Increase the mixer speed to medium and beat 2 minutes more, scraping the sides down again if needed. The batter should look thick and well blended. Pour the batter into the prepared pan, smoothing it out with the rubber spatula. Drain the cherries, reserving the water, and place them on top of the batter, spacing them out in the pan. Place the pan in the oven.

3. Bake the cake until it is golden brown and springs back when lightly pressed with your finger, 43 to 45 minutes. Remove the pan from the oven and place it on a wire rack to cool while you prepare the sauce.

4. For the cherry sauce, place the reserved cherry juice (⅜ cup), water, lemon juice, sugar, cornstarch, and almond extract in a saucepan over low heat, whisking constantly, until the mixture comes to a boil and thickens, 3 to 4 minutes. Remove the pan from the heat.

5. Cut the cake into squares and use a metal spatula to flip them out onto serving plates, upside down. Pour the cherry sauce over the squares and serve.

❋ *Store this cake unsauced, covered in plastic wrap or aluminum foil, at room temperature for up to 3 days or in the refrigerator for up to 1 week. Prepare the cherry sauce right before serving. The cherry water will keep, covered, in the refrigerator for up to 1 week.*

Loaf Pans: Not for Bread Only

Sometimes you just want to loaf around—in the kitchen, that is. You just want to bake another shape of cake instead of the usual round, square, tube, or sheet. That's when it's fun to pull out the loaf pans. Loaf pans have long been used to bake pound cakes and fruitcakes. All you need are two 9- to 10-inch pans, or three 8-inch pans, to accommodate the recipes in this book. Most any recipe going into a tube or Bundt pan will fit into two or three loaf pans. The baking time will differ with the recipe because those cakes calling for sour cream and other heavy ingredients just take longer to bake. Look for the same signs of doneness with loaf pans—tops spring back when lightly pressed with your finger, cakes just start to pull away from the sides of the pan, a toothpick inserted in the center comes out clean. Let a loaf cake cool about 15 to 20 minutes in the pan, then turn it out onto a rack so it can cool on its side. Frost cooled carrot or banana loaves with a cream cheese frosting.

Here's a quick frozen dessert from a simple white, yellow, or chocolate loaf: Split the loaf lengthwise into 3 long slices. Place the bottom slice back into the loaf pan and cover with a layer of softened ice cream. Top with a second slice of cake and smooth on top of it a second flavor of ice cream. Top with the remaining slice of cake and cover the pan with aluminum foil. Place the pan in the freezer until the ice cream refreezes. This will keep for up to 1 month. Slice and serve with a warm Shiny Chocolate Glaze (page 435), Brown Sugar Caramel Glaze (page 437), or Fresh Berry Compote (page 438).

BLUEBERRY STREUSEL COFFEE CAKE

Use whatever blueberries are on hand for this easy coffee cake. In the summertime, that would mean fresh; but in the depths of winter, you will need to add frozen berries or the tiny wild berries that come in a can (not blueberry pie filling!). All varieties taste delicious when paired with cream cheese and when topped with a buttery pecan and brown sugar streusel, such as this one.

SERVES: 18 TO 20
PREPARATION TIME: 20 MINUTES
BAKING TIME: 45 TO 47 MINUTES

Vegetable oil spray for misting the pan

STREUSEL:

½ cup chopped pecans
¼ cup packed light brown sugar
3 tablespoons butter, melted
½ teaspoon ground cinnamon

CAKE:

1 package (18.25 ounces) plain yellow
  cake mix
1 package (8 ounces) cream cheese,
  at room temperature
½ cup vegetable oil, such as canola, corn,
  safflower, soybean, or sunflower
½ cup granulated sugar
¼ cup whole milk
3 large eggs
1½ cups fresh, frozen (unthawed), or canned
  (well drained) blueberries

1. Place a rack in the center of the oven and preheat the oven to 350°F. Lightly mist a 13- by 9-inch baking pan with vegetable oil spray. Set the pan aside.

2. For the streusel, place the pecans, brown sugar, melted butter, and cinnamon in a small mixing bowl and stir until well combined. Set the bowl aside.

3. Place the cake mix, cream cheese, oil, sugar, milk, and eggs in a large mixing bowl. Blend with an electric mixer on low speed for 1 minute. Stop the machine and scrape down the sides of the bowl with a rubber spatula. Increase the mixer speed to medium and beat 2 minutes more, scraping the sides down again if needed. The batter should look thick and well blended. Pour the batter into the prepared pan, smoothing it out with the rubber spatula. Scatter the drained blueberries over the top of the batter. Drop the streusel mixture by the teaspoonful over the blueberries. Place the pan in the oven.

4. Bake the cake until it is golden brown and springs back when lightly pressed with your finger, 45 to 47 minutes. Remove the pan from the oven and place it on a wire rack to cool for 10 minutes. Slice the cake into squares and serve warm.

R

the Cake Doctor says...

You need to ease up a bit on the liquid in a cake-mix recipe when you are adding blueberries. This fruit has a lot of water in it and has a tendency to sink to the bottom of the batter. Fresh blueberries work the best because they are less watery than canned or frozen. The streusel is a nice crunchy contrast to the soft berries and cream cheese.

✳ *Store this cake, covered in plastic wrap or aluminum foil, at room temperature for up to 3 days or in the refrigerator for up to 1 week. Or freeze it, wrapped in foil, for up to 6 months. Thaw the cake overnight on the counter before serving.*

APPLE SOUR CREAM KUCHEN

Whereas *kuchen* is the German word for cake, the type of baked good it refers to in American cooking is a flat, buttery cake on which you layer fresh fruit, sugar, and spices. The beauty of this kuchen is that it uses a cake mix, plus some pantry staples, and whatever fresh fruit is in season. In this

apple kuchen, thinly slice tart cooking apples and season them with sugar, cinnamon, and a drizzling of melted butter. Instead of apples, use fall pears, or even cranberries (a 12-ounce bag). And serve warm with a cup of tea.

SERVES: 20

PREPARATION TIME: 30 MINUTES

BAKING TIME: 30 TO 32 MINUTES

Softened butter for greasing the pan

1 package (18.25 ounces) plain yellow
    cake mix

1 cup sour cream

8 tablespoons (1 stick) butter, melted

1 large egg

3 cups peeled, sliced cooking apples
    (¼-inch-thick slices from 4 large or
    6 small apples)

1 tablespoon fresh lemon juice

½ cup sugar

1 teaspoon ground cinnamon

1. Place a rack in the center of the oven and preheat the oven to 350°F. Lightly grease a 13- by 9-inch baking pan with softened butter. Set the pan aside.

2. Place the cake mix, sour cream, 4 tablespoons melted butter, and the egg in a large mixing bowl. Blend with an electric mixer on low speed until the mixture just

R

the Cake Doctor says...

Prebaking the cake prevents the apples from sinking to the bottom. To save time, you can use a can of apple pie filling mixed with the lemon juice, spreading it on top of the cake batter after prebaking it. Season with a little cinnamon (you won't need any additional sugar) and drizzle with butter.

comes together into a thick dough, 1 minute. Using your fingertips, press the dough evenly over the bottom of the pan so that it reaches the sides of the pan. Place the pan in the oven. Bake the cake for 10 minutes.

3. Meanwhile, toss the apple slices with the lemon juice in a large mixing bowl. Place the sugar and cinnamon in a small mixing bowl and stir until well combined. Remove the cake from the oven, but leave the oven on.

4. Arrange the apples in rows across the top of the warm cake. Sprinkle the sugar mixture evenly over the apples. Drizzle the remaining 4 tablespoons melted butter over the sugar mixture. Return the pan to the oven and bake the cake until it is golden brown and a toothpick inserted in the center comes out clean, 30 to 32 minutes. Remove the pan from the oven and place it on a wire rack to cool for 20 minutes.

5. Slice the warm cake into pieces, and using a metal spatula, remove them from the pan to a serving platter. Serve while still a little warm.

✳ *Store this cake, covered in plastic wrap, for up to 3 days at room temperature or up to 1 week in the refrigerator. Or freeze it, wrapped in aluminum foil, for up to 6 months. Before serving, open the foil and reheat the kuchen in a preheated 300°F oven until warmed through.*

FRESH PEACH PECAN KUCHEN

When summer peaches are in plentiful supply and you're searching for yet another way to enjoy them, try this kuchen. Be sure to drain those fresh, fragrant peaches well (when cut, they will exude plenty of juice), however, or the batter will be a bit heavier and will not bake up crisp on the bottom. Here, cake mix takes on another guise, and the peaches and pecans are just the right addition.

SERVES: 20

PREPARATION TIME: 30 MINUTES

BAKING TIME: 30 TO 32 MINUTES

Softened butter for greasing the pan
1 package (18.25 ounces) plain yellow
*　　cake mix*
1 cup sour cream
10 tablespoons (1¼ sticks) butter, melted
1 large egg
3 cups ripe fresh peaches, peeled, pitted,
*　　and sliced ¼ inch thick (1½ pounds or*
*　　from 4 large peaches)*
½ cup sugar
½ teaspoon ground cinnamon
½ cup chopped pecans

1. Place a rack in the center of the oven and preheat the oven to 350°F. Lightly grease a 13- by 9-inch baking pan with softened butter. Set the pan aside.

2. Place the cake mix, sour cream, 4 tablespoons melted butter, and the egg in a large mixing bowl. Blend with an electric mixer on low speed just until the mixture comes

R

the Cake Doctor says...

In a pinch, you can use frozen or canned peaches in this recipe. Be sure to drain them well and slice them thinly before arranging them on the cake batter after prebaking it. Season with the cinnamon (if using frozen peaches, add the ½ cup sugar; if using canned, ¼ cup sugar is all you need).

together into a thick dough, 1 minute. Using your fingertips, press the dough evenly over the bottom of the pan so that it reaches the sides of the pan. Place the pan in the oven. Bake the cake for 10 minutes.

3. Meanwhile, place the sugar and cinnamon in a small mixing bowl and stir until well combined. Remove the pan from the oven, but leave the oven on.

4. Arrange the peach slices in rows across the top of the warm cake. Sprinkle the sugar mixture evenly over the peaches. Drizzle the remaining 6 tablespoons melted butter over the sugar mixture. Top with the chopped pecans. Return the pan to the oven and bake the cake until it looks golden brown and a toothpick inserted in the center comes out clean, 30 to 32 minutes. Remove the pan from the oven and place it on a wire rack to cool for 20 minutes.

5. Slice the warm cake into pieces and, using a metal spatula, remove them from the pan to a serving platter. Serve while still a little warm.

✳ *Store this cake, covered in plastic wrap, for up to 3 days at room temperature or up to 1 week in the refrigerator. Or freeze it, wrapped in aluminum foil, for up to 6 months. Before serving, open the foil and reheat the kuchen in a preheated 300°F oven until warmed through.*

PUMPKIN SPICE CAKE

I baked this cake the week before Thanksgiving when my thoughts were on pumpkin and cinnamon and ginger. But it didn't upstage the traditional pumpkin pie at Thanksgiving dinner because the cake was long gone, every crumb savored, before turkey day.  You can frost it with Buttercream Frosting or Fresh Orange Cream Cheese Frosting, or simply serve it unadorned.

SERVES: 18 TO 20
PREPARATION TIME: 10 MINUTES
BAKING TIME: 32 TO 35 MINUTES
ASSEMBLY TIME: 10 MINUTES

Vegetable oil spray for misting the pan
1 package (18.25 ounces) plain spice
  cake mix
1 package (3.4 ounces) vanilla instant
  pudding mix
1 cup pumpkin, canned or mashed
  fresh
½ cup vegetable oil, such as canola, corn,
  safflower, soybean, or sunflower
½ cup water
3 large eggs
1 teaspoon ground cinnamon
½ teaspoon ground ginger
Buttercream Frosting (page 416) or
  Fresh Orange Cream Cheese Frosting
  (page 422), optional
½ cup pecans, walnuts, or almonds, toasted
  (see Toasting Nuts, page 134) and
  chopped (if frosting)

1. Place a rack in the center of the oven and preheat the oven to 350°F. Lightly mist a 13- by 9-inch baking pan with vegetable oil spray. Set the pan aside.

2. Place the cake mix, pudding mix, pumpkin, oil, water, eggs, cinnamon, and ginger in a large mixing bowl. Blend with an electric mixer on low speed for 1 minute. Stop the machine and scrape down the sides of the bowl with a rubber spatula. Increase the mixer speed to medium and beat for 2 minutes more, scraping the sides down again if needed. The batter should look thick and well blended. Pour the batter into the prepared pan, smoothing it out with the rubber spatula. Place the pan in the oven.

3. Bake the cake until it springs back when lightly pressed with your finger and a toothpick inserted in the center comes out clean, 32 to 35 minutes. Remove the pan from the oven and place it on a wire rack to cool for 20 minutes. Frost with either of the suggested frostings, if desired. If frosting, sprinkle with the toasted nuts. Slice into squares and serve.

✳ *Place this cake, uncovered, in the refrigerator until the frosting sets, 20 minutes. Cover the cake in waxed paper and store in the refrigerator for up to 1 week. Or freeze it, wrapped in aluminum foil, for up to 6 months. Thaw overnight on the counter before serving.*

the Cake Doctor says...

If you frost this cake, be sure to top it with ½ cup toasted chopped nuts—either pecans, walnuts, or almonds. You'll enjoy the play of crunchy nuts and creamy frosting.

RIPE BANANA LOAVES

It's tough to duplicate the rich, homemade taste of banana bread when you use a cake mix, but these loaves come extremely close. That's because they're jammed with ripe bananas, buttermilk, cinnamon, and brown sugar. They're delicious sliced, toasted, and served with coffee. And they make nice gifts, too.

MAKES TWO 9-INCH LOAVES
PREPARATION TIME: 10 MINUTES
BAKING TIME: 40 TO 45 MINUTES

Solid vegetable shortening for greasing the pan

Flour for dusting the pan

1 package (18.25 ounces) plain yellow cake mix

½ cup packed light brown sugar

2 very ripe medium bananas, peeled and mashed (about 1 cup)

¾ cup buttermilk

½ cup vegetable oil, such as canola, corn, safflower, soybean, or sunflower

3 large eggs

1 teaspoon ground cinnamon

1. Place a rack in the center of the oven and preheat the oven to 350°F. Lightly grease two 9-inch or 10-inch loaf pans with solid vegetable shortening, then dust with flour. Shake out the excess flour. Set the pans aside.

R

the Cake Doctor says...

Add 1 cup miniature chocolate chips to the batter before baking and you'll have a dressed-up banana loaf, suitable for gift-giving or packing for a day's hike in the mountains.

2. Place the cake mix, brown sugar, mashed bananas, buttermilk, oil, eggs, and cinnamon in a large mixing bowl. Blend with an electric mixer on low speed for 1 minute. Stop the machine and scrape down the sides of the bowl with a rubber spatula. Increase the mixer speed to medium and beat 2 minutes more, scraping the sides down again if needed. The batter should look well blended, and the bananas should be well pureed. Divide the batter between the prepared pans and place them in the oven side by side.

3. Bake the loaves until they are golden brown and a toothpick inserted in the center of each loaf comes out clean, 40 to 45 minutes. Remove the pans from the oven and place them on wire racks to cool for 20 minutes. Run a dinner knife around the edge of each pan and invert each loaf onto a rack to cool on its side for 30 minutes more. Slice and serve.

❋ *Store the loaves, covered in aluminum foil, at room temperature for up to 1 week. Or freeze them, wrapped in foil, for up to 6 months. Thaw the loaves overnight on the counter before serving.*

Cakes
with Spirit

• • •

Flip through your grand-mother's cookbooks or old cookbooks at the local library, and you'll find cakes saturated with bourbon, per-fumed with brandy, and reeking of whiskey. Wasn't there Prohibi-tion? Or was all the cake baking done underground?

Obviously these cooks knew the power of spirits. It was not so much the flavor of the spirit before it went into the cake as the flavors the spirit imparted as it baked and perfumed the house. Cakes were, and still are, baked with whiskey in them, and they are baked and then soaked with liquor or liqueur after-wards. Think of the Truman Capote rec-ollection as included in *A Christmas Memory* in 1956. Fruitcakes were being stirred in a country kitchen and baked in a wood-burning stove. "Nose-tingling odors saturate the kitchen," he recalls. "Thirty-one cakes, dampened with whiskey, bask on win-dow sills and shelves."

Whiskey and other spir-its have long afforded cakes a longer shelf life. This is especially help-ful when you're trying to pump a little pizzazz into a bone-dry fruitcake! But in cake-mix cakes where moisture is plen-tiful, spirits are called on to add flavor and ignite conversation. Bake a Harvey Wallbanger Cake, a Bacardi Rum Cake, a Piña Colada Cake, or a Fuzzy Navel Cake and folks will be talking. And eating! The firewater added to these recipes is fun to detect and talk about.

Mixes seem to withstand the punch that liquor adds to cake. And they revel in it. You'll never detect the mix in the Double-Chocolate Rum Cake or the Chocolate Kahlúa Cake. Nor will you think mix when you fork into an Orange Rum Zum Cake or Amaretto Cake.

The combination of cake mix and spirit allows us to create exciting desserts in a very short time. Ingredients are few, baking times are moderate, and preparation—as is typical with mixes—is a breeze.

Enjoy!

HARVEY WALLBANGER CAKE

The Harvey Wallbanger was a 1970s cocktail that supposedly originated at Pancho's Bar in Manhattan Beach, California. It is said that a surfer named Harvey drank several of these concoctions (after losing a surfboard tournament) and accidentally banged his head on the wall as he left the bar. The drink contains a sweet yellow anise-flavored Italian liqueur known as Galliano, as well as orange juice and vodka. It didn't take long for cooks to figure out they could add that same trio to a cake-mix batter and come up with a cake reminiscent of those disco days. So put on your stacked heels, dance your way into the kitchen, and mix up this cake for an impromptu dinner party. Just don't bang your head on the wall!

SERVES: 16
PREPARATION TIME: 5 TO 7 MINUTES
BAKING TIME: 45 TO 50 MINUTES
ASSEMBLY TIME: 5 MINUTES

CAKE:

Vegetable oil spray for misting the pan
Flour for dusting the pan
1 package (18.25 ounces) plain orange
  cake mix
1 package (3.4 ounces) vanilla instant
  pudding mix
4 large eggs
½ cup vegetable oil, such as canola, corn,
  safflower, soybean, or sunflower
½ cup fresh orange juice (from 2 to 3
  oranges) or from the carton
½ cup Galliano liqueur or anisette
2 tablespoons vodka

GLAZE:

1 cup confectioners' sugar, sifted

1 tablespoon orange juice

1 tablespoon Galliano liqueur or anisette

1 teaspoon vodka

1. Place a rack in the center of the oven and preheat the oven to 350°F. Lightly mist a 12-cup Bundt pan with vegetable oil spray, then dust with flour. Shake out the excess flour. Set the pan aside.

2. Place the cake mix, pudding mix, eggs, oil, orange juice, Galliano, and vodka in a large mixing bowl. Blend with an electric mixer on low speed for 1 minute. Stop the machine and scrape down the sides of the bowl with a rubber spatula. Increase the mixer speed to medium and beat 2 minutes more, scraping down the sides again if needed. The batter should look thick and smooth. Pour the batter into the prepared pan, smoothing it out with the rubber spatula. Place the pan in the oven.

3. Bake the cake until it is golden brown and springs back when lightly pressed with your finger, 45 to 50 minutes. Remove the pan from the oven and place it on a wire rack to cool for 20 minutes. Run a long, sharp knife around the edge of the cake and invert it on a serving platter. Poke holes in the top of the cake with a wooden skewer or toothpick.

4. Prepare the glaze. Place the confectioners' sugar, orange juice, Galliano, and vodka in a small bowl and stir until smooth. Spoon the glaze over the warm cake, allowing it to seep into the holes and drizzle down the sides and into the center of the cake. Allow the cake to cool completely before slicing.

✱ *Store this cake, covered in aluminum foil or plastic wrap, at room temperature for up to 4 days. Or freeze it, wrapped in foil, for up to 6 months. Thaw the cake overnight on the counter before serving.*

the Cake Doctor says...

The Harvey Wallbanger is traditionally made with Galliano, but you can substitute anisette instead. You just can't beat the combination of orange juice and an anise liqueur in this sweet and tangy cake. It zaps any cake-mix taste!

CHOCOLATE KAHLUA CAKE

Pairing chocolate and coffee is nothing new. But adding a bit of a coffee-flavored liqueur like Kahlúa to a chocolate cake? Well, it's a match made in food heaven. This formula is similar to Amaretto Cake (page 303) and is from the same cook, Peggy Davis. This recipe would be superb baked in smaller pans because you could unmold the cakes, wrap them in clear cellophane, tie them with a mocha-colored bow, and give them to friends.

SERVES: 16
PREPARATION TIME: 8 MINUTES
BAKING TIME: 45 TO 47 MINUTES
ASSEMBLY TIME: 2 TO 3 MINUTES

CAKE:

Vegetable oil spray for misting the pan
Flour for dusting the pan
1 package (18.25 ounces) plain devil's food
*   cake mix*
1 package (5.9 ounces) chocolate instant
*   pudding mix*
¾ cup Kahlúa
½ cup water
½ cup vegetable oil, such as canola, corn,
*   safflower, soybean, or sunflower*
4 large eggs

GLAZE:

1 cup confectioners' sugar, sifted
¼ cup Kahlúa

1. Place a rack in the center of the oven and preheat the oven to 350°F. Lightly mist a 12-cup Bundt pan with vegetable

R

the Cake Doctor says...

Take care not to overbake chocolate cakes; they bake in less time than their yellow counterparts. If you want to play up the Mexican flavors in this cake, add ½ teaspoon ground cinnamon to the batter.

oil spray, then dust with flour. Shake out the excess flour. Set the pan aside.

2. Place the cake mix, pudding mix, Kahlúa, water, oil, and eggs in a large mixing bowl. Blend with an electric mixer on low speed for 1 minute. Stop the machine and scrape down the sides of the bowl with a rubber spatula. Increase the mixer speed to medium and beat for 2 to 3 minutes more, scraping the sides down again if needed. The batter should look thick and smooth. Pour the batter into the prepared pan, smoothing it out with the rubber spatula. Place the pan in the oven.

3. Bake the cake until it springs back when lightly pressed with your finger and a toothpick inserted into the center comes out clean, 45 to 47 minutes. Remove the pan from the oven and place it on a wire rack to cool for 20 minutes. Run a long, sharp knife around the edge of the cake and invert it on a serving platter.

4. Prepare the glaze. Place the confectioners' sugar and Kahlúa in a small mixing bowl and stir until well combined. Spoon the glaze over the top of the warm cake, allowing it to drizzle down the sides and into the center of the cake. Allow the cake to cool completely before slicing.

✱ *Store this cake, covered in plastic wrap or under a glass cake dome, at room temperature for up to 4 days or in the refrigerator for up to 1 week. Or freeze it, wrapped in aluminum foil, for up to 6 months. Thaw the cake overnight on the counter before serving.*

Time Passages:

COLOR VISION CAKE, SPUMONI CAKE, HARVEY WALLBANGER CAKE, SOCK-IT-TO-ME CAKE, POKE CAKE

*I*f you remember any of the above cakes, then you're divulging your age, for these wacky cakes were all the rage in different decades.

- **Color Vision Cake:** Like looking through a pair of rose-tinted glasses, you chose what shade of cake to eat. You actually tinted the white mix with a little fruit-flavored gelatin, then used the remaining gelatin to tint a simple buttercream frosting. This cake was ahead of its time, born in the early 1950s in the Betty Crocker test kitchen, about the time the flower children were in nursery school.

- **Spumoni Cake:** Fancy layer cakes were all the rage in the 1960s, and this particular cake had pistachio pudding, chocolate pudding, vanilla pudding, as well as candied fruit and nuts in it. It was the beginning of the pudding-and-cake combination, one that would later develop into puddings actually in the cake mixes.

- **Harvey Wallbanger Cake** and **Sock-It-To-Me Cake:** In the disco 70s, the sweet cocktail devised from vodka, orange juice, and an anise-flavored liqueur known as Galliano was known as a Harvey Wallbanger and was it ever hip. It didn't take long for that drink to carry over into the cake-mix bowls of America. And on the television, *Laugh In* was the top-rated show. Its unforgettable phrase, "Sock-It-To-Me," also carried over into cooking, into a legendary cinnamon-flavored coffee cake from the Duncan Hines test kitchen.

- **Poke Cake:** This cake, circa 1980s, has nothing to do with Southern poke sallet. It has everything to do with a straw or a fork that you jab or poke into the cake after it has cooled a bit. Then, you pour dissolved fruit-flavored gelatin or an ice-cream syrup over the cake so it can seep down into the nooks and crannies you've created. Then you chill the cake and garnish it with whipped topping. When sliced, the cake looks pretty and is very moist. The Better Than ? cakes are variations on the poke theme, with sweetened condensed milk or caramel topping or crushed pineapple and syrup among the flavorings.

DOUBLE-CHOCOLATE RUM CAKE

Inspired by the famous Bacardi recipe on page 292, this rendition has a more velvety glaze and lots of luscious chocolate. It begins with a chocolate chip rum cake over which you spoon a raspberry and rum sauce. Then you make a chocolate glaze and spoon this on top. It's triple pleasure, no doubt about it, and the cake seems to improve with flavor day after day.

SERVES: 16
PREPARATION TIME: 8 MINUTES
BAKING TIME: 50 TO 55 MINUTES
ASSEMBLY TIME: 10 MINUTES

CAKE:

Vegetable oil spray for misting the pan
Flour for dusting the pan
1 package (18.25 ounces) plain devil's food
    or chocolate cake mix
1 package (3.9 ounces) chocolate instant
    pudding mix
¾ cup water
½ cup gold rum
½ cup vegetable oil, such as canola, corn,
    safflower, soybean, or sunflower
4 large eggs
1 package (6 ounces; 1 cup) semisweet
    chocolate chips

RASPBERRY SAUCE:

½ cup seedless raspberry jam
¼ cup gold rum

TOPPING:

Shiny Chocolate Glaze (page 435)

R

the Cake Doctor says...

The powerful flavors of chocolate, rum, and raspberry are at work in this dessert, creating a cake that is moist and memorable. You could substitute either light or dark rum for the gold rum, if desired.

1. Place a rack in the center of the oven and preheat the oven to 350°F. Lightly mist a 12-cup Bundt pan with vegetable oil spray, then dust with flour. Shake out the excess flour. Set the pan aside.

2. Place the cake mix, pudding mix, water, rum, oil, and eggs in a large mixing bowl. Blend with an electric mixer on low speed for 1 minute. Stop the machine and scrape down the sides of the bowl with a rubber spatula. Increase the mixer speed to medium and beat for 2 to 3 minutes more, scraping the sides again if needed. The batter should look thick and smooth. Fold in the chocolate chips, distributing them evenly in the batter. Pour the batter into the prepared pan, smoothing it out with the rubber spatula. Place the pan in the oven.

3. Bake the cake until it springs back when lightly pressed with your finger and just starts to pull away from the sides of the pan, 50 to 55 minutes. Remove the pan from the oven and place it on a wire rack to cool for 20 minutes. Run a long, sharp knife around the edge of the cake and invert it on a serving platter to cool.

4. Meanwhile, prepare the raspberry sauce. Place the raspberry jam and rum in a small saucepan over low heat. Heat, stirring constantly, until the jam is melted, 2 minutes.

5. Poke holes in the top of the cake with a wooden skewer or toothpick. Spoon the hot raspberry sauce over the cake, allowing it to seep into the holes and drizzle down the sides and into the center of the cake.

6. Prepare the Shiny Chocolate Glaze. Spoon the glaze over the cake, allowing it to run down the sides of the cake as well. Allow the glaze to set and the cake to cool completely before slicing.

✳ *Store this cake, covered in plastic wrap or in a plastic cake server, in the refrigerator for up to 1 week. Or freeze it, wrapped in aluminum foil, for up to 6 months. Thaw the cake overnight in the refrigerator before serving.*

History of the Bundt Pan

*P*rior to the 1966 Pillsbury Bake-Off contest, few cooks had ever heard of the fluted cake pan we now know as a Bundt. But it was the Tunnel of Fudge Cake, prepared in a Bundt pan by Ella Helfrich of Texas, that knocked the socks off the judges in that 1966 cooking contest and captured the imagination of the country. Pillsbury, alone, received more than 200,000 requests to help locate this mysterious pan.

Bundt pans originated in 1950, according to Jean Anderson in *The American Century Cookbook*, when a group of Minneapolis women contacted Nordic Products chief H. David Dalquist, seeking an aluminum version of the cast-iron kugelhupf pan of Europe. Dalquist agreed to make some for these ladies and a few more to sell to the general public.

In 1960, the *Good Housekeeping Cookbook* showed a pound cake baked in a Bundt pan, which increased sales.

But it was the Tunnel of Fudge Cake that officially launched Bundt-mania, a trend that continued well into the 1970s. Bundt cakes are now an important part of American home baking, and Bundt is a registered trademark of Northland Aluminum Products, Inc., of Minneapolis.

The Bundt pan holds 12 cups of batter, so in recipes it is referred to as a 12-cup Bundt, and it will yield 16 to 24 slices, depending how generous you are. Bundts come in both a light and dark finish on the interior. Take care when baking chocolate cakes in a dark finish pan for they will bake more quickly.

To release a cake from a Bundt pan, simply let it cool in the pan for 20 minutes, then run a long, sharp knife around the edge of the cake to release it from the pan. Or, tap the pan against the palm of your hand to loosen the cake, and invert it onto a rack to finish cooling.

BACARDI RUM CAKE

Dark or light rum is a perfect addition to this easy cake, a classic recipe that has made its way into recipe swaps and cookbooks. As originally written, though, it's my opinion that the cake called for too much glaze—and I'm one who likes a good amount, so you can imagine! Here's that legendary cake but with half as much glaze, which is plenty.

R

the Cake Doctor says...

Because the Bacardi Rum Cake glaze calls for granulated sugar instead of the usual confectioners' sugar, you will need to heat the mixture in order to dissolve the sugar.

SERVES: 16

PREPARATION TIME: 5 TO 7 MINUTES

BAKING TIME: 58 TO 60 MINUTES

ASSEMBLY TIME: 10 MINUTES

CAKE:

Vegetable oil spray for misting the pan

Flour for dusting the pan

1 cup finely chopped pecans or walnuts

1 package (18.25 ounces) plain yellow cake mix

1 package (3.4 ounces) vanilla instant pudding mix

½ cup Bacardi dark rum

½ cup vegetable oil, such as canola, corn, safflower, soybean, or sunflower

½ cup water

4 large eggs

GLAZE:

4 tablespoons (½ stick) butter

2 tablespoons water

½ cup sugar

¼ cup Bacardi dark rum

1. Place a rack in the center of the oven and preheat the oven to 325°F. Lightly

mist a 12-cup Bundt pan with vegetable oil spray, then dust with flour. Shake out the excess flour. Sprinkle the pecans or walnuts in the bottom of the pan. Set the pan aside.

2. Place the cake mix, pudding mix, rum, oil, water, and eggs in a large mixing bowl. Blend with an electric mixer on low speed for 1 minute. Stop the machine and scrape down the sides of the bowl with a rubber spatula. Increase the mixer speed to medium and beat 2 minutes more, scraping the sides down again if needed. The batter should look thick and smooth. Pour the batter into the prepared pan, smoothing it out with the rubber spatula. Place the pan in the oven.

3. Bake the cake until it is golden brown and springs back when lightly pressed with your finger, 58 to 60 minutes. Remove the pan from the oven and place it on a wire rack to cool for 20 minutes. Run a long, sharp knife around the edge of the cake and invert it on a serving platter. Poke holes in the top of the cake with a wooden skewer or toothpick.

4. Prepare the glaze. Place the butter in a small saucepan and melt it over low heat, 2 to 3 minutes. Add the water and sugar, stirring. Increase the heat to medium and bring the mixture to a boil. Reduce the heat slightly and let the glaze simmer until thickened, 4 to 5 minutes, stirring

The Illustrious Bacardi Rum Cake

*I*n 1976 Bacardi president William Walker was entertaining friends at his home in Miami. One of his guests, a neighbor, brought a cake for dessert. It was based on a yellow cake mix and contained Bacardi dark rum in both the cake and the glaze. The cake was such a hit that this neighbor was called on to bake rum cakes again and again. And Walker asked corporate chef Julio Perez to make one of these cakes for Bacardi executives at lunchtime. They, too, loved it, which led to a vigorous ad campaign, and the rest, as they say, is history.

constantly. Remove the pan from the heat and stir in the rum. Spoon the glaze over the warm cake, allowing it to seep into the holes and drizzle down the sides and into the center of the cake. Allow the cake to cool completely before slicing.

❋ *Store this cake, covered in aluminum foil or plastic wrap, at room temperature for up to 4 days or in the refrigerator for up to 1 week. Or freeze it, wrapped in foil, for up to 6 months. Thaw the cake overnight on the counter before serving.*

ORANGE RUM ZUM CAKE

Imagine you're resting under a shade tree on a tropical island. A waiter approaches from out of nowhere carrying a tray, on which is a slice of cake and a tall glass of iced tea. The cake is moist, has strong orange flavors, and is packed with dark rum.

It's both comforting and exotic in the same bite. Well, this cake can take you to that island with little preparation time and no bags to pack! It rings of the tropics and is perfect for spring and summer entertaining outdoors.

SERVES: 16

PREPARATION TIME: 10 MINUTES

BAKING TIME: 45 TO 50 MINUTES

ASSEMBLY TIME: 5 MINUTES

CAKE:

Vegetable oil spray for misting the pan

Flour for dusting the pan

1 package (18.25 ounces) plain yellow cake mix

1 package (3.4 ounces) vanilla instant pudding mix

1 cup fresh orange juice (from about 5 oranges) or from the carton

8 tablespoons (1 stick) butter, melted

¼ cup dark rum

4 large eggs

1 tablespoon grated orange zest (from 1 medium orange)

RUM GLAZE:

4 tablespoons (½ stick) butter

½ cup sugar

¼ cup dark rum

¼ cup fresh orange juice

1. Place a rack in the center of the oven and preheat the oven to 350°F. Lightly mist a 12-cup Bundt pan with vegetable oil spray, then dust with flour. Shake out the excess flour. Set the pan aside.

2. Place the cake mix, pudding mix, orange juice, melted butter, rum, eggs, and orange zest in a large mixing bowl. Blend with an electric mixer on low speed for 1 minute. Stop the machine and scrape down the sides of the bowl with a rubber spatula. Increase the mixer speed to medium and beat for 2 minutes more, scraping the sides down again if needed. The batter should look thick and smooth. Pour the batter into the prepared pan, smoothing it out with the rubber spatula. Place the pan in the oven.

3. Bake the cake until it springs back when lightly pressed with your finger and just starts to pull away from the sides of the pan, 45 to 50 minutes. Remove the pan from the oven and place it on a wire rack to cool for 20 minutes. Run a long, sharp knife around the edge of the cake and invert it on a serving platter to cool.

4. Meanwhile, prepare the glaze. Place butter, sugar, rum, and orange juice in a small saucepan over medium heat. Bring the glaze to a boil, stirring constantly, and cook 2 minutes.

5. Poke holes in the top of the cake with a wooden skewer or toothpick. Spoon the hot rum glaze over the cake, allowing it to soak into the holes and drizzle down the sides and into the center of the cake. Allow the cake to cool completely before slicing.

✳ *Store this cake, covered in plastic wrap, at room temperature for up to 4 days or in the refrigerator for up to 1 week. Or freeze it, wrapped in aluminum foil, for up to 6 months. Thaw the cake overnight in the refrigerator before serving.*

the Cake Doctor says...

In this recipe, you will need more orange juice than is available from the zested orange. Squeeze the juice of the zested orange into a liquid cup measure, then fill with more fresh orange juice or with juice from a carton. Of course, fresh is best, but this cake is delicious made with cartoned juice as well. And if you feel so inclined, use a mixture of citrus juices, such as tangerine and lemon.

PINA COLADA CAKE

T his cake, modeled after the fun cocktail of cream of coconut, pineapple juice, and rum, is one of my favorites. It's a party cake, some-  thing you tote to the gourmet supper club or bring to your best friends' anniver- sary party. Canned cream of coconut goes into the cake, the syrup, and even into a marvelous whipped cream sauce. Then, to gild the lily, this cake is garnished with toasted coconut. It's not for the faint of heart or for the shy of coconut!

....

SERVES: 16

PREPARATION TIME: 10 MINUTES

BAKING TIME: 50 TO 55 MINUTES

ASSEMBLY TIME: 15 MINUTES

....

R the Cake Doctor says...

Although this cake can be stored, it's best to eat it within a day or two because the water in the pineapple will cause the cake to get soggy over time.

CAKE AND SYRUP:

Vegetable oil spray for misting the pan

Flour for dusting the pan

1 can (15 ounces) cream of coconut

1 package (18.25 ounces) plain yellow cake mix

1 package (3.4 ounces) vanilla instant pudding mix

½ cup plus 2 tablespoons light rum

⅓ cup vegetable oil, such as canola, corn, safflower, soybean, or sunflower

4 large eggs

1 can (8 ounces) crushed pineapple packed in juice, drained

1 cup frozen unsweetened grated coconut, thawed

COCONUT WHIPPED CREAM:

1 cup heavy (whipping) cream

1 can (8.5 ounces) cream of coconut

1. Place a rack in the center of the oven and preheat the oven to 350°F. Lightly mist a 12-cup Bundt pan with vegetable oil spray, then dust with flour. Shake out the excess flour. Set the pan aside.

2. Stir the cream of coconut, then pour ½ cup into a liquid measuring cup and reserve the remaining 1 cup for the syrup.

3. Place the cake mix, pudding mix, ½ cup cream of coconut, ½ cup rum, oil, and eggs in a large mixing bowl. Blend with an electric mixer on low speed for 1 minute. Stop the machine and scrape down the sides of the bowl with a rubber spatula. Increase the mixer speed to medium and beat for 2 minutes more, scraping the sides down again if needed. The batter should look thick and smooth. Fold in the crushed pineapple until it is well distributed throughout the batter. Pour the batter into the prepared pan, smoothing it out with the rubber spatula. Place the pan in the oven.

4. Bake the cake until it springs back when lightly pressed with your finger and just starts to pull away from the sides of the pan, 50 to 55 minutes. Remove the pan from the oven and place it on a wire rack to cool for 20 minutes. Place the coconut in an aluminum pie pan and toast it in the oven until lightly browned, 4 to 5 minutes. Remove the pan and set aside. Run a long, sharp knife around the edge of the cake and invert it onto a serving platter.

5. Prepare the rum syrup. Place the reserved 1 cup cream of coconut and the remaining 2 tablespoons rum in a small mixing bowl. Stir until well combined.

6. While the cake is still warm, poke holes in the top with a long wooden skewer or toothpick. Spoon the rum syrup over the top, allowing it to seep into the holes and drizzle down the sides and into the center of the cake. Let the cake cool completely, 30 minutes.

7. For the coconut whipped cream, place the heavy cream and cream of coconut in a large mixing bowl. Beat with an electric mixer on high speed until stiff peaks form, 2 to 3 minutes.

8. Slice and serve the cake topped with coconut whipped cream and garnished with the toasted coconut.

✳ *Store this cake, under a glass cake dome or in a plastic cake saver, at room temperature for up to 4 days or in the refrigerator for up to 1 week. Or freeze it, wrapped in aluminum foil, for up to 2 months. Thaw the cake overnight in the refrigerator. Prepare the coconut whipped cream and toasted coconut just before serving.*

FUZZY NAVEL CAKE

This rich and moist cake has intense orange and peach flavors, perfect for summertime picnic suppers. It's named after the Fuzzy Navel drink, which contains orange juice and peach schnapps. The recipe was shared by Peggy Davis of Nashville, who enjoys jazzing up cake-mix batters. For this recipe, you will use an entire 200-milliliter bottle of peach schnapps.

SERVES: 16

PREPARATION TIME: 5 TO 7 MINUTES

BAKING TIME: 45 TO 50 MINUTES

ASSEMBLY TIME: 5 MINUTES

CAKE:

Vegetable oil spray for misting the pan

Flour for dusting the pan

1 package (18.25 ounces) plain yellow cake mix

1 package (5.1 ounces) vanilla instant pudding mix

¾ cup peach schnapps

½ cup vegetable oil, such as canola, corn, safflower, soybean, or sunflower

½ cup fresh orange juice (from 2 to 3 oranges) or from the carton

4 large eggs

½ teaspoon pure orange extract

GLAZE:

1 cup confectioners' sugar, sifted

4 tablespoons fresh orange juice

2 tablespoons peach schnapps

R

the Cake Doctor says...

For a more intensely flavored cake, add the freshly grated zest of 1 orange to the batter.

1. Place a rack in the center of the oven and preheat the oven to 350°F. Lightly mist a 12-cup Bundt pan with vegetable oil spray, then dust with flour. Shake out the excess flour. Set the pan aside.

2. Place the cake mix, pudding mix, peach schnapps, oil, orange juice, eggs, and orange extract in a large mixing bowl. Blend with an electric mixer on low speed for 1 minute. Stop the machine and scrape down the sides of the bowl with a rubber spatula. Increase the mixer speed to medium and beat for 2 minutes more, scraping the sides down again if needed. The batter should look thick and smooth. Pour the batter into the prepared pan, smoothing it out with the rubber spatula. Place the pan in the oven.

3. Bake the cake until it is golden brown and springs back when lightly pressed with your finger, 45 to 50 minutes. Remove the pan from the oven and place it on a wire rack to cool for 20 minutes. Run a long, sharp knife around the edge of the cake and invert it onto a serving platter.

4. Prepare the glaze. Place the sugar, orange juice, and peach schnapps in a small mixing bowl. Stir until well combined.

5. Poke holes in the top of the cake with a wooden skewer or toothpick. Spoon the glaze over the warm cake, allowing it to seep into the holes and drizzle down the sides and into the center of the cake. Allow the cake to cool completely before slicing.

✻ *Store this cake, covered in plastic wrap or under a glass cake dome, at room temperature for up to 4 days. Or freeze it, wrapped in aluminum foil, for up to 6 months. Thaw the cake overnight on the counter before serving.*

KENTUCKY BUTTERMILK RAISIN CAKE

I n the heartland of Kentucky there is one and only one whiskey suitable for drinking and cooking with, and that is bourbon. And bourbon goes so well in fruitcakes, for the sweetness of the liquor marries with the sugar in the fruit. This cake is based on a buttery from-scratch buttermilk cake that you enliven with golden raisins plumped in warm bourbon and with orange zest. And the glaze has a nip to it, too.

SERVES: 16

PREPARATION TIME: 15 MINUTES

BAKING TIME: 45 TO 50 MINUTES

ASSEMBLY TIME: 5 MINUTES

CAKE:

Vegetable oil spray for misting the pan

Flour for dusting the pan

1 cup golden raisins

½ cup bourbon

1 tablespoon grated orange zest

1 package (18.25 ounces) plain yellow
    cake mix

1 package (3.4 ounces) vanilla instant
    pudding mix

1 cup buttermilk

8 tablespoons (1 stick) butter, melted

4 large eggs

1 teaspoon pure vanilla extract

HOT BUTTERED GLAZE:

4 tablespoons (½ stick) butter

½ cup packed light brown sugar

¼ cup bourbon

¼ cup water

Buttermilk

My grandfather, a long, lean Southern man, was verbal about his love of buttermilk. He drank a glass of buttermilk and ate a wedge of cornbread every day, and he lived well into his 90s. My grandfather's buttermilk was a by-product of churning milk or cream into butter—the way buttermilk is supposed to be. The lightly sour taste of real buttermilk was pleasant to him, and unlike sweet milk (fresh milk) that would sour quickly, buttermilk would keep for several days.

Buttermilk is no longer made the old-fashioned way. Most of what we buy is skim milk that has been treated with lactic acid bacteria to make it taste sour. You can still reap benefits from today's buttermilk even if you don't care to drink a glass. In cake baking, buttermilk contributes to a moist, tender crumb. The recipes in this book have been tested with low-fat buttermilk, although in some Southern supermarkets you can find full-fat buttermilk. And if you can't find buttermilk in your store, look in the baking aisle for a buttermilk powder, which you will need to reconstitute. Or, make your own soured milk by an age-old formula: Stir 1 tablespoon lemon juice or white vinegar into 1 cup of milk (whole, 2%, 1%, or skim). Let it rest on the counter for 15 minutes, or until it looks curdled. Proceed with the recipe.

1. Place a rack in the center of the oven and preheat the oven to 350°F. Lightly mist a 12-cup Bundt pan with vegetable oil spray, then dust with flour. Shake out the excess flour. Set the pan aside.

2. Place the raisins, bourbon, and orange zest in a small saucepan and heat to warm over low heat. Do not boil. Set the pan aside.

3. Place the cake mix, pudding mix, buttermilk, melted butter, eggs, and vanilla in a large mixing bowl. Blend with an electric mixer on low speed for 1 minute. Stop the machine and scrape down the sides of the bowl with a rubber spatula. Increase the mixer speed to medium and beat for 2 minutes more, scraping the sides down again if needed. The batter should look thick and smooth. Fold in the raisin and bourbon mixture until it is well distributed. Pour the batter into the prepared pan, smoothing it out with the rubber spatula. Place the pan in the oven.

R

the Cake Doctor says...

Plumping dried fruit in a liquid such as bourbon in the microwave oven is a fast way to soften and flavor the fruit. Place in a microwave-safe bowl and heat on high power for 30 seconds.

4. Bake the cake until it is golden brown and springs back when lightly pressed with your finger, 45 to 50 minutes. Remove the pan from the oven and place it on a wire rack to cool for 20 minutes. Run a long, sharp knife around the edge of the cake and invert it on a serving platter.

5. Prepare the glaze. Place the butter, brown sugar, bourbon, and water in a small saucepan over medium heat. Bring the glaze to a boil, stirring. Boil for 3 minutes.

6. Poke holes in the top of the cake with a wooden skewer or toothpick. Spoon the hot glaze over the top of the cake, allowing it to seep into the holes and drizzle down the sides and into the center of the cake. Allow the cake to cool completely before slicing.

✱ *Store this cake, covered in plastic wrap or under a glass cake dome, at room temperature for up to 4 days or in the refrigerator for up to 1 week. Or freeze it, wrapped in aluminum foil, for up to 6 months. Thaw the cake overnight on the counter before serving.*

AMARETTO CAKE

Amaretto is an almond-flavored liqueur and is tailor-made for adding to cake batters. Peggy Davis of Nashville shares this recipe, which is packed with almond taste—from the almond extract in the cake, to the Amaretto in both the cake and glaze, to the toasted slivered almonds strewn across the top. Davis prepares this cake not only for entertaining but also for giving at Christmas. My family raves about it, and it has been making the party circuit!

SERVES: 16
PREPARATION TIME: 5 TO 7 MINUTES
BAKING TIME: 48 TO 52 MINUTES
ASSEMBLY TIME: 5 MINUTES

CAKE:

Vegetable oil spray for misting the pan
Flour for dusting the pan
1 package (18.25 ounces) plain yellow
    cake mix
1 package (5.1 ounces) vanilla instant
    pudding mix
¾ cup Amaretto
½ cup water
½ cup vegetable oil, such as canola,
    corn, safflower, soybean, or
    sunflower
4 large eggs
¼ teaspoon pure almond extract

GLAZE AND GARNISH:

1 cup confectioners' sugar, sifted
3½ tablespoons Amaretto
⅓ cup slivered almonds, toasted
    (see Toasting Nuts, page 134)

R

the Cake Doctor says...

This is a pretty boozy cake. If you want to tame the taste, substitute fresh lemon juice for some of the Amaretto.

1. Place a rack in the center of the oven and preheat the oven to 350°F. Lightly mist a 10-inch tube pan with vegetable oil spray, then dust with flour. Shake out the excess flour. Set the pan aside.

2. Place the cake mix, pudding mix, Amaretto, water, oil, eggs, and almond extract in a large mixing bowl. Blend with an electric mixer on low speed for 1 minute. Stop the machine and scrape down the sides of the bowl with a rubber spatula. Increase the mixer speed to medium and beat for 2 minutes more, scraping the sides down again if needed. The batter should look thick and smooth. Pour the batter into the prepared pan, smoothing it out with the rubber spatula. Place the pan in the oven.

3. Bake the cake until it is golden brown and springs back when lightly pressed with your finger, 48 to 52 minutes. Remove the pan from the oven and place it on a wire rack to cool for 20 minutes.

Run a long, sharp knife around the edge of the cake and invert it onto a rack and then again onto a serving platter so that it is right side up.

4. Prepare the glaze. Place the confectioners' sugar and Amaretto in a small mixing bowl and stir until well combined. Spoon the glaze over the top of the warm cake, allowing it to drizzle down the sides. Scatter the toasted almonds over the top to garnish. Allow the cake to cool completely before slicing.

✳ *Store this cake, covered in plastic wrap or under a glass cake dome, at room temperature for up to 4 days or in the refrigerator for up to 1 week. Or freeze it, wrapped in aluminum foil, for up to 6 months. Thaw the cake overnight on the counter before serving.*

Toppings, Quick and Easy

*D*on't want to frost? You can still top off your cake with something special. The first three suggestions are streusels that call for ½ cup of the cake mix. Don't worry. Setting aside this amount won't throw off the other cake proportions.

- **Basic streusel:** Combine ½ cup reserved cake mix or flour, ¼ cup packed light brown sugar, 4 tablespoons softened butter, and ½ teaspoon ground cinnamon in a medium mixing bowl. Mix with a fork, your fingers, or a food processor. Crumble atop the cake before baking.

- **Oat streusel:** Combine ½ cup reserved cake mix or flour, ¼ cup instant or quick-cooking oats, ¼ cup packed light brown sugar, 4 tablespoons softened butter, and ½ teaspoon ground cinnamon in a medium mixing bowl. Mix with a fork, your fingers, or a food processor. Crumble atop the cake before baking.

- **Nut streusel:** Combine ½ cup reserved cake mix or flour, ¼ cup finely chopped pecans, ¼ cup packed light brown sugar, 4 tablespoons softened butter, and ½ teaspoon ground cinnamon or nutmeg in a medium mixing bowl. Mix with a fork, your fingers, or a food processor. Crumble atop the cake before baking.

- **Chocolate chips:** Either semisweet, milk, or white chocolate chips make an easy topper sprinkled on the batter before the cake goes into the oven (but it's better for sheet cakes that you don't plan on frosting). Or, for those tube and Bundt cakes you don't have the time to frost, simply melt some of the chips over low heat and pour over the top of a cooled cake.

- **Nuts:** What an easy topping just plain nuts can be. Scatter chopped pecans, walnuts, or almonds atop a cake before baking and let them toast away and become more flavorful. Plus, they add crunch and color.

CHOCOLATE GRAPPA CAKE

Several years ago our local herb society hosted a holiday dinner with an Italian theme. We prepared a bountiful meal of tenderloin, polenta, salad, bread, Italian wines, and a decadent chocolate cake for dessert. The cake was rich and studded with pine nuts, and raisins, and spoonfuls of velvety chocolate ganache. And the cake was seasoned generously with grappa. Grappa is a colorless Italian brandy made from the grape skins and seeds that are left in the wine press after the juice has been removed to make wine. Here is my quicker version of that from-scratch cake.

SERVES: 16
PREPARATION TIME: 20 MINUTES
BAKING TIME: 48 TO 50 MINUTES
ASSEMBLY TIME: 10 MINUTES

Chocolate Ganache (page 428)
⅓ cup grappa
Softened butter for greasing the pan
Flour or cocoa powder for dusting the pan
½ cup raisins
1 package (18.25 ounces) plain devil's
  food cake mix
½ cup vegetable oil, such as canola, corn,
  safflower, soybean, or sunflower
½ cup whole milk
3 large eggs
1 teaspoon pure vanilla extract
⅓ cup pine nuts

1. Prepare the chocolate ganache using 1 tablespoon grappa in the preparation. Cover the bowl with plastic wrap and place it in the refrigerator to chill while you prepare the rest of the cake.

2. Place a rack in the center of the oven and preheat the oven to 350°F. Lightly

butter a 9-inch springform pan with softened butter, then dust with flour or unsweetened cocoa powder. Shake out the excess flour or cocoa. Set the pan aside.

3. Place the grappa in a small saucepan and heat to warm over low heat. Do not boil. Remove the pan from the heat and stir in the raisins. Set the pan aside while the raisins plump.

4. Place the cake mix, oil, milk, eggs, and vanilla in a large mixing bowl. Blend with an electric mixer on low speed for 1 minute. Stop the machine and scrape down the sides of the bowl with a rubber spatula. Increase the mixer speed to medium and beat 2 minutes more, scraping the sides down again if needed. The batter should look thick and smooth. Fold in the pine nuts, raisins, and grappa. Pour the batter into the prepared pan, smoothing it out with the rubber spatula.

5. Remove the bowl of chocolate ganache from the refrigerator and remove the plastic wrap. With a tablespoon, plop spoonfuls of the soft ganache over the surface of the cake, adding about 20 spoonfuls, or about half of the ganache. Place the pan in the oven. Re-cover the ganache and return it to the refrigerator.

6. Bake the cake until it is still a little soft in the center but the outside edges are firm, 48 to 50 minutes. Remove the pan from the oven and place it on a wire rack to cool for 20 minutes. Run a long, sharp knife around the edge of the cake. Unsnap the ring around the springform pan and remove the sides of the pan. Let the cake cool completely, 20 to 30 minutes more. Run a long, sharp knife between the bottom of the cake and the springform base. Carefully slide the cake onto a serving platter.

7. Spread the remaining chocolate ganache around the sides and on top of the cake. Place the platter, uncovered, in the refrigerator and chill the cake for easier slicing. Slice and serve.

✳ *Store this cake, covered in plastic wrap, in the refrigerator for up to 1 week. Or freeze it, wrapped in aluminum foil, for up to 6 months. Thaw the cake overnight in the refrigerator before serving.*

R
the Cake Doctor says...

When making ganache, if the chocolate hasn't melted after you have added the hot cream and stirred, simply place the chocolate mixture in the microwave oven and cook on medium power for 30 seconds. Stir again until the chocolate is smooth.

JACK APPLE PECAN SPICE CAKE

Yes, leave it to someone from Middle Tennessee to sneak a little sour mash whiskey into a cake! A wee bit of Jack Daniel's flavors the cake, along with buttermilk, chopped apples, and pecans. Jack Daniel's is the nation's oldest registered distillery, located in Lynchburg, Tennessee.

The square bottle was selected by founder Jack Newton Daniel in 1895 and continues to be the company trademark. This rich whiskey cake is suitable any time of year, but it's especially welcome in fall when fresh local apples come into the market.

SERVES: 20

PREPARATION TIME: 10 MINUTES

BAKING TIME: 40 TO 45 MINUTES

ASSEMBLY TIME: 5 MINUTES

CAKE:

Vegetable oil spray for misting the pan

Flour for dusting the pan

1 package (18.25 ounces) plain spice cake mix

1 cup buttermilk

¾ cup vegetable oil, such as canola, corn, safflower, soybean, or sunflower

2 tablespoons Jack Daniel's Tennessee Whiskey

3 large eggs

2 cups finely chopped peeled apples (2 medium apples)

1 cup chopped pecans

GLAZE:

4 tablespoons (½ stick) butter, melted

2 cups confectioners' sugar, sifted

3 tablespoons Jack Daniel's Tennessee Whiskey

1 teaspoon pure vanilla extract

R

the Cake Doctor says...

Whiskey adds a deep, earthy taste to cake recipes and marries well with the spices in the mix. Add a couple tablespoons of your favorite whiskey, such as Jack Daniel's or bourbon, to a spice cake batter and you'll be pleased with the results!

1. Place a rack in the center of the oven and preheat the oven to 350°F. Lightly mist a 13- by 9-inch baking pan with vegetable oil spray, then dust with flour. Shake out the excess flour. Set the pan aside.

2. Place the cake mix, buttermilk, oil, whiskey, and eggs in a large mixing bowl. Blend with an electric mixer on low speed for 1 minute. Stop the machine and scrape down the sides of the bowl with the rubber spatula. Increase the mixer speed to medium and beat for 2 minutes more, scraping the sides down again if needed. The batter should look thick and well blended. Fold in the apples and pecans. Pour the batter into the prepared pan, smoothing it out with the rubber spatula. Place the pan in the oven.

3. Bake the cake until it is light brown and springs back when lightly pressed with your finger, 40 to 45 minutes. Remove the pan from the oven and place it on a rack to cool while you prepare the glaze.

4. For the glaze, place the melted butter, confectioners' sugar, whiskey, and vanilla in a medium mixing bowl and stir with a wooden spoon until the sugar is dissolved and the glaze is smooth. Spoon the glaze over the warm cake, spreading it out to all sides of the pan. Allow the cake to cool about 30 minutes before cutting it into squares and serving.

✳ *Store this cake, covered in aluminum foil, at room temperature for up to 1 week. Or freeze it, wrapped in foil, for up to 6 months. Thaw the cake overnight on the counter before serving.*

Incredible Bars and Comforting Cookies

● ● ●

The way most cooks get their feet wet isn't by baking some grand multi-tiered wedding cake. It is by making a batch of cookies. For the simplicity of a cookie recipe is as appreciated by a novice baker as warm gentle water is by a first-time swimmer.

The recipes in this chapter won't excite a hotel pastry chef. They will, however, excite busy cooks and children who are looking for just a few ingredients, a minimum of equipment, and a short lapse of time.

And that's where cake mixes come into play. They turn a simple from-scratch bar or drop cookie recipe into something even easier. With just an egg or two, a little butter or oil, and some embellishments like chocolate chips, coconut, fruit, or nuts you can turn a simple mix into enough dessert to feed an entire class or half a Boy Scout troop!

When working with cake mixes be aware of a few things. Since they contain a good bit of leavening, and you don't want the rising that you do with a layer cake, you'll only need to add an egg or two. If you want a more crunchy bar, add more fat—butter or oil—than you might add to a layer cake. Many recipes call for a cup of butter! If you want a less crunchy bar, use cake mixes with pudding added. They produce a moister, softer crust.

Drop cookies are a snap to prepare. The batter will look thick, but rest assured the cookies will bake up chewy. In some of these recipes a cup of flour is added to firm up the dough so the cookies will retain their shape after baking.

So bring on the cold milk. The Cranberry Oat Crumble Bars, Sticky Pecan Pie Bars, Peanut Butter Chocolate Bars, Double-Chocolate Chewies, and Applesauce Raisin Cookies are ready and waiting to be savored by cooks of all ages.

LEMON CHEESE BARS

When I was a young food writer in Atlanta, green to the business so to speak, I came upon a recipe for something called "lemon cheese." That sounded like a peculiar type of cheese until I consulted my older, wiser colleague Jean Thwaite, who had lived all her life in Georgia. She laughed and said "lemon cheese" was an old-fashioned Southern term for lemon curd. The light bulb went on in my head and I understood immediately—the creamy consistency of curd reminded early bakers of cheese. Well, this bar recipe has that same lemon-curd consistency, but it gets the texture from the addition of cream cheese. So I guess it is a true lemon cheese!

MAKES: 24 BARS
PREPARATION TIME: 15 MINUTES
BAKING TIME:
27 TO 30 MINUTES

*1 package (18.25 ounces) plain lemon
  cake mix*

*⅓ cup vegetable oil, such as canola,
  corn, safflower, soybean,
  or sunflower*

2 large eggs

*1 package (8 ounces) cream cheese, at room
  temperature*

⅓ cup sugar

*2 tablespoons fresh lemon juice
  (from about 1 lemon)*

R

the Cake Doctor says...

You can prepare these bars with yellow cake mix, but you won't get as intense a lemony taste. To make up for this, add the finely grated zest of a lemon to the crust mixture.

1. Place a rack in the center of the oven and preheat the oven to 350°F. Set aside an ungreased 13- by 9-inch baking pan.

2. Place the cake mix, oil, and 1 egg in a large mixing bowl. Blend with an electric mixer on low speed for 1½ to 2 minutes. Stop the machine and scrape down the sides of the bowl with a rubber spatula. The mixture should be crumbly. Reserve 1 cup for the topping. Transfer the remaining crust mixture to the pan. Using your fingertips, press the mixture evenly over the bottom of the pan so that it reaches all sides. Place the pan in the oven.

3. Bake the crust until it is light brown, 13 to 15 minutes. Remove the pan from the oven and set aside. Leave the oven on.

4. For the filling, place the cream cheese in the same mixing bowl used to prepare the crust, and with the same beaters (no

need to clean either) blend with an electric mixer on low speed until creamy, 30 seconds. Stop the machine and add the sugar, lemon juice, and remaining 1 egg. Beat on low speed until well combined, 1 to 2 minutes. Use the rubber spatula to spread the filling over the baked crust so that it covers the entire surface. Scatter the reserved crust mixture over the filling. Place the pan in the oven.

5. Bake the cake until the crust is golden brown and the filling just starts to set, 14 to 15 minutes. Remove the pan from the oven and place it on a wire rack to cool for 30 minutes.

6. Cut the cake into 24 bars. Remove the bars from the pan with a metal spatula, and serve.

✱ *Store these bars, covered in plastic wrap, at room temperature for up to 4 days or in the refrigerator for up to 1 week. Or freeze them, wrapped in aluminum foil, for up to 6 months. Thaw the bars overnight in the refrigerator before serving.*

APRICOT ALMOND SQUARES

This recipe is adapted from one shared by Cathy Barber, food editor of *The Dallas Morning News.* Barber included it in a column on baking cookies with cake mixes. I found it to be an all-purpose recipe because you can add any type of pre-serves you've got in the refrigerator—raspberry, strawberry, even orange marmalade. With the addition of cream cheese, it has a near cheese-cake consistency.

MAKES: 24 BARS
PREPARATION TIME: 15 MINUTES
BAKING TIME: 33 TO 35 MINUTES

1 package (18.25 ounces) yellow cake
   mix with pudding
8 tablespoons (1 stick) butter, melted
½ cup finely chopped almonds (with skins
   or blanched)
1⅓ cups apricot preserves (12-ounce jar)
1 package (8 ounces) cream cheese,
   at room temperature
¼ cup sugar
2 tablespoons all-purpose flour
½ teaspoon pure almond extract
1 large egg

1. Place a rack in the center of the oven and preheat the oven to 350°F. Set aside an ungreased 13- by 9-inch baking pan.

2. Place the cake mix, melted butter, and almonds in a large mixing bowl. Blend with an electric mixer on low speed for 1½ minutes. Stop the machine and scrape down the sides of the bowl with a rubber

R

the Cake Doctor says...

Instead of almonds, add chopped walnuts or pecans. Then substitute pure vanilla extract for the almond.

spatula. The mixture should be crumbly. Reserve 1 cup for the topping. Transfer the remaining crust mixture to the pan. Using your fingertips, press the mixture evenly over the bottom of the pan so that it reaches all sides. Spread the preserves over the crust. Set the pan aside.

3. For the filling, place the cream cheese in the same mixing bowl used to prepare the crust, and with the same beaters (no need to clean either) blend with an electric mixer on low speed until creamy, 30 seconds. Stop the machine and add the sugar, flour, almond extract, and egg. Beat on low speed until well combined, 1 to 2 minutes. Use the rubber spatula to spread the filling over the preserves so that it covers the entire surface. Scatter the reserved crust mixture over the preserves. Place the pan in the oven.

4. Bake the cake until the crust is golden brown and the filling is set, 33 to 35 minutes. Remove the pan from the oven and place it on a wire rack to cool for 30 minutes.

5. Cut the cake into 24 bars. Remove the bars from the pan with a metal spatula, and serve.

✳ *Store these bars, covered in plastic wrap, at room temperature for up to 4 days or in the refrigerator for up to 1 week. Or freeze them, wrapped in aluminum foil, for up to 6 months. Thaw the bars overnight in the refrigerator before serving.*

RASPBERRY MERINGUE BARS

This bar is faintly reminiscent of linzertorte, the Austrian dessert with raspberry preserves and a buttery crust. But I've topped it with a meringue filled with finely chopped almonds or pecans instead of the customary latticework pastry crust, so you get all the flavor of a linzertorte but in a fraction of the time.

MAKES: 30 BARS;
48 SMALLER PIECES
PREPARATION TIME: 10 MINUTES
BAKING TIME: 40 TO 42 MINUTES

CRUST:

1 package (18.25 ounces) plain yellow
   cake mix
8 tablespoons (1 stick) butter, melted
2 large egg yolks

MERINGUE:

2 large egg whites
½ cup sugar
1½ cups finely chopped almonds
   (with skin or blanched) or pecans

FILLING:

1½ cups seedless raspberry jam or
   raspberry preserves

1. Place a rack in the center of the oven and preheat the oven to 350°F. Set aside an ungreased 13- by 9-inch baking pan.

R

the Cake Doctor says...

Because these bars are so sweet,
you'll only want a small portion. That's
why the recipe yields 30; and you
can cut them into still smaller pieces
to yield 48.

2. Place the cake mix, melted butter, and egg yolks in a large mixing bowl. Blend with an electric mixer on low speed for 1 minute. Stop the machine and scrape down the sides of the bowl with a rubber spatula. The mixture will look like coarse pellets. Using the rubber spatula, spread the crust mixture evenly over the bottom of the pan so that it reaches all sides. Place the pan in the oven.

3. Bake the crust until it is lightly browned, 15 minutes. Remove the pan from the oven and place it on a wire rack to cool. Leave the oven on.

4. For the meringue, place the egg whites in a medium-size bowl and beat with an electric mixer on high speed for 1 minute, or until foamy. Stop the machine and add half of the sugar. Continue beating on high, gradually adding the remaining sugar, until stiff peaks form, 1 to 2 min-

utes. Stop the machine and gently fold in the nuts until they are well distributed. Set aside.

5. Spread the raspberry jam or preserves over the baked crust with the rubber spatula. With a clean rubber spatula, carefully spread the meringue over the jam so that it covers the jam but doesn't blend with it. Place the pan in the oven.

6. Bake the cake until the meringue just starts to brown, 25 to 27 minutes. Remove the pan from the oven and place it on a wire rack to cool completely, 1 hour.

7. Cut the cake into 30 bars or 48 bite-size pieces. Remove the bars from the pan with a metal spatula, and serve.

✳ *Store the bars, covered in plastic wrap, at room temperature for up to 1 week.*

Metal Baking Pans for Bars

Bars need to be baked in metal pans in order to become crisp on the bottom and easy to remove. Glass causes bars to stick.

CINNAMON BLUEBERRY CRUMBLE BARS

When blueberries come into season in your part of the country, turn them into these crumb-topped bars. What's nice about this recipe is that the fruit is the star—and you get an unmistakably blueberry taste when you take a bite. Plus, since blueberries are soft they are quick to cook, shaving the preparation time of this recipe.

MAKES: 24 BARS
PREPARATION TIME: 10 MINUTES
BAKING TIME: 40 TO 45 MINUTES

1 package (18.25 ounces) plain yellow
   cake mix
1 cup (2 sticks) butter, melted
1 cup old-fashioned oatmeal
½ cup packed light brown sugar
2 large eggs
1 teaspoon ground cinnamon
2 cups fresh blueberries, rinsed
   and drained
½ cup granulated sugar

1. Place a rack in the center of the oven and preheat the oven to 350°F. Set aside an ungreased 13- by 9-inch baking pan.

2. Place the cake mix, melted butter, oatmeal, brown sugar, eggs, and cinnamon in a large mixing bowl. Blend with an electric mixer on low speed for 1 to 1½ minutes. Stop the machine and scrape down the sides of the bowl with a rubber spatula. The mixture will be thick. Reserve 1½ cups for the topping. Transfer the remaining crust mixture to the pan. Using your fingertips, press the mixture evenly over the bottom of the pan so that it reaches all sides.

3. For the filling, place the blueberries and granulated sugar in a small bowl and stir to combine. Pour the blueberries onto the crust, and spread with a spoon so that the berries are evenly distributed. Pinch off pieces of the reserved crust mixture and scatter them over the filling. Place the pan in the oven.

4. Bake the cake until it is light brown and bubbling, 40 to 45 minutes. Remove the pan from the oven and place it on a wire rack to cool, 30 minutes.

5. Cut the cake into 24 bars. Remove the bars from the pan with a metal spatula, and serve.

✱ *Store these bars, covered in plastic wrap, at room temperature for up to 3 days or in the refrigerator for up to 1 week. Or freeze them, wrapped in aluminum foil, for up to 6 months. Thaw the bars overnight in the refrigerator before serving.*

the Cake Doctor says...

For a lemony flavor, spread prepared lemon curd thinly onto the crust before adding the sugared blueberries. For a dressy look, sprinkle granulated sugar over the topping before the pan goes in the oven.

CRANBERRY OAT CRUMBLE BARS

Just because everyone associates cranberries with the fall doesn't mean you can't capitalize on their flavor at other times of the year. Do buy them in the fall, but then freeze the bags for up to a year. Just turn those frozen cranberries right into the filling for this delightful recipe.

MAKES: 24 BARS

PREPARATION TIME: 20 MINUTES

BAKING TIME: 35 TO 40 MINUTES

1 package (12 ounces; 3 cups) whole
    cranberries, fresh or frozen

1 cup granulated sugar

¾ cup water

1 package (18.25 ounces) plain yellow
    cake mix

1 cup (2 sticks) butter, melted

1 cup old-fashioned oatmeal

½ cup packed light brown sugar

2 large eggs

1 teaspoon ground ginger

1. Place a rack in the center of the oven and preheat the oven to 350°F. Set aside an ungreased 13- by 9-inch baking pan.

2. Pick over the cranberries, and discard any that are shriveled or discolored. Place the remaining cranberries, granulated sugar, and water in a medium-size heavy saucepan over medium heat. Cook, stirring, until the mixture is thickened and all the cranberries pop, 10 to 15 minutes. Remove the pan from the heat, pour the cranberry filling into a shallow freezer-proof glass dish, and place it in the freezer to cool.

3. Place the cake mix, melted butter, oatmeal, brown sugar, eggs, and ginger in a large mixing bowl. Blend with an electric mixer on low speed for 1 to 1½ minutes. Stop the machine and scrape down the sides of the bowl with a rubber spatula. The mixture will be thick. Reserve 1½ cups for the topping. Transfer the remaining crust mixture to the pan. Using your fingertips, press the mixture evenly over the bottom of the pan so that it reaches all sides.

4. Remove the chilled cranberry filling from the freezer and pour it over the crust, spreading it out with the rubber spatula. Pinch off pieces of the reserved crust mixture and scatter them over the filling. Place the pan in the oven.

R
the Cake Doctor says...

If the flavor of orange in the cranberry filling appeals to you, use orange juice in place of the water and add 1 teaspoon grated orange zest.

5. Bake the cake until it is light brown and bubbling, 35 to 40 minutes. Remove the pan from the oven and place it on a wire rack to cool for 30 minutes.

6. Cut the cake into 24 bars. Remove bars from the pan with a metal spatula, and serve.

✳ *Store these bars, covered in plastic wrap, at room temperature for up to 3 days or in the refrigerator for up to 1 week. Or freeze them, wrapped in aluminum foil, for up to 6 months. Thaw the bars overnight in the refrigerator before serving.*

STICKY PECAN PIE BARS

Down in South Georgia pecan country, where the trees are often a century old and families have been growing pecans

and sharing recipes for generations, pecan pie remains a favorite. This easy bar cookie is a rendition of that classic pecan pie. The corn syrup and brown sugar combination makes the bars sticky, and the cake mix creates a fast crust.

MAKES: 24 BARS
PREPARATION TIME: 10 MINUTES
BAKING TIME: 42 TO 45 MINUTES

CRUST:

1 package (18.25 ounces) plain yellow
    cake mix
8 tablespoons (1 stick) butter, melted
1 large egg

FILLING:

¾ cup dark corn syrup
¼ cup packed light brown sugar
2 large eggs
1 teaspoon pure vanilla extract
1½ cups chopped pecans or pecan halves

1. Place a rack in the center of the oven and preheat the oven to 350°F. Set aside an ungreased 13- by 9-inch baking pan.

2. Place the cake mix, melted butter, and egg in a large mixing bowl. Blend with an electric mixer on low speed for 2 minutes. Stop the machine and scrape down the sides of the bowl with a rubber spatula.

The batter should come together in a thick dough. Using your fingertips, press the crust mixture evenly over the bottom and ½ inch up the sides of the pan, smoothing it out until it is smooth. Place the pan in the oven.

3. Bake the crust until it just begins to brown, 20 minutes. Remove the pan from the oven and set aside. Leave the oven on.

4. Meanwhile, prepare the filling. Place the corn syrup, brown sugar, eggs, and vanilla in the same mixing bowl used to prepare the crust, and with the same beaters (no need to clean either) blend with an electric mixer on medium speed until well combined, 1 minute. Stop the machine, scrape the sides of the bowl down with the rubber spatula, and fold in the pecans until well distributed.

5. Pour the filling over the baked crust and spread with the rubber spatula so that the filling covers the entire surface. Place the pan in the oven.

6. Bake the cake until the crust is golden brown and the filling just starts to set, 22 to 25 minutes. Remove the pan from the oven and place it on a wire rack to cool, 30 minutes.

7. Cut the cake into 24 bars. Remove the bars from the pan with a metal spatula, and serve.

✳ *Store these bars, covered in plastic wrap, at room temperature for up to 4 days or in the refrigerator for up to 1 week. Or freeze them, wrapped in aluminum foil, for up to 6 months. Thaw the bars overnight in the refrigerator before serving.*

the Cake Doctor says...

For a Kentucky flavor, add a tablespoon of bourbon to the filling instead of the teaspoon of vanilla.

BUTTERSCOTCH CASHEW SCOTCHIES

Delightful flavor contrasts are at work here—the salty, crunchy cashews with the creamy butterscotch pieces and the chewy and sweet cake. This is an easy bar recipe that may be adapted to include your favorite nut.

....

MAKES: 24 BARS

PREPARATION TIME: 10 MINUTES

BAKING TIME: 27 TO 29 MINUTES

....

1 package (18.25 ounces) plain yellow
    cake mix

¼ cup packed light brown sugar

8 tablespoons (1 stick) butter, melted

2 large eggs

1 teaspoon pure vanilla extract

1 cup chopped lightly salted cashews

1 cup butterscotch chips

R *the Cake Doctor says...*

Instead of butterscotch chips, use semisweet chocolate.

1. Place a rack in the center of the oven and preheat the oven to 350°F. Set aside an ungreased 13- by 9-inch baking pan.

2. Place the cake mix, brown sugar, melted butter, eggs, and vanilla in a large mixing bowl. Blend with an electric mixer on low speed for 1 minute. Stop the machine and scrape down the sides of the bowl with a rubber spatula. Blend again on low speed for 1 minute. Transfer the batter to the pan, smoothing it out with the rubber spatula so that it reaches all sides. Sprinkle the cashew pieces and butterscotch chips over the batter. Place the pan in the oven.

3. Bake the cake until it is golden brown and a toothpick inserted in the center comes out clean, 27 to 29 minutes.

Remove the pan from the oven and place it on a wire rack to cool for 30 minutes.

4. Cut the cake into 24 bars. Remove the bars from the pan with a metal spatula, and serve.

* *Store the bars, covered in plastic wrap, at room temperature for up to 1 week. Or freeze them, wrapped in aluminum foil, for up to 6 months. Thaw the bars overnight on the counter before serving.*

Betty Crocker

In 1945, the best-known woman in America was First Lady Eleanor Roosevelt. The second best-known lady, according to an article that appeared that year in *Fortune* magazine, was Betty Crocker. Devised in 1921 by the promotional department of General Mills to personalize consumer inquiries about baking, Betty Crocker soon became the fictitious first lady of food. "Betty" was chosen because it sounded friendly, and "Crocker" was to honor a retired director, William G. Crocker.

Just nine years before that magazine article appeared, a long-awaited portrait of Betty was unveiled to the public. It was the first in a string of reincarnations over the years, and this first Betty in the customary red jacket and white blouse looked motherly. But as times changed and cooking changed, so did Betty change. In 1955 she looked softer and happier. In 1965 she appeared more stylish, in a tailored red suit and pearls.

In 1968 her brown hair was longer and for the first time she appeared more professional, beginning the transformation of an at-home Betty into a working Betty. In 1972 she appeared extremely businesslike, whereas eight years later her look had softened. In 1986 she was back in the boardroom looking competent, but in 1996 the take-charge but friendly Betty looked as if she ran a small business out of her home. A busy lady, Betty Crocker has hosted radio programs in the 1920s, responded to consumer demands for meal planning during the Depression, introduced cake mixes in the late 1940s, appeared on television in the 1950s, and published more than 200 cookbooks since 1950. Her name and red spoon have been emblazoned on housewares, flatware, dishes, even appliances. Betty Crocker through the years seems to have embodied the American female cook— the only difference is that as we age she grows younger!

PEANUT BUTTER CHOCOLATE BARS

How could this bar be anything but uncommonly good, for it contains not only peanut butter in the crunchy crust, but a creamy topping of chocolate, coconut, and chopped pecans. And it can be prepared, baked, and in your mouth in under an hour. What could be better?

MAKES: 24 BARS
PREPARATION TIME: 20 MINUTES
BAKING TIME: 20 TO 25 MINUTES

1 package (18.25 ounces) plain yellow
*   cake mix*
1 cup smooth peanut butter
8 tablespoons (1 stick) butter, melted
2 large eggs
1 package (12 ounces; 2 cups) semisweet
*   chocolate chips*
1 can (14 ounces) sweetened condensed milk
2 tablespoons butter
1 cup frozen unsweetened grated coconut,
*   thawed*
1 cup chopped pecans
2 teaspoons pure vanilla extract

1. Place a rack in the center of the oven and preheat the oven to 325°F. Set aside an ungreased 13- by 9-inch baking pan.

2. Place the cake mix, peanut butter, melted butter, and eggs in a large mixing bowl. Blend with an electric mixer on low speed for 1 minute. Stop the machine and

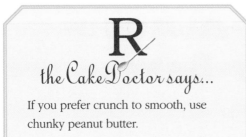

the Cake Doctor says...

If you prefer crunch to smooth, use chunky peanut butter.

scrape down the sides of the bowl with a rubber spatula. The mixture will be thick. Reserve 1½ cups for the topping. Transfer the remaining crust mixture to the pan. Using your fingertips, press the crust evenly over the bottom of the pan so that it reaches all sides. Set aside.

3. For the filling, place the chocolate chips, condensed milk, and 2 tablespoons butter in a medium-size heavy saucepan over low heat. Stir and cook until the chocolate is melted and the mixture is well combined, 3 to 4 minutes. Remove the pan from the heat and stir in the coconut, pecans, and vanilla until well distributed. Pour the chocolate mixture over the crust, and spread it evenly with the rubber spatula so that it reaches the sides of the pan. Using your fingertips, crumble the reserved crust and scatter it evenly over the chocolate. Place the pan in the oven.

4. Bake the cake until it is light brown, 20 to 25 minutes. Remove the pan from the oven and place it on a wire rack to cool for 30 minutes.

5. Cut the cake into 24 bars. Remove the bars from the pan with a metal spatula, and serve.

✳ *Store these bars, covered in plastic wrap, at room temperature for up to 3 days or in the refrigerator for up to 1 week. Or freeze them, wrapped in aluminum foil, for up to 6 months. Thaw the bars overnight in the refrigerator before serving.*

CHOCOLATE-ALMOND-COCONUT BARS

If you love the combination of chocolate, almonds, and coconut, then you'll take to this simple layered bar in which the mix becomes the crust for coconut and chocolate on top.
If you want an even more intense almond flavor, add 1 cup toasted chopped almonds (with skin or blanched) to the crust.

MAKES: 24 BARS

PREPARATION TIME: 10 MINUTES

BAKING TIME:

25 TO 30 MINUTES

CRUST:

1 package (18.25 ounces) plain devil's food
    cake mix

1 cup (2 sticks) butter, melted

1 large egg

½ teaspoon pure almond extract

TOPPING:

2 large eggs

1½ cups frozen unsweetened grated coconut,
    thawed

1 package (6 ounces; 1 cup) semisweet
    chocolate chips

1. Place a rack in the center of the oven and preheat the oven to 350°F. Set aside an ungreased 13- by 9-inch baking pan.

2. Place the cake mix, melted butter, egg, and almond extract in a large mixing bowl. Blend with an electric mixer on low speed for 1 minute. Stop the machine and scrape down the sides of the bowl with a rubber spatula. The batter will be thick. Using the rubber spatula, spread the batter evenly over the bottom of the pan so that it reaches all sides. Set aside.

3. For the topping, place the eggs in a medium-size mixing bowl. Beat with a fork until they are lemon colored. Fold in the coconut until it is well distributed. Pour the mixture over the crust, using the rubber spatula to spread it out evenly. Sprinkle the chocolate chips evenly on top.

4. Bake the cake until the coconut mixture has set, 25 to 30 minutes. Remove the pan from the oven and place it on a wire rack to cool completely, 1 hour.

5. Cut the cake into 24 bars. Remove the bars from the pan with a metal spatula, and serve.

✷ *Store these bars, covered in plastic wrap, at room temperature for up to 4 days.*

the Cake Doctor says...

For a different look, spread the chips into a smooth icing after the pan is removed from the oven. Use a long knife or a thin metal spatula to do the smoothing.

CANDY BARS

This recipe takes me back to my days as editor of the *Atlanta Journal-Constitution* food sections. How we racked our brains to think up yet another story angle for Halloween. One year, I devised recipes using the leftover trick or treat candy, and here is the recipe. You make a

quick chewy bar using a yellow cake mix and then just before baking fold in a cup of chopped chocolate candy bars. Add Snickers, Butterfinger, or toffee pieces—your choice!

MAKES: 24 BARS

PREPARATION TIME: 10 MINUTES

BAKING TIME:

40 TO 45 MINUTES

1 package (18.25 ounces) plain yellow
    cake mix
½ cup packed light brown sugar
8 tablespoons (1 stick) butter, melted
2 large eggs
1 cup chopped candy bar pieces,
    such as Snicker's, Butterfinger,
    and so on

1. Place a rack in the center of the oven and preheat the oven to 350°F. Set aside an ungreased 13- by 9-inch baking pan.

2. Place the cake mix, brown sugar, melted butter, and eggs in a large mixing bowl. Blend with an electric mixer on low speed for 1 minute. Stop the machine and scrape down the sides of the bowl with a rubber spatula. Blend again on low speed for 1 minute. Fold in the candy bar pieces until well distributed. Pour the batter into the pan, smoothing it out with the rubber

4. Cut the cake into 24 bars. Remove the bars from the pan with a metal spatula, and serve.

✳ *Store these bars, covered in plastic wrap, at room temperature for up to 1 week. Or freeze them, wrapped in aluminum foil, for up to 6 months. Thaw the bars overnight on the counter before serving.*

R
the Cake Doctor says...

The brown sugar makes these bars irresistibly chewy. You can substitute dark brown sugar, but the bars will be darker in color and have more of a molasses flavor.

spatula so that it reaches all sides. Place the pan in the oven.

3. Bake the cake until it is golden brown and a toothpick inserted in the center comes out clean, 40 to 45 minutes. Remove the pan from the oven and place it on a wire rack to cool completely, 1 hour.

RUM BALLS

I can't recall a Christmas when there weren't rum balls nudging the decorated sugar cookies for space on the cookie platter. These little gems begin with a square of angel food cake that you smear on all sides (messy!) with a rum, butter, and sugar frosting and then roll in ground pecans. Because the recipe calls for half a cake, it's the best way I can think of to use leftovers. The secret is to cut the cake into tiny squares, for they tend to grow fat as they get covered in frosting and pecans. Pack them in a waxed paper–lined tin for gift giving.

MAKES: 36 RUM BALLS
PREPARATION TIME: 10 MINUTES
ASSEMBLY TIME: 30 MINUTES

One half of an angel food cake, baked
in a 10-inch round tube pan
(see Angel Food Cake From the Box,
facing page)
1 cup (2 sticks) butter, at room temperature
6 cups confectioners' sugar, sifted
½ cup light rum
1 pound pecans, finely ground

R
the Cake Doctor says...

When I was a child, my mother used to grind pecan halves in a hand grinder she would lock onto the edge of the kitchen counter. Now I can easily grind pecans in a food processor fitted with the steel blade.

1. Cut the cooled angel food cake into 6 slices, then cut each slice into 6 squares, 1½ inches each. Discard any scraps. Set aside.

2. Place the butter in a large mixing bowl. Blend with an electric mixer on low speed until creamy, 1 minute. Gradually add the confectioners' sugar, blending on low speed for 1 minute. Stop the machine and scrape down the sides of the bowl with a rubber spatula. Add half the rum, then blend again on low speed for 1 minute, adding more of the remaining rum until you get the right spreading consistency, soft like frosting but not runny. Set aside.

3. Spread out the ground pecans in a shallow pie pan or wide glass dish.

4. Spread rum frosting generously on all sides of the cake squares, then lightly dredge the squares in the ground pecans. Transfer the rum balls in one layer to waxed paper–lined cookie tins or plastic storage containers to chill before serving.

Angel Food Cake From the Box

Angel food cake from the box is so much nicer than a store-bought angel food cake. It bakes up larger and lighter and fresher tasting. And it makes a great beginning for several recipes in this book. All you need is the mix plus 1¼ cups water, a little beating on low speed to incorporate the mix with the water, and then 1 minute of beating on medium to fluff it up. Bake it following box directions and there you are.

✳   *Store the rum balls, wrapped in waxed paper in a tin or plastic airtight storage container, in the refrigerator for up to 2 weeks.*

DOUBLE-CHOCOLATE CHEWIES

With the chewiness of a brownie and the crunch of a cookie, the best of both worlds combine in this speedy chocolate cookie recipe. As you can see, little is needed to turn a devil's food mix into fabulous cookies your family will beg you to bake again. Don't stop with this recipe; try all the variations that follow.

MAKES: 48 (2-INCH) COOKIES
PREPARATION TIME: 5 MINUTES
BAKING TIME: 10 TO 12 MINUTES
ASSEMBLY TIME: 15 MINUTES

Solid vegetable shortening for greasing the pans
1 package (18.25 ounces) plain devil's food cake mix
⅓ cup water
4 tablespoons (½ stick) butter, melted
1 large egg
1 bag (6 ounces; 1 cup) semisweet chocolate chips
½ cup chopped walnuts, pecans, or hazelnuts

1. Place a rack in the center of the oven and preheat the oven to 350°F. Lightly grease 2 cookie sheets with solid vegetable shortening. Set the pans aside.

2. Place the cake mix, water, melted butter, and egg in a large mixing bowl. Blend with an electric mixer on low speed for 1 minute. Stop the machine and scrape down the sides of the bowl with a rubber spatula. Increase the speed to medium and beat for 1 minute more. The cookie dough will be thick. Fold in the chips and nuts until well distributed.

3. Drop heaping teaspoons of the dough 2 inches apart on the prepared cookie sheets. Place the pans in the oven. (If your oven cannot accommodate both pans on the center rack, place one sheet on the top rack and one on the center rack and rotate them halfway through the baking time.)

4. Bake the cookies until they have set but are still a little soft in the center, 10 to 12 minutes. Remove the pans from the oven. Let the cookies rest on the cookie sheets for 1 minute. Remove the cookies with a metal spatula to wire racks to cool completely, 20 minutes. Repeat the baking process with the remaining cookie dough.

✻ *Store the cookies, wrapped in aluminum foil or in an airtight container, at room temperature for up to 1 week. Or freeze them, wrapped in foil and placed in a plastic freezer bag, for up to 3 months. Thaw the cookies overnight on the counter before serving.*

R
the Cake Doctor says...

If you prefer larger cookies, drop the dough by heaping tablespoons, leaving 3 inches of space between the cookies. This will yield about 2 dozen 4-inch cookies.

Tips for Baking Cookies

- Refrigerate bar cookies briefly after cooling to make the slicing easier.

- Cookies can be frozen up to 6 months in the freezer if wrapped in aluminum foil or in a zipper-lock plastic bag.

- To prevent cookies from darkening too much on the bottom, use shiny aluminum cookie sheets. Or double the pans, stacking the pan with the cookies on it on top of another cookie sheet. This slows down the process and results in more even baking. If you must use a dark baking sheet, reduce the oven temperature by 25°F.

- You really don't need to grease the cookie sheet if following a recipe that's high in butter. But if you feel it will prevent the cookies from sticking, go ahead and grease it lightly with solid shortening or vegetable oil spray. If you're reusing a sheet during baking, scrape crumbs from it between baking, but don't regrease.

- Cool the cookie sheets off before putting new cookies on them. Cookie dough spreads on hot surfaces.

- If you like chewy cookies, keep them in the oven a few minutes less than the recipe suggests, or start checking the cookies for doneness about 2 minutes before the end of the recommended baking time.

- Store soft cookies in a tightly covered container so they don't dry out.

- Store crisp cookies in a loosely covered container.

- Wrapping cookies for packing? Wrap cookies in pairs, flat sides together or in small stacks, in aluminum foil or layer cookies in cans using crumpled wax paper to fill the air space.

- Want to keep drop cookies all the same shape? Use a spoon to measure the dough and place it on cooled baking sheets so the cookies don't spread.

- What's the best way to remove a cookie from the baking sheet? Don't let it cool longer than 1 minute on the sheet, then run a metal spatula underneath and transfer it to a rack to cool completely.

CHOCOLATE MOCHA CHEWIES

C offee and chocolate are natural partners. And in this easy recipe you just add one-third cup coffee—a delicious way to use up the leftover coffee sitting in the pot. The milk chocolate chips offer a nice contrast to the stark flavors, but you could easily forgo them or add some chopped walnuts instead.

MAKES: 48 (2-INCH) COOKIES
PREPARATION TIME: 5 MINUTES
BAKING TIME: 10 TO 12 MINUTES
ASSEMBLY TIME: 15 MINUTES

Solid vegetable shortening for greasing
the pans
1 package (18.25 ounces) plain devil's
food cake mix
⅓ cup brewed coffee, at room
temperature
4 tablespoons (½ stick) butter, melted
1 large egg
1 cup milk chocolate chips

1. Place a rack in the center of the oven and preheat the oven to 350°F. Lightly grease 2 cookie sheets with solid vegetable shortening. Set the pans aside.

2. Place the cake mix, coffee, melted butter, and egg in a large mixing bowl. Blend with an electric mixer on low speed for 1 minute. Stop the machine and scrape down the sides of the bowl with a rubber spatula. Increase the speed to medium and beat for 1 minute more. The cookie

Educational Baking: What Kids Learn

When my daughters Kathleen and Litton hear me rattling pans and revving up the electric mixer, believe it or not, they turn off the television set and hurry into the kitchen to help. No, they race. The winner licks raw batter off the spatula, and the loser spoons raw batter from the sides of the mixing bowl. They don't get much, so no tummy aches and luckily no salmonella from the raw eggs.

My girls have inherited a love of baking—the way it tastes, the way it smells, and the way it excites your brain. I have learned that something so simple as baking a cake can teach children valuable lessons in math, language, and science:

- **Fractions:** Have them measure ingredients, both dry and liquid. Have them cut a cake into servings.

- **Addition:** How many ingredients in all? How many minutes longer will the cake be in the oven?

- **Subtraction:** How many eggs are left in the box? How many slices are left on the plate?

- **Multiplication and division:** If I cut this pan of cake into four squares across and five down, how many squares will I have in all? If everyone gets two slices of cake, how many people will this pan feed?

- **Geometry:** Circular pans, square pans, rectangles.

- **Reading:** "Read me the recipe," I ask my girls. They learn to recognize new words and follow directions.

- **Telling time:** The cake needs to bake 30 minutes. It is 1 o'clock. When will the cake be ready?

- **Science:** The three forms of matter—solid (cake mix), liquid (water), gas (steam from the heat of the oven)—as well as simple machines, levers and planes, and countless other science experiments.

dough will be thick. Fold in the chips until well distributed.

3. Drop heaping teaspoons of dough 2 inches apart on the prepared cookie sheets. Place the pans in the oven. (If your oven cannot accommodate both pans on the center rack, place one pan on the top rack and one on the center rack and rotate them halfway through the baking time.)

4. Bake the cookies until they have set but are still a little soft in the center, 10 to 12 minutes. Remove the pans from the oven. Let the cookies rest on the cookie sheets for 1 minute. Remove the cookies with a metal spatula to wire racks to cool completely, 20 minutes. Repeat the baking process with the remaining cookie dough.

✳ *Store the cookies, wrapped in aluminum foil or in an airtight container, at room temperature for up to 1 week. Or freeze them, wrapped in foil and placed in a plastic freezer bag, for up to 3 months. Thaw the cookies overnight on the counter before serving.*

the Cake Doctor says...

If you don't have any leftover brewed coffee, add ⅓ cup tap water and 1 tablespoon instant coffee powder to the recipe instead.

WHITE CHOCOLATE CHEWIES

Forgo the white chocolate chips in frostings and cake batters, but do fold them into cookie recipes like this one. The chips are formulated to withstand high heat, and in cookie recipes they should keep  their shape. In this combination their creamy vanilla taste complements the boldness of the devil's food mix.

....

MAKES: 48 (2-INCH) COOKIES
PREPARATION TIME: 5 MINUTES
BAKING TIME: 10 TO 12 MINUTES
ASSEMBLY TIME: 15 MINUTES

....

R the Cake Doctor says...

If white chocolate chips are not available at your supermarket, buy a 4-ounce bar of white chocolate and chop it into small pieces. If you like nuts in your chip cookies, add ¼ cup chopped almonds (with skins or blanched) or pecans.

Solid vegetable shortening for greasing the pans
1 package (18.25 ounces) plain devil's food cake mix
⅓ cup water
4 tablespoons (½ stick) butter, melted
1 large egg
1 teaspoon pure vanilla extract
1 cup white chocolate chips

1. Place a rack in the center of the oven and preheat the oven to 350°F. Lightly

grease 2 cookie sheets with solid vegetable shortening. Set the pans aside.

2. Place the cake mix, water, melted butter, egg, and vanilla in a large mixing bowl. Blend with an electric mixer on low speed for 1 minute. Stop the machine and scrape down the sides of the bowl with a rubber spatula. Increase the speed to medium and beat for 1 minute more. The cookie dough will be thick. Fold in the chips until well distributed.

3. Drop heaping teaspoons of the dough 2 inches apart on the prepared cookie sheets. Place the pans in the oven. (If your oven cannot accommodate both pans on the center rack, place one pan on the top rack and one on the center rack and rotate them halfway through the baking time.)

4. Bake the cookies until they have set but are still a little soft in the center, 10 to 12 minutes. Remove the pans from the oven. Let the cookies rest on the cookie sheets for 1 minute more. Remove the cookies with a metal spatula to wire racks to cool completely, 20 minutes. Repeat the baking process with the remaining cookie dough.

✳ *Store the cookies, wrapped in aluminum foil or in an airtight container, at room temperature for up to 1 week. Or freeze them, wrapped in foil and placed in a plastic freezer bag, for up to 3 months. Thaw the cookies overnight on the counter before serving.*

CHUNKY OATMEAL MACADAMIA COOKIES

Oatmeal usually keeps company with the likes of cinnamon and raisins, but in this recipe it moves out of its comfortable circle. Here it meets macadamia nuts and white chocolate and bakes  up successfully into a simple cookie just right for springtime picnics.

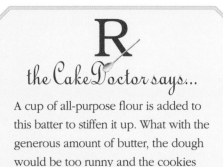

R
the Cake Doctor says...

A cup of all-purpose flour is added to this batter to stiffen it up. What with the generous amount of butter, the dough would be too runny and the cookies would spread too much without it.

MAKES: 48 (2-INCH) COOKIES
PREPARATION TIME: 5 TO 7 MINUTES
BAKING TIME: 12 TO 15 MINUTES
ASSEMBLY TIME: 15 MINUTES

1 package (18.25 ounces) plain yellow
    cake mix
1 cup all-purpose flour
12 tablespoons (1½ sticks) butter, melted
2 large eggs
1 teaspoon pure vanilla extract
1 cup quick-cooking or instant oatmeal
1 cup chopped macadamia nuts
1 cup white chocolate chips

1. Place a rack in the center of the oven and preheat the oven to 375°F. Set aside 2 ungreased cookie sheets.

2. Place the cake mix, flour, melted butter, eggs, and vanilla in a large mixing bowl. Blend with an electric mixer on low speed for 1 minute. Stop the machine and scrape down the sides of the bowl with a rubber spatula. Increase the speed to medium and beat for 1 minute more. The cookie dough will be thick. Fold in the oatmeal, macadamias, and chips until well distributed.

3. Drop heaping teaspoons of the dough 2 inches apart on the cookie sheets. Place the pans in the oven. (If your oven cannot accommodate both pans on the center rack, place one pan on the top rack and one on the center rack and rotate them halfway through the baking time.)

4. Bake the cookies until the edges are golden brown, 12 to 15 minutes. Remove the pans from the oven. Let the cookies rest on the cookie sheets for 1 minute. Remove the cookies with a metal spatula to wire racks to cool completely, 20 minutes. Repeat the baking process with the remaining cookie dough.

❋ *Store the cookies, wrapped in aluminum foil or in an airtight container, at room temperature for up to 1 week. Or freeze the cookies, wrapped in foil and placed in a plastic freezer bag, for up to 3 months. Thaw the cookies overnight on the counter before serving.*

Macadamias

The crunchy, round, and buttery nuts called macadamias that marry so well with chocolate—both white and dark—were first grown in Australia. The evergreen tree was prized for its ornamental beauty and was named after John McAdam, a Scottish chemist who first cultivated it there. Whereas Australia still produces macadamias, as does California, most of the world's crop—90 percent—comes from Hawaii. And about half of the Hawaiian crop is eaten there by locals and tourists—which is understandable because macadamias eaten in Hawaii just seem to taste even better!

I recall first eating macadamias in rainy Hilo, located on the Big Island of Hawaii and dubbed the "Macadamia Nut Capital of the World." Here macadamia orchards have flourished since the 1940s. It's the combination of rich volcanic soil plus humidity and abundant rainfall that makes the climate ideal. And when you drink the Island's local Kona coffee and see chocolate-covered macadamia nuts in every local shop, you understand how well the nuts go with coffee and chocolate flavors.

APPLESAUCE RAISIN COOKIES

These cookies resemble those homey, cakey applesauce cookies your grandmother made. If grandma had only known how simple they are to make with a mix. They are particularly delicious dunked in an icy cold glass of milk or accompanied by a mug of hot chocolate.

MAKES: 48 (2-INCH) COOKIES
PREPARATION TIME: 5 MINUTES
BAKING TIME: 12 TO 15 MINUTES
ASSEMBLY TIME: 15 MINUTES

R the Cake Doctor says...

Dress up these cookies by spreading them with a confectioners' sugar glaze. Stir together 1 cup sifted confectioners' sugar and 2 tablespoons milk until smooth. Spread a thin coating of glaze over each cooled cookie.

Solid vegetable shortening for greasing
    the pans
1 package (18.25 ounces) plain spice
    cake mix
½ cup vegetable oil, such as canola, corn,
    safflower, soybean, or sunflower
½ cup applesauce
1 large egg
1 cup raisins

1. Place a rack in the center of the oven and preheat the oven to 350°F. Lightly grease 2 cookie sheets with solid vegetable shortening. Set the pans aside.

2. Place the cake mix, oil, applesauce, and egg in a large mixing bowl. Blend with an electric mixer on low speed for 1 minute. Stop the machine and scrape down the sides of the bowl with a rubber spatula. Increase the speed to medium and beat for 1 minute more. The cookie dough will be thick. Fold in the raisins until well distributed.

3. Drop heaping teaspoons of dough 2 inches apart on the prepared cookie sheets. Place the pans in the oven. (If your oven cannot accommodate both pans on the center rack, place one pan on the top rack and one on the center rack and rotate them halfway through the baking time.)

4. Bake the cookies until they are light brown and feel firm when lightly pressed with your fingers, 12 to 15 minutes. Remove the pans from the oven. Let the cookies rest on the cookie sheets for 1 minute. Remove the cookies with a metal spatula to wire racks to cool completely, 20 minutes. Repeat the baking process with the remaining cookie dough.

✳ *Store the cookies, wrapped in aluminum foil or in an airtight container, at room temperature for up to 1 week. Or freeze them, wrapped in foil and placed in a plastic freezer bag, for up to 3 months. Thaw the cookies overnight on the counter before serving.*

ORANGE SPICE COOKIES

If you're planning on selling your house anytime during the holiday season, then this is the cookie recipe to bake just before the prospective buyers come calling. It will perfume the rooms with warm holiday smells like orange and ginger. These cookies are delicious served along with ordinary crackers at a wine and cheese party, too. Spread any soft mild-flavored  creamy cheese on top and you're in for a particularly good nibble.

MAKES: 48 (2-INCH) COOKIES
PREPARATION TIME: 5 MINUTES
BAKING TIME: 12 TO 15 MINUTES
ASSEMBLY TIME: 15 MINUTES

Solid vegetable shortening for greasing '
    the pans
1 package (18.25 ounces) plain spice
    cake mix
½ cup vegetable oil, such as canola,
    corn, safflower, soybean,
    or sunflower
½ cup orange marmalade
1 large egg
1 teaspoon ground ginger

1. Place a rack in the center of the oven and preheat the oven to 350°F. Lightly grease 2 cookie sheets with solid vegetable shortening. Set the pans aside.

2. Place the cake mix, oil, orange marmalade, egg, and ginger in a large mixing bowl. Blend with an electric mixer on low speed for 1 minute. Stop the machine and scrape down the sides of the bowl with a

R

the Cake Doctor says...

For fun, vary the type of marmalade, adding lemon, lime, or tangerine marmalade, found at specialty food shops.

rubber spatula. Beat on low speed for 1 minute more. The cookie dough will be thick.

3. Drop teaspoons of dough 2 inches apart on the prepared cookie sheets. Place the pans in the oven. (If your oven cannot accommodate both pans on the center rack, place one pan on the top rack and one on the center rack and rotate them halfway through the baking time.)

4. Bake the cookies until they are light brown and feel firm when lightly pressed with your fingers, 12 to 15 minutes. Remove the pans from the oven. Let the cookies rest on the cookie sheets for 1 minute. Remove the cookies with a metal spatula to wire racks to cool completely, 20 minutes. Repeat the baking process with the remaining cookie dough.

❋ *Store the cookies, wrapped in aluminum foil or in an airtight container, at room temperature for up to 1 week. Or freeze them, wrapped in foil and placed in a plastic freezer bag, for up to 3 months. Thaw the cookies overnight on the counter before serving.*

COOKIE POPS

These cookies are just right for gift giving or for selling at a school bake sale fundraiser. You carefully insert a wooden ice cream pop stick into each warm cookie, then let them cool. Wrap the cookies in clear cellophane and tie a  pretty ribbon around the top of the stick to secure the cellophane.

MAKES: 48 (2-INCH)
COOKIE POPS
PREPARATION TIME: 5 MINUTES
BAKING TIME: 8 TO 12 MINUTES
ASSEMBLY TIME: 15 MINUTES

Solid vegetable shortening for greasing
the pans
1 package (18.25 ounces) plain yellow
cake mix
1 cup all-purpose flour
8 tablespoons (1 stick) butter, melted
¼ cup honey
2 large eggs
1 cup colored sugar sprinkles
48 wooden craft sticks

1. Place a rack in the center of the oven and preheat the oven to 375°F. Lightly grease 2 cookie sheets with solid vegetable shortening. Set the pans aside.

2. Place the cake mix, flour, melted butter, honey, and eggs in a large mixing bowl. Blend with an electric mixer on low speed for 1 minute. Stop the machine and scrape down the sides of the bowl with a rubber spatula. Beat on low speed for 1 minute more. The cookie dough will be thick. With lightly floured hands, shape the dough into 1-inch balls. Pour the colored sprinkles into a shallow bowl and roll the balls in them.

3. Place the dough balls 2 inches apart on the prepared cookie sheets. Place the pans in the oven. (If your oven cannot accommodate both pans on the center rack, place one pan on the top rack and one on the center rack and rotate them halfway through the baking time.)

4. Bake the cookies until the edges are light brown, 8 to 12 minutes. Remove the pans from the oven. Immediately insert a wooden craft stick halfway into the side of each cookie. Let the cookies rest on the cookie sheets for 1 minute. Carefully remove the cookies with a metal spatula to wire racks to cool completely, 30 minutes. Repeat the baking process with the remaining cookie dough and craft sticks.

R

the Cake Doctor says...

Substitute a devil's food or chocolate cake mix for chocolate cookie pops!

❋ *Store the cookies, wrapped in aluminum foil or in an airtight container, at room temperature for up to 1 week. Or freeze them with the sticks in place, wrapped in foil and placed in a plastic freezer bag, for up to 3 months. Thaw the cookies overnight on the counter before serving.*

CHOCOLATE MACADAMIA BISCOTTI

Biscotti are closer than you think when you've got a box of cake mix on hand. All you add to a devil's food mix is butter, eggs, flour, and macadamias, then mix and bake twice for that characteristic crunch of biscotti. Dip these slender cookies into a tall glass of milk and you have a snack suitable for your weekend houseguests.

MAKES: 18 BISCOTTI
PREPARATION TIME: 15 MINUTES
BAKING TIME:
30 TO 35 MINUTES FOR
FIRST BAKING,
10 MINUTES FOR SECOND
RESTING TIME IN OVEN:
30 TO 40 MINUTES

Parchment paper for the pan
1 package (18.25 ounces) plain devil's
    food cake mix
8 tablespoons (1 stick) butter, melted
2 large eggs
1 cup all-purpose flour
½ cup chopped macadamia nuts

1. Place a rack in the center of the oven and preheat the oven to 350°F. Line a baking sheet with parchment paper and set aside.

2. Place the cake mix, melted butter, eggs, flour, and macadamia nuts in a large mixing bowl. Blend with an electric mixer on low speed until well blended, 3 to 4 minutes. Stop the machine and scrape down the sides of the bowl with a rubber spatula. The dough should come together into a ball. Transfer it to the prepared baking sheet. With floured hands, shape the dough into a rectangle about 14 inches long by 4 inches wide by ½ inch thick. Mound the dough so it is slightly higher in the center. Place the baking sheet in the oven.

3. Bake the biscotti rectangle until it feels firm when lightly pressed with your finger and a toothpick inserted in the center comes out clean, 30 to 35 minutes. Remove the baking sheet from the oven and let the biscotti cool 10 minutes. Leave the oven on.

4. Cutting on the baking sheet, use a sharp serrated bread knife to slice the rectangle on the diagonal into 1-inch-thick slices. You should get 14 slices. Carefully turn these slices onto their sides, using the slicing knife to arrange them on the same baking sheet. Return the baking sheet to the oven.

5. Bake the biscotti 10 minutes. Turn the oven off, and let the biscotti remain in the oven until they are crisp, for 30 to 40 minutes more. Remove the baking sheet from the oven, transfer the biscotti to a rack, and allow them to cool completely, 2 hours.

✱ *Store the biscotti in an airtight container at room temperature for up to several weeks.*

R the Cake Doctor says...

Vary the cake mix and the nuts to suit your taste. Hazelnuts could easily stand in for the macadamias. Or, should you want an even more island flavor, add ¼ cup unsweetened grated coconut to the batter.

LEMON PECAN BISCOTTI

The taste of citrus is made for biscotti, as this lemony recipe illustrates. You could add a little grated lemon zest to intensify the flavor. Pack biscotti in a pretty glass jar and attach a ribbon and a couple of tea bags. You have a gift ready to go.

R
the Cake Doctor says...

Biscotti that include nuts can be difficult to slice. That's why a sharp serrated bread knife is the best tool; the sawing motion cuts through the dough. The nuts can be pushed back into the warm slices if they fall out.

MAKES: 18 BISCOTTI
PREPARATION TIME: 15 MINUTES
BAKING TIME:
30 TO 35 MINUTES FOR
FIRST BAKING,
10 MINUTES FOR SECOND
RESTING TIME IN OVEN:
30 TO 40 MINUTES

Parchment paper for the pan
1 package (18.25 ounces) plain lemon
    cake mix
8 tablespoons (1 stick) butter, melted
2 large eggs
1 cup all-purpose flour
½ cup chopped pecans

1. Place a rack in the center of the oven and preheat the oven to 350°F. Line a baking sheet with parchment paper and set aside.

2. Place the cake mix, melted butter, eggs, flour, and pecans in a large mixing bowl. Blend with an electric mixer on low speed until well blended, 3 to 4 minutes. Stop the machine and scrape down the sides of the

Biscotti

*I*f an idea is half-baked, it's no good. But in Italy if a cookie is twice-baked, then it's the wonderful *biscotto* or *biscotti,* the plural. Biscotti can be made from a cake mix in your kitchen, but you must add a cup of flour to the dough to give it structure. Shape the dough into a rectangle to bake the first time, then slice it and bake the pieces a second time. After two trips to the oven biscotti become hard enough to be dipped into coffee, cocoa, milk, or sweet wine and not crumble. But they should never be so hard to crack a tooth. There are no real tricks to making biscotti that aren't revealed in the recipes. Choose a cake mix and extras (nuts, chips, pure vanilla extract) that complement one another. And make sure the biscotti are completely cooled before you store them in a tightly sealed container. Crisp and dry, biscotti will keep at room temperature for 2 to 3 weeks.

bowl with a rubber spatula. The dough should come together into a ball. Transfer it to the prepared baking sheet. With floured hands, shape the dough into a rectangle about 14 inches long by 4 inches wide by ½ inch thick. Mound the dough so it is slightly higher in the center. Place the baking sheet in the oven.

3. Bake the biscotti rectangle until it feels firm when lightly pressed with your finger and a toothpick inserted in the center comes out clean, 30 to 35 minutes. Remove the baking sheet from the oven and let the biscotti cool 10 minutes. Leave the oven on.

4. Cutting on the baking sheet, use a sharp serrated bread knife to slice the rectangle on the diagonal into 1-inch-thick slices. You should get 14 slices. Carefully turn these slices onto their sides, using the slicing knife to arrange them on the same baking sheet. Return the baking sheet to the oven.

5. Bake the biscotti 10 minutes. Turn the oven off, and let the biscotti remain in the oven until they are crisp, 30 to 40 minutes more. Remove the baking sheet from the oven, transfer the biscotti to a rack, and allow them to cool completely, 2 hours.

✻ *Store the biscotti in an airtight container at room temperature for up to several weeks.*

This Can't Contain Cake Mix

• • •

It doesn't look like a cake. It doesn't taste like a cake. But it contains cake mix?

That's precisely the criteria I used in this chapter of marvelous crisp, crumble, and cobbler recipes, plus trifles and even a dessert pizza. The recipe had to contain a cake mix, but it couldn't resemble one.

The early American settlers might have called this chapter salmagundi—or hodgepodge. But I think my name is more descriptive because that's the response you'll get when you tell someone that Nina's Strawberry Crisp, containing whole berries and butter, as well as the Apple Walnut Crisp begin with a yellow cake mix. These cobblers and crisps use a mix, but they employ it in a different way. Instead of combining the mix with the customary eggs, fat, and liquid, the mix is used dry and layered between wet juicy ingredients. In the Sour Cream Pear Buckle, the mix is moistened with eggs and melted butter, then lightly cooked pears, and a sour cream topping are added. In the Fruit Pizza, the cake-mix batter is stiff but spreadable and baked in pizza pans or a shallow jelly-roll pan until browned. After cooling, it is spread with whipped topping and your choice of sliced fresh fruit.

In this chapter you will also find punch bowl cakes, which are essentially trifles—baked cake torn into pieces, then layered with pudding, often fruit or candy pieces, and whipped cream in a pretty glass bowl. For Chocolate Custard Icebox Cake, a baked angel food cake is torn into pieces and layered with rum and chocolate custard, then topped with toasted pecans. The mixture is chilled until serving time.

And lastly, Cherry Dump Cake is the ultimate hodgepodge. You literally dump cans of crushed pineapple and cherry pie filling, dry yellow cake mix, and the rest of the ingredients into a 13-by-9-inch pan and bake away.

There you have it—a salmagundi, a hodgepodge of delicious but unconventional ways to use cake mix!

CHOCOLATE CUSTARD ICEBOX CAKE

Many of the desserts in this book call for an instant pudding mix, but not this one. No, you're going to stir together a simple home-made custard on top of the stove, flavor some of it with  rum, some of it with chocolate, and then use them as layers over heavenly hunks of angel food cake. And although it takes about 1 hour to put it together, you've got a stellar dessert for company that can be tucked in the icebox (refrigerator) a day ahead.

SERVES: 16

PREPARATION TIME: 25 MINUTES

BAKING TIME: 40 TO 45 MINUTES

ASSEMBLY TIME: 10 MINUTES

CAKE:

1 box (16 ounces) angel food cake mix

1¼ cups water

CUSTARD:

1½ cups whole milk

2 large eggs, lightly beaten

½ cup sugar

¼ teaspoon salt

1 envelope (1 ounce) unflavored gelatin

⅓ cup cold water

¾ cup semisweet chocolate chips

2 tablespoons light rum

1½ cups heavy (whipping) cream

½ cup chopped pecans, toasted
(see Toasting Nuts, page 134)

1. Remove the top oven rack and move the other rack to the lowest position. Preheat the oven to 350°F. Set aside an ungreased 10-inch tube pan.

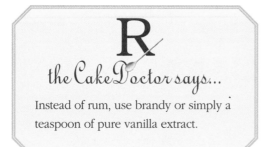

R

the Cake Doctor says...

Instead of rum, use brandy or simply a
teaspoon of pure vanilla extract.

2. Prepare the cake mix according to the
package instructions, using 1¼ cups
water. The batter should look well combined. Pour the batter between the pan,
smoothing it out with the rubber spatula,
and place the pan in the oven.

3. Bake the cake until it is golden brown
and feels firm when lightly pressed with
your finger, 40 to 45 minutes. Remove the
pan from the oven and invert the pan onto
the neck of a heatproof glass bottle until it
is completely cool, from 1 to 1½ hours.
Run a long, sharp knife around the edge
of the cake and invert it onto a platter. Set
aside.

4. Meanwhile, prepare the custard. Place
the milk, eggs, sugar, and salt in a medium
saucepan over medium-low heat. Whisk
and cook until the froth has disappeared
and the mixture is smooth, thickened, and
coats the back of a spoon, 4 to 5 minutes.
Remove the pan from the heat and set
aside. Dissolve the gelatin in the cold water
in a small bowl. Stir into the custard.

5. Working quickly, measure out 1 cup of
the warm custard and place it in a small
bowl with the chocolate chips. Stir until
the chips have melted. Place the chocolate
custard, uncovered, in the refrigerator to
chill. Stir the rum into the remaining custard in the saucepan. Pour the rum custard into a medium-size mixing bowl, and
place the bowl, uncovered, in the refrigerator to chill.

6. Chill a large mixing bowl and beaters
in the freezer for 1 minute. Pour the heavy
cream into the chilled bowl and with an
electric mixer on high speed, beat the
cream until stiff peaks form, 2 to 3 minutes. Remove the rum custard from the
refrigerator and gently fold in the whipped
cream. Return to the refrigerator.

7. Tear the angel food cake into bite-size
pieces and place in the bottom of a 13- by
9-inch baking pan. Spread the rum custard evenly over the cake with the rubber
spatula. Drizzle the chocolate custard
evenly over the rum custard. Cover the
pan with plastic wrap or waxed paper and
place in the refrigerator. Chill at least 1
hour before serving. Spoon individual
servings onto pretty plates, then sprinkle
the top with the toasted pecans.

✳ *Store this cake, covered in plastic
wrap or waxed paper, in the refrigerator for
up to 4 days.*

CHERRY DUMP CAKE

Look at the meager ingredient list and the unflattering name of this time-tested recipe and you might wonder about the outcome. True to its name, you simply dump the ingredients into the pan one by one. But when you smell this dessert baking, you'll only wonder why it took you so long to try it. More like a cobbler than a cake, this classic dump cake is best served warm with vanilla ice cream.

SERVES: 18 TO 20
PREPARATION TIME: 10 MINUTES
BAKING TIME: 55 TO 60 MINUTES

1 can (20 ounces) crushed pineapple, undrained
1 can (21 ounces) cherry pie filling
1 package (18.25 ounces) plain yellow cake mix
12 tablespoons (1½ sticks) butter, melted
½ cup frozen unsweetened grated coconut, thawed
1 cup chopped pecans
Vanilla ice cream, for serving

1. Place a rack in the center of the oven and preheat the oven to 350°F.

2. Spoon the pineapple evenly over the bottom of an ungreased 13- by 9-inch baking pan (see "the Cake Doctor says," page 361). Cover the pineapple with the cherry pie filling. Pour the dry cake mix evenly over the fruit mixture so that it reaches all the sides of the pan. Drizzle the entire pan with the melted butter.

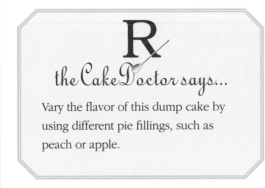

R

the Cake Doctor says...

Vary the flavor of this dump cake by
using different pie fillings, such as
peach or apple.

Sprinkle the coconut and pecans evenly
over the top of the cake. Place the pan in
the oven.

3. Bake the cake until it is deep brown
and a toothpick inserted into the center of
the cake topping comes out clean, 55 to
60 minutes. Remove the pan from the
oven and place it on a wire rack to cool for
10 minutes.

4. Spoon the warm dump cake into
bowls, top with a scoop of vanilla ice
cream, and serve.

✳ *Store this cake, covered in plastic
wrap, for up to 1 day in the refrigerator if
using a metal pan, or for up to 1 week if
using a glass pan. If using a metal pan, let
the cake cool, then transfer it to a glass or
plastic container and it will keep, covered,
for up to 1 week in the refrigerator.*

APPLE WALNUT CRISP

Men just love cobblers and crisps, those down-home deep-dish fruit pies that have a lot of crust or topping. They'll spoon out a huge portion of a warm dessert such as this, load the top with vanilla ice cream, sit back and envision, as they lick the spoon and clean their bowl, that this is the way mama's apple pie tasted. Even if their mama never cooked! And considering that it's no trouble at all to assemble one of these quick apple crisps—it's the same easy preparation as the Cherry Dump Cake—why not go ahead and let 'em dream?

SERVES: 18 TO 20
PREPARATION TIME: 12 MINUTES
BAKING TIME: 55 TO 60 MINUTES

2 cans (21 ounces each) apple pie filling
1 lemon
1 teaspoon ground cinnamon, divided
1 package (18.25 ounces) plain yellow
    cake mix
1 cup chopped walnuts
1 cup (2 sticks) butter, melted

1. Place a rack in the center of the oven and preheat the oven to 350°F (see "the Cake Doctor Says," facing page).

2. Spoon the apple pie filling evenly onto the bottom of an ungreased 13- by 9-inch baking pan. Grate the zest from the lemon and sprinkle it over the apples. Cut the lemon in half and squeeze the juice over the apples. Sprinkle the apples with ½ teaspoon cinnamon. Pour the dry cake mix evenly over the apples so that it reaches all the sides of the pan. Sprinkle the cake mix with the remaining ½ teaspoon cinnamon. Sprinkle the walnuts on top and drizzle the melted butter over the entire pan. Place the pan in the oven.

3. Bake the crisp until it is golden brown and bubbly and the walnuts have browned, 55 to 60 minutes. Remove the pan from the oven and place it on a wire rack to cool for 10 minutes.

4. Spoon the crisp into bowls, top with a scoop of vanilla ice cream, and serve.

✻ *Store this crisp, covered in plastic wrap, for up to 1 day in the refrigerator if using a metal pan, or for up to 1 week if using a glass pan. If using a metal pan, let the crisp cool, then transfer it to a glass or plastic container and it will keep, covered, for up to 1 week in the refrigerator.*

R
the Cake Doctor says...

You can bake crisps, cobblers, and cakes that have a layer of fruit on the bottom in a metal pan, but I find it better to use glass. Although the crisp will bake up nicely in either, the storage time will be less in a metal pan. If left too long in metal, especially aluminum, the acidity in the fruit will corrode the pan (I know from experience!). If using a glass baking pan, reduce the oven temperature to 325°F.

SOUR CREAM PEAR BUCKLE

If you've got a bowl of pears ripening quickly and you're searching for a way to turn them into a quick dessert, here's your answer. This old-fashioned cake, called a buckle, is built on a cake mix, but includes lightly cooked pears, brown sugar, and cinnamon, as well as a topping of sour cream. The pears can be quickly precooked in a microwave oven or steamed in a little water on top of the stove.

SERVES: 18 TO 20

PREPARATION TIME: 15 MINUTES

BAKING TIME: 45 TO 50 MINUTES

CAKE:

Solid vegetable shortening for greasing the pan

Flour for dusting the pan

1 package (18.25 ounces) plain yellow cake mix

4 tablespoons (½ stick) butter, melted

2 large eggs

½ teaspoon ground cinnamon

5 medium pears, peeled, cored, and sliced ¼ inch thick (5 cups sliced)

½ cup packed light brown sugar

½ cup chopped pecans or raisins

½ teaspoon ground cinnamon

TOPPING:

1 cup sour cream

1 large egg

1 teaspoon pure vanilla extract

1. Place a rack in the center of the oven and preheat the oven to 350°F. Lightly grease a 13- by-9-inch baking pan with solid vegetable shortening, then dust with flour. Shake out excess flour. Set the pan aside.

2. Place the cake mix, melted butter, eggs, and cinnamon in a large mixing bowl. Blend with an electric mixer on low speed until the mixture just comes together into a stiff dough, 1 minute. Using wet fingertips, press the dough evenly over the bottom of the prepared pan, so that it reaches the sides of the pan. Set the pan aside.

3. Place the pear slices in a medium-size glass mixing bowl and place in the microwave oven (see "the Cake Doctor says," below). Cook, uncovered, on high power for 2 minutes. Remove the bowl and stir the pear slices. Return the bowl to the oven and cook on high power for 2 minutes more. Remove the bowl and pour the pears over the crust, spreading them evenly with a spoon. Sprinkle the brown sugar over the pears. Sprinkle the nuts and cinnamon over the brown sugar.

4. For the topping, place the sour cream, egg, and vanilla in a small mixing bowl. Whisk to combine, and then pour the mixture over the top of the cake so that it has a drizzled effect and isn't spread neatly from edge to edge. Place the pan in the oven.

5. Bake the cake until the sour cream topping firms up and the cake springs back when lightly pressed with your finger, 45 to 50 minutes. Remove the pan from the oven and place it on a wire rack to cool for 20 minutes.

6. Slice the warm buckle into pieces and, using a metal spatula, remove them from the pan to a serving platter. Serve warm.

✳ *Store this cake, covered in plastic wrap, at room temperature for up to 3 days or in the refrigerator up to 1 week. Or freeze it, wrapped in aluminum foil, for up to 6 months. Before serving, open the foil and reheat the cake in a preheated 300°F oven until warmed through.*

R
the Cake Doctor says...

It is easier to spread the dough onto the bottom of the pan if you press with wet fingertips. If the dough begins to stick to your fingers, just rinse them under running water.

Also, instead of pears, you can substitute lightly cooked peeled, cored apple slices, zapped in the microwave.

If you choose to precook the pears or apples on top of the stove, place them in a medium-size saucepan with ½ cup water. Cover and cook over low heat, stirring occasionally, until soft, 8 to 10 minutes. Drain well before spreading the fruit over the crust.

NINA'S STRAWBERRY CRISP

Nina Long is a Nashville photographer who likes to prepare this easy crisp using frozen straw-berries. It's a recipe she first tasted at her hus-band's family reunion. And whereas the flavor would be spectacular with locally grown berries, it's a dandy of a recipe even if assembled with the frozen supermarket variety. In fact, two 16-ounce bags of frozen unsweetened berries cover a 13- by 9-inch pan perfectly. Layer cake mix and butter on top, then get the bowls ready, for the scent of this crisp baking in the kitchen is truly irresistible.

SERVES: 18 TO 20
PREPARATION TIME: 5 MINUTES
BAKING TIME: 60 TO 65 MINUTES

2 bags (16 ounces each) frozen
    whole unsweetened strawberries,
    thawed, or 6 cups fresh whole
    strawberries, rinsed, drained,
    and capped
1 package (18.25 ounces) plain yellow
    cake mix
1 cup (2 sticks) butter
Vanilla ice cream, for serving
    (optional)

R the Cake Doctor says...

Cake mix will sweeten up unsweet-ened berries, but if you have frozen whole berries in light syrup, don't fret. Just drain the berries of the sugar syrup and save it to pour over pancakes.

1. Place a rack in the center of the oven and preheat the oven to 350°F.

2. Place the strawberries in the bottom of an ungreased 13- by 9-inch baking pan (see "the Cake Doctor says," page 361). Cover the strawberries with half of the dry cake mix. Cut the butter into ½-inch pieces and scatter half of these over the mix. Cover with the remaining cake mix, then scatter the remaining butter pieces on top. Place the pan in the oven.

3. Bake the crisp until it is golden brown and crisp on top, 60 to 65 minutes. Remove the pan from the oven and place it on a wire rack to cool for 10 minutes.

4. Spoon the warm crisp into bowls, top with a scoop of vanilla ice cream if desired, and serve.

❋ *Store this crisp, covered in plastic wrap, for up to 1 day in the refrigerator if using a metal pan or for up to 1 week if using a glass pan. If using a metal pan, let the crisp cool, then transfer it to a glass or plastic container and it will keep, covered, for up to 1 week in the refrigerator.*

What's the Difference?

- **Cobbler:** Fruit and sugar topped with a pastry crust.

- **Crisp:** Fruit and sugar covered with sweet buttery crumbs, and often nuts.

- **Crumble:** Similar to a crisp except the topping is denser and might contain oats.

- **Buckle:** A sweet batter baked up around a fruit topping.

- **Betty:** Similar to cobbler, but made with buttered bread cubes instead of pastry.

PUNCH BOWL CAKE

The English have a proper name for this layered dessert—a trifle. In the classic English trifle, sponge cake is soaked with sherry, then layered with jam and custard in a glass bowl and covered with whipped cream and candied fruit. In this American rendition—called a punch bowl cake because that is the best container in which to display this dessert—a simple yellow cake mix is layered with pie filling, pineapple, pudding, and bananas before being topped with whipped cream. It's heavy and it's wonderful, and I am sure my English friends would approve!

SERVES: 16 TO 20

PREPARATION TIME: 10 MINUTES

BAKING TIME: 30 TO 35 MINUTES

ASSEMBLY TIME: 10 MINUTES

Vegetable oil spray for misting the pan

1 package (18.25 ounces) plain yellow cake mix

1⅓ cups water

⅓ cup vegetable oil, such as canola, corn, safflower, soybean, or sunflower

3 large eggs

2 packages (3.4 ounces each) banana instant pudding mix

4 cups whole milk

2 cans (21 ounces each) cherry pie filling

1 can (20 ounces) crushed pineapple, drained

4 ripe bananas, sliced ½ inch thick

1 container (12 ounces) frozen whipped topping, thawed

1 cup chopped pecans, toasted (see Toasting Nuts, page 134)

R

the Cake Doctor says...

For a change of taste, vary the cake mix and fruits to suit the occasion. With a pineapple cake mix, for example, you might enjoy tropical fruits like mango and pineapple chunks, as well as sliced banana. In the summer, bake up a lemon cake mix and layer it with blueberries, blackberries, raspberries, and strawberries.

1. Place a rack in the center of the oven and preheat the oven to 350°F. Lightly mist a 13- by 9-inch baking pan with vegetable oil spray. Set the pan aside.

2. Place the cake mix, water, oil, and eggs in a large mixing bowl. Blend with an electric mixer on low speed for 1 minute. Stop the machine and scrape down the sides of the bowl with a rubber spatula. Increase the mixer speed to medium and beat for 2 minutes more, scraping the sides down again if needed. The batter should look thick and well blended. Pour the batter into the prepared pan, smoothing it out with the rubber spatula. Place the pan in the oven.

3. Bake the cake until it is golden brown and springs back when lightly pressed with your finger, 30 to 35 minutes. Remove the pan from the oven and place it on a wire rack to cool completely, 40 minutes.

4. Meanwhile, place the banana pudding mix and milk in a large bowl and blend according to the package directions. Set aside.

5. Remove the cooled cake from the pan and crumble it into 1-inch pieces with your hands. Place half of the crumbles in the bottom of a large glass punch bowl. Top with 1 can cherry pie filling, half of the crushed pineapple, and half of the pudding. Add half of the banana slices, half of the whipped topping, and half of the pecans. Repeat the layers, beginning with the remaining cake crumbles and ending with the pecans. Cover the bowl with plastic wrap and place in the refrigerator. Chill at least 1 hour before serving.

6. Serve up portions of the cake with a long spoon.

✳ *Store this cake, covered in plastic wrap, in the refrigerator for up to 4 days.*

CHOCOLATE PUNCH BOWL CAKE

Kathy Sellers passed along this recipe, which she described as "so-ooo good." She's right. There is something so-ooo good about spooning deep into a punch bowl and bringing up layers of Kahlúa-soaked chocolate cake, pudding, whipped topping, and crushed toffee candy. This is Saturday night potluck supper fare, for it is a snap to assemble when you'd rather be digging in your garden than cooking.

SERVES: 16 TO 20

PREPARATION TIME: 10 MINUTES

BAKING TIME: 30 TO 35 MINUTES

ASSEMBLY TIME: 10 MINUTES

Vegetable oil spray for misting the pan

1 package (18.25 ounces) plain devil's food cake mix

1⅓ cups water

⅓ cup vegetable oil, such as canola, corn, safflower, soybean, or sunflower

3 large eggs

2 packages (3.9 ounces each) chocolate instant pudding mix

4 cups whole milk

½ cup Kahlúa or other coffee liqueur

1 container (8 ounces) frozen whipped topping, thawed

1 cup crushed toffee candy bar pieces

1. Place a rack in the center of the oven and preheat the oven to 350°F. Lightly mist a 13- by 9-inch baking pan with vegetable oil spray. Set the pan aside.

R

the Cake Doctor says...

For an elegant change, scatter crumbled Italian amaretti cookies over the whipped topping on the cake instead of the toffee candy pieces.

2. Place the cake mix, water, oil, and eggs in a large mixing bowl. Blend with an electric mixer on low speed for 1 minute. Stop the machine and scrape down the sides of the bowl with a rubber spatula. Increase the mixer speed to medium and beat for 2 minutes more, scraping the sides down again if needed. The batter should look thick and well blended. Pour the batter into the prepared pan, smoothing it out with the rubber spatula. Place the pan in the oven.

3. Bake the cake until it springs back when lightly pressed with your finger and a toothpick inserted in the center comes out clean, 30 to 35 minutes. Remove the cake from the oven and place it on a rack to cool completely, 40 minutes.

4. Meanwhile, place the chocolate pudding mix and milk in a large bowl and blend according to the package directions. Set aside.

5. Remove the cooled cake from the pan and crumble it into 1-inch pieces with your hands. Place all the crumbles in the bottom of a large glass punch bowl. Pour the Kahlúa evenly over the cake. Stir the crumbles to evenly distribute the Kahlúa-soaked ones. With the rubber spatula, spread the chocolate pudding on top of the Kahlúa-soaked cake, then spread the whipped topping over the pudding. Scatter the toffee candy pieces over the whipped topping. Cover the bowl with plastic wrap and place in the refrigerator. Chill at least 1 hour before serving.

6. Serve up portions of the cake with a long spoon.

✳ *Store this cake, covered in plastic wrap, in the refrigerator for up to 4 days.*

FRUIT PIZZA

You couldn't find a more kid-friendly recipe, as children marvel at anything that resembles pizza. And when they bite into the chewy crust, the soft whipped topping and then strawberries, grapes, kiwi, and banana, they may never order pepperoni again!

Prebake

the crust,

then set out

the whipped topping and bowls of sliced fruits for a great backyard birthday party activity.

....

SERVES: 16

PREPARATION TIME: 10 MINUTES

BAKING TIME: 18 TO 22 MINUTES

ASSEMBLY TIME: 10 MINUTES

....

CRUST:

Vegetable oil spray for misting the pans

Parchment or waxed paper for the pans

Flour for dusting the parchment or waxed paper

1 package (18.25 ounces) plain yellow cake mix

¼ cup water

¼ cup packed light brown sugar

4 tablespoons (½ stick) butter, melted

2 large eggs

TOPPING:

1 container (16 ounces) frozen whipped topping, thawed

2 cups sliced fresh strawberries

2 cups thinly sliced bananas

1 cup sliced kiwi

1 cup seedless grapes, halved

GLAZE:

½ cup apricot preserves

2 tablespoons water

R

the Cake Doctor says...

Brown sugar makes the pizza crust nice and chewy. The glaze gives the pizza the look of a European fruit tart.

1. Place one rack in the top of the oven and another in the center and preheat the oven to 350°F. Lightly mist two 12- to 14-inch pizza pans or one 16½- by 11½- by 1-inch jelly-roll pan with vegetable oil spray. Line the pans with parchment paper or waxed paper. Lightly mist the paper with vegetable oil spray, then dust with flour. Hold onto the edges of the paper and shake off the excess flour. Set the pans aside.

2. For the crust, place the cake mix, water, brown sugar, butter, and eggs in a large mixing bowl. Blend with an electric mixer on low speed until well blended, 1 to 2 minutes. The dough will be stiff and sticky. With a rubber spatula, spread the dough onto the bottom and sides of the prepared pans. Place one pizza pan on the top rack in the oven and place the second pan on the center rack. If using a jelly-roll pan, use the center rack.

3. Bake the pizza crust until it is light brown and feels firm in the center when lightly pressed with your finger, 18 to 22 minutes. Take care not to overbake the crust on the top rack. Remove the pans from the oven and place them on wire racks to cool completely, 1 hour.

4. For the topping, spread the cooled pizza crusts with the whipped topping and then arrange the fruit over the top in concentric circles. If using a jelly-roll pan, mix the fruit together in a medium-size mixing bowl and spoon it evenly over the topping. Place the apricot preserves and the water in a small saucepan over low heat, and stir until mixture warms. Remove the pan from the heat and strain, discarding the apricot solids. Brush the strained apricot glaze over the fruit. Place the pizzas in the refrigerator and chill, uncovered, until serving time, at least 1 hour.

✷ *Store this pizza, lightly covered in plastic wrap, in the refrigerator for up to 1 week.*

Lighter Cakes

• • •

In the twentieth century, we've savored sponge cakes, ginger cakes, wartime cakes (made without eggs, milk, or butter), chiffon cakes, Bundt cakes, bar cakes, cheesecakes, flourless chocolate cakes, and the nearly fat-free cakes of the 1990s. Following closely on the heels of those decadent 1980ish cakes rich with whipping cream and caramel, the objective for most of the century's final decade was to excommunicate the fat.

As a result, prune purees replaced butter, and on the back of the box even the cake-mix manufacturers came out with recipes for lighter versions of their cakes. But just so you don't think these folks invented the wheel, consider that for many years cooks have been relying on fruit purees to add flavor, body, and moisture to a batter. Consider the humble banana bread, made rich from a puree of overripe bananas. Consider grandmother's applesauce cake, most likely made with her homemade applesauce.

For years fruit purees have shown they can improve a cake. In this chapter I share recipes that do just that, with purees of prune, pear, apple, and cranberry. Be aware, however, that fruit-based cakes are dense and will not rise as much or brown as easily as cakes containing more eggs and fat.

Other lighter cakes included in this chapter are the chiffon and angel food cake. Chiffons are glorious cakes, middle of the road cakes, encompassing the richness of the sponges and the airiness of the angels. One bite of the Classic Orange, Apricot Lemon, or Dark Chocolate Chiffon Cakes and you'll be baking more chiffons, I promise!

Angel food cakes contain not a smidgen of fat. And all the egg whites you need are dried and already in the mix. All you add is water. But to turn the mix into a signature dessert, you need to add flavorings carefully. The trick is to season without deflating the cake, relying on juice concentrates for some of the water, and grated fruit zest or pure extracts for flavor. Both the chiffon and angel cakes bake up high and mighty in an ungreased tube pan. And both need to cool upside down, with the pan inverted over the neck of a glass bottle for 1 hour.

As the recipes in this chapter prove, you don't have to give up luscious flavor and texture when you bake with less fat.

BETTER-FOR-YOU POUND CAKE

This recipe comes from Kathy McClanahan of Kingston Springs, Tennessee, who believes now is the time to start eating healthier! She incorporates buttermilk and applesauce for richness and uses egg whites instead of whole eggs to cut back on fat. McClanahan stores this cake in the refrigerator overnight and serves it cold with fresh sliced peaches or berries. The cake becomes more moist as it is allowed to rest in the refrigerator.

SERVES: 16

PREPARATION TIME:
5 TO 7 MINUTES

BAKING TIME: 35 TO 40 MINUTES

ASSEMBLY TIME: 5 MINUTES

Vegetable oil spray for misting the pan
1 package (18.25 ounces) yellow cake
    mix with pudding
1¼ cups buttermilk
⅓ cup sweetened applesauce
4 large egg whites
1 tablespoon all-purpose flour
½ cup nonfat sweetened condensed milk
½ cup sliced almonds, toasted
    (see Toasting Nuts, page 134)

1. Place a rack in the center of the oven and preheat the oven to 350°F. Lightly mist a 12-cup Bundt pan with vegetable oil spray. Set the pan aside.

2. Place the cake mix, buttermilk, applesauce, egg whites, and flour in a large mixing bowl. Blend with an electric mixer on low speed for 1 minute. Stop the machine and scrape down the sides of the bowl with a rubber spatula. Increase the mixer speed to medium and beat 2 minutes more, scraping the sides down again if needed. The batter should look well combined and thickened. Pour the batter into the prepared pan, smoothing it out with the rubber spatula. Place the pan in the oven.

3. Bake the cake until it is golden brown and springs back when lightly pressed with your finger, 35 to 40 minutes. Remove the pan from the oven and place it on a wire rack to cool for 20 minutes.

4. Run a long, sharp knife around the edge of the cake and invert it onto a serving platter. Poke holes in the top and sides of the cake with a wooden skewer or toothpick. Brush the cake generously all over with the sweetened condensed milk. Sprinkle with the toasted almonds. Lightly cover the cake with plastic wrap and store in the refrigerator overnight.

5. The next day, slice and serve, with fresh fruit.

❋ *Store this cake, covered in plastic wrap, for up to 1 week in the refrigerator. Or freeze it, wrapped in aluminum foil, for up to 6 months. Thaw the cake overnight on the counter before serving.*

the Cake Doctor says...

This cake benefits from the pudding-enhanced mix. Since you have omitted the egg yolks, the pudding helps to keep the cake moist and makes up for that missing fat. Buttermilk also keeps the cake moist and adds a nice nip.

STRAWBERRY APPLESAUCE CAKE

A lighter cake than the other strawberry cakes in this book, this one is based on applesauce and calls for a package of frozen berries, pureed. You could easily use fresh berries, but do go ahead and slice and sweeten them with sugar first before pureeing (1 tablespoon sugar per 1 cup berries). You will need about a cup of pureed berries for the cake.

SERVES: 16
PREPARATION TIME: 5 MINUTES
BAKING TIME: 30 TO 35 MINUTES
ASSEMBLY TIME: 5 MINUTES

CAKE:

*Vegetable oil spray for misting
    the pan*
Flour for dusting the pan
*1 package (18.25 ounces) plain white
    cake mix*
*1 package (10 ounces) frozen strawberries
    in syrup, thawed and pureed*
½ cup sweetened applesauce
2 large eggs

FROSTING:

*4 ounces neufchâtel cheese (reduced-
    fat cream cheese), at room
    temperature*
*½ cup strawberry preserves or sweetened
    sliced strawberries*
½ cup confectioners' sugar, sifted
1 drop red food coloring (optional)

R

the Cake Doctor says...

This cake is delicious unfrosted. So if you're in a hurry, just dust it with 2 teaspoons confectioners' sugar. Or, if you have fresh strawberries on hand, omit the frosting and fill the center of the cake with 1 cup low-fat vanilla yogurt topped with those gorgeous berries.

1. Place a rack in the center of the oven and preheat the oven to 350°F. Lightly mist a 12-cup Bundt pan with vegetable oil spray, then dust with flour. Shake out the excess flour. Set the pan aside.

2. Place the cake mix, strawberry puree, applesauce, and eggs in a large mixing bowl. Blend with an electric mixer on low speed for 1 minute. Stop the machine and scrape down the sides of the bowl with a rubber spatula. Increase the mixer speed to medium and beat 2 minutes more, scraping the sides down again if needed. The batter should look well combined and thickened. Pour the batter into the prepared pan, smoothing it out with the rubber spatula. Place the pan in the oven.

3. Bake the cake until it is light brown and springs back when lightly pressed with your finger, 30 to 35 minutes. Remove the pan from the oven and place it on a wire rack to cool for 20 minutes. Run a long, sharp knife around the edge of the cake and invert it onto a serving platter to cool completely, 20 minutes more.

4. Meanwhile, prepare the frosting. Place the neufchâtel cheese and the strawberry preserves in a medium-size mixing bowl. Blend with an electric mixer on low speed until just combined, 30 seconds. Stop the machine, scrape down the sides of the bowl with the rubber spatula, and add the confectioners' sugar and red food coloring, if desired. Increase the mixer speed to medium and beat until fluffy, 1 minute more.

5. Spread the frosting over top and sides of the cooled cake with clean, smooth strokes. Slice and serve.

✳ *Store this cake, covered in waxed paper, in the refrigerator for up to 1 week.*

ZESTY CRANBERRY CAKE

This cake is so moist that you'd never guess it is made without oil. Thank the cranberry sauce for that contribution! Serve the cake at those cranberry times of year—Thanksgiving and on through the winter holidays. But don't rule it out for spring and summer, too, since the sauce is available year-round on the grocer's shelf. But unlike the vivid red cranberry sauce, this cake turns pinkish tan as it bakes.

SERVES: 16

PREPARATION TIME: 5 TO 7 MINUTES

BAKING TIME: 30 TO 35 MINUTES

ASSEMBLY TIME: 2 TO 3 MINUTES

Vegetable oil spray for misting the pan
Flour for dusting the pan
1 can (16 ounces) jellied cranberry sauce
1 package (18.25 ounces) plain white
    cake mix
½ cup fresh orange juice (from 2 to 3
    oranges) or from the carton
1 tablespoon grated orange zest (from
    1 medium orange)
2 large eggs
½ cup confectioners' sugar, sifted

1. Place a rack in the center of the oven and preheat the oven to 350°F. Lightly mist a 12-cup Bundt pan with vegetable oil spray, then dust with flour. Shake out the excess flour. Set the pan aside.

2. Reserve ¼ cup of the cranberry sauce for the glaze and place the remaining sauce, the cake mix, orange juice, zest,

the Cake Doctor says...

It's easy to overbake a fruit-based lighter cake since it doesn't brown as much as its higher-fat counterparts. Plus, the lighter cakes bake up dense and don't rise as much in the pan. So do make sure to start testing at the light brown stage.

and eggs in a large mixing bowl. Blend with an electric mixer on low speed for 1 minute. Stop the machine and scrape down the sides of the bowl with the rubber spatula. Increase the mixer speed to medium and beat 2 minutes more, scraping the sides down again if needed. The batter should look well combined and thickened. Pour the batter into the prepared pan, smoothing it out with the rubber spatula. Place the pan in the oven.

3. Bake the cake until it is light brown on top and springs back when lightly pressed with your finger, 30 to 35 minutes. Remove the pan from the oven and place it on a wire rack to cool for 20 minutes. Run a long, sharp knife around the edge of the cake and invert it onto a serving platter to cool completely, 20 minutes more.

4. Meanwhile, prepare the glaze. Place the reserved cranberry sauce and confectioners' sugar in a small mixing bowl. Blend with a fork until well combined and smooth.

5. Spoon the glaze over the cooled cake so that it drizzles down the sides and into the center. Slice and serve.

✳ *Store this cake, covered in waxed paper or in a plastic cake saver, in the refrigerator for up to 1 week. Or freeze it, wrapped in aluminum foil, for up to 6 months. Thaw the cake overnight in the refrigerator before serving.*

PEAR AND TOASTED PECAN BUTTERMILK CAKE

I saw this idea for pureeing canned pears in *Eating Well* magazine. After you puree the pears you cook down the mixture for about 20 minutes on top of the stove to concentrate the flavors. This puree adds body, flavor, and rich- ness to a simple yellow cake mix. Spoon the reserved pear syrup onto the cake as it cools or simply dust with confectioners' sugar.

SERVES: 16

PREPARATION TIME: 30 MINUTES

BAKING TIME: 30 TO 35 MINUTES

ASSEMBLY TIME: 2 TO 3 MINUTES

Vegetable oil spray for misting the pan
Flour for dusting the pan
2 cans (15 ounces each) pear halves
    packed in light syrup, drained,
    syrup reserved
1 package (18.25 ounces) plain yellow
    cake mix
½ cup buttermilk
2 large eggs
2 teaspoons pure vanilla extract
½ cup finely chopped toasted pecans
    (see Toasting Nuts, page 134)

1. Place a rack in the center of the oven and preheat the oven to 350°F. Mist a 12-cup Bundt pan with vegetable oil spray, then dust with flour. Shake out the excess flour. Set the pan aside.

2. Place the drained pear halves in a food processor fitted with a steel blade. Process

R

the Cake Doctor says...

Reducing the pear puree intensifies its flavor. If you are pressed for time, you can omit this step. You will need a generous cup of pear puree for the recipe.

until the pears are pureed, about 10 seconds. Transfer the pear puree to a small saucepan and place over medium heat. Cook, stirring occasionally, until the pear puree has reduced by half its volume, 15 to 20 minutes. You should have about 1 cup puree. Remove the pan from the heat and let the puree cool.

3. Place the cake mix, buttermilk, eggs, vanilla, and cooled pear puree in a large mixing bowl. Blend with an electric mixer on low speed for 1 minute. Stop the machine and scrape down the sides of the bowl with a rubber spatula. Increase the mixer speed to medium and beat for 2 minutes more, scraping the sides down again if needed. The batter should look well blended. Fold in the pecans until well distributed. Pour the batter into the prepared pan, smoothing the top with the rubber spatula. Place the pan in the oven.

4. Bake the cake until it is light brown and springs back when lightly pressed with your finger, 30 to 35 minutes. Remove the pan from the oven and place it on a rack to cool for 20 minutes. Run a long, sharp knife around the edge of the cake and invert it onto a serving platter.

5. Poke holes in the top of the cake with a wooden skewer or toothpick. Spoon 1 cup of the reserved pear syrup on the top of the cake and allow it to seep into the holes and drizzle down the sides and into the center. Allow the cake to cool completely, 30 minutes more. Slice and serve.

✷ *Store this cake, covered in plastic wrap, at room temperature for up to 1 week. Or freeze it, wrapped in aluminum foil, for up to 6 months. Thaw the cake overnight on the counter before serving.*

Vanilla

In the humid tropical forests of the world, a giant climbing orchid vine called *Vanilla planifolia* grows. But on only one day of the year do the orchid blossoms open. When they do, they are quickly hand-pollinated, for their only natural pollinator is the overworked and vanishing Melipona bee. (Pesticides have killed much of the Melipona bee population.) In about 10 months, the orchid produces mature pods, which are hand-picked while green, boiled, dried, and fermented to take on the characteristic brown color that we know as vanilla beans. After these beans are chopped and soaked in an alcohol and water solution, they become the pure vanilla extract we use in baking and cooking.

Pure vanilla is twice as expensive as artificial vanillin, which is used in cake-mix formulation and comes from pine, fir, and other wood pulp by-products. The first vanilla substitute was developed in Germany in 1876. This is not to be confused with natural vanillin, however, a powdery substance or bloom (what the French call *givre*) that occurs on the better vanilla beans after fermentation.

You can improve your cake-mix batters by using pure vanilla extract. Here are some suggestions:

- Vanilla extract makes a batter foam, so add it at the end of the preparation.

- Flavor confectioners' sugar with vanilla to use in frostings and glazes. Place a whole vanilla bean in a glass jar filled with confectioners' sugar. Fasten the lid and let it sit for a week on the kitchen counter before using.

- To make your own pure vanilla extract, coarsely grind vanilla beans in a food processor. Place them in a glass jar and cover with brandy or dark rum (2 vanilla beans for each ½ cup liquid). Fasten the lid and let sit on the counter for a month. Strain and use.

CLASSIC ORANGE CHIFFON CAKE

I f I had to name the perfect flavor match for the chiffon cake, it would be orange. And there is no better way to impart an orange oomph in cake than to add thawed frozen orange juice concentrate. My family raved about this cake, pristine in color and captivating in flavor. It reminded me of the orange cake my grandmother used to bake.

SERVES: 16
PREPARATION TIME: 15 MINUTES
BAKING TIME:
48 TO 52 MINUTES
ASSEMBLY TIME: 5 MINUTES

CAKE:

5 large egg whites

½ teaspoon cream of tartar

1 package (18.25 ounces) plain yellow cake mix

3 large egg yolks

¾ cup orange juice

½ cup vegetable oil, such as canola, corn, safflower, soybean, or sunflower

¼ cup thawed frozen orange juice concentrate (see "the Cake Doctor says," page 385)

1 teaspoon grated orange zest

GLAZE:

2 cups confectioners' sugar, sifted

3 tablespoons orange juice

The Chiffon Cake

In chiffon cakes you have the best of both cake worlds—the moistness and tenderness of a cake made with fat and the lightness of a cake made with beaten egg whites.

The idea of incorporating beaten egg whites into a batter prepared with yolks and vegetable oil belonged to a Los Angeles insurance salesman named Harry Baker. He is said to have developed the cake in 1927, and he baked it for celebrities until he was able to sell his "little secret" to General Mills in 1948. This gossamer, light from-scratch cake called the chiffon was heralded by G.M. as the "cake discovery of the century." It was light, it was airy, it was moist and velvety, and it baked high in the pan. It was far more tender than the angel food cake. And happily, in the time before electric mixers, the chiffon took only 10 minutes of manual beating to come together, compared to the rigorous 25 minutes of the angel food.

The chiffon is a perfect cake to begin with a mix because it can rely on the mix's built-in leavening agents and not just the leavening power of the eggs. Oil tends to make a from-scratch chiffon cake heavy unless it is added in a stream so that it suspends throughout the batter. With cake-mix chiffons you don't have to be so careful, and you can blend the yolks, oil, liquid, flavorings, and cake mix and then fold in the beaten egg whites.

1. Place a rack in the center of the oven and preheat the oven to 325°F. Set aside an ungreased 10-inch tube pan.

2. Place the egg whites and cream of tartar in a medium mixing bowl. Beat with an electric mixer on high speed until stiff peaks form, 2 to 3 minutes. Set the bowl aside.

3. Place the cake mix, egg yolks, orange juice, oil, orange juice concentrate, and orange zest in a large mixing bowl, and with the same beaters used to beat the egg whites (no need to clean them) blend with the electric mixer on low speed for 1 minute. Stop the machine and scrape down the sides of the bowl with a rubber spatula. Increase the mixer speed to medium and beat for 2 minutes more, scraping the sides down again if needed. The batter should look well blended. Turn the beaten egg whites out on top of the batter, and with the

R

the Cake Doctor says...

After you measure out ¼ cup of the thawed orange juice concentrate, prepare orange juice with the remaining concentrate by adding half as much water as the package directs. Use this orange juice in the cake batter and glaze.

rubber spatula fold the whites into the batter until the mixture is light but well combined. Pour the batter into the prepared pan, smoothing the top out with the rubber spatula. Place the pan in the oven.

4. Bake the cake until it is golden brown and springs back when lightly pressed with your finger, 48 to 52 minutes. Remove the pan from the oven and immediately turn it upside down over the neck of a glass bottle to cool for 1 hour. Remove the pan from the bottle. Run a long, sharp knife around the edge of the cake and invert it once onto a rack, then invert it again on a serving platter, so that it is right side up.

5. For the glaze, place the confectioners' sugar and orange juice in a medium mixing bowl. Blend with an electric mixer on low speed for 1 minute. Spread the glaze over the top and sides of the cake with clean, smooth strokes. Let the glaze set for 20 minutes, then slice and serve.

✳ *Store this cake, covered loosely in plastic wrap, at room temperature for up to 1 week. Or freeze it, wrapped in aluminum foil, for up to 6 months. Thaw the cake overnight on the counter before serving.*

APRICOT LEMON CHIFFON CAKE

can of apricot nectar in the pantry reminded me of a flavor combination I adore—apricots and lemons. Team these two up in a chiffon cake and you have a cake that is worthy of dinner party fare, and certainly will take highest bids at the bake sale! This chiffon cake tastes best when simply glazed. It is also superb unglazed, with just a cold glass of milk.

SERVES: 16

PREPARATION TIME: 10 TO 12 MINUTES

BAKING TIME: 48 TO 52 MINUTES

ASSEMBLY TIME: 5 MINUTES

CAKE:

5 large egg whites

½ teaspoon cream of tartar

1 package (18.25 ounces) plain white cake mix

3 large egg yolks

¾ cup apricot nectar

½ cup vegetable oil, such as canola, corn, safflower, soybean, or sunflower

2 tablespoons fresh lemon juice

1 teaspoon grated lemon zest

GLAZE:

2 cups confectioners' sugar, sifted

2 tablespoons fresh lemon juice

1 tablespoon apricot nectar

1 teaspoon grated lemon zest

Egg Whites:

THE KEY TO A CHIFFON'S SUCCESS

Egg whites are crucial to the moist-textured chiffon cake. So here are some things to remember:

- **Temperature:** Traditionally you can get more volume from room temperature egg whites, but with cake-mix chiffons, egg whites right out of the refrigerator work just fine.

- **Cream of tartar:** The addition of this acidic powder stabilizes the egg whites as they are beaten to stiff peaks.

- **Equipment:** Use an electric mixer on the highest setting, making sure the beaters are clean, without a trace of fat. It will take from 2 to 3 minutes to beat 5 large egg whites.

- **Stiff peaks:** Stop the electric mixer and pull the beaters out of the egg whites. The foam that clings to the beaters should be straight and stiff, not curved as in soft peaks.

- **Folding:** This is the down-across-up-over motion used to incorporate beaten egg whites into a heavier batter without losing precious air in the egg whites. Turn the beaten egg whites out of the bowl on top of the beaten egg yolk, cake mix, and oil mixture. Beginning at the back of the bowl, cut down through the egg whites and batter with a rubber spatula, across the bottom of the bowl and up to the side nearest you. Rotate the bowl a quarter of a turn after a few strokes. Fold only until the batter has lightened and no traces of white remain.

1. Place a rack in the center of the oven and preheat the oven to 325°F. Set aside an ungreased 10-inch tube pan.

2. Place the egg whites and cream of tartar in a medium mixing bowl. Beat with an electric mixer on high speed until stiff peaks form, 2 to 3 minutes. Set the bowl aside.

3. Place the cake mix, egg yolks, apricot nectar, oil, lemon juice, and lemon zest in a large mixing bowl, and with the same beaters used to beat the egg whites (no

R
the Cake Doctor says...

You will need about 2 lemons for this cake. I've mentioned this before but it's worth noting again: To extract more juice from a lemon, roll it back and forth between your palm and the kitchen counter before cutting and squeezing.

need to clean them) blend with an electric mixer on low speed for 1 minute. Stop the machine and scrape down the sides of the bowl with a rubber spatula. Increase the mixer speed to medium and beat for 2 minutes more, scraping the sides down again if needed. The batter should look well blended. Turn the beaten egg whites out on top of the batter, and with the rubber spatula fold the whites into the batter until the mixture is light but well combined. Pour the batter into the prepared pan, smoothing out the top with the rubber spatula. Place the pan in the oven.

4. Bake the cake until it is golden brown and springs back when lightly pressed with your finger, 48 to 52 minutes. Remove the pan from the oven and immediately turn it upside down over the neck of a glass bottle to cool for 1 hour. Remove the pan from the bottle. Run a long, sharp knife around the edge of the cake and invert it onto a rack, then invert it again onto a serving platter so that it is right side up.

5. For the glaze, place the confectioners' sugar, lemon juice, apricot nectar, and lemon zest in a medium-size mixing bowl. Blend with an electric mixer on low speed for 1 minute. Spread the frosting on the top and sides of the cake with clean, smooth strokes. Let the frosting set for 20 minutes, then slice and serve.

✳ *Store this cake, covered loosely in plastic wrap, at room temperature for up to 1 week. Or freeze it, wrapped in aluminum foil, for up to 6 months. Thaw the cake overnight on the counter before serving.*

DARK CHOCOLATE CHIFFON CAKE

I already know that this is the cake I would like for my birthday—not just this year, but every year. So I am teaching my daughter Kathleen how to beat egg whites so she can make it for me! In fact, I enjoy it so much, I'm hoping Kathleen keeps it in mind for Mother's Day as well. Cakes don't get much more down to earth than an enjoyable chocolate chiffon.

SERVES: 16
PREPARATION TIME: 10 MINUTES
BAKING TIME: 48 TO 52 MINUTES
ASSEMBLY TIME: 5 MINUTES

CAKE:

5 large egg whites

½ teaspoon cream of tartar

1 package (18.25 ounces) plain devil's food cake mix

3 large egg yolks

¾ cup water

½ cup vegetable oil, such as canola, corn, safflower, soybean, or sunflower

1 tablespoon instant coffee powder

1 teaspoon pure vanilla extract

FROSTING:

3 tablespoons butter, at room temperature

3 tablespoons unsweetened cocoa powder

1 cup confectioners' sugar, sifted

2 tablespoons milk

1 teaspoon pure vanilla extract

R

the Cake Doctor says...

For a more adult flavor, add 1 tablespoon brandy to the frosting instead of the vanilla. Add a little extra confectioners' sugar if needed to make the frosting of a nice spreading consistency.

1. Place a rack in the center of the oven and preheat the oven to 325°F. Set aside an ungreased 10-inch tube pan.

2. Place the egg whites and cream of tartar in a medium mixing bowl. Beat with an electric mixer on high speed until stiff peaks form, 2 to 3 minutes. Set the bowl aside.

3. Place the cake mix, egg yolks, water, oil, coffee powder, and vanilla in a large mixing bowl, and with the same beaters used to beat the egg whites (no need to clean them) blend with an electric mixer on low speed for 1 minute. Stop the machine and scrape down the sides of the bowl with a rubber spatula. Increase the mixer speed to medium and beat for 2 minutes more, scraping the sides down again if needed. The batter should look well blended. Turn the beaten egg whites out on top of the batter, and with the rub-

ber spatula fold the whites into the batter until the mixture is light but well combined. Pour the batter into the prepared pan, smoothing the top out with the rubber spatula. Place the pan in the oven.

4. Bake the cake until it springs back when lightly pressed with your finger and a toothpick inserted in the center comes out clean, 48 to 52 minutes. Remove the pan from the oven and immediately turn it upside down over the neck of a glass bottle to cool for 1 hour. Remove the pan from the bottle. Run a long, sharp knife around the edge of the cake and invert it onto a rack, then invert it again onto a serving platter so that it is right side up.

5. For the frosting, place the butter and cocoa in a medium-size mixing bowl. Blend with an electric mixer on low speed for 30 seconds. Stop the machine and add the confectioners' sugar, milk, and vanilla. Increase the mixer speed to medium and beat until fluffy, 1 minute more. Spread the frosting on the top and sides of the cake with clean, smooth strokes. Slice and serve.

✱ *Store this cake, covered with a glass cake dome, at room temperature for up to 4 days or in the refrigerator for up to 1 week. Or freeze it, wrapped in aluminum foil, for up to 6 months. Thaw the cake overnight in the refrigerator before serving.*

ORANGE ALMOND ANGEL FOOD CAKE

Angel food cake mix has a decidedly almond taste, so I built on this flavor by adding almond extract and orange juice concentrate. This cake bakes up tall and beautiful in the pan and is delicious sliced and served along with frozen yogurt. If you feel the urge to splurge—and who doesn't once in a while—frost with the easy almond-enhanced whipped cream I suggest in this recipe.

SERVES: 16

PREPARATION TIME: 10 MINUTES

BAKING TIME: 38 TO 42 MINUTES

ASSEMBLY TIME: 5 TO 7 MINUTES

....

CAKE:

1 package (16 ounces) angel food cake mix

1 cup water

¼ cup thawed frozen orange juice concentrate

1 teaspoon pure almond extract

TOASTED ALMOND CREAM (OPTIONAL):

1 cup heavy (whipping) cream

1 tablespoon confectioners' sugar

¼ teaspoon pure almond extract

¼ cup sliced almonds, toasted (see Toasting Nuts, page 134)

R

the Cake Doctor says...

The acid in the orange juice concentrate has a beneficial effect on the egg whites in the cake mix. You get maximum rise and a soft, pillowy texture.

Angels in the Icebox

Hilda Chapin of Vero Beach, Florida, sent in this recipe for a special angel food cake: Carefully cut a 1-inch slice off the top of a cooled angel food cake in one piece. Use your hands to hollow out the cake, leaving a 1-inch shell. Fill it with frozen yogurt. Replace the top slice and freeze the cake. Frost with fat-free whipped topping and cover with crushed peanut brittle.

1. Place a rack in the center of the oven and preheat the oven to 325°F. Set aside an ungreased 10-inch tube pan.

2. Place the cake mix, water, orange juice concentrate, and the almond extract in a large mixing bowl. Beat with an electric mixer on low speed for 1 minute. Stop the machine and scrape down the sides of the bowl with a rubber spatula. Increase the mixer speed to medium and beat for 1 minute more, scraping the sides down again if needed. The batter should look well blended. Pour the batter into the prepared pan, smoothing the top with the rubber spatula. Place the pan in the oven.

3. Bake the cake until it is deep brown and springs back when lightly pressed with your finger, 38 to 42 minutes. Remove the pan from the oven and immediately turn it upside down over the neck of a glass bottle to cool for 1 hour. Remove the pan from the bottle. Run a long, sharp knife around the edge of the cake and invert it onto a rack, then invert it again onto a serving platter so that it is right side up.

4. Prepare the Toasted Almond Cream, if desired. Place a large mixing bowl and the beaters for the electric mixer in the freezer to chill for a few minutes. Place the cream in the chilled bowl and beat with the mixer on high speed until slightly thickened, or soft peaks form, 2 minutes. Add the confectioners' sugar and the almond extract and continue beating at high speed until stiff peaks form, 1 to 2 minutes more. Fold in the toasted almonds until well distributed.

5. Spread the Toasted Almond Cream over the top of the cake or serve it in a bowl on the side. Slice and serve.

❋ *Store this cake, covered in plastic wrap, at room temperature for up to 1 week. Or freeze it, wrapped in aluminum foil, for up to 6 months. Thaw the cake overnight on the counter before serving.*

CHOCOLATE-SPECKLED PEPPERMINT ANGEL FOOD CAKE

When I think of chocolate and peppermint and angel food cake, I envision a ladies' lunch on the terrace with starched linen tablecloths, sterling silver spoons, and freshly cut roses in crystal vases. Serve this cake with scoops of chocolate nonfat frozen yogurt and dig in guilt-free. If you wish to omit the schnapps, increase the water to 1¼ cups and the extract to ½ teaspoon.

R *the Cake Doctor says...*

This cake is delicious as is or topped with frozen yogurt or with scoops of peppermint or chocolate chip ice cream. It is also good with whipped cream flavored with crushed peppermint candy. Add the candy once the cream is at the soft peak stage, then continue beating until stiff peaks form. For chocolate lovers, serve this cake with chocolate syrup.

SERVES: 16

PREPARATION TIME: 10 MINUTES

BAKING TIME:

40 TO 45 MINUTES

6 Ways to Tweak an Angel Food Cake

Angel food cake mixes rely on water to get them going. Make your cake special by adding one of the following to the batter.

- **Toasted coconut:** Add ½ cup.

- **Unsweetened cocoa powder:** Add up to ¼ cup.

- **Pure almond extract:** Add 1 teaspoon.

- **Peppermint schnapps:** Add 2 tablespoons.

- **Coffee:** Add up to ¼ cup, brewed and cooled, replacing the same amount of the water.

- **Orange juice concentrate:** Add up to ¼ cup, replacing the same amount of water.

---

1 package (16 ounces) angel food cake mix

1 cup water

¼ cup peppermint schnapps

¼ teaspoon pure peppermint extract

1 square (1 ounce) semisweet chocolate, grated

1. Place a rack in the center of the oven and preheat the oven to 325°F. Set aside an ungreased 10-inch tube pan.

2. Place the cake mix, water, peppermint schnapps, and peppermint extract in a large mixing bowl. Beat with an electric mixer on low speed for 1 minute. Stop the machine and scrape down the sides of the bowl with a rubber spatula. Increase the mixer speed to medium and beat for 1 minute more, scraping the sides down again if needed. The batter should look well blended. Fold in the grated chocolate until well distributed. Pour the batter into the prepared pan, smoothing out the top with the rubber spatula. Place the pan in the oven.

3. Bake the cake until it is light brown and springs back when lightly pressed with your finger, 40 to 45 minutes. Remove the pan from the oven and immediately turn it upside down over the neck of a glass bottle to cool for 1 hour. Remove the pan from the bottle. Run a long, sharp knife around the edge of the cake and invert it onto a rack, then invert it again onto a serving platter so that it is right side up. Slice and serve.

✳ *Store this cake, covered in plastic wrap, at room temperature for up to 1 week. Or freeze it, wrapped in aluminum foil, for up to 6 months. Thaw the cake overnight in the refrigerator before serving.*

CINNAMON AND PINEAPPLE CARROT SHEET CAKE

Most carrot cakes are heavy with oil—but not this one. A fast puree of prunes and hot water yields a healthy substitute. You also add crushed pineapple and freshly grated carrots, providing a delicious mingling of flavors and textures. The creamy frosting is really much lighter than what would ordinarily top a carrot cake. Neufchâtel is lower in fat than cream cheese and marshmallow creme fluffs without fat.

SERVES: 20

PREPARATION TIME: 10 MINUTES

BAKING TIME: 33 TO 37 MINUTES

ASSEMBLY TIME: 5 MINUTES

CAKE:

Vegetable oil spray for misting the pan

½ cup pitted prunes (12 prunes)

¼ cup hot water

1 package (18.25 ounces) plain yellow
    cake mix

¼ cup vegetable oil, such as canola, corn,
    safflower, soybean, or sunflower

2 large eggs

1 teaspoon ground cinnamon

1 can (8 ounces) crushed pineapple in
    juice, drained

1 cup grated carrots (3 medium carrots)

FROSTING:

4 ounces neufchâtel cheese (reduced-fat
    cream cheese), at room temperature

½ cup marshmallow creme

GARNISH:

½ cup chopped pecans, toasted
    (see Toasting Nuts, page 134)

R

the Cake Doctor says...

Neufchâtel cheese is a less fatty stand-in for full-fat cream cheese. If you desire a lot of frosting, double the recipe. This cake recipe also works well as cupcakes. Fill pan cups three-quarters full; it will make about 12 cupcakes that need from 25 to 30 minutes to bake.

1. Place a rack in the center of the oven and preheat the oven to 350°F. Lightly mist a 13- by 9-inch baking pan with vegetable oil spray. Set the pan aside.

2. Place the prunes and hot water in a food processor fitted with the steel blade. Process with on and off pulses until the prunes are finely chopped. Scrape down the sides of the processor with the rubber spatula. Set the prune puree aside.

3. Place the cake mix, oil, eggs, cinnamon, and prune puree in a large mixing bowl. Blend with an electric mixer on low speed for 1 minute. Stop the machine and scrape down the sides of the bowl with a rubber spatula. Increase the mixer speed to medium and beat for 2 minutes more, scraping the sides down again if needed.

The batter will be thick. Fold in the drained pineapple and carrots until well distributed. Pour the batter into the prepared pan, smoothing the top with the rubber spatula. Place the pan in the oven.

4. Bake the cake until it is golden brown and springs back when lightly pressed in the center, 33 to 37 minutes. Remove the pan from the oven and place it on a wire rack to cool.

5. Meanwhile, prepare the frosting. Place the neufchâtel cheese and the marshmallow creme in a medium-size mixing bowl. Blend with an electric mixer on low speed until just combined, 30 seconds. Stop the machine and scrape down the sides of the bowl with the rubber spatula. Increase the mixer speed to medium and beat until fluffy, 1 minute more.

6. When the cake has cooled, spread the top with a thin layer of frosting. Sprinkle with the toasted chopped pecans. Cut into squares and serve.

✻ *Store this cake, covered in plastic wrap, in the refrigerator for up to 1 week.*

Just the Basics

• • •

eet the bare bones. Without the chocolate chips, the fluffy frostings, and the extravagant fillings, these recipes are the beginnings of many a recipe in this book. And they are assembled here for all of you who—on occasion—want just the basics because you'd rather do your own creative doctoring.

Well, here are the canvases, so to speak. I've already doctored the mixes, but feel free to tweak them to your own taste. Use the ingredients you've got in the pantry, adding a smidgen of ginger or a pinch of cinnamon; mix in orange juice and zest, chocolate chips or sprinkles, raisins or dried cranberries. Be your own Cake Mix Doctor.

BASIC SOUR CREAM WHITE CAKE

I love this cake plain just as I love a cup of plain hot tea. The tender, colorless cake has a comforting quality just like that unadulterated tea. It is the foundation for Snowballs (page 215) and also the Plum and Cardamom Cake baked in a Bundt pan (page 87).

the Cake Doctor says...

This recipe is made in a 13- by 9-inch pan, but you can easily bake it in layers (see Pan Changes, page 405).

SERVES: 16 TO 20

PREPARATION TIME: 6 MINUTES

BAKING TIME: 35 TO 40 MINUTES

Solid vegetable shortening for greasing the pan
Flour for dusting the pan
1 package (18.25 ounces) plain white cake mix
1 cup sour cream
½ cup vegetable oil, such as canola, corn, safflower, soybean, or sunflower
3 large eggs
1 teaspoon pure vanilla extract

1. Place a rack in the center of the oven and preheat the oven to 350°F. Generously grease a 13- by 9-inch baking pan with solid vegetable shortening, then dust with flour. Shake out the excess flour. Set the pan aside.

2. Place the cake mix, sour cream, oil, eggs, and vanilla in a large mixing bowl. Blend with an electric mixer on low speed for 1 minute. Stop the machine

Freezing Unfrosted Cakes

With time being your most precious commodity, it makes sense to bake cakes ahead and freeze them for later consumption. And one of the best ways to do this and still allow for that last-minute spontaneity is to bake and freeze unfrosted layers. To prepare unfrosted cakes for freezing, first make sure they have cooled completely on the kitchen counter. Then, wrap well in heavy-duty aluminum foil and place them in a large zipper-lock freezer bag and seal. Or, if you don't have any bags, wrap them twice in heavy-duty aluminum foil. Place in the coldest part of your freezer—the back or the bottom— where they will keep for up to 2 months.

To thaw for frosting, remove the layers from the plastic bag and unwrap the foil at the top so the cake can breathe as it thaws on the counter. This will allow the moisture to escape so the cake won't get soggy. When the cake is completely thawed, frost the layers and serve.

and scrape down the sides of the bowl with a rubber spatula. Increase the mixer speed to medium and beat 2 minutes more, scraping the sides down again if needed. The batter should look well combined and thickened. Pour the batter into the prepared pan, smoothing it out with the rubber spatula. Place the pan in the oven.

3. Bake the cake until it is light brown and springs back when lightly pressed with your finger, 35 to 40 minutes. Remove the pan from the oven and place it on a wire rack to cool for 20 minutes. Run a dinner knife around the edge of the cake and invert it onto a rack, then invert it again onto another rack so that the right side is up. Allow the cake to cool completely, 30 minutes. Frost as desired.

❋ *Store this cake, unfrosted, covered in aluminum foil, at room temperature for up to 4 days or in the refrigerator for up to 1 week. For freezing unfrosted cake, see box above.*

BASIC YOGURT WHITE CAKE

What a moist and flavorful cake yogurt makes! This cake formula is found in the Charleston Poppy Seed Cake (page 124) and the Lemon Buttermilk Poppy Seed Cake (page 127). It's so delicious, no glaze is needed, although a little sifted confectioners' sugar sprinkled over the top is a nice touch.

R
the Cake Doctor says...

Yogurt gives this cake the same rich texture as sour cream but without so much fat.

SERVES: 16

PREPARATION TIME: 5 TO 7 MINUTES

BAKING TIME:
45 TO 50 MINUTES

Vegetable oil spray for misting the pan
Flour for dusting the pan
1 package (18.25 ounces) plain white
  cake mix
1 package (3.4 ounces) vanilla instant
  pudding mix
1 cup low-fat vanilla yogurt
½ cup vegetable oil, such as canola, corn,
  safflower, soybean, or sunflower
½ cup liquid, such as water, dry sherry,
  or orange juice
4 large eggs

1. Place a rack in the center of the oven and preheat the oven to 350°F. Lightly mist a 10-inch tube pan with vegetable oil spray, then dust with flour. Shake out the excess flour. (For other sizes of this cake, see Pan Changes, page 405.) Set the pan aside.

Is It Possible for a Cake Mix to Flop?

*Y*es. The three most common mistakes consumers make in preparing a cake using a mix are:

1. ***Not measuring accurately:*** In spite of the road tests on cake mixes, you need to measure correctly. That means glass measuring cups for liquids and spoons and cups for dry measures.

2. ***Not timing properly:*** If you keep forgetting to jot down what time you placed the cake in the oven, buy an inexpensive timer and set it when you place the cake in the oven. You're bound to remember to do one or the other.

3. ***Baking with an oven temperature that is too high:*** As ovens age, so do thermostats. Most often these older ovens bake at 25 degrees and up higher than normal. Invest in an oven thermometer and either bake with a reduced oven temperature or, better still, have your oven recalibrated.

2. Place the cake mix, pudding mix, yogurt, oil, liquid of choice, and eggs in a large mixing bowl. Blend with an electric mixer on low speed for 1 minute. Stop the machine and scrape down the sides of the bowl with a rubber spatula. Increase the mixer speed to medium and beat 2 minutes more, scraping the sides down again if needed. The batter should look well combined and thickened. Pour the batter into the prepared pan, smoothing it out with the rubber spatula. Place the pan in the oven.

3. Bake the cake until it is golden brown and springs back when lightly pressed with your finger, 45 to 50 minutes. Remove the pan from the oven and place it on a wire rack to cool for 20 minutes. Run a long, sharp knife around the edge of the cake and invert it onto a wire rack, then invert again onto another rack so that the cake is right side up. Allow the cake to cool completely, 30 minutes more. Frost as desired.

✳ *Store this cake, unfrosted, covered in aluminum foil, at room temperature for up to 4 days or in the refrigerator for up to 1 week. For freezing unfrosted cake, see page 399.*

BASIC
BUTTER CAKE

Turn this formula into birthday layer cakes, such as Mom's Layer Cake with Fluffy Chocolate Frosting (page 106). Or bake in a Bundt pan, as in Five-Flavor Cake (page 165).

SERVES: 16

PREPARATION TIME:
5 TO 7 MINUTES

BAKING TIME: 27 TO 29 MINUTES

Solid vegetable shortening for greasing
   the pans
Flour for dusting the pans
1 package (18.25 ounces) plain white
   cake mix
1 cup whole milk
8 tablespoons (1 stick) butter, melted
3 large eggs
2 teaspoons pure vanilla extract

R

the Cake Doctor says...

These are the layers to bake ahead and freeze to frost later for birthdays. When you're busy with other party preparations, you'll be glad to have one less thing to get done.

1. Place a rack in the center of the oven and preheat the oven to 350°F. Generously grease two 9-inch round cake pans with solid vegetable shortening, then dust with flour. Shake out the excess flour. Set the pans aside.

2. Place the cake mix, milk, melted butter, eggs, and vanilla in a large mixing bowl. Blend with an electric mixer on low speed for 1 minute. Stop the machine and scrape down the sides of the bowl with a rubber spatula. Increase the mixer speed to medium and beat 2 minutes more, scraping the sides down again if needed. The batter should look well blended. Divide the batter between the prepared pans, smoothing it out with the rubber spatula. Place the pans in the oven side by side.

3. Bake the cake until it is golden brown and springs back when lightly pressed with your finger, 27 to 29 minutes. Remove the pans from the oven and place them on a wire rack to cool for 10 minutes. Run a dinner knife around the edge of each layer and invert each onto a rack, then invert them again onto another rack so that the cakes are right side up. Allow the cakes to cool completely, 30 minutes more. Frost as desired.

✱ *Store this cake, unfrosted, covered in aluminum foil, at room temperature for up to 4 days or in the refrigerator for up to 1 week. For freezing unfrosted cakes, see page 399.*

BASIC SOUR CREAM YELLOW CAKE

This recipe is the basis for the famous Sock-It-To-Me Cake (page 260). It's a dandy of a Bundt or tube cake recipe, easily tweaked with your favorite spices and flavorings. To dress it up, spread with Shiny Chocolate Glaze (page 435), or, more simply, with confectioners' sugar moistened with a little milk.

R
the Cake Doctor says...

For a super-easy taste change, substitute pure almond extract for the vanilla. Serve it up as Almond Sour Cream Pound Cake. Terrific!

SERVES: 16
PREPARATION TIME: 5 TO 7 MINUTES
BAKING TIME: 50 TO 55 MINUTES

Vegetable oil spray for misting the pan
Flour for dusting the pan
1 package (18.25 ounces) plain yellow
*   cake mix*
1 cup sour cream
⅓ cup vegetable oil, such as canola,
*   corn, safflower, soybean, or*
*   sunflower*
¼ cup water
¼ cup sugar
4 large eggs
1 teaspoon pure vanilla extract

1. Place a rack in the center of the oven and preheat the oven to 350°F. Lightly mist a 10-inch tube pan with vegetable oil spray, then dust with flour. Shake out the excess flour. Set the pan aside.

2. Place the cake mix, sour cream, oil, water, sugar, eggs, and vanilla in a large mixing bowl. Blend with an electric mixer

Pan Changes

Let's say you need a layer cake but the recipe you'd like to try calls for a Bundt pan. Or, let's say you don't have time to fuss with frosting a layer cake and would rather make a sheet cake instead. It's possible to break the mold and pour that batter into a different-shaped pan. Just follow my guidelines below. Layers bake most quickly, followed by the 13- by 9-inch sheet pan, followed by Bundts and tubes. Pay close attention to your cake and look for light browning, the center that springs back when lightly pressed, and edges that start to pull away from the sides of the pan—all signs of doneness.

- For 9-inch cake layers, plan on from 27 to 32 minutes.
- For a 13- by 9-inch pan, plan on from 30 to 45 minutes.
- For 12-cup Bundts or 10-inch tubes, plan on 40 to 55 minutes.

on low speed for 1 minute. Stop the machine and scrape down the sides of the bowl with a rubber spatula. Increase the mixer speed to medium and beat 2 minutes more, scraping the sides down again if needed. The batter should look thick and smooth. Pour the batter into the prepared pan, smoothing it out with the rubber spatula. Place the pan in the oven.

3. Bake the cake until it is golden brown and springs back when lightly pressed with your finger, 50 to 55 minutes. Remove the pan from the oven and place it on a wire rack to cool for 20 minutes. Run a long, sharp knife around the edge of the cake and invert it onto a wire rack, then invert it again onto another rack so that the cake is right side up. Allow the cake to cool completely, 30 minutes more. Frost as desired.

✳ *Store this cake, unfrosted, covered in aluminum foil, at room temperature for up to 4 days or in the refrigerator for up to 1 week. For freezing unfrosted cake, see page 399.*

BASIC YELLOW POUND CAKE

W e used this multi-purpose recipe in Stacy's Chocolate Chip Cake (page 42), but it's good on its own. Bake in a Bundt, in a tube, or in layer pans and spread with your favorite frosting.

R

the Cake Doctor says...

For a delicious summertime tweak, substitute 1 cup melted lemon sorbet for the milk. Serve it with additional scoops of sorbet and fresh berries.

SERVES: 16
PREPARATION TIME:
5 TO 7 MINUTES
BAKING TIME: 58 TO 60 MINUTES
FOR A 10-INCH TUBE
OR 12-CUP BUNDT PAN

*Vegetable oil spray for misting
  the pan*
Flour for dusting the pan
*1 package (18.25 ounces) plain yellow
  cake mix*
*1 package (3.4 ounces) vanilla instant
  pudding mix*
1 cup whole milk
*1 cup vegetable oil, such as canola,
  corn, safflower, soybean, or
  sunflower*
4 large eggs

1. Place a rack in the center of the oven and preheat the oven to 325°F. Lightly mist a

10-inch tube pan with vegetable oil spray, then dust with flour. Shake out the excess flour. Set the pan aside.

2. Place the cake mix, pudding mix, milk, oil, and eggs in a large mixing bowl. Blend with an electric mixer on low speed for 1 minute. Stop the machine and scrape down the sides of the bowl with a rubber spatula. Increase the mixer speed to medium and beat 2 minutes more, scraping the sides down again if needed. The batter should look well blended. Pour the batter into the prepared pan, smoothing it out with the rubber spatula. Place the pan in the oven.

3. Bake the cake until it is golden brown and springs back when lightly pressed with your finger, 58 to 60 minutes for a tube pan. Remove the pan from the oven and place it on a wire rack to cool for 20 minutes. Run a long, sharp knife around the edge of the cake and invert it onto a wire rack, then invert it again onto another rack so that the cake is right side up. Allow to cool completely, 30 minutes more. Frost.

✳ *Store this cake, unfrosted, covered in aluminum foil, at room temperature for up to 4 days or in the refrigerator for up to 1 week. For freezing unfrosted cakes, see page 399.*

BASIC BUTTERMILK SPICE CAKE

Use this formula to make the Tennessee Jam Cake (page 116). It naturally goes with the Quick Caramel Frosting (page 430), and is marvelous with the Fresh Orange Cream Cheese Frosting (page 422).

R

the Cake Doctor says...

Turn this spice cake into an easy coffee cake. Bake it in a 13- by 9-inch pan (see Pan Changes, page 405 for the correct baking time) and frost it with Cinnamon Buttercream Frosting (page 417).

SERVES: 16

PREPARATION TIME: 5 TO 7 MINUTES

BAKING TIME: 26 TO 28 MINUTES

Solid vegetable shortening for greasing the pans

Flour for dusting the pans

1 package (18.25 ounces) plain spice cake mix

1 cup buttermilk

⅓ cup sweetened applesauce

⅓ cup vegetable oil, such as canola, corn, safflower, soybean, or sunflower

3 large eggs

¼ teaspoon ground cinnamon

1. Place a rack in the center of the oven and preheat the oven to 350°F. Lightly grease two 9-inch round cake pans with solid vegetable shortening, then dust with flour. Shake out the excess flour. Set the pans aside.

2. Place the cake mix, buttermilk, applesauce, oil, eggs and cinnamon in a large mixing bowl. Blend with an electric mixer on low speed for 1 minute. Stop the machine and scrape down the sides of the bowl with a rubber spatula. Increase the mixer speed to medium and beat for 2 minutes more, scraping the sides down again if needed. The batter should look thick and well combined. Divide the batter between the prepared pans, smoothing it out with the rubber spatula. Place the pans in the oven side by side.

3. Bake the cakes until they spring back when lightly pressed with your finger, about 26 to 28 minutes. Remove the pans from the oven and place them on a wire rack to cool for 10 minutes. Run a dinner knife around the edge of each layer and invert each onto a rack, then invert them again onto another rack so that the cakes are right side up. Allow them to cool completely, 30 minutes more. Frost as desired.

✳ *Store the cake, unfrosted, covered in aluminum foil, at room temperature for up to 4 days or in the refrigerator for up to 1 week. For freezing unfrosted cake, see page 399.*

10 Cake Doctor Flavor Favorites

Any of these ingredients will enliven cake mix batter; the list isn't in any particular order.

1. Lemon zest
2. Coffee
3. Semisweet chocolate chips
4. Bananas
5. Orange zest
6. Sherry
7. Buttermilk
8. Cream of coconut
9. Pure almond extract
10. Canned pumpkin

BASIC BUTTERMILK DEVIL'S FOOD CAKE

Frosted with White Chocolate Frosting (page 424), this cake becomes a fetching birthday cake. But it could just as easily be donned with either Sour Cream Chocolate Frosting (page 425) or Peppermint Buttercream Frosting (page 418).

R
the Cake Doctor says...

Substitute ½ teaspoon pure orange extract for the vanilla and frost the finished cake with Fresh Orange Cream Cheese Frosting (page 422). The results are elegant—a perfect ending to a seafood meal.

SERVES: 16
PREPARATION TIME: 5 TO 7 MINUTES
BAKING TIME:
28 TO 30 MINUTES

Solid vegetable shortening for greasing
    the pans
Flour or unsweetened cocoa powder
    for dusting the pans
1 package (18.25 ounces) plain devil's
    food cake mix
3 tablespoons unsweetened cocoa
    powder
1⅓ cups buttermilk
½ cup vegetable oil, such as canola,
    corn, safflower, soybean, or
    sunflower
3 large eggs
1 teaspoon pure vanilla extract

1. Place a rack in the center of the oven and preheat the oven to 350°F. Generously grease two 9-inch round cake pans with solid vegetable shortening, then dust with flour or cocoa powder. Shake out the excess flour. Set the pans aside.

2. Place the cake mix, 3 tablespoons cocoa powder, buttermilk, oil, eggs, and vanilla in a large mixing bowl. Blend with an electric mixer on low speed for 1 minute. Stop the machine and scrape down the sides of the bowl with a rubber spatula. Increase the mixer speed to medium and beat 2 minutes more, scraping the sides down again if needed. The batter should look well blended. Divide the batter evenly between the prepared pans, smoothing it out with the rubber spatula. Place the pans in the oven side by side.

3. Bake the cakes until they spring back when lightly pressed with your finger and just start to pull away from the sides of the pan, 28 to 30 minutes. Remove the pans from the oven and place them on a wire rack to cool for 10 minutes. Run a dinner knife around the edge of each layer and invert each onto a rack, then invert them again onto another rack so that the cakes are right side up. Allow them to cool completely, 30 minutes more. Frost as desired.

✳ *Store this cake, unfrosted, covered in aluminum foil, at room temperature for up to 4 days or in the refrigerator for up to 1 week. For freezing unfrosted cake, see page 399.*

BASIC CHOCOLATE POUND CAKE

T his chocolate cake grows moister by the day. It's the basis for the Darn Good Chocolate Cake (page 36). It's so rich you need little frosting or glaze, just patience to let it rest and cool before you slice.

R

the Cake Doctor says...

For an intensely chocolate flavor, dust the pan with unsweetened cocoa powder instead of flour.

SERVES: 16

PREPARATION TIME:
8 TO 10 MINUTES

BAKING TIME: 45 TO 50 MINUTES

*Vegetable oil spray for misting
    the pan*
Flour for dusting the pan
*1 package (18.25 ounces) plain
    devil's food or dark chocolate
    fudge cake mix*
*1 package (3.9 ounces) chocolate instant
    pudding mix*
4 large eggs
1 cup sour cream
½ cup warm water
*½ cup vegetable oil, such as canola,
    corn, safflower, soybean, or
    sunflower*

1. Place a rack in the center of the oven and preheat the oven to 350°F. Lightly mist a 12-cup Bundt pan with vegetable oil spray, then dust with flour.

Shake out the excess flour. Set the pan aside.

2. Place the cake mix, pudding mix, eggs, sour cream, water, and oil in a large mixing bowl. Blend with an electric mixer on low speed for 1 minute. Stop the machine and scrape down the sides of the bowl with a rubber spatula. Increase the mixer speed to medium and beat 2 to 3 minutes more, scraping the sides down again if needed. The batter should look thick and well combined. Pour the batter into the prepared pan, smoothing it out with the rubber spatula. Place the pan in the oven.

3. Bake the cake until it starts to pull away from the sides of the pan and springs back when lightly pressed with your finger, 45 to 50 minutes. Remove the pan from the oven and place it on a wire rack to cool for 20 minutes. Run a long, sharp knife around the edge of the cake and invert it onto a wire rack to finishing cooling, 20 minutes more. Or invert it onto a serving platter to slice and serve while still warm.

✳ *Store this cake, unfrosted, covered in aluminum foil, at room temperature for up to 4 days or in the refrigerator for up to 1 week. For freezing unfrosted cake, see page 399.*

Frostings, Glazes, and One Compote

• • •

I have a confession to make. My editor asked me to do a little research and taste some of the instant supermarket frostings to see if I found them either usable as is or if they could be doctored up themselves, with the addition of some cinnamon or lemon zest. After sampling a half dozen of these ready-made products my research abruptly ended. I dumped the entire mess in the garbage can and muttered, "You will not set foot on my cakes."

Indeed, the role of the frosting and glaze isn't an afterthought. To me, they are a forethought, something I plan on deliciously as I create a cake. A carrot cake must be frosted with an orange and cream cheese combination. A deep chocolate buttermilk layer cake cries out for a soft white chocolate frosting. A spice cake should take a smooth caramel frosting. And these made-in-heaven combinations seemed to snowball as this book progressed.

Basically, the frostings and glazes in this book fall into two categories—cooked and uncooked. The cooked frostings are few—caramel, chocolate pan frosting, penuche, and marshmallow meringue. For the ganache, you quickly bring cream to a boil before pouring it over chopped chocolate. And for a berry compote, you briefly bake berries and sugar. But most of the recipes in this grouping are for uncooked frostings, either buttercreams or cream cheese frostings or quick glazes. They're fast, reliable, and easy. In addition, uncooked frostings such as the ones that follow are a breeze to assemble the day before you need to frost the birthday cake or the sea of cupcakes for your child's class party. Store, covered, in the refrigerator and just bring the bowl to room temperature to make spreading easier.

Whether of chocolate, cream cheese, peanut butter, brown sugar, or marshmallows, frostings are the icing on the cake, so to speak. They may be our last stroke, our last mark as a cook, but they are the first bite, the first flavor that meets the critical taste bud.

BUTTERCREAM FROSTING

This is a basic and necessary frosting that will take you places and open doors for you. It goes with just about any cake flavor and lends itself easily to doctoring up. For example, add freshly grated lemon zest and juice and you have a lemon buttercream. Add cinnamon and you have Cinnamon Buttercream. Add peppermint candy and you have Peppermint Buttercream (page 418), so delicious on chocolate cake.

the Cake Doctor says...

Don't try to sneak margarine into this recipe. You'll be caught! Not only is butter in the name, it's also in the soul of this simple recipe that relies on flavor, flavor, flavor.

MAKES 3½ CUPS, ENOUGH TO FROST
A 2- OR 3-LAYER CAKE
PREPARATION TIME:
5 MINUTES

8 tablespoons (1 stick) butter, at room
   temperature
3¾ cups confectioners' sugar,
   sifted
3 to 4 tablespoons milk
2 teaspoons pure vanilla extract

1. Place the butter in a large mixing bowl. Blend with an electric mixer on low speed until fluffy, 30 seconds. Stop the machine and add the confectioners' sugar, 3 tablespoons milk, and vanilla. Blend with the mixer on low speed until the sugar is incorporated, 1 minute. Increase the speed to medium and beat until light and fluffy, 1 minute more. Blend in up to 1 tablespoon milk if the frosting seems too stiff.

2. Use to frost the top and sides of the cake of your choice.

✸ **Variation: Cinnamon Buttercream Frosting:** *Cinnamon is a natural addition to a buttercream frosting. Its rich, exotic aroma pairs particularly well with spice* cakes, such as carrot or banana. To make this frosting, decrease the amount of vanilla extract to 1 teaspoon and add 1 teaspoon ground cinnamon after you add the vanilla.

The Professional Froster

It isn't difficult to give your cake a professional look with a few frosting tricks:

1. For a fluffy top on your cake, gently press the back of a spoon in and out of the frosting, working your way across the top.

2. For smooth sides, run a thin, flat, long spatula under the hot water tap, dry it well, then drag it around the sides of the frosted cake.

3. For a wavy look on the sides, place that spatula vertical to the cake and gently press it in toward the cake, then out, creating a rippled look. Turn the cake with your other hand as you work.

HOW MUCH FROSTING IS ENOUGH?

Nothing is more frustrating than running out of frosting right in the middle of the job! Here's what you will need:

- For 12 cupcakes: 1 cup

- For the top of a 13- by 9-inch pan or a 2-layer cake (8-inch layers): 1¼ to 2¼ cups

- For the top and sides of a 13- by 9-inch pan, 2-layer cake (9-inch layers), or 3-layer cake (8-inch layers): 2½ cups

- For a 10-inch tube pan, 12-cup Bundt pan, or a 3-layer cake (9-inch layers): 3 to 4 cups

If you'll be glazing your cake, you'll need smaller amounts:

- For a 13- by 9-inch pan: ½ to 1 cup

- For a 10-inch tube pan or 12-cup Bundt pan: 1½ to 2 cups

PEPPERMINT BUTTERCREAM FROSTING

I can't think of a prettier or more festive frosting for a simple chocolate layer cake than this peppermint-flavored buttercream. It's just right for birthdays and holiday buffets, and no matter what your age, you will clamor for another slice and another glass of milk! Peppermint schnapps lends a sophisticated tone to this frosting, and the alcohol in the frosting also makes it spreadable. But if you prefer, omit the schnapps and add ½ teaspoon peppermint extract and a little extra milk to pull the frosting together.

R the Cake Doctor says...

An easy way to crush peppermint candy and not have it fly across the kitchen is to place it on a cutting board and cover with a clean kitchen towel. Pound the covered candy with a meat cleaver or a heavy rolling pin until the candy is finely crushed.

MAKES 3½ CUPS,
ENOUGH TO FROST
A 2- OR 3-LAYER CAKE
PREPARATION TIME: 10 MINUTES

---

8 tablespoons (1 stick) butter, at room m
 temperature
½ cup finely crushed peppermint candy
 (about 7 peppermint sticks)
3 cups confectioners' sugar, sifted
2 to 3 tablespoons milk
1 to 2 tablespoons peppermint schnapps or
 ½ teaspoon peppermint extract

Country Buttercream or City Buttercream

It's plain and simple: There are two kinds of buttercream frosting. The first, the country version, if you will, is what is included in this book. These are uncooked frostings made of softened butter, confectioners' sugar, vanilla extract, and a little milk. The city version, on the other hand, is cooked buttercream, containing egg yolks, water, granulated sugar, and a higher ratio of butter. The sugar syrup made by heating the sugar and water combines with the egg yolks and creates a creamy, rich frosting that is more delicate on the palate and complements light cakes known as *genoise.*

Here are some easy ways to jazz up an uncooked buttercream:

- **Almond Buttercream:** Add 2 teaspoons pure almond extract instead of vanilla.

- **Apricot Buttercream:** Use apricot nectar or strained apricot preserves instead of milk.

- **Lemon Buttercream:** Add 1 teaspoon grated lemon zest for the vanilla and use ¼ cup fresh lemon juice instead of milk.

- **Mocha Buttercream:.** Use ⅓ cup unsweetened cocoa powder and 3 to 4 tablespoons brewed coffee instead of the milk.

1. Place the butter in a large mixing bowl. Blend with an electric mixer on low speed until fluffy, 30 seconds. Stop the machine and add the peppermint candy, confectioners' sugar, 2 tablespoons milk, and 1 tablespoon peppermint schnapps. Blend with the mixer on low speed until the sugar is well incorporated, 1 minute. Increase the speed to medium and beat until the frosting lightens and is fluffy, 1 minute more. Blend in up to 1 tablespoon milk or peppermint schnapps if the frosting seems too stiff.

2. Use to frost or fill the cake of your choice.

CREAM CHEESE FROSTING

A perennial favorite, this cream cheese frosting enhances cakes of all flavors—from carrot to Hummingbird (page 74) to chocolate. It, too, is open to variation as are the Chocolate Cream Cheese Frosting (facing page) and the Fresh Orange Cream Cheese Frosting (page 422). And there is a little trick to making this frosting without having to have your cream cheese and butter at room temperature before blending: Simply put them in a glass bowl and soften them in the microwave on high power for 20 to 30 seconds.

MAKES 3 CUPS, ENOUGH TO FROST
A 2- OR 3-LAYER CAKE
PREPARATION TIME:
5 TO 7 MINUTES

R
the Cake Doctor says...

You can easily substitute reduced-fat cream cheese for the full-fat cream cheese in this recipe.

1 package (8 ounces) cream cheese,
    at room temperature
8 tablespoons (1 stick) butter, at room
    temperature
3¾ cups confectioners' sugar, sifted
1 teaspoon pure vanilla extract

1. Place the cream cheese and butter in a large mixing bowl. Blend with an electric mixer on low speed until combined, 30 seconds. Stop the machine. Add the confectioners' sugar, a bit at a time, blending with the mixer on low speed until the sugar is well incorporated, 1 minute. Add the vanilla, then increase the mixer speed to medium and blend the frosting until fluffy, 1 minute more.

2. Use at once to frost the top and sides of the cake of your choice.

CHOCOLATE CREAM CHEESE FROSTING

I first tasted a chocolate cream cheese frosting at the Tennessee State Fair about five years ago. It was a revelation—chocolate and cream cheese were natural partners! Since then, I flavor this frosting with pure almond extract if I'm making a chocolate almond cake or with pure vanilla extract for a buttermilk devil's food cake, a yellow layer cake, or brownies.

R
the Cake Doctor says...

When you fork into a cake that has been deliciously enrobed with this frosting, the cake world is your oyster. It's *the* one to always keep in mind.

MAKES 4 CUPS, ENOUGH TO FROST
A 2- OR 3-LAYER CAKE
PREPARATION TIME: 10 MINUTES

1 package (8 ounces) cream cheese,
    at room temperature
8 tablespoons (1 stick) butter, at room
    temperature
½ cup unsweetened cocoa powder
1 teaspoon pure almond extract or pure
    vanilla extract
4 cups confectioners' sugar, sifted

1. Place the cream cheese and butter in a large mixing bowl. Blend with an electric mixer on low speed until combined, 30 seconds. Stop the machine. Add the cocoa powder, extract, and confectioners' sugar and blend with the mixer on low speed until the ingredients are moistened, 30 seconds. Increase the speed to medium and beat until the frosting is fluffy, 2 minutes more.

2. Use at once to frost the top and sides of the cake of your choice.

FRESH ORANGE CREAM CHEESE FROSTING

Nothing tops an orange for delivering intense flavor and outstanding color, especially when you add the juice and zest from an orange to a basic cream cheese frosting. This frosting is superb with Carrot Cake (page 109), but also with Mom's Layer Cake (page 106), Buttermilk Devil's Food Cake (page 28), and the Basic Buttermilk Spice Cake (page 408).

R
the Cake Doctor says...

Substitute the same amount of lemon juice and zest for the orange, if you like, and use atop a carrot cake or spice cake.

MAKES 3 CUPS, ENOUGH TO FROST
A 2- OR 3-LAYER CAKE
PREPARATION TIME: 10 TO 12 MINUTES

*1 package (8 ounces) cream cheese,
    at room temperature*
*8 tablespoons (1 stick) butter, at room
    temperature*
3 cups confectioners' sugar, sifted
2 tablespoons fresh orange juice
*1 tablespoon grated orange zest
    (from 1 medium orange)*

1. Place the cream cheese and butter in a large mixing bowl. Blend with an electric mixer on low speed until combined, 30 seconds. Stop the machine. Add the confectioners' sugar, a bit at a time, blending with the mixer on low speed until the sugar is well combined, 1 minute. Then add the orange juice and zest to the mixture. Increase the mixer speed to medium and beat until the frosting lightens and is fluffy, 1 minute more.

2. Use at once to frost the top and sides of the cake of your choice.

COCONUT PECAN CREAM CHEESE FROSTING

When you want a frosting with some real substance to it, then choose this marvelous cream cheese frosting to which you add coconut and chopped pecans. It's just the right touch for a Sweet Potato Cake (page 114) or an orange or banana cake.

....

MAKES 3½ CUPS, ENOUGH TO FROST
A 2- OR 3-LAYER CAKE
PREPARATION TIME: 5 TO 7 MINUTES

....

1 package (8 ounces) cream cheese,
    at room temperature
8 tablespoons (1 stick) butter, at room
    temperature
2½ cups confectioners' sugar, sifted
1 teaspoon pure vanilla extract
½ cup frozen unsweetened grated coconut,
    thawed
½ cup finely chopped pecans

R
the Cake Doctor says...

And you thought frozen grated coconut was confined to coconut cake! Keep coconut in your freezer, then remove what you need and let it thaw while you assemble the ingredients for this frosting. You can substitute the canned sweetened coconut, but the flavor is not as intense as the frozen.

1. Place the cream cheese and butter in a large mixing bowl. Blend with an electric mixer on low speed until combined, 30 seconds. Stop the machine. Add the confectioners' sugar, a bit at a time, blending with the mixer on low speed until the sugar is well incorporated, 1 minute. Add the vanilla, then increase the mixer speed to medium and blend the frosting until fluffy, 1 minute more. Fold in the coconut and the pecans.

2. Use at once to frost the top and sides of the cake of your choice.

WHITE CHOCOLATE FROSTING

This is such an elegant frosting, especially when you spread it on a chocolate cake. Or, for a pristine look all in white, pair it with the Basic Sour Cream White Cake (page 398).

....

MAKES 3 CUPS, ENOUGH TO FROST
A 2- OR 3-LAYER CAKE
PREPARATION TIME: 10 MINUTES

....

6 ounces white chocolate, coarsely
    chopped
1 package (8 ounces) cream cheese,
    at room temperature
4 tablespoons (½ stick) butter, at room
    temperature
1 teaspoon pure vanilla extract
2½ cups confectioners' sugar, sifted

1. Place the white chocolate in a small saucepan and melt over low heat, 4 minutes, stirring constantly. Remove the pan

R
the Cake Doctor says...

I just love how cream cheese cuts through the sweetness of this frosting. Be sure to use bar white chocolate, not white chocolate chips (they would lend a gummy texture to the frosting).

from the heat and let the chocolate cool.

2. Place the cream cheese and butter in a large mixing bowl. Beat with an electric mixer on low speed until well combined, 30 seconds. Stop the machine. Add the melted white chocolate and blend on low for 30 seconds. Add the vanilla and confectioners' sugar and blend on low speed for 30 seconds more. Increase the mixer speed to medium and beat until the frosting is fluffy, 1 minute more.

3. Use to frost the the top and sides of the cake of your choice. Refrigerate the frosted cake until serving time.

SOUR CREAM CHOCOLATE FROSTING

This is adult frosting, not X-rated mind you, just appealing to adults because it's not so sweet and has that nice tang of sour cream. Plus, it's a soft brown color that complements the dark deep color of devil's food.

....

MAKES 2½ CUPS, ENOUGH TO FROST
A 2- OR 3-LAYER CAKE
OR 24 CUPCAKES
PREPARATION TIME: 10 MINUTES

....

4 tablespoons (½ stick) butter
3 ounces semisweet chocolate, finely chopped
½ cup sour cream
2¼ cups confectioners' sugar, sifted
2 tablespoons hot water
1 teaspoon pure vanilla extract

1. Place the butter and chocolate in a small saucepan and melt over low heat, 3 to 4 minutes. Stir the mixture until the chocolate is melted and smooth. Let cool slightly, then stir in the sour cream.

2. Transfer the mixture to a large mixing bowl. With an electric mixer on low speed, add half the confectioners' sugar and 1 tablespoon hot water, beating to incorporate. Then add the remaining sugar and water and continue beating until the frosting comes together into a spreadable consistency without lumps. Stop the machine, add the vanilla, and blend well, 30 seconds.

3. Use at once on the cake or cupcakes of your choice.

R
the Cake Doctor says...

It's important to add the sugar and hot water alternately so that the hot tap water dissolves the sugar, thus preventing any lumps in the frosting.

FLUFFY CHOCOLATE FROSTING

When I was a little girl, I couldn't keep my fingers out of the mixing bowl when my mother made this frosting. It was just so buttery and so chocolatey, and so good! This is birthday cake frosting, plain and simple, terrific on Mom's Layer Cake (page 106), the Buttermilk Devil's Food Cake (page 28), the Sour Cream Chocolate Cupcakes (page 60), or just on the tip of your finger!

the Cake Doctor says...

You can pull together buttercream frostings more easily if both the butter and the milk are at room temperature.

MAKES 3 CUPS, ENOUGH TO FROST
A 2- OR 3-LAYER CAKE
OR 30 CUPCAKES
PREPARATION TIME: 10 MINUTES

8 tablespoons (1 stick) butter, at room
    temperature
⅔ cup unsweetened cocoa powder
3 cups confectioners' sugar, sifted, plus
    additional if needed
⅓ cup whole milk, plus additional if needed
2 teaspoons pure vanilla extract
¼ teaspoon salt

1. Place the butter and cocoa powder in a large mixing bowl. Blend with an electric mixer on low speed until the mixture is soft and well combined, 30 seconds. Stop the machine. Place the confectioners' sugar, ⅓ cup milk, vanilla, and salt in the bowl, and beat with the mixer on low speed until the frosting lightens and is fluffy, 2 to 3 minutes. Add more milk if the frosting is too thick or confectioners' sugar, 1 tablespoon at a time, if the frosting is too thin.

2. Use the frosting to frost the cake or cupcakes of your choice.

PEANUT BUTTER FROSTING

I don't know how I could have gotten through those pregnant months without peanut butter. It is the most comforting, satisfying spoonful around, and it has found its place in this frosting recipe. Sweetened with just enough sugar to balance the salt in the peanut butter and with a smidgen of vanilla and milk to make it spreadable, this frosting is a go-anywhere, do-anything kind of recipe. Smooth it over Chocolate Sheet Cake (page 52) or spread it over a simple butter layer cake.

MAKES 3 CUPS, ENOUGH TO FROST A
2- OR 3-LAYER CAKE OR THE TOP OF
A 13- BY 9-INCH SHEET CAKE
PREPARATION TIME: 5 MINUTES

R
the Cake Doctor says...

Omit the milk and you have a decadent peanut butter filling to sandwich in between chocolate cake layers.

1 cup creamy peanut butter

8 tablespoons (1 stick) butter, at room temperature

2 cups confectioners' sugar, sifted

3 to 4 tablespoons milk

2 teaspoons pure vanilla extract

1. Place the peanut butter and butter in a large mixing bowl. Blend with an electric mixer on low speed until fluffy, 30 seconds. Stop the machine. Add the confectioners' sugar, 3 tablespoons milk, and the vanilla. Blend with the mixer on low speed until the sugar is well combined, 1 minute. Increase the speed to medium and beat until the frosting lightens and is fluffy, 1 minute more. Blend in up to 1 tablespoon milk if the frosting seems too stiff.

2. Use at once to frost a cake of choice.

CHOCOLATE GANACHE

Once you make ganache and taste a spoonful, you know you'll never be the same again. It is downright simple in its list of ingredients, and it is pure ecstasy in your mouth. And just wait until you spread it around the edges of a layer cake. It glides on effortlessly, seductively. And then it firms up magically before your eyes. Amazing stuff!

MAKES 2 CUPS, ENOUGH TO THINLY
FROST A 2- OR 3-LAYER CAKE
PREPARATION TIME: 5 MINUTES

¾ cup heavy (whipping) cream
8 ounces semisweet chocolate, finely chopped
1 tablespoon liqueur such as Grand Marnier,
    framboise, or peppermint schnapps
    (optional)

R *the Cake Doctor says...*

If the ganache gets too thick for using as a glaze or frosting, simply set the pan in a larger pan of water that's simmering on the stove (double boilers are perfect for this) and stir until the ganache softens.

1. Place the cream in a small heavy saucepan over medium heat. Bring to a boil, stirring. Meanwhile, place the chopped chocolate in a large mixing bowl. Remove the pan from the heat and pour the hot cream over the chopped chocolate. Stir until the chocolate is melted. Stir in the liqueur, if desired.

2. To use this ganache as a glaze, let it stand at room temperature for 10 minutes before spooning over a cooled cake. To use the ganache as a frosting or filling, let it stand at room temperature for 4 hours, or chill it until it thickens and is spreadable.

CHOCOLATE PAN FROSTING

I was raised on fudge cakes and brownies frosted with a cooked chocolate frosting, similar to this one. But the method my mother used was time-consuming and called for a candy thermometer. This is a simpler, and just as delicious, version in which you bring a cocoa mixture to a boil, then stir in sugar. And it's luscious on brownies, layer cakes, and chocolate sheet cakes.

························

MAKES 4 CUPS, ENOUGH TO FROST
A 2- OR 3-LAYER CAKE
PREPARATION TIME: 10 MINUTES

························

8 tablespoons (1 stick) butter

4 tablespoons unsweetened cocoa powder

⅓ cup whole milk

4 cups confectioners' sugar, sifted

1. Place the butter in a medium saucepan and melt over low heat, 2 to 3 minutes. Stir in the cocoa powder and milk. Let the mixture come just to a boil, stirring, and then remove the pan from the heat. Stir in the confectioners' sugar until the frosting is thickened and smooth.

2. Pour the warm frosting over the top of a cooled cake of your choice, spreading it with a spatula so that it reaches all sides of the cake. Work quickly because this frosting goes on best while still warm.

R

the Cake Doctor says...

When made with milk, this is a basic pan frosting. With cola and pecans, it becomes the frosting for the Old-Fashioned Cola Cake (page 55). There are only four ingredients, but don't scrimp on or make substitutions for any of them or you won't have the deep and decadent flavor of the original. For added flavor, scatter toasted pecans on top of the cake. (See page 134 for instructions on toasting pecans.)

QUICK CARAMEL FROSTING

I f you had to leave at once on an around-the-world cooking trip, which recipes would you pack? No doubt about it, I'd pack this caramel frosting, but then, it's so simple I've memorized it! You'll do the same as you discover how wonderful it is atop Banana Cake (page 72), Caramel Cake (page 112), Tennessee Jam Cake (page 116), or just about any other layer cake imaginable.

MAKES 3 CUPS, ENOUGH TO FROST
A 2- OR 3-LAYER CAKE
PREPARATION TIME: 10 MINUTES

8 tablespoons (1 stick) butter
½ cup packed light brown sugar
½ cup packed dark brown sugar
¼ cup whole milk
2 cups confectioners' sugar, sifted
1 teaspoon pure vanilla extract

R
the Cake Doctor says...

This is far simpler to make than the old-fashioned cooked caramel frosting in which you caramelize granulated sugar in a cast-iron skillet. Plus, this is a lighter frosting, and it doesn't weigh down delicate cake layers.

1. Place the butter and brown sugars in a medium-size heavy saucepan over medium heat. Stir and cook until the mixture comes to a boil, about 2 minutes. Add the milk, stir, and bring the mixture back to a boil, then remove the pan from the heat. Add the confectioners' sugar and vanilla. Beat with a wooden spoon until the frosting is smooth.

2. Use immediately (while still warm) to frost the cake of your choice or the frosting will harden. If it does harden while you are frosting the cake, simply place the pan back over low heat and stir until the frosting softens up.

PENUCHE FROSTING

I wasn't raised on penuche frosting, so it wasn't until I tried this recipe that I tasted how much it resembled the caramel frosting of my childhood. It's a bit more sugary, more candy-like. Try it spread over Zucchini Spice Cake (page 131), a simple yellow layer cake, or Tennessee Jam Cake (page 116).

....

MAKES 3 CUPS, ENOUGH TO FROST
A 2- OR 3-LAYER CAKE
OR A BUNDT OR TUBE CAKE
PREPARATION TIME: 10 MINUTES

....

1 cup packed light brown sugar

8 tablespoons (1 stick) butter

¼ cup whole milk

2 cups confectioners' sugar, sifted

1. Place the brown sugar and butter in a medium-size heavy saucepan over medium heat. Simmer, stirring constantly,

R

the Cake Doctor says...

Take the time to sift the confectioners' sugar. Use a flour sifter or a fine-mesh strainer. Lumps are a lot of trouble to get out once they're in the frosting.

until well combined, 2 minutes. Carefully pour in the milk, stirring, and bring the mixture to a boil. Remove the pan from the heat and cool slightly.

2. Place the confectioners' sugar in a large mixing bowl. Pour the hot brown sugar mixture over the confectioners' sugar. Beat with an electric mixer on low speed until the frosting is smooth and creamy, 2 to 3 minutes.

3. Use immediately (while still warm) to frost the cake of your choice or the frosting will harden. If it does harden while you are frosting the cake, simply place the pan back over low heat and stir until the frosting softens up.

SWEETENED CREAM

Nothing tastes so simple and yet so luxurious as fresh cream whipped with a little confectioners' sugar. Plain, unadorned, yet elegant, this whipped cream can be the crowning glory to a fancy Peaches and Cream Cake (page 70) or Chocolate Praline Cake (page 33).

R the Cake Doctor says...

If you enjoy the taste of vanilla, add ½ teaspoon pure vanilla extract along with the confectioners' sugar to the soft whipped cream and continue beating until stiff peaks form.

MAKES 2 CUPS,
ENOUGH TO GENEROUSLY FILL OR
THINLY FROST A 2-LAYER CAKE,
12-CUP BUNDT CAKE,
10-INCH TUBE CAKE, OR
13- BY 9-INCH SHEET CAKE

1 cup heavy (whipping) cream
¼ cup confectioners' sugar

1. Place a clean, large mixing bowl and electric mixer beaters in the freezer for a few minutes while you assemble the ingredients. Pour the whipping cream into the chilled bowl and beat with the electric mixer on high speed until the cream has thickened, 1½ minutes. Stop the machine and add the sugar. Beat the cream and sugar on high speed until stiff peaks form, 1 to 2 minutes more.

2. Use to frost the cake of your choice.

MARSHMALLOW FROSTING

This is a speedier version of the classic seven-minute frosting, which, ironically, used to seem a snap to prepare. It's perfect for slathering onto coconut cake, spice cake, or a sour cream white layer cake. But be extra careful while preparing this frosting: When you are beating the frosting on the stove, be sure to keep the mixer cord away from the burner.

MAKES 3½ CUPS, ENOUGH TO FROST
A 2- OR 3-LAYER CAKE
PREPARATION TIME: 5 MINUTES

½ cup sugar

2 tablespoons water

2 large egg whites

1 jar (7 ounces; 1½ cups) marshmallow creme

1. Place the sugar, water, and egg whites in a medium-size heavy saucepan. Cook

R
the Cake Doctor says...

This frosting seems miraculous. The ingredient amounts appear slim, yet they expand and lighten to yield plenty of frosting with a rich mouthfeel. The secret lies in the marshmallow creme, which keeps the mixture stabilized.

over low heat, beating continuously with an electric hand mixer on high speed until soft peaks form, 2 to 3 minutes. If your hand mixer has a cord, make sure to keep it away from the burner.

2. Remove the pan from the heat. Add the marshmallow creme and beat the mixture with the mixer on high speed until stiff peaks form, 2 minutes more.

3. Use at once to frost the cake of your choice.

CHOCOLATE MARSHMALLOW FROSTING

What is it about chocolate and marshmallows that is so enticing? Perhaps it dates back to my youth in Girl Scouts and eating s'mores at the campfire. This frosting is perfect for spreading on tube and Bundt cakes. The recipe is easy to double for a layer or a 13- by 9-inch cake.

MAKES 1½ CUPS, ENOUGH TO FROST
THE TOP OF A TUBE CAKE
OR BUNDT CAKE
PREPARATION TIME: 10 MINUTES

2 cups confectioners' sugar

½ cup unsweetened cocoa powder

6 large marshmallows

4 tablespoons (½ stick) butter

⅓ cup plus 1 tablespoon milk

1 teaspoon pure vanilla extract

R the Cake Doctor says...

Marshmallows add a miraculous texture to frostings. And they turn an ordinary chocolate frosting into something fudgelike in consistency. This frosting will dress up marbled cakes and chocolate chip cakes, any cake where you feel you need to crank up the flavor one notch more.

1. Sift the sugar and cocoa powder together into a large mixing bowl. Set aside.

2. Place the marshmallows, butter, and milk in a medium-size heavy saucepan over low heat. Stir until the marshmallows are melted, 3 to 4 minutes. Remove the pan from the heat. Pour the confectioners' sugar and cocoa mixture over the marshmallow mixture. Add the vanilla and stir until the frosting is smooth and satiny.

3. Use at once to frost the top of the cake of your choice.

SHINY CHOCOLATE GLAZE

This recipe is so simple you really don't need a recipe, but that's precisely the type of glaze this is—when you desire just a bit on the top, nothing flashy that might detract from your cake. Use this glaze to crown the Chocolate Marble Cake (page 44), the Chocolate Pistachio Cake (page 40), and the Incredible Melted Ice-Cream Cake (page 163). It's yummy served hot over vanilla ice cream, too!

MAKES 1½ CUPS,
ENOUGH TO GLAZE 1 BUNDT OR
TUBE CAKE
PREPARATION TIME: 10 MINUTES

2 tablespoons butter
2 tablespoons unsweetened cocoa powder
¼ cup heavy (whipping) cream
1 cup confectioners' sugar, sifted
1 teaspoon pure vanilla extract

1. Melt the butter in a small heavy saucepan over low heat. Add the cocoa powder and cream and stir until the mixture thickens, 2 minutes. Do not boil. Remove the pan from the heat and stir in the confectioners' sugar and vanilla until the mixture is smooth.

2. Spoon the glaze over the cooled cake of your choice.

R
the Cake Doctor says...

For a flavor variation, use ¼ cup brewed coffee instead of the cream. If you want to add toasted nuts on top of the cake, scatter the nuts over the glaze while it is still soft. That way, they adhere better to the glaze.

HOT BUTTERMILK GLAZE

The baking soda added to the buttermilk in this recipe begins what looks like a science experiment. As the glaze heats up, it foams, but don't worry—no explosions! The soda thickens the glaze, and the buttermilk and sugar provide flavor. This is just the sort of glaze needed for a dense, spicy cake.

R

the Cake Doctor says...

Pair this glaze with fruit-based cakes or spice cakes.

MAKES 2 CUPS, ENOUGH TO GLAZE
THE TOP OF A 13- BY 9-INCH CAKE
PREPARATION TIME: 10 MINUTES

1 cup sugar
½ cup buttermilk
6 tablespoons (¾ stick) butter
1 tablespoon light corn syrup
½ teaspoon baking soda
½ teaspoon pure vanilla extract

1. Place the sugar, buttermilk, butter, corn syrup, baking soda, and vanilla in a medium saucepan over medium heat. Bring to a boil, stirring constantly. The glaze will foam up and thicken as the sugar dissolves and the butter melts, 3 to 4 minutes.

2. Poke holes in the cooled cake of your choice and pour the hot glaze over it.

BROWN SUGAR CARAMEL GLAZE

This recipe is a staple at our house, poured atop apple cake in the fall and served with fresh peaches and ice cream in the summertime. Or try it with pound cake or angel food cake. Most anything improves with a spoonful of this glaze!

R
the Cake Doctor says...

This glaze takes the average cake to a higher level. The combination of butter, sugar, and cream is velvety in your mouth. Why, this glaze would be delicious on just about any cake, even pancakes!

MAKES ½ CUP, ENOUGH TO GLAZE THE TOP OF A 12-CUP BUNDT CAKE OR A 13- BY 9-INCH CAKE
PREPARATION TIME: 5 MINUTES

3 tablespoons butter or margarine
3 tablespoons packed light brown sugar
3 tablespoons granulated sugar
3 tablespoons heavy (whipping) cream
½ teaspoon pure vanilla extract

1. Place the butter, sugars, cream, and vanilla in a medium-size saucepan over medium heat. Bring the mixture to a boil, stirring. Let boil for 1 minute, stirring often.

2. Remove the pan from the heat and spoon or spread the warm glaze onto the cake of your choice.

FRESH BERRY COMPOTE

If you're searching for just the right topping for that simple slice of pound cake or angel food cake, look no farther. Sure, sliced peaches sweetened with a little sugar are scrumptious, but so is this easy baked compote of summer berries. Choose an assortment or just whatever you can get your hands on.

....

MAKES 5 CUPS,
ENOUGH FOR 16 SERVINGS
PREPARATION TIME: 20 MINUTES

....

2 cups fresh strawberries, rinsed, drained,
    and capped
2 cups fresh blackberries, rinsed and
    drained
2 cups fresh blueberries, rinsed and drained
½ cup sugar
1½ cups fresh raspberries, rinsed and
    drained

1. Place a rack in the center of the oven and preheat the oven to 350°F.

2. Place the strawberries, blackberries, blueberries, and sugar in a shallow 12-inch baking dish. Stir the berries to combine them. Place the dish in the oven and bake until the fruit is soft and the juices begin to run, 10 minutes. Remove the dish from the oven and stir in the raspberries. Taste the compote and add more sugar if it is needed.

3. Serve the compote warm, or let it cool and then serve.

R
the Cake Doctor says...

I just love warm fruit compotes. Use seasonal favorites, adding fresh ripe diced, peeled plums or peaches. Or flavor the fruits with a little fresh lemon zest or mint. You can make and store a compote in the refrigerator for up to 1 week. Reheat before serving.

Conversion Table

Liquid Conversions

US	IMPERIAL	METRIC
2 TBS	1 FL OZ	30 ML
3 TBS	1 1/2 FL OZ	45 ML
1/4 CUP	2 FL OZ	60 ML
1/3 CUP	2 1/2 FL OZ	75 ML
1/3 CUP + 1 TBS	3 FL OZ	90 ML
1/3 CUP + 2 TBS	3 1/2 FL OZ	100 ML
1/2 CUP	4 FL OZ	125 ML
2/3 CUP	5 FL OZ	150 ML
3/4 CUP	6 FL OZ	175 ML
3/4 CUP + 2 TBS	7 FL OZ	200 ML
1 CUP	8 FL OZ	250 ML
1 CUP + 2 TBS	9 FL OZ	275 ML
1 1/4 CUPS	10 FL OZ	300 ML
1 1/3 CUPS	11 FL OZ	325 ML
1 1/2 CUPS	12 FL OZ	350 ML
1 2/3 CUPS	13 FL OZ	375 ML
1 3/4 CUPS	14 FL OZ	400 ML
1 3/4 CUPS + 2 TBS	15 FL OZ	450 ML
1 PINT (2 CUPS)	16 FL OZ	500 ML
2 1/2 CUPS	1 PINT	600 ML
3 3/4 CUPS	1 1/2 PINTS	900 ML
4 CUPS	1 3/4 PINTS	1 LITER

Weight Conversions

US / UK	METRIC	US / UK	METRIC
1/2 OZ	15 G	7 OZ	200 G
1 OZ	30 G	8 OZ	250 G
1 1/2 OZ	45 G	9 OZ	275 G
2 OZ	60 G	10 OZ	300 G
2 1/2 OZ	75 G	11 OZ	325 G
3 OZ	90 G	12 OZ	350 G
3 1/2 OZ	100 G	13 OZ	375 G
4 OZ	125 G	14 OZ	400 G
5 OZ	150 G	15 OZ	450 G
6 OZ	175 G	1 LB	500 G

Oven Temperatures

FAHRENHEIT	GAS MARK	CELSIUS
250	1/2	120
275	1	140
300	2	150
325	3	160
350	4	180
375	5	190
400	6	200
425	7	220
450	8	230
475	9	240
500	10	260

Note: Reduce the temperature by 20°C (68°F) for fan-assisted ovens.

Approximate Equivalents

1 stick butter = 8 TBS = 4 OZ = 1/2 CUP

1 CUP all-purpose presifted flour or dried bread crumbs = 5 OZ

1 CUP granulated sugar = 8 OZ

1 CUP (packed) brown sugar = 6 OZ

1 CUP confectioners' sugar = 4 1/2 OZ

1 CUP honey/syrup = 11 OZ

1 CUP grated cheese = 4 OZ

1 CUP dried beans = 6 OZ

1 large egg = 2 OZ = about 1/4 CUP

1 egg yoke = about 1 TBS

1 egg white = about 2 TBS

Note: All the conversions shown here are approximate but close enough to be useful when converting from one system to another.

Bibliography

• • •

Ihave savored cakes, frostings, and many ideas from the following good books. These sources were especially helpful in planning, developing, and writing *The Cake Mix Doctor.*

Anderson, Jean. *The American Century Cookbook: The Most Popular Recipes of the 20th Century.* New York: Clarkson Potter, 1997.

Beranbaum, Rose Levy. *The Cake Bible.* New York: William Morrow and Company, Inc., 1988.

Calling All Cooks. Telephone Pioneers of America, Alabama Chapter No. 34. Nashville, TN: Favorite Recipes Press, 1982.

Corriher, Shirley O. *CookWise: The Hows and Whys of Successful Cooking.* New York: William Morrow and Company, Inc., 1997.

Cunningham, Marion. *The Fannie Farmer Cookbook,* 13th ed. New York: Alfred A. Knopf, 1996.

Farrell-Kingsley, Kathy and the Editors of Woman's Day. *The Woman's Day Cookbook.* New York: Viking Penguin, 1995.

FitzGibbon, Theodora. *The Food of the Western World: An Encyclopedia of Food from North America and Europe.* New York: Quadrangle/The New York Times Book Co., 1976.

Herbst, Sharon Tyler. *The New Food Lover's Companion: Comprehensive Definitions of Over 4,000 Food, Wine and Culinary Terms,* 2nd ed. Hauppauge, NY: Barron's Educational Services, Inc., 1995.

Kentucky Kitchens Volume II. Telephone Pioneers of America, Kentucky Chapter No. 32. Nashville, TN: Favorite Recipes Press, 1989.

Lapchick, J. Michael. *The Label Reader's Pocket Dictionary of Food Additives.* Minneapolis, MN: Chronimed Publishing, 1993.

LeSueur, Sadie. *Recipes, Party Plans, and Garnishes.* New York: Hearthside Press, Inc., 1970.

Mariani, John. *The Dictionary of American Food & Drink.* New Haven, CT: Ticknor & Fields, 1983.

Martha White's Southern Sampler. Martha White Foods, Inc. Nashville, TN: Rutledge Hill Press, 1989.

McGee, Harold. *On Food and Cooking: The Science and Lore of the Kitchen.* New York: Charles Scribner's Sons, 1984.

Pillsbury Best of the Bake-Off Cookbook: 350 Recipes from America's Favorite Cooking Contest. The Pillsbury Company. New York: Clarkson Potter, 1996.

Pregnall, Teresa. *Treasured Recipes from the Charleston Cake Lady.* New York: Hearst Books, 1996.

Rosenberg, Judy. *Rosie's Bakery All-Butter, Fresh Cream, Sugar-Packed, No-Holds-Barred Baking Book.* New York: Workman Publishing, 1991.

The Southern Heritage Cakes Cookbook. Southern Living. Birmingham, AL: Oxmoor House, Inc., 1983.

Trager, James. *The Food Chronology: A Food Lover's Compendium of Events and Anecdotes, From Prehistory to the Present.* New York: Henry Holt and Company, 1995.

Villas, James with Martha Pearl Villas. *My Mother's Southern Desserts.* New York: William Morrow and Company, Inc., 1998.

Walter, Carole. *Great Cakes.* New York: Clarkson Potter, 1991.

Yamaguchi, Roy. *Roy's Feasts from Hawaii.* Berkeley, California: Ten Speed Press, 1995.

Index

• • •

A

ACNielsen survey, 6
Add-ins, 176, 409
    for angel food cake, 394
    for carrot cake, 110
    zest or fruit juice, 78
Air bubbles, avoiding, 268
Almond(s):
    Amaretto cake, 303-4
    apricot squares, 314-15
    buttercream, 419
        and caraway cake, Irish,
        190-91
    chocolate cake with
        chocolate cream cheese
        frosting, 26-27
    chocolate-coconut bars,
        328-29
    cream cheese pound cake,
        129-30
    extract, as add-in, 394
    gooey butter cake, 242-43
    orange angel food cake,
        391-92
    toasted, cream, 391-92
    toasting, 134
Aluminum foil, 12
Amaretto cake, 303-4
Ambrosia cake, 212-14
Angel food cake, 268, 333
    add-ins for, 394
    chocolate custard icebox
        cake, 356-57

chocolate-speckled
    peppermint, 393-94
filled with frozen yogurt, 392
orange almond, 391-92
red, white, and blue,
    ice-cream cake, 197-98
rum balls, 332-33
Anisette, in Harvey Wall-
    banger cake, 284-85
Apple(s), 90
    Jack pecan spice cake, 308-9
    skillet cake, upside-down,
        100-101
    sour cream kuchen, 274-75
    walnut crisp, 360-61
Applesauce:
    raisin cookies, 344-45
    spice cake, 89-91
    strawberry cake, 376-77
Apricot(s):
    almond squares, 314-15
    buttercream, 419
    cinnamon-chocolate coffee
        cake, 254-56
    friendship cake, 179-81
    glaze, 85-86, 370-71
    lemon chiffon cake, 386-87
    nectar cake, favorite, 85-86

B

Bacardi rum cake, 292-93
Bake sales, 253, 259
Baking cakes:

most common mistakes in,
    401
oven temperature and,
    12, 14, 17, 401
in quantity, 249
rack position and, 12-13, 17
with children, 338
Banana(s):
    cake with caramel frosting,
        72-73
    foster upside-down cake,
        102-3
    fruit pizza, 370-71
    hummingbird cake, 74-75
    pudding cake, 139-40
    punch bowl cake, 366-67
    ripe, loaves, 280-81
Bars, 310-33
    apricot almond squares,
        314-15
    butterscotch cashew
        scotchies, 324-25
    candy, 330-31
    chocolate-almond-coconut,
        328-29
    cinnamon blueberry crumble,
        318-19
    cranberry oat crumble,
        320-21
    lemon cheese, 312-13
    metal baking pans for, 317
    peanut butter chocolate,
        326-27
    pecan pie, sticky, 322-23

raspberry meringue, 316-17
rum balls, 332-33
wrapping, 217
Basic cakes, 397-413
   butter, 402-3
   buttermilk devil's food,
      410-11
   buttermilk spice, 408-9
   chocolate pound, 412-13
   sour cream white, 398-99
   sour cream yellow, 404-5
   yellow pound, 406-7
   yogurt white, 400-401
Berry:
   buttercream frosting, 184-85
   fresh, compote, 438
   see also specific berries
Better than _?_ cake, 171-72
   chocolate, 169-70
Betty, 365
Birthday cake, 68
   cones, 195-96
Biscotti, 353
   chocolate macadamia,
      350-51
   lemon pecan, 352-53
Blackberry jam cake, Tennessee,
      116-17
Blueberry:
   cinnamon crumble bars,
      318-19
   muffin cake, 94-95
   streusel coffee cake, 272-73
Bourbon, in Kentucky
   buttermilk raisin cake,
      300-302
Bowls, 11
Brandied whipped cream,
      209-10
Breakfast cake, Kathy's
   cinnamon, 257-58
Bride's cake with raspberry
      filling and white
      chocolate frosting, 192-93

Brownies, wrapping, 217
Brown sugar caramel glaze, 437
Buckle, 365
   sour cream pear, 362-63
Bundt cakes, 10, 12-13, 17, 405
   frosting needed for, 421
   history of, 291
   turning out of pan, 16, 291
   wrapping, 217
Butter, 8-9, 14, 15
   cake, basic, 402-3
   glaze, five-extract, 165-66
   layer cake with sweet lime
      curd, 76-77
   see also Gooey butter cake
Buttercream frosting, 19, 416-17
   almond, 419
   apricot, 419
   berry, 184-85
   cinnamon, 417
   country vs. city, 419
   lemon, 419
   mocha, 419
   peppermint, 418-19
Buttered glaze, hot, 300-301
Butterfinger candy bars,
   in holy cow cake, 177-78
Buttermilk, 10, 301
   devil's food cake, basic,
      410-11
   devil's food cake with
      white chocolate
      frosting, 28-29
   glaze, hot, 436
   lemon poppy seed cake,
      127-28
   pear and toasted pecan cake,
      380-81
   raisin cake, Kentucky,
      300-302
   spice cake, basic, 408-9
Butterscotch:
   cashew scotchies, 324-25
   hornet's nest cake, 175-76

C

Cake-mix batter, holding and
   baking later, 203
Cake mixes:
   ACNielsen survey on, 6
   choosing, 4-8
   common mistakes with, 401
   doctoring, 1-3
   history of, 20-23
   pudding-enhanced, 5
"Cake-mix taste," 8
Cake pans, 10-11, 16, 268
   changing size or shape of,
      405
   flouring, 13
   getting 20 servings from,
      181
   greasing, 13, 14, 268
   special coatings for, 178
   turning cake out of, 16
Candy bars, 330-31
Cannoli cake, 199-201
Caramel(s):
   brown sugar glaze, 437
   cake, 112-13
   frosting, 430
   holy cow cake, 177-78
   penuche frosting, 431
   turtle cake, 48-49
Caraway and almond cake, Irish,
      190-91
Cardamom and plum cake, 87-88
Carrot cake, 111
   cinnamon and pineapple,
      sheet, 395-96
   with orange cream cheese
      frosting, 109-11
Cashew butterscotch
      scotchies, 324-25
Cast-iron skillets, caring for,
      101
Charleston poppy seed cake,
      124-25

Cheesecake, 222-39
    cherry, sweet-tart, 232-33
    chocolate mocha swirl,
       234-35
    doneness tests for, 228
    history of, 225
    lime, 230-31
    New York–style, 224-25
    pumpkin spice, 227-29
    ricotta, Mindy's, 238-39
    storing and serving, 229
    toffee crunch, 236-37
Cherry(ies):
    cake, happy valley, 269-70
    cheesecake, sweet-tart,
       232-33
    chocolate-covered, cake,
       50-51
    dump cake, 358-59
    filling, 187-88
    maraschino, in friendship
       cake, 179-81
    Mount Vernon cake, 187-89
    punch bowl cake, 366-67
    sauce, 270
Chiffon cake, 384
    apricot lemon, 386-87
    dark chocolate, 389-90
    orange, classic, 383-84
    tips for, 387
Chocolate, 9
    almond-coconut bars, 328-29
    chip lemon picnic cake, 96-97
    chips, as topping, 305
    cinnamon-apricot coffee
       cake, 254-56
    coating, for cake pans, 178
    cookies, as add-ins, 176
    curls, 107
    custard icebox cake, 356-57
    double-, chewies, 334-35
    glaze, 50-51
    glaze, shiny, 435
    history of, 39

    macadamia biscotti, 350-51
    melting, 34
    mocha chewies, 337-38
    mocha swirl cheesecake,
       234-35
    peanut butter bars, 326-27
    speckled peppermint angel
       food cake, 393-94
    syrup cake, Mom's, 264-65
    tips on working with, 54
    toffee crunch cheesecake,
       236-37
    see also White chocolate
Chocolate cake, 24-61
    almond, with chocolate cream
       cheese frosting, 26-27
    better than ?, 169-70
    birthday, cones, 195-96
    buttermilk devil's food, basic,
       410-11
    buttermilk devil's food, with
       white chocolate
       frosting, 28-29
    hocolate chip, Stacy's, 42-43
    chocolate-covered cherry,
       50-51
    cola, old-fashioned, 55-56
    dark, chiffon, 389-90
    darn good, 36-37
    devilishly good, 202-3
    earthquake, 173-74
    grappa, 306-7
    holiday yule log, 209-11
    holy cow, 177-78
    Kahlúa, 286-87
    love, 184-86
    macadamia fudge torte,
       136-37
    milk, pound, 38-39
    Mississippi mud, 46-47
    peppermint, lethal, 30-31
    pistachio, 40-41
    pound, basic, 412-13
    praline, 33-35

    punch bowl, 368-69
    red velvet, 152-55
    sheet, with peanut butter
       frosting, 52-54
    sour cream, cupcakes with
       sour cream chocolate
       frosting, 60-61
    turtle, 48-49
    white, pound, 58-59
Chocolate cake mix:
    double-chocolate rum cake,
       289-90
    see also Dark chocolate
       fudge cake mix; Devil's
       food cake mix; German
       chocolate cake mix
Chocolate frosting, 389-90
    cola, 55-56
    cream cheese, 421
    fluffy, 426
    ganache, 32, 428
    marshmallow, 434
    pan, 429
    sour cream, 425
    white, 424
Chocolate marble cake:
    Fiddler on the Roof, 161-62
    gooey butter, 244-46
    with shiny chocolate glaze,
       44-45
Cinnamon, 255
    blueberry crumble bars,
       318-19
    breakfast cake, Kathy's,
       257-58
    buttercream frosting, 417
    chocolate-apricot coffee
       cake, 254-56
    orange poppy seed cake,
       Mattie's, 262-63
    and pineapple carrot sheet
       cake, 395-96
    snickerdoodle cake, 121-23
Classics, cake-mix, 148-81

better than ?, 171-72
chocolate better than ?, 169-70
earthquake, 173-74
Fiddler on the Roof, 161-62
finger lickin' good, 150-51
five-flavor, 165-66
friendship, 179-81
holy cow, 177-78
hornet's nest, 175-76
lemon-lime, with pineapple
    curd, 158-60
melted ice-cream, incredible,
    163-64
orange dreamsicle, 167-68
red velvet, 152-55
tomato soup spice, with
    cinnamon buttercream
    frosting, 156-57
Cobbler, 365
Cocoa powder:
    as add-in, 394
    coating cake pan with, 178
Coconut, 9
    ambrosia cake, 212-14
    better than ? cake, 171-72
    cherry dump cake, 358-59
    chocolate-almond bars,
        328-29
    earthquake cake, 173-74
    frosting, 119
    icebox cake, Grandma's,
        118-20
    peanut butter chocolate
        bars, 326-27
    pecan cream cheese frosting,
        423
    pecan gooey butter cake,
        250-51
    piña colada cake, 296-97
    pistachio, and pineapple
        frosting, 150-51
    snowballs, 215-16
    toasted, in angel food cake,
        394

toasted, sour cream cake,
    142-43
whipped cream, 297
Coffee:
    as add-in, 394
    see also Mocha
Coffee cakes, 252-81
    apple sour cream kuchen,
        274-75
    banana loaves, 280-81
    blueberry streusel, 272-73
    cherry, happy valley, 269-70
    chocolate syrup, Mom's,
        264-65
    cinnamon breakfast, Kathy's,
        257-58
    cinnamon-chocolate-apricot,
        254-56
    honey bun, 266-67
    orange cinnamon poppy seed,
        Mattie's, 262-63
    peach pecan kuchen, 276-77
    pumpkin spice, 278-79
    sock-it-to-me, 260-61
Coffee liqueur.
    See Kahlúa
Cola cake, old-fashioned, 55-56
Colorings, 7
Color vision cake, 288
Compote, fresh berry, 438
Confectioners' sugar, 243
Conversion table, 439
Cookie(s), 310-11, 334-53
    applesauce raisin, 344-45
    chocolate macadamia
        biscotti, 350-51
    chocolate mocha chewies,
        337-38
    double-chocolate chewies,
        334-35
    lemon pecan biscotti, 352-53
    oatmeal macadamia, chunky,
        342-43
    orange spice, 346-47

pops, 348-49
tips for baking, 336
white chocolate chewies,
    340-41
Cooling racks, 11, 16, 17
Cranberry:
    cake, zesty, 378-79
    oat crumble bars, 320-21
    orange cake, festive, 81-82
Cream.
    See Whipped cream
Cream cheese, 10
    almond pound cake, 129-30
    creamy filling, 204-5
    lemon bars, 312-13
Cream cheese frosting,
    19, 142-43, 420
    chocolate, 421
    coconut pecan, 423
    lighter, 395-96
    orange, 422
    strawberry, 65-66
    strawberry, lighter, 376-77
Cream of tartar, 388
Crème de menthe, as add-in, 176
Crisp, 365
    apple walnut, 360-61
    strawberry, Nina's, 364-65
Crocker, Betty,
    5, 21, 22-23, 325
Crowds, cakes for, 245, 249
Crumble, 365
Cupcakes, 174
    frosting needed for, 421
    sour cream chocolate, with
        sour cream chocolate
        frosting, 60-61
Curd:
    lemon, as add-in, 176
    lime, 76-77
    pineapple, 159
Custard, chocolate, icebox
    cake, 356-57
Cutting frosted cakes, 268

D

Dark chocolate fudge cake mix:
chocolate cake, darn good,
36-37
chocolate pound cake, basic,
412-13
Devil's food cake, 53
buttermilk, basic, 410-11
buttermilk, with white
chocolate frosting, 28-29
Devil's food cake mix, 53
birthday cake cones, 195-96
buttermilk devil's food
cake, basic, 410-11
buttermilk devil's food cake
with white chocolate
frosting, 28-29
chocolate almond cake with
chocolate cream cheese
frosting, 26-27
chocolate-almond-coconut
bars, 328-29
chocolate better than ? cake,
169-70
chocolate cake, darn good,
36-37
chocolate-covered cherry
cake, 50-51
chocolate grappa cake,
306-7
chocolate Kahlúa cake,
286-87
chocolate macadamia
biscotti, 350-51
chocolate mocha chewies,
337-38
chocolate mocha swirl
cheesecake, 234-35
chocolate pound cake, basic,
412-13
chocolate praline cake, 33-35
chocolate punch bowl cake,
368-69

chocolate sheet cake with
peanut butter frosting,
52-54
dark chocolate chiffon cake,
389-90
devilishly good chocolate
cake, 202-3
double-chocolate chewies,
334-35
double-chocolate rum cake,
289-90
holiday yule log, 209-11
holy cow cake, 177-78
macadamia fudge torte,
136-37
Mississippi mud cake, 46-47
peppermint chocolate cake,
lethal, 30-31
sour cream chocolate
cupcakes with sour cream
chocolate frosting,
60-61
white chocolate chewies,
340-41
Doneness, testing for,
11, 15-17
Double-chocolate:
chewies, 334-35
rum cake, 289-90
Doubling recipes, 249
Dreamsicle cake, orange, 167-68
Dump cake, cherry, 358-59
Duncan Hines, 5, 20-23

E

Earthquake cake, 173-74
Educational baking, 339
Egg(s), 9, 14
whites, in chiffon cake, 388
Eggnog, as add-in, 176
Emulsifiers, 7
Equipment, 10-12
Extracts, 9-10

F

Fiddler on the Roof cake,
161-62
Filberts, toasting, 134
Fillings:
cherry, 187-88
creamy, 204-5
lime curd, 76-77
pineapple, 110
pineapple curd, 159
pineapple-orange, 212-13
Finger lickin' good cake,
150-51
Five-flavor cake, 165-66
Flavor favorites, 409
Flavorings, 7-8, 9-10
Flouring pans, 13
Fluffy chocolate frosting, 427
Folding egg whites, 388
Freezing unfrosted cakes, 399
Friendship cake, 179-81
Frostings, 414-35
amount needed, 417
caramel, 430
coconut, 119
cola, 55-56
marshmallow, 433
peanut butter, 427
penuche, 431
pistachio, coconut, and
pineapple, 150-51
spreading on cake, 16-18
storage and, 19
strawberry, 67-69, 376-77
tricks for, 417
see also Buttercream
frosting; Chocolate
frosting; Cream cheese
frosting; Whipped cream
Fruit, cakes with, 62-103
applesauce spice, 89-91
apple skillet, upside-down,
100-101

apricot nectar, favorite, 85-86

banana, with caramel frosting, 72-73

bananas foster, upside-down, 102-3

blueberry muffin, 94-95

butter layer, with sweet lime curd, 76-77

cran-orange, festive, 81-82

friendship, 179-81

hummingbird, 74-75

lemon, Susan's, 83-84

lemon chip picnic, 96-97

orange, fresh, 79-80

peaches and cream, 70-71

pear and ginger, old-fashioned, 98-99

pineapple inside-out, 92-93

plum and cardamom, 87-88

strawberry, triple-decker, 67-69

strawberry, with strawberry cream cheese frosting, 64-66

Fruit desserts, baked, 354-55

apple walnut crisp, 360-61

cherry dump cake, 358-59

fruit pizza, 370-71

names for, 365

punch bowl cake, 366-67

sour cream pear buckle, 362-63

strawberry cobbler, Nina's, 364-65

Fudge:

macadamia torte, 136-37

see also Dark chocolate fudge cake mix

Fuzzy navel cake, 298-99

G

Galliano, in Harvey Wallbanger cake, 284-85

Ganache, 32

chocolate, 428

General Mills, 5, 20-23, 325

German chocolate cake mix:

earthquake cake, 173-74

red velvet cake, 152-55

turtle cake, 48-49

Ginger:

as add-in, 110

and pear cake, old-fashioned, 98-99

Gingerbread house, 218-21

Glass cake domes or bells, 12

Glazes, 16, 17, 414

Amaretto, 303-4

apricot, 85-86, 370-71

apricot lemon, 386-87

brown sugar caramel, 437

butter, five-extract, 165-66

buttermilk, hot, 436

chocolate, 50-51

chocolate, shiny, 435

ganache, 32

hot buttered, 300-301

lemon, 83-84, 96-97

lemon whiskey, 191

orange, 79-80, 81-82, 167-68, 383-84

orange marmalade, 110

rum, 292-93, 294-95

sugar, 266-67

whiskey, 309

Golden cake mix:

almond cream cheese pound cake, 129-30

upside-down bananas foster cake, 102-3

Gooey butter cake, 240-41

almond, 242-43

chocolate marble, 244-46

coconut-pecan, 250-51

lemon chess, 247-48

Grapes, in fruit pizza, 370-71

Grappa chocolate cake, 306-7

Greasing pans, 13, 14, 268

Groom's cake, 194

H

Happy valley cherry cake, 269-70

Harvey Wallbanger cake, 284-85, 288

Hazelnuts, toasting, 134

High-altitude baking, 14

Holiday yule log, 209-11

Holy cow cake, 177-78

Honey bun cake, 266-67

Hornet's nest cake, 175-76

Hot buttered glaze, 300-301

Hummingbird cake, 74-75

I

Icebox cake:

chocolate custard, 356-57

coconut, Grandma's, 118-20

Ice cream:

cake, red, white, and blue angel food, 197-98

melted, cake, incredible, 163-64

Icing, royal, 219-20

Ingredients:

in cake mix, 4-8

measuring, 17

mixing, 14-15, 17

pantry items, 8-10

Irish almond and caraway cake, 190-91

Italian-style desserts:

cannoli cake, 199-201

chocolate macadamia biscotti, 350-51

lemon pecan biscotti, 352-53
tiramisù cake, easy, 146-47

J

Jack apple pecan spice cake,
    308-9
Jam:
    cake, Tennessee, 116-17
    raspberry, as add-in, 176

K

Kahlúa:
    chocolate cake, 286-87
    chocolate punch bowl cake,
        368-69
Kentucky buttermilk raisin
    cake, 300-302
Kiwi, in fruit pizza, 370-71
Knives, serrated, 11
Kuchen:
    apple sour cream, 274-75
    peach pecan, 276-77

L

Layer cakes:
    baking, 14, 405
    frosting needed for, 421
    wrapping, 217
Leavening, 7
Lemon(s):
    apricot chiffon cake, 386-87
    buttercream, 419
    buttermilk poppy seed cake,
        127-28
    cake, Susan's, 83-84
    cheese bars, 312-13
    chess gooey butter cake,
        247-48
    chip picnic cake, 96-97
    curd, as add-in, 176
    glaze, 83-84, 96-97

lime cake with pineapple
    curd, 158-60
pecan biscotti, 352-53
pineapple inside-out cake,
    92-93
whiskey glaze, 191
zesting, 78
Lemon cake mix:
    cherry cake, happy valley,
        269-70
    lemon cheese bars, 312-13
    lemon pecan biscotti, 352-53
    pineapple inside-out cake,
        92-93
Lighter cakes, 372-96
    apricot lemon chiffon,
        386-87
    chocolate-speckled
        peppermint angel food,
        393-94
    cinnamon and pineapple
        carrot sheet, 395-96
    cranberry, zesty, 378-79
    dark chocolate chiffon,
        389-90
    orange almond angel food,
        391-92
    orange chiffon, classic,
        383-84
    pear and toasted pecan
        buttermilk, 380-81
    pound, better-for-you,
        374-75
    strawberry applesauce,
        376-77
Lime(s):
    cheesecake, 230-31
    curd, 76-77
    lemon cake with pineapple
        curd, 158-60
    zesting, 78
Loaves, cake, 271
    wrapping, 217
Love cake, 184-86

M

Macadamia(s), 343
    as add-in, 110
    chocolate biscotti, 350-51
    fudge torte, 136-37
    oatmeal cookies, chunky,
        342-43
    toasting, 134
Marble cake, chocolate:
    Fiddler on the Roof, 161-62
    gooey butter, 244-46
    with shiny chocolate glaze,
        44-45
Margarine, 8-9
Marshmallow(s), 14, 57
    chocolate frosting, 434
    cola cake, old-fashioned,
        55-56
    frosting, 433
    Mississippi mud cake, 46-47
Measuring, 16, 401
Melted ice-cream cake,
    incredible, 163-64
Meringue bars, raspberry, 316-17
Milk, 9
Milk chocolate pound cake, 38-39
Mississippi mud cake, 46-47
Misters, 11, 13
Mixers, 11, 15
Mixing ingredients, 14-15, 16
Mocha:
    buttercream, 419
    chocolate chewies, 337-38
    chocolate swirl cheesecake,
        234-35
Mom's layer cake with fluffy
    chocolate frosting, 106-8
Mount Vernon cake, 187-89

N

New York–style cheesecake,
    224-25

Nut(s), 9
    streusel, 305
    toasting, 134
    as topping, 305
    see also specific nuts

O

Oat(meal):
    cranberry crumble bars,
        320-21
    macadamia cookies, chunky,
        342-43
    streusel, 305
Orange(s):
    almond angel food cake,
        391-92
    ambrosia cake, 212-14
    cake, fresh, 79-80
    chiffon cake, classic,
        383-84
    cinnamon poppy seed cake,
        Mattie's, 262-63
    cranberry cake, festive,
        81-82
    cream cheese frosting, 423
    dreamsicle cake, 167-68
    fuzzy navel cake, 298-99
    glaze, 79-80, 81-82, 167-68,
        383-84
    Harvey Wallbanger cake,
        284-85
    juice concentrate, as add-in,
        394
    mandarin, in finger lickin'
        good cake, 150-51
    marmalade glaze, 110
    and pineapple filling,
        212-13
    rum zum cake, 294-95
    spice cookies, 346-47
    zesting, 78
Oven temperature, 12, 14, 16,
        401

P

Pans.
    See Cake pans
Pantry items, 8-10
Parchment, 13
Pastry combs, 11
Peach(es):
    and cream cake, 70-71
    pecan kuchen, 276-77
    schnapps, in fuzzy navel
        cake, 298-99
Peanut butter:
    chocolate bars, 326-27
    frosting, 427
Pear:
    and ginger cake, old-
        fashioned, 98-99
    sour cream buckle, 362-63
    and toasted pecan buttermilk
        cake, 380-81
Pecan(s):
    banana cake with caramel
        frosting, 72-73
    better than ? cake, 171-72
    cherry dump cake, 358-59
    chocolate better than ? cake,
        169-70
    chocolate praline cake,
        33-35
    coconut cream cheese
        frosting, 424
    coconut gooey butter cake,
        250-51
    cola cake, old-fashioned,
        55-56
    earthquake cake, 173-74
    hornet's nest cake, 175-76
    Jack apple spice cake, 308-9
    lemon biscotti, 352-53
    Mississippi mud cake, 46-47
    peach kuchen, 276-77
    pie bars, sticky, 322-23
    pie cake, 133-35

pumpkin pie crumble cake,
        207-8
    sock-it-to-me cake, 260-61
    toasted, and pear buttermilk
        cake, 380-81
    toasting, 134
    turtle cake, 48-49
Penuche frosting, 431
Peppermint:
    buttercream frosting, 418-19
    chocolate cake, lethal, 30-31
    chocolate-speckled angel
        food cake, 393-94
    schnapps, as add-in, 394
Pillsbury, 20-23
    Bake-Off, 5, 22, 23, 50, 136,
        138, 291
Piña colada cake, 296-97
Pineapple:
    ambrosia cake, 212-14
    better than ? cake, 171-72
    cherry dump cake, 358-59
    and cinnamon carrot sheet
        cake, 395-96
    curd, 159
    filling, 110
    friendship cake, 179-81
    hummingbird cake, 74-75
    inside-out cake, 92-93
    and orange filling, 212-13
    piña colada cake, 296-97
    pistachio, and coconut
        frosting, 150-51
    punch bowl cake, 366-67
Pine nuts, toasting, 134
Pistachio:
    chocolate cake, 40-41
    coconut, and pineapple
        frosting, 150-51
Pizza, fruit, 370-71
Plastic cake savers, 11-12
Plastic wrap, 12
Plum and cardamom cake, 87-88
Poke cake, 288

Poppy seed cake:
   Charleston, 124-25
   lemon buttermilk, 127-28
   orange cinnamon, Mattie's,
      262-63
Potlucks, 15 cakes for, 57
Pound cake:
   almond cream cheese, 129-30
   better-for-you, 374-75
   chocolate, basic, 412-13
   milk chocolate, 38-39
   white chocolate, 58-59
   yellow, basic, 406-7
Praline chocolate cake, 33-35
Prune cake with hot buttermilk
      glaze, old-fashioned,
      144-45
Pudding cake, banana, 139-40
Pudding-in-the-mix cakes, 5
Pumpkin:
   pie crumble cake, 207-8
   roulade, 204-6
   spice cake, 278-79
   spice cheesecake, 227-29
Punch bowl cake, 366-67
   chocolate, 368-69

R

Rack position, in oven, 12-13, 17
Racks, cooling, 11, 16, 17
Raisin(s):
   applesauce cookies, 344-45
   buttermilk cake, Kentucky,
      300-302
   friendship cake, 179-81
Raspberry:
   buttercream frosting, 184-85
   filling, bride's cake with
      white chocolate frosting
      and, 192-93
   jam, as add-in, 176
   meringue bars, 316-17
   sauce, 289-90

Red, white, and blue angel food
      ice-cream cake, 197-98
Red velvet cake, 152-55
Rich cakes, 104-47
   almond cream cheese pound,
      129-30
   banana pudding, 139-40
   caramel, 112-13
   carrot, with orange cream
      cheese frosting, 109-11
   coconut icebox, Grandma's,
      118-20
   jam, Tennessee, 116-17
   lemon buttermilk poppy seed,
      127-28
   macadamia fudge torte,
      136-37
   Mom's layer, with fluffy
      chocolate frosting, 106-8
   pecan pie, 133-35
   poppy seed, Charleston,
      124-25
   prune, with hot buttermilk
      glaze, old-fashioned,
      144-45
   snickerdoodle, 121-23
   sweet potato, with coconut
      pecan cream cheese
      frosting, 114-15
   tiramisù, easy, 146-47
   toasted coconut sour cream,
      142-43
   zucchini spice, with penuche
      frosting, 131-32
Ricotta:
   cannoli cake, 199-201
   cheesecake, Mindy's, 238-39
Roulades, 13, 268
   holiday yule log, 209-11
   pumpkin, 204-6
Royal icing, 219-20
Rum:
   Bacardi, cake, 292-93
   balls, 332-33

double-chocolate cake,
   289-90
glaze, 292-93, 294-95
piña colada cake, 296-97
zum cake, orange, 294-95

S

Sauces:
   cherry, 270
   raspberry, 289-90
Shakers, 11
Sheet cakes, 16, 405
   chocolate, with peanut
      butter frosting, 52-54
   cinnamon and pineapple
      carrot, 395-96
   fast toppers for, 249
   frosting needed for, 421
Sherry, 125
Shipping cakes, 217
Skillet(s):
   cake, upside-down apple,
      100-101
   cast-iron, caring for, 101
Snickerdoodle cake, 121-23
Snowballs, 215-16
Sock-it-to-me cake, 260-61, 288
Sour cream, 10
   apple kuchen, 274-75
   chocolate cupcakes with sour
      cream chocolate frosting,
      60-61
   chocolate frosting, 426
   coconut frosting, 119
   pear buckle, 362-63
   toasted coconut cake, 142-43
   white cake, basic, 398-99
   yellow cake, basic, 404-5
Spatulas, 11
Special occasion cakes, 182-221
   almond and caraway, Irish,
      190-91
   ambrosia, 212-14

birthday cake cones, 195-96

bride's, with raspberry
    filling and white
    chocolate frosting, 192-93

cannoli, 199-201

chocolate, devilishly good,
    202-3

gingerbread house, 218-21

holiday yule log, 209-11

love, 184-86

Mount Vernon, 187-89

pumpkin pie crumble, 207-8

pumpkin roulade, 204-6

red, white, and blue angel
    food ice-cream, 197-98

snowballs, 215-16

Spice(s), 10

    applesauce raisin cookies,
        344-45

    orange cookies, 346-47

    pumpkin cheesecake, 227-29

Spice cake:

    applesauce, 89-91

    buttermilk, basic, 408-9

    gingerbread house, 218-21

    Jack apple pecan, 308-9

    jam, Tennessee, 116-17

    pear and ginger, old-
        fashioned, 98-99

    pumpkin, 278-79

    tomato soup, with cinnamon
        buttercream frosting,
        156-57

    zucchini, with penuche
        frosting, 131-32

Spice cake mix:

    applesauce raisin cookies,
        344-45

    applesauce spice cake, 89-91

    buttermilk spice cake, basic,
        408-9

    gingerbread house, 218-21

    Jack apple pecan spice cake,
        308-9

jam cake, Tennessee, 116-17

orange spice cookies, 346-47

pear and ginger cake, old-
    fashioned, 98-99

pumpkin roulade, 204-6

pumpkin spice cake, 278-79

pumpkin spice cheesecake,
    227-29

sweet poato cake with
    coconut pecan cream
    cheese frosting, 114-15

tomato soup spice cake with
    cinnamon buttercream
    frosting, 156-57

upside-down apple skillet
    cake, 100-101

Spirits, cakes with, 282-309

    almond and caraway, Irish,
        190-91

    Amaretto, 303-4

    Bacardi rum, 292-93

    chocolate grappa, 306-7

    chocolate Kahlúa, 286-87

    chocolate punch bowl,
        368-69

    chocolate-speckled
        peppermint angel
        food, 393-94

    double-chocolate rum,
        289-90

    fuzzy navel, 298-99

    Harvey Wallbanger, 284-85

    Jack apple pecan spice,
        308-9

    Kentucky buttermilk raisin
        cake, 300-302

    orange rum zum, 294-95

    piña colada, 296-97

Spumoni cake, 288

Stencils, 11

Sticky pecan pie bars, 322-23

Storing cakes, 19

    equipment for, 11-12

    unfrosted, freezing, 399

Strawberry(ies):

    applesauce cake, 376-77

    buttercream frosting, 184-85

    cake, triple-decker, 67-69

    cake with strawberry cream
        cheese frosting, 64-66

    cream cheese frosting, 65-66

    crisp, Nina's, 364-65

    frosting, 67-69, 376-77

    fruit pizza, 370-71

Streusel:

    basic, 305

    blueberry coffee cake, 272-73

    nut, 305

    oat, 305

Sugar:

    coating, for cake pans, 178

    confectioners', 243

    glaze, 266-67

Sweetened cream, 433

Sweet potato cake with coconut
    pecan cream cheese
    frosting, 114-15

T

Tennessee jam cake, 116-17

Timers, 401

Tiramisù, easy, 146-47

Toffee:

    candy bar pieces, in
        chocolate punch bowl
        cake, 368-69

    crunch cheesecake, 236-37

Tomato soup spice cake with
    cinnamon buttercream
    frosting, 156-57

Toppings:

    chocolate chips, 305

    nuts, 305

    streusel, 305

    see also Frostings;
        Glazes; Sauces; Streusel;
        Whipped cream

Torte, macadamia fudge, 136-37
Triple-decker strawberry cake, 67-69
Tube cakes, 10, 12-13, 16, 17
    frosting needed for, 421
    wrapping, 217
Turtle cake, 48-49

U

Upside-down cake:
    apple skillet, 100-101
    bananas foster, 102-3

V

Vanilla, 382
Vegetable oil, 7, 9, 13, 15

W

Walnut(s):
    apple crisp, 360-61
    earthquake cake, 173-74
    toasting, 134
Waxed paper, 12
Wedding cake:
    bride's cake with raspberry
        filling and white
        chocolate frosting,
        192-93
    groom's cake, 194
Whipped cream, 141
    brandied, 209-10
    coconut, 297
    sweetened, 432
    toasted almond, 391-92
Whiskey:
    almond and caraway cake,
        Irish, 190-91
    glaze, 309
    Jack apple pecan spice cake,
        308-9
    lemon glaze, 191

White cake, basic:
    sour cream, 398-99
    yogurt, 400-401
White cake mix, 4
    ambrosia cake, 212-14
    apricot lemon chiffon cake,
        386-87
    blueberry muffin cake, 94-95
    bride's cake with raspberry
        filling and white
        chocolate frosting, 192-93
    butter cake, basic, 402-3
    butter layer cake with sweet
        lime curd, 76-77
    cannoli cake, 199-201
    caramel cake, 112-13
    cherry cheesecake,
        sweet-tart, 232-33
    chocolate pistachio cake,
        40-41
    cinnamon-chocolate-apricot
        coffee cake, 254-56
    coconut icebox cake,
        Grandma's, 118-20
    cola cake, old-fashioned,
        55-56
    cranberry cake, zesty, 378-79
    enriching, 122
    lemon buttermilk poppy seed
        cake, 127-28
    love cake, 184-86
    melted ice-cream cake,
        incredible, 163-64
    Mom's layer cake with fluffy
        chocolate frosting, 106-8
    Mount Vernon cake, 187-89
    New York–style cheesecake,
        224-25
    poppy seed cake, Charleston,
        124-25
    ricotta cheesecake, Mindy's,
        238-39
    snickerdoodle cake, 121-23
    snowballs, 215-16

sour cream white cake, basic,
    398-99
strawberry applesauce cake,
    376-77
strawberry cake, triple-
    decker, 67-69
strawberry cake with
    strawberry cream cheese
    frosting, 64-66
tiramisù, easy, 146-47
toasted coconut sour cream
    cake, 142-43
white chocolate pound cake,
    58-59
yogurt white cake, basic,
    400-401
White chocolate, 54
    chewies, 340-41
    frosting, 425
    love cake, 184-86
    pound cake, 58-59
Wrapping cakes as gifts, 217

Y

Yellow cake, basic:
    pound, 406-7
    sour cream, 404-5
Yellow cake mix, 4
    almond and caraway cake,
        Irish, 190-91
    almond gooey butter cake,
        242-43
    Amaretto cake, 303-4
    apple sour cream kuchen,
        274-75
    apple walnut crisp, 360-61
    apricot almond squares,
        314-15
    apricot nectar cake, favorite,
        85-86
    Bacardi rum cake, 292-93
    banana cake with caramel
        frosting, 72-73

banana loaves, 280-81

banana pudding cake, 139-40

better than ? cake, 171-72

blueberry muffin cake, 94-95

blueberry streusel coffee
cake, 272-73

butterscotch cashew
scotchies, 324-25

candy bars, 330-31

carrot cake with orange
cream cheese frosting,
109-11

cherry dump cake, 358-59

chocolate chip cake, Stacy's,
42-43

chocolate marble cake with
shiny chocolate glaze,
44-45

chocolate marble gooey
butter cake, 244-46

chocolate syrup cake, Mom's,
264-65

cinnamon and pineapple
carrot sheet cake,
395-96

cinnamon blueberry crumble
bars, 318-19

cinnamon breakfast cake,
Kathy's, 257-58

coconut-pecan gooey butter
cake, 250-51

cookie pops, 348-49

cranberry oat crumble bars,
320-21

cran-orange cake, festive,
81-82

Fiddler on the Roof cake,
161-62

finger lickin' good cake,
150-51

five-flavor cake, 165-66

friendship cake, 179-81

fruit pizza, 370-71

fuzzy navel cake, 298-99

gooey butter cake, 240-41

honey bun cake, 266-67

hornet's nest cake, 175-76

hummingbird cake, 74-75

Kentucky buttermilk raisin
cake, 300-301

lemon cake, Susan's, 83-84

lemon chess gooey butter
cake, 247-48

lemon chip picnic cake,
96-97

lime cheesecake, 230-31

milk chocolate pound cake,
38-39

oatmeal macadamia cookies,
chunky, 342-43

orange cake, 79-80

orange chiffon cake, classic,
383-84

orange cinnamon poppy seed
cake, Mattie's, 262-63

orange dreamsicle cake,
167-68

orange rum zum cake,
294-95

peaches and cream cake,
70-71

peach pecan kuchen,
276-77

peanut butter chocolate
bars, 326-27

pear and toasted pecan
buttermilk cake,
380-81

pecan pie bars, sticky,
322-23

pecan pie cake, 133-35

piña colada cake, 296-97

plum and cardamom cake,
87-88

pound cake, better-for-you,
374-75

prune cake with hot
buttermilk glaze, old-

fashioned, 144-45

pumpkin pie crumble cake,
207-8

punch bowl cake, 366-67

raspberry meringue bars,
316-17

sock-it-to-me cake, 260-61

sour cream pear buckle,
362-63

sour cream yellow cake,
basic, 404-5

strawberry crisp, Nina's,
364-65

toffee crunch cheesecake,
236-37

yellow pound cake, basic,
406-7

zucchini spice cake with
penuche frosting, 131-32

Yogurt, 10

frozen, angel food cake
filled with, 392

white cake, basic, 400-401

Yule log, holiday, 209-11

Z

Zest, adding to cakes, 78

Zesty cranberry cake, 378-79

Zucchini spice cake with
penuche frosting, 131-32